ISBN 978-0-428-97929-4
PIBN 10064441

THE

CHICAGO * LAW * TIMES

VOLUME III.

Edited by CATHARINE V. WAITE.

————

CHICAGO
C. V. WAITE & COMPANY
1889

Joseph Story

THE

CHICAGO * LAW * TIMES

VOLUME III.

Edited by CATHARINE V. WAITE.

CHICAGO
C V. WAITE & COMPANY
1889.

THE CHICAGO LAW TIMES.

CONTENTS OF VOLUME THREE.

INDEX TO SUBJECTS.

Contents to Volume III.

INDEX TO WRITERS.

JOSEPH STORY

Was born in Marblehead, Massachusetts, on the eighteenth
day of September, 1779.* He was the eldest child of a second
marriage. His father, Dr. Elisha Story, had served as a surgeon in the army of the Revolution, and afterward engaged
in the practice of medicine in Marblehead, with distinguished
success, till his death in 1805. His second wife, the mother of
Judge Story, was Mehitable Pedrick, the daughter of an opu-
lent merchant of Marblehead. She was married at the age of
nineteen, and lived to an advanced age, surviving her eminent
son by a few years. She was a woman of sense and energy,
with an active mind and a cheerful spirit. Left, at the death of
her husband, with a numerous family and a very moderate
income, she showed an admirable tact and method in the management of her household, and the education of her children.

Young Story was prepared for college in his native town,
and entered the Freshman Class in Harvard College, in January, 1795, about half a year in advance. His college life was
in all respects honorable to him. His studies embraced not
merely the prescribed course of the college, but ranged over a
wide field of English literature. Among his classmates were
Dr. Tuckerman and Dr. Channing. With the latter he contended for the highest honors of his class, but always acquiesced
in the decision that gave the first place to his friend.

* In the preparation of this sketch, we have made free use of the material in
the "Memoir of Joseph Story, LL. D.," by George S. Hillard, published in the
Proceedings of the Massachusetts Historical Society, Boston, 1869.

The profession of the law had been his first and only choice, and he entered upon the study of it immediately after leaving college, first at Marblehead, in the office of Chief-Justice Sewall, and afterward at Salem, with Judge Putnam. His love of literature, and especially poetry, and his enthusiastic temperament, made the study of the law at first distasteful to him; and he was obliged to struggle desperately over "Coke on Littleton" and other treatises of the kind, which were placed before the law students of that day. But these difficulties soon vanished before his resolute industry, and in the three years of his preparation he laid a strong and sure foundation of knowledge, on which to build in after years.

He was admitted to the bar in 1801, and immediately began the practice of the law in Salem. His industry, the fidelity with which he served his clients, and his frank and engaging manners soon secured him a fair and steadily increasing amount of business, notwithstanding the fact that he had espoused the unpopular side in politics. He was a democrat, while the wealth, the cultivation and social influence of Salem, and indeed of all Massachusetts, were with the Federal party.

During the year 1803, the post of naval officer of the port of Salem was offered to him, but declined on the ground that its duties would interfere with his professional prospects. His pen was actively employed at this time, and not always in the line of his profession. His imaginative faculty found vent in poems and orations.

During the same year, he prepared for the press and published a "Selection of Pleadings in Civil Actions," a useful and accurate manual, and for a long time, during the reign of special pleading, almost the only book of forms used in this country.

In December, 1804, Mr. Story was married to Miss Mary Lynde Oliver, a young lady to whom he had been long and tenderly attached; but this domestic happiness was destined to be of brief duration, for his wife's health began to decline soon after their marriage, and she died in June, 1805, to the inexpressible grief of her husband. She had pleasing manners, a cultivated mind, and an amiable and gentle disposition. Her image he always recalled with affectionate tenderness.

In 1805, he was chosen a member of the Legislature of Massachusetts, to represent the town of Salem, and was annually re-elected until his appointment to the bench. He soon came to be recognized as the leader of his party in the House, and was often obliged to contest, almost single-handed, against the powerful array of ability and influence which supported the federal cause. In these contests he bore himself with a courage and eloquence which extorted hearty praise from the more generous of his opponents. He was an ardent, but not a bitter or an unscrupulous partisan. In 1806, he so far broke away from party ties as to support Theophilus Parsons for Chief-Justice of the Supreme Court of Massachusetts, though Parsons was an uncompromising federalist; and Mr. Story even twice used his influence to raise the salary of the office, so that the Chief-Justice could afford to continue to hold the position. He was for a long time denounced by some of the journals of his own party for the part he took in these measures.

In January, 1806, he drew up an able memorial from the inhabitants of Salem to the President and Congress, on the infringement of the neutral trade of this country by Great Britain.

In the month of August, 1808, he was married to Miss Sarah Waldo Wetmore, a lady with whom he lived in great happiness during the remainder of his life.

In the autumn of 1808, he was elected a member of Congress. He served only for the remainder of a broken term for which he had been chosen, and declined a re-election; his hopes and aspirations being professional rather than political. While in Congress, he manifested his usual independence by giving his support to propositions to increase the navy and to repeal the embargo; upon both questions acting against the party to which he belonged. Mr. Jefferson was displeased at his course, and in one of his letters calls him a "pseudo-republican."

In 1809, he edited a new edition of "Chitty on Bills of Exchange and Promissory Notes;" appending to it a large number of valuable annotations. In 1810, he prepared an edition of "Abbott on Shipping," and in 1811, an edition of "Lawes on

Assumpsit;" to both works adding copious notes.

In January, 1811, he was chosen Speaker of the House of Representatives of Massachusetts, and on the organization of the new House, in the succeeding May, he was re-elected to the same position .

In 1810, the seat of Associate Justice of the Supreme Court of the United States became vacant by the death of Mr. Justice Cushing. The place was first offered by President Madison to the Hon. Levi Lincoln, who declined it; and then to the Hon. John Quincy Adams, at that time in Russia, by whom it was also declined. In the month of November, 1811, the appointment was. very much to his surprise, offered to Mr. Story, and after some reflection, accepted.

Mr. Story, when he went upon the bench, was only thirty-two years old; an almost unprecedented age for a lawyer to be advanced to a seat upon the highest judicial tribunal of his country. Mr. Justice Buller is perhaps the only exception. There was in some quarters some apprehension on account of his youth and his previous political partisanship; but from the moment he assumed his judicial office, he shook the dust of politics from his feet, and bore himself with absolute impartiality.

From 1811 to 1829, when he removed to Cambridge, the life of Judge Story flowed on in a uniform and uneventful current. About three months of every year were spent with the Supreme Court in Washington, and several weeks were devoted to the judicial duties of his circuit, embracing Maine, New Hampshire, Massachusetts and Rhode Island. His life was useful, laborious and happy. His duties were eminently congenial to his tastes and to the structure of his mind. His domestic and social nature found satisfaction in a happy home, and in a large circle of relatives and friends, by whom he was regarded with equal pride and affection. His lot was not, however, free from trials. Four of his seven children were taken from him during these years. His letters show how acutely he felt these losses, and with what Christian resignation he sustained them.

During this period, he was not idle in the intervals of his judicial labors. His time was occupied in preparing addresses, biographical sketches and memorials, and in literary work of a miscellaneous character. He contributed to the North American Review various law articles of great value, and filled many of the titles in the Encyclopedia Americana, such as Congress, Contract, Courts of the United States, Criminal Law, Equity, Jury, Lien, Natural Law, National Law, etc. The elaborate notes in "Wheaton's Reports," occupying nearly two hundred closely printed pages, were written by Judge Story.

To this period of his life also belongs his impressive charge to the grand jury at Portland, in 1821, on the horrors of the slave trade.

In 1820, after the separation of Maine from Massachusetts, a convention was called to revise the Constitution of the latter State. To this convention—a body remarkable for wisdom, ability, and comprehensive patriotism—Judge Story was sent as a delegate from the town of Salem. He took an active and influential part in its proceedings, maintaining on one occasion, in a powerful argument, the independence of the judiciary.

In 1829, an important change took place in his life and labors. In this year, the Dane Professorship of Law in Harvard College was established, and Judge Story, though he had previously declined to accept the Royal Professorship of Law at Cambridge, was induced to fill the chair of the Dane Professorship in Harvard. He left Salem in September, and immediately entered upon the duties of his new position. Under the influence of the name and reputation of Judge Story, the number of students in the Law School, increased the first year from eight to thirty.

On the 10th of May, 1831, his youngest daughter, Louisa— a child singularly lovely in person and attractive in character, died of scarlet fever. This loss he felt most keenly, and it appeared to cast a shadow over his subsequent life.

In the autumn of 1831, the chief-justiceship of the Supreme Court of Massachusetts became vacant by the death of Chief-Justice Parker, and Judge Story was much pressed to accept the vacant office, but declined to do so.

In the beginning of the year 1832, Judge Story published his "Commentaries on the Law of Bailments," the first of the series of text books prepared by him while incumbent of the professor's chair, for the use of the bar and bench, and as aids in the teaching of the elementary principles of law. Nothing on the subject had previously appeared in English except the meager outline of Sir William Jones. The new treatise, received with great favor alike in America and England was introduced into the Law School as a text book.

In 1833, Judge Story published his "Commentaries on the Constitution," in three volumes, which were received with great and general favor. A just and appreciative tribute was paid to this work by the eminent man to whom it was so appropriately dedicated—John Marshall—in a letter of acknowledgment to the author: "I have finished reading your great work, and wish it could be read by every statesman, and every would-be statesman in the United States. It is a comprehensive and an accurate commentary on our Constitution, formed in the spirit of the original text."

In the early part of 1834, the "Commentaries on the Conflict of Laws" were published. It was the first systematic treatment of the subject in the English language; and its admirable method, its copious learning, and the liberal spirit which pervaded it were warmly recognized by professional readers both in England and America. It was reprinted in England, and soon translated into German and French; and it was received by the jurists and juridical writers of the Continent with a welcome which was the best proof of the substantial merit of the work.

We pass over, as of less importance to the professional reader, many other literary works of Judge Story during this period—essays, lectures, eulogies, etc. Among these was a glowing but discriminative tribute to Chief-Justice Marshall, who had died on the sixth of July, 1835.

During the year 1835, Judge Story prepared for the "Kritische Zeitschrift"—a periodical published at Heidelberg, an elaborate article on the Constitutional and Public Law of the United States; and subsequently he furnished for the "Revue Etrangére," at Paris, an article on the Organization and Jurisdiction of National Courts in the United States.

In the latter part of 1835, Judge Story revised and published a selection from his miscellaneous writings, which was dedicated to Mr. Josiah Quincy, then President of Harvard College.

In the early part of 1836, the first volume of his "Commentaries on Equity Jurisprudence" was published, which was followed by the second in the summer of the same year. This is a work of profound and exact learning; and in practical value to the profession, has not been surpassed by any of Judge Story's legal treatises. He found a peculiar pleasure alike in the study and the administration of equity law. Its broad and comprehensive principles, which were in unison with his own liberal and enlightened views of jurisprudence, were expounded by him with a fullness of illustration and a depth of research which showed that his mind was working in a congenial sphere. His "Commentaries" took a place in the literature of the profession which no previous work on the same subject had occupied, and from which it has not since been removed.

In the year 1838, Judge Story published a treatise on "Equity Pleadings," a work supplementary to the "Commentaries on Equity Jurisprudence," and marked by similar thorough research and luminous method.

In the spring of 1839, his "Commentaries on the Law of Agency" were published, which met with the same success, at home and abroad, as his previous works. The same may be said of the "Commentaries on Partnership," which appeared in 1841. In the interval between the publication of these treatises, new editions were prepared of the works on "Bailments," on "Equity Pleadings," and on the "Conflict of Laws," involving much labor and comprising extensive additions.

In 1842, his health gave way under his unremitted labors, and he had a serious fit of illness. He recovered very slowly, and was obliged to give up his usual course of judicial duties at Washington, and remain at home during the winter. This was the only session of the Supreme Court which he failed to attend, from his appointment to the time of his death—a period of thirty-three years.

In the early part of 1843, his "Commentaries on Bills of Exchange" appeared, and this was followed, two years afterward by his "Commentaries on the Law of Promissory Notes," both of which were received with the same favor as his earlier works.

For some time before his death, Judge Story had been meditating a resignation of his seat upon the bench. He wished to devote his whole time and energies to the Law School, in which he felt an ever increasing interest, and to the preparation of the legal treatises which he had meditated, but had not yet written. Besides, though his personal relations with his brethren of the bench were entirely agreeable, Washington was no longer to him what it had been in the days of Marshall. A change had come over the spirit of the Court; and the constitutional opinions of that illustrious man; and his own, no longer swayed the tribunal. He had been compelled, in more than one instance, to dissent from the judgment of the Court, and he felt that in the future the divergence was more likely to increase than to diminish.

Returning from Washington early in 1845, with a fixed determination of resigning his judicial position, he addressed himself to the task of clearing the docket of the Circuit Court, so as to leave no legacy of unfinished work to his successor. Many of the cases were intricate and difficult, and the arduous labors they required bore heavily upon his strength and upon his vital energies, which doubtless had already been overtaxed. Such was the buoyancy of his spirit, however, that the effect was not perceived at the time.

The last time he appeared in public was on the third of July, 1846, when a festival was given in celebration of the completion of a large addition to the Law Building of the College. On that occasion he appeared in excellent health and spirits, and made a speech, in which he gave a history of the foundation and growth of the Law School, and paid a generous tribute to Mr. Dane.

By the beginning of September he had finished the hearing of all the cases pending before him, and had drawn up opinions in all but one, and that was nearly completed. The severe labor which these tasks imposed, and the heat of the summer, had greatly exhausted him; and while in this prostrated condition, he took a slight cold, which was followed by a violent internal stricture, from which he was not relieved until after many hours of great suffering. But now his exhausted system could not rally. His strength daily declined, in spite of the best medical advise and the most careful nursing, and he died, without consciousness or pain, on the 10th of September, 1846, at the age of sixty-seven years.

The news of his death threw a gloom over the community, all the deeper from the fact that none but those who lived in his immediate neighborhood were prepared for it. Resolutions were adopted, and speeches expressive of the highest respect and admiration were made at the opening of every court over which he had presided, and also of the Supreme Court at Washington. On the 18th of September, the sixty-seventh anniversary of his birth, a beautiful and impressive eulogy was delivered by his colleague, Professor Greenleaf, before the pupils of the Law School. In the Courts of the United States, in New York, Pennsylvania, Tennessee, Louisiana and Mississippi, his death was appropriately noticed.

Judge Story was about five feet eight inches in height, with rather broad shoulders, and a compact and active figure. He was very animated in his movements, and to the last, maintained the elastic step of youth. His complexion was fair, his eyes were blue. His hair in youth was auburn, but in early manhood he became bald. His mouth was large and full of expression. His countenance was easily lighted with smiles, and glowed with kindliness and unaffected sympathy. His manners were simple, unassuming and cordial.

He was a man of large capacity and various faculties; and with such intellectual force, that whatever might have been the sphere allotted to him, he could hardly have failed to have risen to eminence in it. His perceptions were wonderfully quick, and his knowledge was as enduring as it was readily acquired. His memory was "wax to receive and marble to retain." His crowning and conspicuous quality was his industry, wherein few equalled and none excelled. Many men will work hard in order to secure the prizes of life, wealth, office or fame; and when these are won, they begin to grow self-indulgent, and are content to live on their intellectual capital, without adding to its stores. Not so Judge Story; for labor was a necessity of his nature, and he must have ceased to live before he ceased to work. The profession of the law, which he chose, was that which afforded the best scope and sphere to this persevering industry; for of eminence in the law it is not too much to say, that three parts out of four are made up of hard work.

There is, in our opinion, a moral to be drawn from the manner of his death, which should not be lost upon the judges of our day, and especially in this City. Had Judge Story performed, during the last twenty years of his life, but two-thirds of the labor which he did, more than twenty years would probably have been added to a career already glorious, but which by a prudent expenditure of vital energy, would then have been at its zenith.

Judge Story, though fond of general literature, was mainly, almost exclusively, a lawyer, and presented an example of undeviating devotion to his profession, more common in England than in this country. Here professional eminence is apt to prove the stepping-stone to the more showy, and to many natures the more tempting, honors of politics.

That Judge Story was a great lawyer, both in the original force of his mind and in his prodigious attainments, is what no man competent to judge, and free from prejudice, will for a moment deny. Judge Prescott, a man careful of his words, and not inclined to overpraise, said of him, in a letter written in 1840: "I believe him the greatest jurist now living in either country," meaning England or America. That this would not be too much to claim for him, even in England, may be inferred from the fact that Lord Campbell, in the course of a debate in the House of Lords, characterized him as "the first of living writers on the law." If among his contemporaries there were some who were not inferior to him, if there were some who were even superior to him in grasp of legal principles, in logical power, in accuracy of legal perception, and in simplicity and clearness of expression, there was no one who equaled him in the range and depth of his learning.

In England, the division of legal employments limits the professional attainments of their lawyers and judges to a narrower sphere. One man devotes himself to equity law and one to common law, and neither intrudes upon the province of the other. Take the two brothers, Lord Stowell and Lord Eldon, for instance; the former was confined to ecclesiastical and admiralty law, and the latter to equity law. But the jurisdiction of the courts of the United States compelled Judge Story to range over a far wider region of legal investigation than any English judge. He had to hear and determine questions in equity law, in commercial law, in admiralty law, in criminal law, in constitutional law, in the law of copyright, and patent law. In all these departments his learning was accurate, ready and profound. He was at home, also, in the technical and recondite learning of real property. He had made himself master of the uncouth lore of "Coke upon Littleton." With every department of equity law he was familiar—with the obsolete science of special pleading he was perfectly acquainted, and his opinions on constitutional law have in their careful analysis, luminous exposition, and vigorous grasp, but few rivals, and no superiors, unless it be the immortal judgments of Marshall. In knowledge of admiralty law, alike of its origin, history, and practical application, there is no one but Lord Stowell to rival him; and in learning, at least, the finished opinions of this great lawyer and accomplished scholar are not superior to those of Story.

To the important department of patent law. as administered and understood in America, Judge Story's contributions were more abundant and weighty than those of any other judge, or perhaps those of all the judges on the bench during his time. The system of patent law was wanting in symmetry and proportions. The courts of America at that time had contributed almost nothing to the science. It was a department of the law which he took particular pleasure in studying and administering, where his quickness of apprehension and discriminating faculty found a congenial sphere.

Upon the kindred subject of copyright, several important questions came before him during his judicial life; and his opinions on them have the same merits of liberal interpretation and equitable construction as mark his judgments in patent cases.

To understand Judge Story's merits as a lawyer and a jurist, he must be studied in his opinions, as contained in the reports of Gallison, Mason, Sumner and Story, exclusively devoted to his own circuit, as well as those found in the volumes of Cranch, Wheaton and Peters, of the U. S. Supreme Court Reports. His text books, admirable as they are—affluent in learning, luminous in exposition, and abundant in illustration —can hardly claim the same comparative rank as his recorded opinions. No man in America has done more to determine the law; and there is no one whose conclusions have been accepted with more general assent by the profession.

Some of his conclusions, however, though they were the law in his time, must be looked upon, especially in these Western States, only as connecting links between the common law and that more complete modification of it which is necessary to adapt it to our social and political condition.

As a *nisi prius* judge, presiding over jury trials, Judge Story was remarkable for the quickness of his perceptions and the correctness of his decisions, and for the uniform courtesy with which he treated all who appeared before him. He never indulged in sneers or sarcasm, and did not allow himself those judicial sallies, which, though they may make the by-standers smile, rarely fail to disconcert a sensitive advocate, and when too frequent, detract from the dignity of the bench.

He was sometimes accused of indicating, in his charges to the jury, a little too distinctly on which side he thought their verdict ought to be. A similar criticism has been made of the charges of some of the most eminent jurists of this State. The fault is a very natural one. The abler the judge and the clearer his views of the law, the more danger of his falling into it. As the jury, being accustomed to dealing with facts, are apt to consider more closely the facts, so the judge, being more accustomed to consider questions of law, is apt to give to them his closest attention, and, anxious that the verdict should be in accordance with the law when applied to the facts as he views them, he sometimes does not leave to the jury sufficient latitude in determining the facts themselves. Though he may base his charge upon hypothetical conclusions of fact, in such a way that the charge is legally unobjectionable, he couches it in such language as to foreshadow his actual opinion as to what the verdict should be.

Whether we view Judge Story in his private and social life —as a lecturer—as a writer—as a lawyer—as a jurist—as a judge upon the bench, in all these respects he was great; and while some have been his equals and superiors in one or another of these departments, yet when all are taken and viewed together, it is safe to give him pre-eminence in those respects, among the men whom our country has produced.

SOURCE AND EXTENT OF LEGISLATIVE POWER.

The extent of legislative power depends upon its source. That the Legislature derives its power from the people, all admit; but there is not entire uniformity in the modes of thought as to the manner in which the Legislature comes into possession of the power. Some lawyers and even some jurists are in the habit of looking upon the State Constitution as the medium through which the power is transmitted from the people to the legislative bodies, and which is, therefore, to determine its extent.

A correct solution of this question must depend upon three others: the relation between the people of a State and a Constitutional Convention;—the relation between such Convention and the Legislature, and the relation between the Legislature and the people. Let us examine them in their order.

I. The relation between the people and the Convention.

A Constitutional Convention having been called, under an established form of government, nothing is more absurd than the doctrine that as soon as it has assembled, the government is resolved into its original elements, and the members of the Convention become clothed with complete political power for all purposes. It is somewhat surprising that a doctrine so dangerous and so revolutionary should have obtained any foothold among an intelligent and patriotic people.

The Convention is a mere agency of the established government. It is chosen and assembled for a definite purpose, and clothed with definite powers. It is not a legislative body. It

has no legislative powers beyond what are absolutely necessary
for the accomplishment of its special work, which is, either
a general revision of the Constitution, or the considering and
maturing of certain special changes in the fundamental law.

The relation is that of principal and agent. The Convention
is the special political agent of the people. After its work
of general revision or of maturing special amendments has been
done, it should be submitted to the principal, the people, for
approval; and such is now the universal practice in this country.

The mere statement of this relation is sufficient to show that
it is not competent for the Constitutional Convention to confer
any political rights upon the people. To attempt to do that
would be for the agent to undertake to clothe his principal
with authority. "A Constitution" says Dwarris, "grants no
right to the people, but is the creature of their power, the
instrument of their convenience."—(Dwarris on Statutes, p.
347.)

But while an agent cannot confer power upon his principal,
he can provide for establishing more firmly the power already
possessed, and guard against its overthrow. And so, while
a Convention cannot clothe the people with political rights, it
can provide safeguards for the exercise of those they already
have.

As an illustration, take the question of the suffrage. The
people do not acquire their right of suffrage from the Constitution. That this is the case in reference to the Federal Constitution, was expressly decided by the Supreme Court of the
United States in Minor v. Happersett. It is equally true of
a State Constitution. If any one is disposed for a moment
to think otherwise, let him ask himself whether, in voting for
delegates to a Constitutional Convention, he intends to clothe
those delegates with the power of saying in their discretion,
whether he shall or shall not have the right to vote again.
Does he intend to surrender his right of suffrage into the hands
of the Convention? Before delegates were sent to the Convention he had the right to the suffrage—that right he retains
during its deliberations, and after it adjourns the right is exer-

cised in approving or disapproving the result. And after the Convention adjourns, though he may find his right to vote recognized and guarantied in the new Constitution, his *title* to the suffrage is no better than it was before. A man may be protected by law in the possession of his farm, but that has nothing to do with the title to the farm. And this brings us to the proper construction which should be placed upon the suffrage clauses in a State Constitution.

Though a Convention cannot confer any political rights upon the people, it can provide safeguards against their violation. If it cannot grant rights, it can guaranty them. And this is what it does do when it specifies in the Constitution certain classes of persons "who shall be entitled to vote," or "who shall be qualified electors." This, properly construed, is a guaranty of the right of suffrage in the classes mentioned. It is equivalent to saying that the Legislature must not interfere with their right to vote. Such a clause is not to be construed as a grant of the right of suffrage, because the Convention is not competent to grant such a right; nor should it be construed as a regulation, because the regulation of the suffrage is an ordinary act of legislation which is peculiarly within the province of a legislative assembly. It is not to be presumed that the Convention has undertaken an ordinary act of legislation, if any other construction can be placed upon the Constitution.

The construction which makes such a clause a guaranty, is therefore, the only one which is consistent with the relation between the people and the Convention and with the proper exercise of legislative power. And what is true of the suffrage, is true of every other political right specified in the Constitution. It matters not though the language may be that of a grant, or of a regulation; since the language is to be construed consistently with the power which the Convention possesses, and not with a power which it does not possess.

The conclusion therefore is, that in its relation to the people, a Constitution is a guaranty of their natural and political rights. In its relation to the people it is this and nothing more. It is not the source of the rights of the people.

II. The relation between the Convention and the Legislature.

The Constitution is not a grant of legislative power. No such grant is necessary. The Legislature was antecedent to the Constitutional Convention and was invested with full power of legislation before the Convention assembled. The Legislature did not derive its power from any Convention. Its power comes from the people; not indirectly through a Constitution, but directly. The power to legislate is implied in the word "Legislature," *ex vi termini.* The people, having the right to govern themselves, elect members of a legislative assembly for the very purpose of exercising through them the right of self-government. All the rightful governing power that the people have, the Legislature has.

But the people have no right to oppress each other, or to deprive each other of any civil or political rights, and it is not to be presumed that they intended to authorize the Legislature to do what they had no right to do themselves. Legislators, however, do not always bear in mind these maxims. They are apt to forget that they are the servants of the people and to imagine themselves their masters. Hence the necessity of placing limits upon legislative power; and this is one of the functions of the Constitutional Convention. The people do not need a Convention to confer rights upon themselves or power upon a legislative assembly which they have chosen for the very purpose of exercising legislative power for the preservation of their rights. But they do need checks and restraints upon legislative authority, and they call a Convention for the purpose of establishing such checks and restraints as may be necessary.

When the Constitution says, as in Article IV, Sec. I, of the Constitution of Illinois, "The legislative power shall be vested in a general assembly," etc., the meaning is, not that it shall be now vested, *de novo,* but that it shall *remain* vested. It is a mere recognition of power already possessed.

Sometimes there is in a Constitution what appears to be a grant of power upon some special subject, as, for instance, the provision in Sec. 30 of Article V of the Constitution of 1870, concerning the establishing and opening of roads and cartways, connected with a public road, for private and public use.   All such provisions are to be construed as qualifications of some more general provision which is in the form of a limitation. It will be found, upon examination that there is no difficulty in thus construing the section referred to.   And it matters not though the language of the Constitution may be that of a grant of power.   For here, again, the principle will be applied, that the Convention will be deemed to have acted within the scope of its legitimate powers, and not to have undertaken to do that which it was not competent to do.   It is not competent for a Convention, which is only a special agent of the people, to confer power upon the Legislature, which is the general agent of the same principal.

There is to be found, also, in the Constitution, various directions for the exercise of legislative power upon certain subjects. These may generally be construed in accordance with the legitimate function of a Convention as a restraining and guarantying body, and are therefore generally obligatory, in a moral sense, upon the Legislature.   In cases where they cannot fairly be thus construed, it may well be doubted how far a Convention has power to dictate to future assemblies the character of their legislation.   If the Convention cannot legislate itself, except for a special purpose, how can it say what laws shall be enacted thereafter, otherwise than by way of prohibiting the passage of certain laws, or providing for such as shall make effectual the guaranties of the Constitution?

By a directory provision contained in the Constitution of 1870, Art. VII Sec. 7, it is provided that "The General Assembly shall pass laws excluding from the right of suffrage persons convicted of infamous crimes."   This provision is at the same time a recognition of the power of the Legislature to regulate the suffrage, and a restriction upon that power.   It is equivalent to saying, "The Legislature will have power to regulate the suffrage subject to the guaranty in this article contained, but in making such regulations persons convicted of infamous crimes shall be excluded from the elective franchise." [That is, the Legislature shall not permit them to vote.]

This is the only construction that will explain the fact of Sec. 7 standing by itself, and being in the form of a direction to the General Assembly. If the suffrage article of the Constitution were a grant or a regulation of the suffrage, or both, then the Section would have read as follows:

"Every person having resided in this State one year," etc. "who shall not have been convicted of an infamous crime, shall be entitled to vote at such election."

This would have indicated an intention to regulate the suffrage. If Section 1 is a regulation, and if the regulation is complete except as to criminals, what necessity of an act of the Legislature to exclude them from the suffrage? Why not incorporate the exclusion into the body of the regulation?

Thus it will be seen that however the various provisions of the Constitution may be worded, so far as they relate to the action of the Legislature, they may all be reduced to modes of restriction upon legislative power.

This doctrine, which is thus so plainly to be deduced from the principles upon which a State government is founded and from an analysis of the relation between a State Convention and the Legislature, has been recognized and announced by the various Courts throughout the country whenever the question has come up for adjudication.

The Courts have held with great unanimity that a State Constitution is not a grant of legislative power but a limitation upon its exercise.

One of the earliest decisions to that effect was in 1831, in Connecticut, Starr v. Pease, 8 Conn. Rep. 541; which was indorsed eight years afterward in Pratt v. Allen, 13 Conn. 119. Since then the decisions have been uniform.

The principal cases outside of our own State have been,

In New Hampshire, in 1845, Concord Railroad v. Greely, 17 N. H. 55;

In Michigan, in 1849, Scott v. Smart's Exrs., 1 Mich. (Manning), 306, and in 1865, Twitchell v. Blodgett, 13 Mich. 127;

In California, in 1854, The People v. Coleman, 4 Cal. Rep. 49, and in 1859, People v. Rodgers, 13 Cal. 159;

In Indiana, in 1856, Doe *ex dem.* Chandler v. Douglas, 8

Black. 10, and in 1870, Lafayette etc. R. R. Co. v. Geiger, 34 Ind. 185;

In Iowa, in 1858, McMillen v. Lee, 6 Iowa 391, and in 1863, Wright J. in Morrison v. Springer, 15 Iowa 342;

In Virginia, in 1858, Commonwealth v. Drewry, 15 Gratt. 5;

In Wisconsin, in 1860, Bushnell v. Beloit, 10 Wisconsin 225;

In New York, in 1861, People v. N. Y. Cent. R. R. Co., 34 Barb. 138; in 1865, Justice Brown in Sill v. The Village of Corning, 15 N. Y. 303, and in 1871, People v. Flagg, 46 N. Y. 401;

In Pennsylvania, in 1868, Page v. Allen, 58 Pa. St. 345, and in 1870, Lewis' Appeal, 67 Pa. St. 153;

In Ohio, in 1871, Walker v. Cincinnati, 21 Ohio St. 14;

In Kansas, in 1871, Leavenworth Co. v. Miller, 7 Kans. 479;

In Texas, in 1878, Re Mabry, 5 Tex. Ap. 93, and Logan v. State, Id. 315.

See also Cooley's Const. Limitations, p. 173.

In Illinois, it has been repeatedly held by the Supreme Court that the Constitution is not a grant but a limitation of power. —(Field v. The People, 2 Scam. 79; People v. Wall, 88 Ill. 79; Harris v. Whiteside Co., 105 Ill. 145; Winch v. Tobin, 107 Ill. 212.)

If any doctrine may be considered settled in this country it is this. It is clearly stated by Justice Walker, in Harris v. Whiteside Co. in the following language:

"The question of legislative power, and its extent, depends on the limitations contained in the Constitution. When a State is created it is invested with complete sovereign power, unless restricted by constitutional limitation. * * When we have to determine whether an act is within the scope of legitimate power, we do not look for an express delegation of the power in the fundamental law, but we look to see whether the general power has been limited."—(105 Ill. Rep. 145.)

The relation, then, of the Convention to the Legislature, is that of a special to a general agent. The special agent has been appointed for the purpose of limiting the powers of the general agent. That, therefore, is the function of the Constitutional Convention, in its relation to the Legislative Assembly.

III.   The relation between the Legislature and the people.

This relation is the most direct, the most simple, and the most easily comprehended of any under our form of government.   The most ignorant voter understands that when he casts his ballot for a member of the Legislative Assembly, he is appointing an agent to act with other agents of the people in like manner appointed, in making laws for the State.

As the Convention is the special agent of the people, appointed for a special purpose, so the Legislature is their general political agent, appointed for the purpose of realizing self-government.   This is effected through the exercise by this agency, in behalf of the people, of general legislative authority.   And it is because a special agent cannot invest a general agent with any power which is already within the purview of his general authority, that a Convention cannot, in a Constitution, grant power to the Legislative Assembly.

It is true that in some cases Courts have, from a habit already referred to, spoken of a general grant of legislative power in the Constitution, but it is manifest that the true meaning to be attached to their language is that the general legislative power is recognized in the Constitution; since, frequently the same Courts and the same Judges, in other cases lay down the true doctrine, so well established, both by reason and authority.

The legislative power comes, not from the Constitution, but from the people direct.   It is implied in the very act of electing members of the Legislative Assembly.   It is not a special but a general authority, and is unlimited except by the nature of our government, and by the express prohibitions of the Federal and State Constitutions.

To illustrate the nature of this power, let us recur again to one of the most important objects upon which it can be exercised—the suffrage.

The regulation of the suffrage is an ordinary act of legislation.   It involves direct relations between the Legislature and the people, and should be performed by a Legislative Assembly consisting of two houses.   Hence it is not the function of a single body like a Constitutional Convention.   Such a body meets only at rare intervals, while a wise and prudent regulation of the suffrage must have reference to the exigencies of the times. Is there a great and sudden influx of people into a State from other portions of the country? Then it may be well to require a longer residence in the State. And so of residence in a county or a district. Such questions are peculiarly within the province of a Legislative Assembly.

But the Legislature must not under pretense of regulating the suffrage, interfere with the right.

"All regulations of the elective franchise," says Judge Cooley, "must be reasonable, uniform and impartial; they must not have for their purpose directly or indirectly to deny or abridge the constitutional right of citizens to vote, or unnecessarily to impede its exercise; if they do they must be declared void."—(Cooley's Constitutional Limitations, p. 602.)

And in reply to objections which had been made to certain registry laws on the ground that they violated the foregoing rule, he says:

"The provisions for a registry deprives no one of his right, but is only a reasonable regulation under which the right may be exercised."—(Ibid. p. 602.)

By "the constitutional right of citizens to vote," the learned judge undoubtedly refers to the right which is guarantied by the State Constitution. It is a right under our form of government, and is recognized and made the subject of constitutional guaranty.

Suffrage is the mode in which the citizen participates in the government. He cannot, ordinarily, participate in it in any other way. To say that the people have the right to govern themselves, and at the same time to deny that they have the right of suffrage, is a mere contradiction, in different terms. If it be said that the suffrage cannot be a right because it can ot be exercised until regulations have been made and classes designated to vote, so may it be said with equal truth and propriety that self-government cannot be realized except through forms and modes of action to be prescribed by legislative enactment. And by the same line of reasoning it would follow, therefore, that there can be no such thing as self-government.

So, also, with the right to liberty, and property, and with

all other civil and political rights, none of which can be realized and enjoyed except under the regulations and restraints imposed by the necessities of law and order.

What, then, is a legitimate exercise of the power to regulate the suffrage? It must not arbitrarily interfere with the right of the citizen to participate in the government. Every provision in the way of a regulation must, in the language of Judge Cooley, be "reasonable, uniform and impartial." It must have for its object the good of the State, and must find its justification in the nature of things.

The Legislature of a State has not an absolute, arbitrary control over the suffrage. Suppose it should be provided that a native of Indiana should not have a right to vote in Illinois. Would not such a discrimination against citizens of another State residing in Illinois, be a violation of the Federal Constitution, which provides that the citizens of each State shall be entitled to all privileges and immunities of citizens in the several States? But without going further into this at the present time, let us take another case.

Suppose it should be provided that only citizens between the ages of thirty and fifty could vote, thus excluding more than half of those ordinarily invested with the suffrage. Would not such a so called regulation be held invalid as an attempt to build up an aristocracy and subvert our government? These extreme cases show that there must be a limit to the power, and that suffrage is a right to be regulated, but not arbitrarily taken away. The limit is stated by the learned jurist already cited, and will be established by the Courts when necessary.

As to the extension of the suffrage by legislative action, that may be considered from two points of view. There may be classes of citizens, who are, according to the principles of our government, entitled to the suffrage, who have been wrongfully excluded from it. In such cases, the Legislature not only has the power, but it is its imperative duty to recognize the right in such classes at the earliest opportunity. This would be, properly speaking, no regulation of the suffrage, but the performance of an act of justice.

Again, there may be a class, who have not necessarily a

right to vote, but whom it would still be competent for the Legislature, in the exercise of a sound discretion, to clothe with the elective franchise. Such an extension would be a legitimate regulation.

For instance, those who, being entitled and qualified in other respects, have resided in the county sixty days but not ninety days. This class might by legislative enactment be permitted to vote, and that would be a regulation of the suffrage. If the person seeking to exercise the elective franchise, is a citizen of the United States and has resided in the State a year and in the county ninety days, his right to vote is guarantied to him by the Constitution of the State. But that does not prevent the Legislature from extending the suffrage to those who have resided in the county but sixty days. In regard to legislative power, there is an essential difference between an extension of the suffrage and a restriction of it. In this case, the essence of the Constitutional provision is, that the Legislature shall not require a longer residence than ninety days in the County. Hence a law requiring four months would be a violation of this provision of the Constitution. But a law requiring only sixty days would stand on an entirely different footing.

Indeed, upon principle, it would follow from the propositions which I have endeavored to maintain, that the Legislature would have full power to extend the suffrage to any class not specified in the Constitutional guaranty; since in case of a guaranty, the maxim, *expressio unius est exclusio alterius*, does not apply. In order that A should be guarantied the right to vote, it is not necessary that B should be excluded; hence the Legislature may afterward recognize the right in B.

The Courts have, up to this time, it is true, been inclined to look upon the Constitutional provision as exclusive; but some of these decisions have been mere *dicta*. When it has only been necessary to say that the Legislature could not add to the Constitutional requirements, the Court has held that the Legislature could require neither more nor less than what was specified. The "less" was a *dictum* and a *non sequitur*. The adjudicated cases have not been sufficiently numerous nor have they been sufficiently well considered, to settle the law upon a question of such vast importance.

It may be said that the construction here contended for would enable the Legislature to extend to foreigners the elective franchise, notwithstanding the guaranty to "citizens" in the Constitution. It is true that such a conclusion would follow from the premises. But if such power in the Legislative Assembly be thought a dangerous one, it is easy to guard against it, as some of the States have already done, by inserting in the Constitution a prohibitory clause, forbidding the Legislature to permit aliens to vote. The very fact that such prohibition is found in the Constitutions of some of the States, is sufficient to show that the designation of "citizens" in the Constitution was not considered of itself sufficient; it being looked upon as a guaranty, and not necessarily exclusive of other classes.

Why should the Constitutional Convention, which is not properly a legislative body, undertake the exclusive regulation of the suffrage? Such an assumption of power, if attempted, is something to which no legislative body should submit. And the history of the country shows that the Legislatures have not felt willing to have their hands thus tied upon a legitimate subject of legislation. There have been repeated instances of the extension of the suffrage to classes not specified in the Constitution of the State.

In New York, various acts were passed extending the franchise to classes not within the Constitutional guaranty. One of these only will be mentioned;

An act passed April 21, 1818, provided for a brigade to be called "The First Brigade of New York State Artillery;" and Sec. 56 provided that every non-commissioned officer, musician and private of said brigade, "shall, provided he be a citizen of this State, and of lawful age, be entitled to vote at elections in the same manner as if he had actually paid taxes to this State;" and this although the Constitution expressly specified, as one of the qualifications of the guarantied class, that the elector be rated and "actually pay taxes to the State."

One of the first acts of this character was vetoed by the Governor on the express ground that the provisions of the Constitution were exclusive, but it was passed by the requisite majority over the veto. The Legislature of New York thus insisted upon its power to regulate the suffrage, notwithstanding the guaranty of the Constitution. Similar laws have been passed in various other States.

Such action in different States indicates a sensitiveness on the part of the State Legislatures, and an unwillingness to be deprived of their legitimate power to regulate the suffrage.

Other questions might be taken to illustrate the nature and extent of legislative power. In this article its application to the suffrage has been considered, because the question is now much under discussion, and because of its great importance.

The conclusions upon the general question are:

1. That a State Constitution, in its relation to the people, is a guaranty of their natural and political rights; while, in its relation to the Legislature, it is a restriction upon legislative power.

2. That the legislative power of a State is not derived from the State Constitution, but directly from the people.

3. That in its extent, this power is unlimited, except,

First, by the nature of our government, which forbids any violation of the natural rights of the people.

Secondly, by the restrictions placed upon the legislative power of the States by the people of the United States in the Federal Constitution.

Thirdly, by the restrictions placed upon the State Legislature by the people of the State in their own Constitution.

That the limitation first herein mentioned, the one depending upon the nature of our government, is a legitimate and valid one, has been maintained in a previous article in the "TIMES," in which it was shown that such a limitation upon legislative power has the sanction of the greatest jurists of this country, and has been established by numerous decisions, not only in the State Courts, but also in the Supreme Court of the United States.

Charles B. Waite.

LAW REFORM IN PLEADING AND PRACTICE IN CIVIL CASES.—THE QUESTION OF COSTS.

To refer again to the matter of costs, as not unimportant either to the payee or payor, what are known as interlocutory costs seem to me a subject worthy of consideration. Apart from the costs of the whole cause, which should in my judgment, be, as I have said, paid by the unsuccessful litigant, and thus fall on the party who has needlessly created them, there are sundry items of costs which arise from mispleading, malpractice, neglect, oversight, or some cause altogether apart from the general merits of the case at issue. These, if none other ought assuredly to fall upon the party whose act, or want of care, or lack of diligence or knowledge, causes them to be incurred. And over these the judges, under the present constitution of the courts, apparently have a discretionary jurisdiction and no further legislation would seem to be necessary to invest them with it.

In some cases the judges, very properly I think, exercise such jurisdiction. The writer is conversant with a case in which a cause was dismissed for want of prosecution, no one being present to represent the plaintiff when the case was reached on the calendar. A motion was made to reinstate, which was granted conditionally on payment of five dollars costs,—not costs so called, meaning simply the disbursements paid to clerk of court, but a counsel fee of that amount, to be paid to the defendant's attorney. Now if this can be done in one cause, it could with great propriety be done in very many cases; and if it were made the rule of practice instead of merely

an exception, how much more prompt attorneys would become
in having their cases ready for trial when called, and how
many less continuances would be made than take place, to the
loss of the time of the court, the attorneys and the suitors, and
not infrequently to the detriment of the course of justice.

Interlocutory costs are very often caused by bad pleading.
When a demurrer is filed and properly allowed, the filer of the
faulty pleading gets leave to amend, almost if not always, as a
matter of course; but is never as far as I can learn, ordered to
pay costs; (i. e. attorneys fees.) Thus the attorney who de-
murs and whose demurrer is allowed, has the pleasure of setting
his adversary right, but gets nothing for his own time or trouble, unless he charges his own client, who may or may not
be in the right on the merits, but who has to pay in either
case. It strikes one that this is not justice. Attorneys should
be made to file correct pleadings, or if a mistake will occasionally occur, let the party who makes it or on whose part it
is made, pay all costs of having it corrected and set right. It
is or should be the one great object and aim of all judicial
tribunals to have all matters that come before them for trial,
come up on clear, regular and sufficient pleadings, and it would
greatly aid in bringing about this great desideratum, if the care-
less or inexpert pleader were made to pay the expense of successful demurrers and orders for leave to amend. Apart from
which, the courts would be saved very much time and labor in
not having insufficient pleadings to deal with. If such jurisdiction exists as that exercised in the case alluded to above,
then a judge might as well, I think, make an order for costs
in allowing a demurrer, and no legislation is needed. The
whole subject could be covered by a few rules of court *strictly
carried out.*

Such order for costs should include, as the term costs do
in other places, not merely disbursements but attorney's fees.
This could surely be done under the general jurisdiction exercised by the courts, and without regard to the construction of
sec. 10, c. 33 of the Illinois Statutes relating to "Costs."

Before leaving the question of the establishing of a regular
tariff of costs, a very fair argument in its favor would seem

to me to be—apart from its effect as between litigant parties —the confidence it would tend to establish between attorneys and clients. Where tariffs exist there are two sets of costs, one as between attorney and client, the other between party and party. Whilst it is only fair and just, as I have contended, that the unsuccessful litigant should pay the expenses to which he has put his opponent, that is, the fees and disbursements he has put him to in defending against an unjust or unfounded claim, it is equally fair that these costs should be limited to the actual necessary fees and costs that the successful litigant has had to lay out. They should not include payment for time, labor and trouble which clients incur in dealing with their counsel in the conduct or defense of causes, a very large portion of which is altogether unnecessary, and seems to have for its object, to seek a salve for their own wounded feelings by obtaining assurances of a successful issue, etc. Therefore, in giving costs—fees and disbursements— against a suitor bringing a false claim or setting up an unsustainable defense, the costs given are costs as between party and party, and the successful litigant has to pay for any extra trouble incurred in his intercourse with his attorney in the shape of fees and costs as between attorney and client. This is certainly a much fairer practice than making the successful litigant pay the whole of his own fees and disbursements in any case, as is done here. As to the effect of the tariff system as between attorney and client, there is nothing that tends so much to the fair and honorable management and settlement of legal disputes as a thorough and distinct understanding and perfect confidence between the client and his legal representative. There may be nothing improper between the parties in making a bargain or agreement as to the recompense to be given for services performed, or to be performed, but it is much easier to arrange such terms after the services have been performed, and this is more readily and satisfactorily done when a tariff is in force to estimate them by.

There may or may not be any dispute as to the amount claimed, but for mutual satisfaction the intervention of a taxing master or clerk may be called in. Either party may obtain an order to tax; thé client if he thinks himself overcharged, can file his petition to tax, which is granted as a matter of course, he submitting to pay what may be taxed against him, and an order is made to that effect, enforceable as any other order. Under our practice an attorney seeking to recover costs, has to recover them by suit, if the amount is disputed, and is put to the trouble of proving each item, and the value of the service performed. Our courts are constantly troubled to decide squabbles between suitors and attorneys, which in case of a tariff might be disposed of by a taxing officer in very much less time, without the services of learned and high priced counsel, but by clerks of a year's standing. The correct fees are very quickly learned when they are established by rule.

These may perhaps seem minor details in the discussion of an important subject, but if, as I contend they will, they help to keep up a proper and more confidential footing and a kinder and better feeling between attorneys and clients, they are worthy of consideration. Such a system as I suggest would, in my humble judgment be very beneficial, and conducive to the interest of both of these classes.

Chas. W. Cooper.

REFORM IN THE ADMINISTRATION OF
THE CRIMINAL LAW IN THE STATE OF ILLINOIS.
II.

THE JURY SYSTEM AN ESSENTIAL PART OF OUR FREE INSTITUTIONS.—We consider trial by jury an essential part of our political system which belongs to free institutions. It is protected from legislative violation by the federal and State Constitutions, and in the estimation of some jurists so sacred is this right that it is impossible to be waived by any person charged with a felony.

In criminal cases there is no substitute that would be accepted by the profession or endured by the people. A jury represents the people and when acting under the guidance of a capable judge their verdicts can generally be relied upon.

In civil controversies the verdicts of juries are much less satisfactory and are in many instances subject to just complaints. But the causes are obvious.

1. Jurors should be composed of the best citizens in respect to intelligence, moral character and business experience, but they are not.

2. Judges in this State have been deprived of much of the power necessary to enable them to secure a true verdict. Here in this State they are not allowed as they are in England and in most of the old States; to sum up a case or express any opinion as to the value of the testimony, but are required to confine themselves to marking "given" or "refused," instructions which the counsel in the case have drawn up for them, and which, if not designed to befog the jury, in nine cases out of ten have that tendency.

3. The condition of affairs was bad enough in this State prior to the last session of the General Assembly, but at that time a law was passed providing for "special findings," the result of which is, in many cases, to reduce all trials to a farce, and to create error and thereby lay the foundation of reversing the case. There is no objection to a jury rendering a *special verdict* in a case, that is, finding the facts from all of the evidence and then letting the judge apply the law—but that is not what this new law provides for at all. It provides for a special examination of the jury in advance by putting to them a series of interrogatories, something like the ancient examination of persons charged with crime in the Court of High Commission in the days of the Stuarts, called an examination *ex officio mero*, and if not as disastrous in its results, is attended by many inconveniences and is a burlesque on the whole jury system.

The trial by jury in civil cases will not be satisfactory until our judges are restored to the position that they occupied at common law, and are invested with such legal discretion as they are justly entitled to in carrying out the real object and design of a jury trial.

TRIAL BY JURY IN THE UNITED STATES COURTS.—Justice Gray, in deciding the case of the United States v. the Reading Railroad, 123 U. S. 114, says:—"Trial by jury in the courts of the United States is a trial presided over by a *judge with authority*, not only to rule upon objections to evidence, and to instruct the jury upon the law, but also, when in his judgment the due administration of justice requires it, to aid the jury by explaining and commenting upon the testimony, and even giving them his opinion upon the question of fact, provided only he submits those questions to their determination."—(Vicksburg & Meriden Railroad Co. v. Putnam, 118 U. S. 545. St. Louis Railway v. The Vickers 122 U. S. 360.) We would like for some one to define what a court is in Illinois under our practice. We think that a short definition of a court in Illinois may be as follows:. A court is composed of an individual called a judge assisted by a clerk whose chief duty and functions are to look wise and keep order. He has no power to sum up a case or explain anything to a jury and the only aid or assistance that he can render them is to mark "given" or "refused" on all instructions or conundrums presented to him by the attorneys in the case.

AMENDMENTS TO THE JURY LAW.—1. We think that the jury law should be amended so as to make it incumbent upon some particular person or persons to prepare a jury list of all persons qualified to serve and have them ready to be drawn from in order to supply the courts with the requisite number for the trial of cases both civil and criminal. The best law that was ever devised may be rendered inoperative by incompetent persons or by neglecting to execute the same. It is not so essential who shall do this, but somebody should do it, whose mind cannot be distracted by other pursuits or other engagements.

2. We would change the limit of the age of jurors and instead of fixing 60 years as the limit, make it 65. This city, like most of our older cities, is beginning to have a class of men who have through toil and industry obtained a competency at that early period, and are ready to retire although possessed of all their faculties, sound in mind and body, who would be perfectly willing and perfectly capable of performing the duties of jurors. The time has gone by when jurors are treated with unbecoming brutality and made to endure hunger and thirst, heat and cold, without rest or sleep; and therefore we believe that hundreds of men could be found who would be able to render most valuable services to the State and their fellow men, who are now entirely excluded from all participation in the administration of the laws.

3. We would repeal the law making it incumbent upon courts in criminal cases to grant continuances and changes of venue whenever one charged with crime wishes to postpone the day or select his judges. We would leave that matter where it rightly belongs, and that is to the wise discretion and humane instincts of the trial judge, who acting under the solemnities of his oath, is bound to see that each and every human being receives not only a speedy, but a fair and impartial trial. Also that he has compulsory process for bringing his

witnesses into court, and every right which the Constitution and Bill of Rights entitle him to. To say that such a discretion may be abused, is no argument against its use, because every power with which a court is endowed may be subject to abuse.

4. We would have every *nisi prius* judge who presides in the trial of a criminal case, invested with the absolute power of controlling the examination of jurors and impanelling the same, and not allow the attorneys in any case to control this matter. Of all the abuses of the present day in the trial of criminal cases, especially capital cases, the abuse of privilege with which an attorney at law is invested, is the greatest. Those who understand this matter know that their main object is to educate the jury to their theory of the case, and to pledge them in advance to act in their behalf. The vast interests of the public are no concern of theirs. They are there to win, and to win at all hazards, and under all circumstances, whether their client is innocent or guilty of the crime with which he stands charged.

5. In order to have a jury trial, as known and understood by the common law, we would allow a judge to take some part in it. In other words we would make it a trial by *judge and jury*, and when the evidence is all in and counsel has addressed the jury, we would then have the judge take his appropriate place in this great drama, and would have him sum up the case and analyze the evidence. We would have him state the issues, and explain to the jury the relation of the several parts of the case, and the rules of law by which they are governed. We would have him fulfill the high mission which society has appointed for him, and see to it that justice is done between the prisoner at the bar and the people of the State. Let him so execute his office that the jury may, in the language of the oath which has come down to us from three centuries' use, "well and truly try and a true deliverance make between the people of the State, and the prisoner at the bar, so help them God."

6. The law in regard to charging an habitual criminal in an indictment, ought to be so changed, that if the direct state_ ment and averment is made in the indictment that said party

is charged *as an habitual criminal*, it shall be sufficient. The provisions of the New York Code upon this subject, are well worth considering.

7.   The law making juries judges of the law and the facts should be repealed. Almost every one that has given this subject any attention, agrees that it is absurd and should no longer be continued. As Chief-Justice Shaw said in the case of the Commonwealth v. Auther, "In my judgment, the true glory and excellence of the trial by jury is, that the power of deciding fact and law is wisely divided; that the authority to decide questions of law is placed in a body well qualified by a suitable course of training to decide all questions of law, and another body well qualified for the duty, is charged with deciding questions of fact definitely; and while each within its own sphere performs the duty intrusted to it, such trial affords the best possible security for a safe administration of justice and the security of public and private rights."

In the case of United States v. Battiste, 2 Sumner, 243, Mr. Justice Story says:

"My opinion is that the jury are no more judges of the law in a capital or other criminal case, upon the plea of not guilty, than they are in every civil case tried upon the general issue. In each of these cases their verdict, when general, is necessarily compounded of law and fact and includes both. In each they must necessarily determine the law as well as the fact. In each they have the physical power to disregard the law as laid down to them by the court. But I deny that in any case, civil or criminal, they have the moral right to decide the law according to their own notions or pleasure."

8.   The distinction between misdemeanors and felonies should be more clearly defined, and it should be declared in unmistakable terms that all persons who occupy any fiduciary relation, office of trust or emolument, and who enter into any conspiracy to defraud the public, shall upon conviction be declared guilty of felony, and punished by imprisonment in the penitentiary, not less than one nor more than twenty years.   In such cases, and in fact in all criminal cases, writs of error should be taken directly to the Supreme Court, and nowhere else.   To take any criminal case to the appellate court, where, if the case is reversed the State has no right of appeal or right

of review, is the very height of injustice.

If a writ of error is allowed in any criminal case from the criminal court of Cook County to the appellate court, then the same right should in case of a reversal be allowed the State to the Supreme Court. But we submit that as the only final judgment or conclusion can be reached in the Supreme Court, the case should be taken to the Supreme Court in the very first instance and nowhere else.

Finally, some additional restrictions should be provided in regard to the uses and abuses of the writ of habeas corpus. Writs of habeas corpus were never meant to be used as writs of error—but no sooner does one judge decide a question or sentence a prisoner who has been tried and convicted by a jury, than some other judge of concurrent jurisdiction issues a writ of habeas corpus to review his action, and if he should happen not to agree with the brother, he forthwith declares that "manifest error hath intervened," and releases the prisoner from jail and sets him free.

The most common use to which this writ is now being applied, is to get persons out of the bridewell because the commitment does not recite all the proceedings of the court and the judgment, and to release fraudulent debtors from jail because the attorney of the creditor pays his board bill, or because the the sheriff receives his pay for dieting the refractory prisoner, in advance—and the reason assigned is because the judge is opposed to *imprisonment for debt*, and everything is to be construed *in favorem vitæ*. All these reasons may be good, but we never heard of any one being imprisoned *for debt* in the State of Illinois, and never heard that the doctrine of "in favorem vitæ" applied to either torts or frauds. It is the settled law of this country that where a court has jurisdiction of the parties and subject matter, a writ of habeas corpus cannot be made use of to release a person who is wrongfully convicted, and the judgment cannot be questioned collaterally.—(Ex parte Watkins, 3 Pet. 193; Ex parte Crouch, 112 U. S. 178; Ex parte Carll, 106 U. S. 521; Ex parte Virginia, 100 U. S. 339; State v. Towle, 42 N. H. 540; Ex parte Hartman, 44 Cal. 32.)

AMENDMENTS TO THE CRIMINAL CODE.—We would amend the Criminal Code as follows:

PUNISHMENT BY FINE.—The Statute in regard to fines inflicted by way of punishment as provided in the Criminal Code, shou'd not be avoided by allowing the defendant to schedule out of jail. When a person has been convicted of a misdemeanor there should be no premium offered for his depravity, and he should not be awarded immunity simply because he has not a bank account to draw on, to atone for the wrongs that he may have committed. The criminal code contains several provisions relating to this matter. They are, Sections 448, 452 and 455 of the criminal code, as they appear in Cothran's edition of the statutes.

1. Fines may be fixed by a jury. (See Sec. 445 of the criminal code.)

2. Fines may be imposed by a court.

3. Persons who are convicted and fined in either way may, by virtue of 448, be committed to a workhouse; or by Sec. 452, committed to the jail, there to remain until the fine and costs are fully paid, or he is discharged according to law. By Sec. 168 b. p. 479 of Cothran's statutes, the culprit may work out his fine in the workhouse, or on the streets of public roads, etc., "at the rate of \$1.50 per day."

4. But by Sec. 455, it is provided that whenever it shall be made to appear satisfactorily to the court, after all legal means have been exhausted, that any person who is confined in jail for any fine or costs of prosecution, for any criminal offence, has no estate wherewith to pay such fine and costs or costs only, it shall be the duty of the court to discharge him from further imprisonment for such fine and costs, which discharge shall operate as a complete release of such fine and costs, etc.

No such conflicting provisions ought to exist; and it ought to be clearly declared that no person who has been convicted of any misdemeanor or criminal offense and fined, shall be allowed to be discharged under Sec. 455, but shall work out the same at \$1.50 a day.

Another thing. In counties where there is a city workhouse or city bridewell where work is performed, and the counties, as in Cook County, make arrangements by which persons found guilty of petty larceny and all sorts of misdemeanors are sent there to be kept at so much per capita, can a court order a person who has been fined, to be sent to the bridewell or workhouse or to the county jail? It will require judicial construction to solve the doubt.

These statutes ought to be made perfectly clear, so that there could be no room for doubt. There are several other matters which require attention, but we will refer to only a few.

1.   Length of time in which a person charged with crime should be kept in jail before trial.

2.   No law against forging decree of divorce.

8.   Punishment of the crimes of burglary and robbery.

4.   Amend the law as to the proof of former conviction of a person charged with a second offense.

5.   Evidence of *de facto* corporation in certain cases.

1.   It is provided by Sec. 438 of the criminal code, Cothran's edition, that "Any person committed for a criminal or supposed criminal matter, and not admitted to bail, and not tried at or before the second term of the court having jurisdiction of the offense, shall be set at liberty by the court unless the delay shall happen on the application of the prisoner. If such court at the second term, shall be satisfied that due exertions have been made to procure the evidence for and on behalf of the people, and there are reasonable grounds to believe that such evidence may be procured at the third term, it shall have power to continue such case till the third term." Now take the case of counties where there is a term of court every month, as in Cook County, and an indictment is found, say, at the November term, during the last week, and the December term commences in a week after the indictment found, and expires without the possibility of its being reached for trial, owing to the immense business on hand. By the strict letter of the statute, there being no exception in it, a defendant can come into court and demand his discharge.

The State may have all its witnesses there, but be unable to try the case because other cases are being tried;—then if the State can convince the court that "due exertions have been made to procure the evidence, etc; that there are reasonable grounds to believe that such evidence may be procured at the third term, it shall have power to continue such case till the third term;" but if not, what becomes of the case? Suppose, however, that under any construction of the statute that three or four full terms expire, then surely the prisoner is to be discharged. Now, under this statute, as it reads, a prisoner may be kept in jail in any county in the State of Illinois, outside of Cook County, for at least one year and a half, if not two years, without any exertion on the part of anybody, and without the prisoner being allowed to go free; while in Cook County if he is kept in jail three months, he may demand his discharge. The cases of Brooks v. The People, 88 Ill., 329; Gallagher v. The People, 88 Ill., 337, when properly understood, show just the difficulties we have above alluded to, and the statute ought not to exist a day without amendment. There are times in the criminal history of Cook County when the influx of criminals from other States and counties is such, that the business cannot be kept up by any two judges sitting in continuous session, and the time afforded to do the business ought at least to be as great here as in any other county.

When a single murder trial consumes a month, and when a single grand jury brings in 249 indictments in one month, some idea of the magnitude of the business and obstructions which occasionally ensue, can be obtained.

2. There is no law in this State making it a crime to forge a decree of divorce. This ought to be remedied.—(See Brown v. The People, 86 Ill., 239.)

As things are at the present day, a man may be deprived of his wife by any one skilled in stylography, and become an "orphan" before he knows it.

3. There is a disproportion in the punishment in the crimes of burglary and robbery.

Burglary is punished by confinement in the penitentiary, not less than one or more than twenty years, while simple robbery is not less than one or more than fourteen years. It is true

that the statute provides that if the person "is armed with
a dangerous weapon with intent, if resisted, to kill or maim
such person, or being so armed, he wounds or strikes him, or if
he has any confederate present so armed, to aid or abet him,
he may be imprisoned for any term of years, or for life." But
this does not always appear in cases of highway robbery, and
robbery from the person by violence should be as severely
punished as stealing from the house or building in the night
time.

4.   Amend Sec. 110 of the criminal law, so that in all cases
of larceny, burglary or any crime committed against a corporation its existence may be proved by general reputation.—
(Wharton's Criminal Ev., Sec. 164 a; Wharton's Criminal Pl.
& Prac. Sec. 110.)

HABITUAL CRIMINAL ACT.—The 169th Sec. of the criminal
code, which provides that in order to convict a person of a
second offense, the "former conviction and judgment shall be
set forth in apt words in the indictment" should be amended so
as to dispense with any such thing whatever. . In no other case
that we ever heard of was it necessary to plead the evidence
in the case, and it is perfectly useless and a most unnecessary
piece of labor.

Every writer upon evidence holds to the doctrine that the
same rules of evidence apply in criminal as in civil cases, and
Roscoe in his work on "Criminal Evidence" asserts this in
the very opening sentence of his treatise. We think that the
same provision of the statute in substance which exists in regard to evidence in civil cases—should be made to apply to
criminal cases, and the section as adapted to criminal cases
should be made to read "that no person shall be disqualified as
a witness in any action, suit, criminal proceeding or criminal
prosecution whatever, carried on in the name of the people,
by reason of his or her interest in the event thereof as a party
or otherwise or by reason of his conviction of any crime or misdemeanor; but such interest or conviction may be shown for
the purpose of affecting the credibility of such witness or for
the purpose of establishing the fact that a party has been convicted of a prior offense when he is being prosecuted for said

second offense, and the fact of such conviction or his having been incarcerated in the penitentiary, workhouse or bridewell, may be proven like any fact not of record either by the witness himself or any other witness cognizant of such conviction, as impeaching testimony or by any other competent evidence."

The case of Bartholomew v. The People, 104 Ill. 607, is a most perfect illustration of the necessity of some such provision as we have above set forth. In that case the court held, contrary to what they did in the case of Chase v. The People, 40 Ill. 355, that the presence of the defendant in the penitentiary even, could not be shown, but that before this matter could be even gone into, the State must show a conviction, and in order to a conviction they must produce a full and complete record of the court that convicted him, or an authenticated copy thereof, including the caption, the indictment by the grand jury, the return of the indictment into court, the arraignment of the defendant, his plea, his trial, verdict, conviction, sentence and judgment. We wonder that they did not require the production of the witnesses, and the presence of the court and jury in order to establish the identity and remove all possibility of doubt. The statement of this case will in our judgment show the absurdity of the present practice, and will, moreover, account for the reason why it is that prosecutions do not oftener take place in the case of old offenders under the habitual criminal act.

The next thing that we would do would be to amend Sec. 110 of the criminal code, so that in all cases of larceny, burglary, embezzlement, or any other crime against a corporation its existence may be proved by general reputation.

CHALLENGING JURORS FOR READING NEWSPAPERS.—Sec. 14 of the jury law, which enumerates the cause of challenge should be amended by striking out the words "about the truth of which he has expressed no opinion" in the latter part of the section, so that it shall read as follows: "That in the trial of any criminal cause, the fact that a person, called as a juror, has formed an opinion or impression based on rumor, or upon newspaper statement, shall not disqualify him to serve as a juror in such case, if he shall, upon oath, state that he believes he can fairly and impartially render a verdict therein, in accordance with the law and the evidence, and the court shall be satisfied with the truth of such statement." The words "about the truth of which he has expressed no opinion" are found in practice to be nothing but a source of trouble and confusion, and add nothing whatever to the sanctity of conscience nor the security of defendant's rights.

They are found in no other statute upon the subject that we are aware of, and should be stricken out. It is not necessary that a juror should be a saint or an angel, and all that any one charged with a crime can demand is to be tried by jurors as fair and impartial as the lot of humanity allows. Every body that is not an idiot reads the newspaper, and may form an impression about anything he reads, but if a man can swear on his oath that he has no fixed opinion, and has no prejudice or bias, and that whatever he had read would not influence and control his judgment against the evidence produced at the trial, and he could go into the jury box and render a verdict according to the facts as given on the trial, without regard to what he had heard or read before, and that he could fairly and impartially judge the case according to the law and evidence, ought to be regarded as a competent juror, anywhere and everywhere.—(Wilson v. The People, 94 Ill., 305–6; Plummer v. The People, 74 Ill., 366; Abbot v. The People, 86 N. Y., 465.)

In no case should it be a ground of error sufficient to reverse a case because counsel are restricted in their examination of jurors. This matter should above all things, be within the discretion of the court.

In no State in the American Union, neither in Canada nor England, nor anywhere else on earth, is there such latitude allowed and such an examination into the life and times and into the mental, moral, physical and metaphysical condition of jurors, as in this State.

Intelligence in jurors should not be regarded as a disqualification, but yet that is the ruling in criminal cases.

No better illustration can be given than this: A shrewd criminal lawyer, who was in great fear of obtaining a juror who had a fixed opinion, after spending some time in interrogating him upon every subject he could think of, proceeded as follows:

Counsel:—Are you a member of any church?

Juror:—No.

Counsel:—Do you drink?

Juror:—Yes, when I am dry.

Counsel:—Would you convict a man on doubtful and unsatisfactory evidence?

Juror:—Yes.

Counsel:—Would you guess a man into the penitentiary?

Juror:—Yes.

Counsel:—Suppose the evidence is equally balanced, what then would you do?

Juror:—Balance it.

Counsel:—Have you fixed an opinion about the merits of this case?

Juror:—No.

Counsel:—Have you any fixed opinion about anything?

Juror:—No.

Counsel:—Is your mind so porous that it can leach out all the facts, memory, impression and sense of justice?

Juror:—It can.

Counsel:—Would you acknowledge on due evidence that you were not yourself, but somebody else?

Juror:—I would.

Counsel:—Are you sure, without due legal proof, that it is I who am speaking to you now?

Juror:—I am not.

Counsel:—You assume that this is the year 1888, A. D. but are open to the conviction, on due and sufficient evidence, that it may be 1882 B. C., are you not?

Juror:—I am.

Counsel:—You are of the masculine gender?

Juror:—I am.

Counsel:—But, on due and sufficient evidence being produced, you would, even in this respect, be willing to admit you might be mistaken?

Juror:—I might.

Counsel:—Swear this gentleman. He is the juror we long have sought, and mourned because we found him not.

This is the model juror of the period, made so by the highest tribunals in the land; and any *nisi prius* judge who holds otherwise will find himself in error.

The recent case of the People v. Spies and others, which was taken to the United States Supreme Court and which is reported in volume 123 of that court, decides expressly that the ruling of the trial court which held that "it is not a test question whether the juror will have the opinion which he has formed from the newspapers changed by the evidence, but whether the verdict will be based only upon the account which may be here given by witnesses under oath" was correct and that such a ruling did not, and such an interpretation of the statute did not deprive the persons accused, of a right to trial by an impartial jury and was not repugnant to either the constitution of this State or the constitution of the United States, and further that carrying into effect a sentence of conviction in accordance with the verdict of the jury, did not deprive the persons of their lives without due process of law.

We have been making law pretty fast during the last few years and if we were to have one more anarchist trial and one more boodler trial, we should without the aid of any positive statute arrive at the same goal through the rulings of the courts that New York has reached by legislative enactment.

In its improved condition in England and especially in its improved and varied condition in this country, under the benign influence of an expanded commerce, of enlightened justice, of republican principle, and of sound philosophy, the common law has become a code of matured ethics and enlarged civil wisdom, admirably adapted to promote and secure the freedom and happiness of social life. It has proved to be a system replete with vigorous and healthy principles, eminently conducive to the growth of civil liberty; and it is in no instance disgraced by such a slavish political maxim as that with which the Institutes of Justinian are introduced. It is the common jurisprudence of the United States, and was brought with them as colonists from England and established here so far as it was adapted to our institutions and circumstances. It was claimed by the Congress of the united colonies in 1784, as a branch of those indubitable rights and liberties to which the respective colonies were entitled. It fills up every interstice and occupies every wide space which our statute law cannot occupy. Its principles may be compared to the influence of the liberal arts and sciences; and to use the words of De Ronceau "We live in the midst of the common law, we inhale it at every breath, inbibe it at every pore; we meet with it when we wake and when we lay down to sleep, when we travel and when we stay at home, and it is interwoven with the very idiom that we speak. We cannot learn another system of laws without learning at the same time another language."

As the Supreme Court of the United States say in quito a recent decision, (17 Wallace, 664), "twelve men of the average community, of little education, men of learning and men whose learning consists only of what they have themselves seen and heard, the merchant, the mechanic, the farmer, the laborer, there sit together, consult, apply their separate experience of the affairs of life to the facts proven, and draw a unanimous conclusion.

"This average judgment, thus given, it is the great effort. of the law to obtain. It is assumed that twelve men know more of the common affairs of life than does one man; that they can draw wiser and safer conclusions from admitted facts thus occurring than a single judge." And in this we agree with them.

"This mode of trial" says Livingston, "diffuses the most valuable information amongst every rank of our citizens. It is a school of which every jury that is impaneled is a separate class; where the dictates of the laws and the consequences of disobedience to them are practically taught. The frequent exercise of these important functions, moreover, gives a sense of dignity and self-respect, not only becoming the character of a free citizen, but which adds to his private happiness.

"Neither party spirit nor power can deprive him of his share in the administration of justice, though they can humble the pride of every officer and vacate every other place. Everytime he is called to act in this capacity he must feel that though perhaps placed in the humblest station, he is yet the guardian of the life, the liberty and reputation of his fellow citizens against justice and oppression; and that his plain understanding has been found the best refuge for innocence, and his incorruptible integrity is relied upon as a sure pledge that guilt will not escape. A State whose most obscure citizens are thus individually elevated to perform those august functions—who are alternately the defenders of the injured, the dread of the guilty, the vigilant guardians of the constitution—without whose consent no punishment can be inflicted, no disgrace incurred—who can by their voice arrest the blow of oppression and direct the hand of justice where to strike—such a State can never sink into slavery or easily submit to oppression. Corrupt rulers may pervert the constitution, and vicious demagogues may violate its precepts, foreign influence may control its operation; but while the people enjoy the trial by jury taken by lot from among themselves, they cannot cease to be free.

"The information it spreads, the sense of dignity and independence it inspires, the courage it creates, will always give them an energy of resistance that can grapple with encroachment and a renovating spirit that will make arbitrary power despair."

Can we too religiously guard this sanctuary, into which liberty may retire in times when corruption may pervert and faction overturn every other institution framed for its protection?

.Elliott Anthony.

SUFFRAGE IN WASHINGTON TERRITORY.

The validity of the law defining the qualifications of voters of Washington Territory approved Jan. 18, 1888, was questioned by Judge Nash, of the Fourth Judicial District, in the case of Nevada M. Bloomer v. John Todd, et al. He decided against the law, but filed no written opinion. The case was appealed to the Supreme Court of the Territory, and the judgment was affirmed. This statute is essentially the same as that of 1886, which was annulled by the Supreme Court on account of defects in its title. It makes the essential qualifications for voters, citizenship or a declaration of citizenship, without repect to sex, as it recites that "all citizens of the United States, male and female, above the age of 21 years having a residence of six months previous to the day of election in the Territory," etc., "shall be entitled to vote." The opponents of the law admit that the legislature had ll power to enfranchise all citizens and all persons who had declared their intentions to become citizens, provided that they were adult males. They insist that the word "male" must be interpolated in the law, because at the time the Organic Act was passed [1853] women were not considered entitled to the right of suffrage, and were not properly included in the term "citizens of the United States." They contend that the term "citizens of the United States," so far as suffrage was concerned, was intended to mean only *male* citizens.

The points involved are as follows:

1. The legislative power conferred upon the legislature of the Territory of Washington.

2. The meaning of the term "citizens of the United States."

3. The political rights of a citizen of the United States.

4. The effect of the Fourteenth Amendment.

5. The effect of the revision of the Statutes of the United States.

6· The true rule of interpretation.

THE LEGISLATIVE POWER CONFERRED UPON THE TERRITORY OF WASHINGTON.—The legislative power conferred by the Organic Act, extended "to all rightful subjects of legislation."—(Sec. 6, Act of March 2, 1853.)

In Sec. 5, the qualifications for electors at the first election were prescribed, and it was also enacted: "but the qualifications of voters and of holding office shall be such as shall be prescribed by the legislative assembly: Provided, That the right of suffrage and of holding office shall be exercised only by citizens of the United States above the age of twenty-one years," etc. There was no limitation as to sex.

This was the law up to Dec., 1873, when the Revised Statutes of the United States were adopted.

The first part of Sec. 5, which had ceased to be operative as to Washington Territory, was revised for territories thereafter to be organized. The latter part of the section is now Section 1860, R. S. U. S., which reads:

"The right of suffrage and of holding office shall be exercised only by citizens of the United States above the age of twenty-one years, and by those above that age who have declared on oath, before a competent court of record, their intention to become such, and have taken an oath to support the constitution and government of the United States," etc.

This grant of legislative power over suffrage is subject only to the limitations imposed by Sec. 1860. What Congress has not forbidden, is a valid exercise of legislative power. This clause of the Organic Act is similar to that of Wisconsin, except that under that, only citizens of the United States could vote.

Under that provision of the Organic Act of Wisconsin, the territorial legislature defined the qualifications for voters for the constitutional convention. The Enabling Act passed by Congress, August 6, 1846, contained no restriction as to the qualifications of voters. The people rejected the constitution of 1846, and a new convention was held, and a new constitution framed, which was adopted in March, 1848.

That constitution limited suffrage to adult male persons of the following classes:

First—White citizens of the United States.

Second—White aliens who had declared their intention to become citizens.

Third—Persons of Indian blood who had once been declared by act of Congress to be citizens.

Fourth—Civilized persons of Indian descent, not members of any tribe.

And the section provided "that the legislature may at any time extend by law the right of suffrage to persons not herein enumerated, but no such law shall be in force until the same shall have been submitted to a vote of the people at a general election, and approved by a majority of all the votes cast at such election."

The word "white" was stricken out by a vote of the people of the State at the general election held November 6, 1849.

The word "male" was stricken out as to school elections by virtue of Chap. 211, Laws of 1885.

In Brown v. Phillips, 36 N. W. Reporter, 244, this law was sustained on the ground that "This preservation of power to so extend the right of suffrage, was manifestly intended to relieve the legislature to that extent from the limitations which otherwise would have fastened upon it. To that extent, then, the power of the legislature, when so approved, was left unlimited. The exercise of such power is not restricted to males, nor prohibited from being exercised as to females, unless by implication of a remote and argumentative character. The question is not whether the constitution conferred the power to so extend the right of suffrage to women, but whether it anywhere expressly, or by *necessary* implication, prohibited the exercise of such power. It is not contended that there is any prohibition upon the exercise of such power in the constitution of the United States."

This decision sustains the right of the legislature of the

Territory of Washington to pass a law placing females upon
the same footing as males in regard to the right of suffrage—
provided they are included within the definition of the term
"citizens of the United States." That term as used by the
people of the Territory of Wisconsin in 1848, included women
as well as men, and the Supreme Court of Wisconsin so held.

The Supreme Court of the United States in the case of Murphy v. Ramsey, 114 U. S Reports, 39, had before them the Act
of Congress which amended the suffrage laws of Utah so far as
to provide that neither polygamists, bigamists or females
cohabiting with such persons, should be entitled to vote. Congress did not in that law of March, 22, 1882, attempt to annul
the suffrage laws of Utah by denying the power of the legislature to pass a law conferring suffrage upon both sexes upon
equal terms. Congress provided as follows:

"Sec. 8. That no polygamist, bigamist, or any person cohabiting with more than one woman, and no women cohabiting
with any of the persons described as aforesaid in this section,
in any Territory or other place over which the United States
have exclusive jurisdiction, shall be entitled to vote at any
election held in any such Territory or other place, or be eligible for election or appointment to or be entitled to hold any
office or place of public trust, honor or emolument, in, under,
or for any such Territory or place, or under the United States "

This law was construed in Murphy v. Ramsey, 114 U. S. 39,
where it was held that Mary Ann M. Pratt and Mildred E.
Randall met the requirements of the law, and that they were
entitled to their action against the judges of election for refusing to allow them to vote.

As Congress has not annulled any law of the Territories
of Washington or Wyoming which declared female as well
as male citizens entitled to suffrage on equal terms, these equal
suffrage laws are recognized as fully within the legislative
power conferred upon those Territories.

II. THE MEANING OF THE TERM "CITIZEN OF THE UNITED
STATES."—In The Slaughter House Cases, 16 Wall. 72, the
Supreme Court of the United States say: "The first section of
the fourteenth article, to which our attention is more specially

invited, opens with a definition of citizenship—not only citizenship of the United States, but citizenship of the States. No such definition was previously found in the Constitution, nor had any attempt been made to define it by act of Congress. It had been the occasion of much discussion in the courts, by the executive departments, and in the public journals. It had been said by eminent judges that no man was a citizen of the United States, except as he was a citizen of one of the States composing the Union. Those, therefore, who had been born and resided always in the District of Columbia, or in the territories, though in the United States, were not citizens. Whether this proposition was sound or not had never been judicially decided. But it had been held by this Court, in the celebrated Dred Scott case, only a few years before the outbreak of the civil war, that a man of African descent, whether a slave or not, was not and could not be a citizen of a State or of the United States. * * *

"It declares that persons may be citizens of the United States without regard to their citizenship of a particular State, and it overturns the Dred Scott decision by making *all persons* born within the United States and subject to its jurisdiction, citizens of the United States."

From the date of the adoption of that amendment, every statute containing the words "citizens of the United States," has had the meaning of that section; and if the Statute originally had a different meaning, that amendment defined its true reading thereafter. The Supreme Court of the United States held in Neal v. Delaware, 103 U. S. 389, that "the adoption of the Fifteenth Amendment had the effect, in law, to remove from the State Constitution, or render inoperative, that provision which restricts the right of suffrage to the white race."

The same rule makes all acts of Congress, all organic laws of the territories, conform to the definition of citizen in the first section of the Fourteenth Amendment.

That section, as construed by the Supreme Court of the United States, does not regulate the right of suffrage in a State. But where the qualification for a voter is that of being a "citizen of the United States," it defines the meaning of that term.   As it is a term used with reference to civil and not political rights in that section, the term cannot be used to disqualify women from voting.   The section knows no sex. "Citizen" is used in the sense of a member of the "body politic."

In Ex Parte Yarbrough, 110 U. S. 664, the Supreme Court of the United States qualify the expression in the case of Minor v. Happersett, 21 Wall. 162, that "The Constitution of the United States does not confer the right of suffrage upon any one," by saying:

"But the court was combating the argument that this right was conferred on all citizens, and therefore upon women as well as' upon men."

In the case of Baldwin v. Franks, 120 U. S. 690, where a Chinaman, who was a resident of California, claimed the benefit of the statutes protecting the civil rights of "citizens," the court held: "The person on whom the wrong to be punishable must be inflicted, is described as a citizen.   In the Constitution and laws of the United States the word 'citizen' is generally, if not always, used in a political sense, to designate one who has the rights and privileges of a citizen of a State or of the United States.   It is so used in section 1 of Art XIV of the amendments of the Constitution, which provides that 'all persons born or naturalized in the United States, and subject to the jurisdiction thereof, are citizens of the United States and of the State wherein they reside,' and that 'no State shall make or enforce any law which shall abridge the privileges or immunities of citizens of the United States.' But it is also sometimes used in popular language to indicate the same thing as resident, inhabitant, or person."

The statute referred to, made no distinction of sex as to civil rights.   Nor did the court.

III.   THE POLITICAL RIGHTS OF A CITIZEN OF THE UNITED STATES.—All the territory of the United States originally belonged to the States.   The right to vote in the States was regulated by State constitutions.   The right to vote in the Territories depended on the acts of Congress, or on the acts of the Territorial legislatures.   Some of the Territorial courts claim that under the full legislative power given them, the Territories can disfranchise classes of citizens for other causes than crime.

The question is not involved in this case. Sec. 1860 has imposed the limitations upon the power of the Territorial legislatures, and does not require that the voters shall be "males."

Under the second section of the Fourteenth amendment, the right to vote within the States, on the part of adult male citizens of the United States, residents of the State, is protected against encroachments on the part of Congress or of the State legislatures, except for crime. This amends the old constitution. The section did not forbid States to enfranchise women. It did prohibit the States from disfranchising any adult male citizen of the United States, resident in the State, except for crime.

IV. The Effect of the Fourteenth Amendment.—As held by the court in Neal v. Delaware, 103 U. S. 389, this amendment became the supreme law, and defined the meaning of the term "citizens of the United States" in the first section.

The second section defined and protected the rights of "male inhabitants" of a State, who were "citizens" of the United States within the meaning of the first section of the amendment. It does not limit the political rights of citizens of the United States to "male" voters.

As held by Judge Cranch of the Supreme Court of the District of Columbia, in The United States v. More, 3 Cranch, 162, "The constitution was made for the benefit of every citizen of the United States, and there is no such citizen, whatever may be his condition, or wherever he may be situated within the limits of the territory of the United States, who has not a right to the protection it affords."

The unlimited legislative power over the rights of citizens claimed by some courts, was denied by the Supreme Court of the United States in Loan Association v. Topeka, 20 Wall. 662, in which the court held: "It must be conceded that there are such rights in every free government beyond the control of the State. A government which recognized no such rights, which held the lives, the liberty, and the property

of its citizens subject at all times to the absolute disposition
and unlimited control of even the most democratic depository
of power, is after all but a despotism."

This was re-affirmed in Maynard v. Hill, 8 S. C. Reporter,
p. 726.

There can be no question, therefore, of the power of a Territorial legislature to define the qualifications of electors within
the limitation, that the elector must be a citizen, or a person
who has declared his intention to become such.

V. THE EFFECT OF THE REVISION OF THE STATUTES OF
THE UNITED STATES.—This is to be determined by the repeal
clauses and the interpretation clauses of the Revised Statutes,
in connection with the Constitution.

Sec. 5596, R. S. U. S. repealed the Organic acts of all the
Territories then existing, and left in force only the sections of
the Revised Statutes applicable to the several Territories.

The word "citizen" is then to be determined by the Revised
Statutes of 1874.

The word "citizen" is used generically in these statutes; and
provisions where it is so used—where masculine pronouns are
used, as in the naturalization law—are to be construed as including both sexes. This is a well-known rule of law; and
is enforced in the enacting clause of the Revised Statutes:

"In determining the meaning of the Revised Statutes, or of
any act or resolution of Congress passed subsequent to Feb.
25, 1871, words importing the singular number may extend
and be applied to several persons or things; words importing
the plural number may include the singular; *words importing
the masculine gender may be applied to females.*"—(R. S. p. 1.)

"The Revised Statutes must be treated as the legislative
declaration of the statute law on the subjects which they embrace on the first day of December, 1873. When the meaning
is plain, the courts cannot look to the statutes which have
been revised, to see if Congress erred in that revision, but may
do so when necessary to construe doubtful language used in ex-
pressing the meaning of Congress."—(United States v. Bowen,
100 U. S. 513; Arthur v. Dodge, 101 U. S. 36.)

"No reference, therefore, can be had to the original statutes

to control the construction of any section of the Revised Statutes, when its meaning is plain, although in the original statutes it may have had a larger or more limited application than
that given to it in the revision."—(Deffeback v. Hawke, 115
U. S. 402.)

The power of the legislature of Washington Territory is to
be determined by the letter of the Revised Statutes, unless
controlled by the interpretation clauses or by the constitution.
As the term "citizen of the United States" was not limited
to males prior to the Revision, and is not so limited by the
Revision, it cannot by any true rule of interpretation be limited
in Sec. 1860, to "male" persons only.

As to declaratory statutes, the Supreme Court of the United
States held:

"Both in principle and authority, it may be taken to be
established, that a legislative body may by statute declare the
construction of previous statutes so as to bind the courts in
reference to all transactions occurring after the passage of the
law, and may in many cases thus furnish the rule to govern
the courts in transactions which are past, provided no constitutional right of the party is violated."—(Stockdale v. Insurance Companies, 20 Wall. 331.)

VI. THE TRUE RULE OF INTERPRETATION.—Where the legislative meaning is plain, there is not only no occasion for
rules to aid the interpretation, but it is contrary to the rules to
employ them. The judges have simply to enforce the statute
according to its obvious terms.—(Bishop on Statutory Crimes,
sec. 72; Hyatt v. Taylor, 42 N. Y., 258, 260; Benton et al. v.
Wickwire, 54 N. Y. 328; McCluskey v. Cromwell, 11 N. Y.
601; Rosenplaenter v. Roessle, 54 N. Y. 262; Wilkinson v. Le-
land, et al. 2 Pet. 662.)

"In construing these laws, it has been truly stated to be
the duty of the court to effect the intention of the legislature;
but this intention is to be searched for in the words which the
legislature has employed to convey it."—(Schooner Paulina's
Cargo v. United States, 7 Cranch, 60.)

"The courts must give effect to the intention of Congress
as manifested by the statute. They cannot make, but can only

declare the law."—(Burnett v. United States, 116 U. S. 161.)

"But with language clear and precise and with its meaning evident, there is no room for construction, and consequently no need of anything to give it aid."—(United States v. Graham, 110 U. S. 221.)

"Our duty is to read the statute according to the natural and obvious import of the language, without resorting to subtle and forced construction for the purpose of either limiting or extending its operation."—(Waller v. Harris, 20 Wend. [N. Y.] 561; Pott v. Arthur, 104 U. S. 735.)

"When the language is plain, we have no right to insert words and phrases so as to incorporate in the statute a new and distinct provision."—(United States v. Temple, 105 U. S. 99.)

Vattel's first general maxim of interpretation is that 'it is not allowable to interpret what has no need of interpretation,' and he continues: "When a deed is worded in clear and precise terms—when its meaning is evident and leads to no absurd conclusion—there can be no reason for refusing to admit the meaning which such deed naturally presents. To go elsewhere in search of conjectures, in order to restrict or extend it, is but to elude it."—(Vattel's Law of Nations, 244.) Here the words are plain and interpret themselves.—(Ruggles v. Illinois, 108 U. S. 534.)

There is, therefore, no reason founded on the language or policy of the clause to insert a restriction and locality which have not been expressed by the legislature. On the contrary, upon general principles of interpretation, when the words are general, the court is not at liberty to insert limitations not called for by the sense, or the objects, or the mischiefs of the enactment.—(United States v. Coombs, 12 Pet. 80. Also see Maillard v. Lawrence, 16 How. 261.)

Another rule of interpretation is that words are to be interpreted for the protection of rights, and a liberal construction is adopted for that reason. This applies as well to political rights as to civil rights.

In many States the courts have held that the right to regulate suffrage, especially in regard to registration laws, must not be used to disfranchise any voter who has the constitutional qualifications. Under this rule, the essential qualifications for suffrage in the territories are: Citizenship, or a declaration of intention to become a citizen, residence, and having attained the age of twenty-one years.

This confers no authority to disfranchise any one on account of sex; and beyond question does not demand that it shall be done. · Under this rule, the legislation of Congress in regard to the disfranchisement of women in Utah, affects that Territory alone. That was an amendment of the law of 1882, which disfranchised bigamists and polygamists, and the women who cohabited with them. The same rule was applied to both sexes. This law did not prevent an amendment of the election laws in any territory which might abolish sex as a disqualification for voting or for holding office.

The Organic law of Washington Territory, Sec. 1860, R. S. U. S., is ample authority for the Act of January 18, 1888, defining the qualifications of voters. The words, "citizens of the United States" have included both sexes since the nation existed, and especially since the adoption of the Fourteenth Amendment. The courts are bound by that Amendment, and have no authority to interpolate the word "male," under any pretense that the history of the times in 1853, excluded women from political rights, and they are, therefore, not citizens of the United States. The words are plain. Their duty is equally plain. The question is not the policy or the impolicy of granting women the right to vote on equal terms with men; but the duty of courts to follow the plain language of the Constitution of the United States in construing laws made by Congress.

Seattle, W. T.   *W. S. Bush.*

JAMES R. DOOLITTLE.

Side by side with ex-Senator Trumbull, and scarcely less distinguished, stands ex-Senator Doolittle. A parallel might be drawn, which would exhibit many points in common.—Both having been upon the bench—both having had a brilliant career in the United States Senate—both going into the Senate as republicans, and retiring therefrom as democrats—both when returning to the practice of their profession, gravitating to the queen city of the West as the one offering the best field for the exercise of their forensic powers, and for the enjoyment of the rewards of a well-earned reputation.

James R. Doolittle was born in Hampton, Washington County, New York, January 3, 1815. His father was Reuben and his mother Sarah (Rood) Doolittle. His father was a farmer and mill-owner, the founder of a school and church, and a man of beneficent and generous impulses.

After going through the ordinary course of preparatory education, James R. entered Geneva College in Western New York, and graduated in 1834, taking the highest honors of his class in scholarship.

He then studied law in Rochester, and was admitted to the bar in 1837, by the Supreme Court of New York. Moving to Wyoming County, he there engaged in a successful practice. Though a democrat, he was elected district attorney in a whig county, and served with general satisfaction. In those days he was an active politician.

(58)

In 1848, General Cass was the candidate of the Democratic, and General Taylor of the Whig party, for President of the United States. Before his nomination Gen. Cass had written the celebrated "Nicholson Letter," in which he had said the best way to destroy slavery, was to spread it all over the territories. A good many in the Democratic party were opposed to this principle of "diffusion," and Mr. Doolittle was among the number. He was in the State Convention of New York, and though at that time a very young man, he introduced in the Convention the following resolution:

"Resolved, That while the democracy of New York, represented in this convention, will faithfully adhere to all the compromises of the Constitution, and maintain all the reserved rights of the States, they declare—since the crisis has arrived when that question must be met—their uncompromising hostility to the extension of slavery into any territory now free, which may be hereafter acquired by any action of the government of the United States."

This was the doctrine of the famous Wilmot Proviso; and to understand the full import of the resolution it must be borne in mind that our armies were then in possession of Mexico, and a treaty was pending by which we were about to acquire California and New Mexico—free territories, into which the "diffusion" doctrine of Gen. Cass was intended to introduce slavery.

The resolution was rejected by a majority of one vote. By the president of the convention it was indignantly torn in pieces. On that rejected resolution a convention was called and the Free-soil party was organized. The result was, the nomination of Van Buren as the Free-soil candidate for president. As a consequence Gen. Taylor was elected—the "diffusion" of slavery was defeated, and California admitted as a free State.

In 1851, Mr. Doolittle removed to Wisconsin, and there engaged in the practice of his profession. His decided abilities and noble traits of character were at once recognized, and he entered upon an eventful and successful career. He soon ranked among the ablest and best lawyers in the State. He was retained by Governor Farwell in important cases involving the interests of the State, and in other important litigations. He successfully competed in the courts with older attorneys and held his own among the able lawyers for which Wisconsin was noted at that time.

In 1852, he gave his support to Gen. Pierce for president, not considering there was longer any ground of controversy between himself as a Free-soil democrat, and the Democratic party, as the compromise of 1851 excluded·slavery from all the Territories acquired from Mexico, and both political parties pledged themselves to abide by it, and not agitate the slavery. question, *in or out of Congress.*

In 1853, after a residence in the State of but two years, he was elected judge of the First Judicial Circuit, the most populous judicial district in the State. As a jurist he ranked among the ablest and most impartial in the Northwest. He brought to the bench a thorough knowledge of law; varied learning, and a clear perception of right and justice. In March, 1856, he resigned his office and retired from the bench.

In the summer of 1856, occurred the border-ruffian invasion and subjugation of Kansas, and the subsequent dead-lock in the two houses of Congress. The House had inserted a provision in the army appropriation bill, that no part of the money should be used to enforce the laws passed in Kansas by the border-ruffian Legislature; laws by which slavery was declared to be a divine institution, and any man who questioned it was.liable to be fined and imprisoned. The Senate struck it out. There was a tremendous struggle. At last the law was passed, and means were put into the hands of the President to sustain slavery in the Territory of Kansas, from which it had been excluded by the Missouri Compromise.

The time had now come when Mr. Doolittle must again break with his party. Until the last moment he had hoped the House would prevail. But when that noble band with whom his sympathies were so strongly enlisted, were overcome —when finally the Senate had prevailed, he could not longer remain silent. His first speech was at Racine. Referring to this speech afterward, he said:

"When I came to speak my soul went out with all the earnestness and intensity of thought, feeling and expression of which it is capable; all the more earnest and intense because I had hoped till Congress adjourned, that the House would prevail—that the Senate would yield. I spoke at Racine to an immense crowd. I stripped myself as a farmer does to his work. It was no child's play with me; it was work—earnest work—to save freedom to the Territories and freedom to ourselves."

His next speech was in Milwaukee. Concerning that effort we will again let him speak for himself:

"I took off my coat there; I gave free utterance to all the indignation of my soul. The thought that the federal government would enforce that usurpation, and thereby force slavery into the free territory of Kansas; was the power that moved me."

He now found himself in the Republican party, which was organized the same year, upon the corner-stone of the non-extension of slavery.

In January, 1857, Judge Doolittle was elected to the Senate of the United States, and at the expiration of his term was re elected, serving continuously until 1869. During those politically exciting and stormy years, he was a conspicuous figure in the councils of the nation. His senatorial career is too well known to require any extended notice in this place. His period of service covered the election of Lincoln—the breaking out of the war, and its prosecution to the close—the impeachment of Andrew Johnson, and much of the work of reconstruction. He was a hard and effective worker, serving on the committee of foreign affairs, and of military affairs; also as chairman of the committee on Indian affairs. In 1861, he was a member of the committee of thirteen distinguished senators who were appointed to confer with a like committee of the House to devise some plan to settle the threatened disruption, without resort to arms.

In the Senate, his moderation, urbanity, dignity of manner and personal character won him the esteem of his political opponents, who recognized in him an antagonist who always fought fairly, who never lost his temper, and never struck a foul blow. He would not condescend to tricks in debate, and earnestly opposed all irregular strategy in party action. In the impeachment and trial of Andrew Johnson, and in some of the reconstruction measures resulting from the war, he felt obliged to oppose in Congress the party with which he had been acting.

During the summer recess of 1865, as a member of a joint

committee of both houses, of which he was chairman, he visited
Kansas, Colorado and New Mexico, to inquire into the condition of the Indians west of the Mississippi, and reported their
condition and wants, suggesting reforms in their management,
and gained much information which aided him in future legislation. The inquiry and investigation were thorough, and
the results were published in a volume which contained much
valuable information concerning the various Indian tribes.

Senator Doolittle had, in 1860, framed the call for the Republican Convention at Chicago, which nominated Lincoln,
and in 1866, he drew the call for and presided over the national Union Convention held in Philadelphia.

After his retirement from the Senate in 1869, he engaged in
the practice of his profession in Chicago, retaining his residence in Racine. His partner in the practice in Chicago, was
the Hon. Jesse O. Norton, who had been a member of the
House. After the fire of 1871, the firm was dissolved, and
a partnership was formed with his son, James R. Doolittle, Jr.
In 1876, Henry McKey came into the partnership, under the
firm name of Doolittle and McKey, and this firm has since
continued. The office is at 169 Jackson St.

In 1876, Judge Doolittle was one of the distinguished visitors
to Louisiana, to investigate the circumstances attending the
result of the presidential election in that State.

He was a member of the board of trustees of the University
of Chicago so long as the institution had an existence, and has
lectured upon equity jurisprudence in the Union College of
Law.

On the 4th of February, 1875, Judge Doolittle, at the request of many friends, made a speech in the Assembly Chamber,
at Madison, Wisconsin, in vindication of his political course,
and in reply to bitter attacks which had been made upon him
because of his leaving the Republican party. In that address he gave a graphic sketch of the rise and progress of political parties from the organization of the government. The
election of Washington unanimously, without any party—the
difference in his cabinet between Hamilton and Jefferson—the
formation of the Federal school of politics under Hamilton

and the Republican under Jefferson—the election of Adams in 1796 as a Federalist, and of Jefferson in 1800 as a Republican —the re-election of Jefferson in 1804—the election of Madison as a Republican in 1808 and his re-election in 1812—so of Monroe in 1816 and in 1820—the disappearance of the Federal party in 1816, after the war with England, and the merger of nearly everything into the Republican party—the various Republican candidates in 1824, resulting in no election by the people, and the election of John Quincy Adams by the House —the election of Jackson by the people in 1828 and again in 1832—the first national party convention, and the organization of the Democratic party in 1832, and of the Whig party in 1834—the election of Van Buren as a Democrat in 1836 and of Harrison as a Whig in 1840—of Polk, Democrat, in 1844, and Taylor, Whig, in 1848—this last result being largely due to the organization of the Free-soil party already mentioned; and finally the election of Pierce, Democrat, in 1852, and of Buchanan, in 1856, thus coming down to the memory of most of those whom he was addressing, and to the events in which he had himself been a prominent actor.

A noble feature of this address was the calm and dispassionate manner in which he met the personal abuse which had been heaped upon him, absolutely refusing to participate in that mode of political warfare.

Judge Doolittle is a man of great intellectual power. The writer of this sketch well remembers sitting within the bar of the Supreme Court at Washington, many years ago, observing somewhat listlessly, the proceedings, when an attorney arose and commenced, in a quiet manner, and with a calm and distinct voice, the argument of an admiralty case. As the statement of facts proceeded, showing the situation of two vessels which had collided, and the different movements of the various parties connected with the vessels, the audience became more and more interested, until finally, all, including every judge upon the bench, were listening, eagerly, intent to catch every word of this glowing picture which was being painted upon the imagination.

This was Judge Doolittle, and from that time, the writer

has considered him the intellectual peer of any man in this country.

Judge Doolittle is universally respected and revered by the bar of this City, toward whom he maintains the attitude of friend and counsellor. We but echo the voice of the bar in wishing him many years of enjoyment of a well-earned fame.

WILLIAM B. KEEP.

The great railway system of which Chicago is the center, has rendered necessary the study and practice of railroad law as a specialty. The railroad litigation has been immense, and must for many years to come, occupy much of the time and attention of the courts.

The more important Companies have general solicitors, who act principally as counsel, going into court only in the more important cases. Such are Judge Beckwith, and Messrs. Ayer and Goudy. At the same time they have attorneys who take charge of the current legal business, and of the ordinary litigation in the courts. Among these none are more active, able and efficient than William B. Keep, General Attorney of the Chicago and Northwestern Railway Company.

Mr. Keep was born at Beloit, Wisconsin, March 13, 1852. His father was Judge of the First Judicial Circuit of Wisconsin. He died when William was but nine years old.

The son developed in early life a desire and determination to have a good education, and to be properly prepared and equipped for the struggle before him—to be in fact among those fittest to survive, while others should be going down.

Having prepared himself by the usual preliminary course, he entered Beloit College, from which institution he graduated, in 1873. The same summer he commenced reading law at Omaha, Nebraska. He completed his studies in the spring of 1874, in the office of Ayer and Kales, of this City.

In 1875 he was admitted to the bar, and soon afterward commenced practice. In 1881, he became associated with Mr.

Royse, Attorney of the Lake Shore and Michigan Southern Railroad Company. In September, 1883, he was employed by the Northwestern Railway Company, as an Attorney for that road, acting as assistant Counsel with the Hon. Burton C. Cook, then the General Solicitor of the Company.

In 1885, he was made the General Attorney of the Company, which position he now holds, Hon. William C. Goudy being the General Counsel. Mr. Keep also tries the cases of the North Side Horse Railroad Company and of the West Division Horse Railroad Company. He has been extremely successful in the litigated cases, his Companies thus far not having been obliged to pay but one judgment since the business came into his hands. Office at 22—5th Avenue.

During the last five years Mr. Keep has probably tried more railroad cases than any attorney in the City. He has a remarkable memory, and more than once has astonished the judge on the bench as well as the attorneys in court by repeating after the jury has been empaneled, the name of every juryman, and giving his residence and occupation.

Mr. Keep is a clear and correct thinker, and is exhaustive in his researches into the law of a case. He has one quality which might well be emulated by the younger members of the bar—modesty. Without relying upon the tinsel of superficial eloquence, he is willing to take his place in the profession, wherever the qualities of his mind, aided and supported by close application and thorough research, may assign him.

EDWARD F. DUNNE.

Edward F. Dunne, of the firm of Hynes and Dunne, was born Oct. 12, 1853, at Waterville, Conn. He is a son of the Hon. P. W. Dunne, ex-member of the Illinois Legislature. He received his early education at the public schools of Peoria, graduating from the High School at the age of 16. In 1870, he entered St. Jarlath's College, taking first honors in all departments at the end of the term. He matriculated in Trinity

College, Dublin University, Oct. 7, 1871. He had for a classmate, Oscar Wilde, the ex-esthete. While in the University, Mr. Dunne was a first honor man for several successive terms, but owing to family reverses he was compelled to leave Trinity before completing his course. He engaged in business in Peoria, without, however, abandoning his intention of studying for the bar. Coming to Chicago in 1875, he attended lectures at the Union Law College for a year. With the design of acquiring practical experience in a law office, he entered the office of O' Brien & Kettelle, remaining with the firm until his admission to the bar in Mount Vernon, in 1877. In the same class with him were Harry Rubens, Esq., Levy Mayer, Esq., and other active members of the Chicago bar.

Mr. Dunne devoted himself immediately to his profession with diligence and success. He has never permitted politics to interfere with his professional business. He has never held office, nor sought it.

In 1878, he went into partnership with the ex-Justice of the Supreme Court, Walter B. Scates, and the Hon. W. J. Hynes, under the firm name of Scates, Hynes & Dunne.

About 1880, a partnership was formed between Messrs. Hynes and Dunne and William J. English, whose partner, Judge T. A. Moran, had been elevated to the bench. The new firm continued under the name of Hynes, English & Dunne until July, 1887, when Mr. Dunne and Mr. Hynes organized the present firm of Hynes & Dunne.

The business of the firm is large and prosperous. It has carried to a successful termination many important cases, among them the St. Clara Female Academy v. Sullivan and the Moran breach of promise suit. It counts among its clients the Hibernian Banking Association, Fortune Bros. Brewing Co., Keeley Brewing Co., Order of the Servite Sisters, the Catholic Archbishop of Chicago, Warren Springer Manufacturing Works, P. F. Ryan & Co., D. M. and R. J. Goodwillie, H. D. Kelly & Co., the Gault House, the late Vicar General Conway, etc. The firm has a large probate and real estate practice, and has the management of several large estates.

Office, 22—79 Clark St.

The subject of this sketch was married in 1881, to Elizabeth J. Kelly, daughter of E. F. Kelly, Esq., of Enright & Kelly.

He has been a member of the Irish American Club since its organization.

Mr. Dunne is very persistent in every thing he undertakes. He has already attained a large degree of success, a success which has been legitimate, and not as in some cases, to be traced to adventitious or transitory causes.

He is one of our most substantial, reliable attorneys.

EPHRAIM BANNING

Was born near Bushnell, McDonough County, Illinois, July 21, 1849. His father was originally from Virginia and his mother from Kentucky. His father, after whom he was named, was a plain, sturdy farmer, without much education, except as acquired in the school of life, but with a spirit always full of hope, courage and determination. His mother, who was a sister of the late Judge Pinkney H. Walker of the Supreme Court of Illinois, was a woman of much character, distinguished among her acquaintances for quiet common sense and a most amiable disposition. On his mother's side, were a number of distinguished men, among others his grandfather, Gilmer Walker, an able and honored lawyer, and his great-uncle, Cyrus Walker, said to have been one of the ablest lawyers in Kentucky, and afterward one of the ablest in Illinois.

His father's circumstances were such that from his earliest childhood young Banning was necessarily deprived of many of the opportunities and privileges generally considered indispensable to the proper development of boyhood life. This was particularly so in the matter of education, for in this respect he was always required to contend against adverse circumstances. Nevertheless, being an apt scholar, quick and anxious to learn, he acquired knowledge readily, and on more than one occasion in his boyhood and youth took the prizes in his school.

When about seventeen years of age, and for two or three

years afterward, he studied the languages, and higher branches generally, under the tutorship of Rev. J. P. Finley, D. D., at Brookfield, Missouri.

After leaving Dr. Finley's academy, Mr. Banning taught school a few months, and during this period began the study of law. He afterward continued his legal studies in the office of Hon. Samuel P. Huston of Brookfield, and then, in the spring of 1871, came to Chicago and entered the office of Messrs. Rosenthal & Pence as a clerk and student. In June, 1872, he was admitted to the bar by the Supreme Court of Illinois, and in October of the same year he opened an office and began practice for himself.

The building up of a practice by a young lawyer is generally slow work, especially in a large city, and in this respect Mr. Banning had the usual experience. His business gradually increasing, in the course of a few years he came to be recognized in the courts and at the bar as a lawyer in fair general practice.

About this time, however, several cases came to him involving questions of patent law. On this account, and because of its constantly involving the study and application of beautiful scientific principles, he formed a special liking for this branch of jurisprudence. His first argument in a patent cause was made before Judge Blodgett in 1877, and from about this time, or a little later, may be dated his withdrawal from general practice to devote himself exclusively to patent law. It was also about this time that he was joined by his brother, Thomas A. Banning, with whom he has ever since been in partnership. In a short time, the firm of Banning & Banning became widely known as successful patent lawyers. Its business covering every thing in the line of patent and trade-mark law, it has within the last ten years, argued a very large number of cases of this kind, and it now has a large practice in the Supreme Court of the United States, as well as in the lower federal courts in Chicago and elsewhere. One of their cases recently argued in the Supreme Court, involved over a hundred thousand dollars; another case, still pending, relates to a manufacturing business claimed to be worth more than half that amount every year;. while others, in one of the Circuit Courts, involve the question whether a single company shall be allowed to control the entire air-brake business of the country. The firm still continues as at first organized, except that Mr. George S. Payson has been recently admitted as a member.

Mr. Banning was married in October, 1878, to Lucretia T. Lindsley, an accomplished lady, of earnest christian character, descended from an old and respected family, of whom one was the first president of Yale College, and others prominent figures in colonial and revolutionary times. Mrs. Banning died in February 1887, leaving three small children, boys, all of whom are still living.

Mr. Banning is an elder in the Presbyterian Church, a republican in politics, a member of the Union League Club, and connected with several organizations interested in the material and moral progress of the city. In addition to his legal work, he continues to keep up the study of language, and devotes much time to the reading of history and general literature; and during the past year he has traveled extensively in various European countries.

JOHN C. SIMONDS

Was born near Cairo, Illinois, June 28, 1848. Hon. Cyrus G. Simonds, his father, was one of the leading lawyers of Illinois. He had been a member of the Illinois Legislature, and acquired distinction as a brilliant and powerful advocate. A large proportion of the cases in that section of country found him retained on one side or the other.

John C. was educated at various academic institutions, and in the University of Michigan. He was admitted to the Michigan Bar in the spring of 1873, and to the New York Bar two years later. After some years of successful practice in the New York courts, Mr. Simonds came to Chicago in 1881, where he has since been an esteemed and successful practitioner.

For several years after his arrival in Chicago, Mr. Simonds' practice consisted largely in the preparation of opinions upon statements of facts submitted for his consideration, and of arguments on appeals. For such intellectual effort he is well endowed.

His mind is clear and incisive, and his judgment good. He is adroit in the art of dialectic fence, well grounded in the principles of the law, and skillful in their application. The merit of distinguishing cases, and noting wherein those that resemble differ, is his in a high degree. Lord Bacon held it the sacred duty of the lawyer to master some legal principles and adjudged cases thereon, to reduce them to system, and give to his profession the ripe fruit of his severer studies. Mr. Simonds has paid this debt to the profession in his "History, Methods and Law of the Produce Exchange." He has also written just and discriminating pictures of Western lawyers in Biographical Sketches.

It was long ago remarked by the great Burke, that the study and practice of the law tended rather to the strength than the liberality and culture of the mind. Mr. Simonds with his legal faculties and acquisitions, has also a rare love for *belle-lettres* and the arts, a mind and heart thoroughly in sympathy with the great ennobling movements of the times, and an ear attuned to "the still sad music of humanity." In his valuable and eloquent "History of Manual Labor in all Lands and Ages," he has undertaken authentically to tell the story of the common people—their past progress, present conditions and future hopes.—With rare eloquence and truth, he "has essayed to do for the nameless heroes of all time—those masses of the people that have fought the battles, builded the cities, and wrought the fabric of our civilization, what has already been done for the monarch, the warrior, the nobleman and the statesman." Truly a noble and worthy end.

A list of his contributions to leading magazines on a great variety of topics in literature, law and economics would occupy too much space. They are all characterized by culture, thought and research. He has draped his ideas with the vesture of a clear and classic English.

Recently Mr. Simonds has been chosen as lecturer on "Medical Jurisprudence" at the Chicago College of Physicians and Surgeons. He is also engaged in active practice with Messrs. Edward Maher and Samuel D. Snow, well known and prosperous Chicago lawyers.

Office, 47—187 Lasalle St.

HENRY V. FREEMAN

Of the Chicago Bar, was born Dec. 20, 1842, of New England ancestry, coming from Cape Cod, Mass. One of his grandfathers, about eight generations ago, was Elder William Brewster of Plymouth Colony. His father is Henry Freemen now of Rockford in this State, who for nearly a third of a century, first at Freeport and then at Rockford, was one of the best known superintendents of schools in Northern Illinois. Retired now from professional work, he enjoys in well earned rest all that Shakespeare says should accompany old age.

At sixteen years of age, Henry V. began teaching a country district school. He varied this occupation with work on a farm, and attendance at the preparatory department of Beloit College, until the summer of 1862, when, having just completed his preparation and been admitted to college, he enlisted in Co. K. of the 74 Ill. Vol. Infy. He served three years with the Army of the Cumberland in this and other organizations, coming home at the end of the war in 1865, with the rank of Captain. He entered Yale College in the fall of that year and graduated in the class of 1869. He came to Chicago in the following October, and was admitted to the bar in 1870. Immediately after the great fire of October 9, 1871, the prospects for a young lawyer for the next year in the burned up city, not looking attractive, he was offered and accepted the position of principle of the High School at Charleston, Illinois. Returning to Chicago at the end of the school year in 1872, he was employed in the law offices of King, Scott & Payson, and Rich & Noble, until January 1st, 1873, when he began independent practice. He has continued ever since in the enjoyment of what has grown to be an excellent practice.

Mr. Freeman has been three times appointed attorney for Hyde Park, an office which he has filled with distinguished success. It is said that during the last two years he has not finally lost a single case for the Village. Though occasionally beaten in the lower courts, he succeeded in reversing the decision in every such case in the appellate or Supreme Court.

When this fact was referred to in Mr. Freeman's presence, he ascribed it to "good luck" mainly. While this is true to some extent, because the lawyer cannot make his facts, yet it is also true that "good luck" alone is not sufficient to account for such a record, when we consider the large number and varied character of the suits, which have been in the last few years brought for and against the large municipal corporation of Hyde Park. Mr. Freeman's "good luck" seems to have followed him before the Supreme Court. The reports of cases in which he has been counsel show that in the last ten years he has been on the successful side in nearly every case. The history of the "annexation" litigation is familiar to the people of Cook County. In this, although contending against greater odds than in most cases of public interest that have occurred here within our recollection, the views urged by Mr. Freeman were completely sustained by the Supreme Court. Probably no cases have ever arisen in Cook County of a civil nature where more pressure from the public and the press had to be overcome. It requires no small quantity of backbone, to stand up for one's convictions of duty under such circumstances. But the fight was completely successful. Annexation will doubtless come in time, but under better and wiser legislation than that which the Supreme Court was compelled to declare unconstitutional.

The law firm is Freeman & Walker, his partner being Mr. George R. Walker.

Office, 54—107 Dearborn St.

It will be remembered that when in June of last year, the Bar Association were called upon to nominate candidates for the Bench at a "Bar Primary," Mr. Freeman received within twelve of a majority of the votes cast by his professional brethren, although he was not previously a candidate, and his name was not suggested until a large vote had already been polled.

Among well known and important cases in which Mr. Freeman has been employed as counsel, may be mentioned the case of Smythe v. Holmes, involving the constitutionality of the act under which Building Associations are incorporated in this State. The Supreme Court had decided the act invalid. Mr. Freeman was retained to apply for a rehearing. This was obtained, and after reargument the Supreme Court took back its former decision, and sustained the validity of the act. This decision has been very important in its consequences. Since it was rendered, the Building Associations have increased greatly through the State, and are doing for Chicago what Judge Sharswood of Pennsylvania said they had done for Philadelphia—making it "a city of comfortable homes for the poor."

Mr. Freeman is in the prime of life, physically, but scarcely yet in the maturity of his intellectual powers, which will constantly strengthen with exercise, for many years to come. Already occupying a commanding position at the bar, his future is easily to be predicted.

With a mind strong and clear, with untiring industry, and a noble ambition, it is scarcely possible to doubt that he will not only maintain his present position, but make it a stepping stone to other successes.

THE WOMAN LAWYER.

By Doctor Louis Frank, of the Faculty of Law at Bologna, Advocate at the Bar of Brussels.

Translated by Mary A. Greene, LL. B., Member of the Massachusetts Bar.

TRANSLATOR'S PREFACE.

This pamphlet was prepared and published by Dr. Frank in view of the application in September, 1888, of Mlle. Marie Popelin for admission to the Order of Advocates at Brussels. Mlle. Popelin is a recent graduate of the law department of the University of Brussels, and has passed all her examinations with a very high rank. The Court of Appeal is considering her case.

Dr. Frank reviews the history of woman in her attempts at recognition at the bar, shows the present state of the question in Europe and America, gives a brief biographical sketch of some women who have distinguished themselves in the law, and closes with a critical examination of the right of woman to plead in court.

He has kindly granted permission to me to make the translation for the purpose of publishing it in the Chicago Law Times.

HISTORICAL ASPECT OF THE QUESTION.

Among the Ancient Gauls, women were consulted upon public affairs, and took part in the labors of the men. According to Strabo, the distribution of occupations among men and women was exactly the reverse of that among the Greeks and

Romans, and this, adds the Greek geographer, is a peculiarity which asserts itself among many other barbarous nations.—(Strabo, Geography, Lib. IV, ch. IV, 3.)

In spite of their participation in the discussion of the public interests, the women were remarkably fruitful, and also excellent nurses.—(Id. Lib. IV, ch. IV, 5.)

Woman, among the Celts, was not excluded from religious functions, the Druidess being no exception. It is well known that the judging of the crime of murder was a right pertaining to the office of Druid; women then, could be called upon to try these crimes.

IN ANCIENT EGYPT descent was reckoned by the mother's side. The Egyptian law accorded to woman a privileged position which always excited the astonishment of the Greeks. The law of marriage favored the wife, who, free from any marital authority, enjoyed her property without any restraint. Nay more, the wife had charge of and managed the property of the family. Between husband and wife there was a complete equality of rights. According to Herodotus, "the women go into the public square, transact business, and occupy themselves with industrial pursuits."—(Herodotus, II. 35.)

Although we possess no affirmative testimony on this point, we may presume that this preponderating power of woman, which, among the Egyptians was evident as well in the family as upon the throne, did also exist in the administration of justice.—(Upon the ancient Egyptian law, see Les Origines du mariage et de la famille, by Giraud—Teulon, Professor in the University of Geneva. Geneva, Cherbuliez, 1884, ch. IX.)

AMONG THE JEWS, the equality of the sexes was far from being admitted. In the Bible and in the Talmud, the legal inferiority of the Jewish woman is clearly affirmed. The wife, submitted to the perpetual authority of her father or her husband, was a negative quantity in the community. If the Talmud, sanctioning an immemorial custom, imposed upon the father the obligation to endow his daughters, it was because they were incompetent to inherit.

A law refused to women the right to testify.—(M. Schebouoth, IV, 1.) According to the Mischna, the Jewish woman, in this respect on a level with a slave, could not be a witness, except in certain matrimonial questions, and when her own individual interests were involved. She had no right to be instructed. The schools were closed against her, and even in the bosom of the family the study of the law was forbidden her, because according to some of the rabbis, it was not suitable "to the fragility of her spirit, the delicacy of her feelings, and the especial modesty of her sex."

The Pentateuch commanded that children should be instructed in the law of God; tradition has taken care to inform us that this should only apply to male children.—(Talmud Kidouschin, f. 29, b.)

"'As far as one teaches the law to a woman, so far does he teach her impiety," say several doctors.—(Mischna Sota, III. 4.) It was necessary to make this study inaccessible to woman's comprehension, and to spare her the difficulties of legal and sacred science.

It is not surprising that under the influence of such principles, the doctors should pronounce in favor of excluding women from judicial and priestly functions.—(M. Kidouschin, I. 8; M. Sebahim, III. 1; T. Nidda, 50, a.) However, in spite of these prohibitions, several Jewish women did succeed in breaking from the very small circle of their legal capacity, and in distinguishing themselves in the domain of theology and of law. Anna and the prophetess Deborah have left to us sublime sayings, inspired by the most noble sentiments, and expressed in a language of most striking beauty. The prophetess Deborah gave evidence of great genius; her renown was such that Barak offered to her the command of the army of Israel.—(Judges, IV, 9.) Deborah even filled the office of judge among the Jews.

The Talmud cites to us a line of educated women, deeply versed in science. The rabbis had recourse to their light, and deferred greatly to their opinions.—(T. H'oulin, 109, b.)

Among those Jewish women who were particularly distinguished in the study of juridical and sacred science, we content ourselves with mentioning Beruria, who lived in the time of Hadrian, Maria, in the fifteenth century, El Muallima, Mirjam

Shapira, in the twelfth century, Sara Coppia Sullam, Eva Bacharach, Bella Falk Cohen and Mirjam Loria of Padua, in the seventeenth.

The subject of this sketch does not permit us to recall the numerous Jewesses who shone in politics, in medical science, arts, letters and benevolence, or who delivered admirable polemics in defence of the rights of the Jews.

In GREECE, M. Dupin contents himself with saying, women were excluded from the bar.—(Dupin, Profession d'avocat, Edit. belge, p. 27.) We shall endeavor to interpret this statement by pointing out the portion of error and the depth of exactness concealed in it.

Among the Greeks, particularly at Athens, every citizen had a right and an obligation to fill all public offices and functions. He was at the same time warrior and legislator, judge, and public accuser and defender. The administration of justice was considered an accessary of legislative action. Justice was meted out in the assemblies of the people, and the number of the judges varied from five hundred to six thousand.

In penal matters a purely accusatorial system was in use. Criminal prosecutions were public. In case of a transgression to the injury of the State, any citizen whatever was authorized to prosecute the guilty party; if the wrong was committed to the injury of one only, the right to prosecute belonged to the injured party alone.

Each accused citizen conducted his defense in person. The bar, in the modern sense of the word, was a thing absolutely unknown in Greece. A party could obtain the assistance of one of his relatives, of a friend, or a trustworthy person. The party began by defending himself, then the assistant followed, taking care always to justify his intervention in the debate by invoking the bonds of parentage or friendship which united him to the party to the cause.

As to women, they were considered inferior and subordinate beings with a weak and inefficient will. From the instant of their birth to the moment of their death, they were bowed down under the guardianship of their father, their husband, or of the heir at law of the father. They were the disgraced victims of a tyrannical legislation. During the day they could only go out from their homes in certain exceptional cases, and they were submitted to the authority of special functionaries whose duty it was to watch over them. Under a pretext of regulating their journeys, Solon imposed divers obligations upon them; among others that they should not go out at night unless in a chariot, and preceded by a torch, intended to give light and warning at each step.—(Plutarch, Life of Solon, XXVIII.)

Women received no instruction,—at the very most they were taught dancing and singing, in order to allow them to take part in the choruses in certain religious ceremonies. Most of the women of Athens did not know how to read or to write.

Relegated to the women's apartments they dwelt as total strangers to the splendor of that Hellenic civilization whose brilliancy we admire. They lived in ignorance of city affairs, and in indifference to them, and kept themselves at a distance from political strife and legal debates. One class of women alone, the courtesans, succeeded in enjoying a privileged position, in taking part in philosophical conversations and the discussions of the men, and in acquiring an influence in the government of the republic, indirect, but nevertheless actually powerful.

The most renowned of these courtesans was Aspasia, who instructed both Socrates and Plato in eloquence. Celebrated for her brilliant beauty, remarkable for the charm of her conversation, Aspasia exercised a veritable fascination over the people of Athens. The charms of her wit, the depth of her conceptions, the power of her eloquence, permitted her to rule over all who came in contact with her. This learned and able woman became the legitimate wife of Pericles, after having been his mistress. She inspired her former lover with several of his ideas; history even attributes to her one of the most beautiful orations of Pericles, that delivered in honor of the citizens of Athens slain in the war against the Samians.—(Plutarch, Life of Pericles. Diodorus Siculus, Hist., Lib. XII.)

A prodigy among all women, Aspasia plead causes before the people of Athens.

IN ROME, an unmarried woman was placed under the authority of her father or of her guardian. Deprived of the free disposition of her property, she was held under the perpetual guardianship of her male kindred.

When married, she came under the power of her husband, and remained incapable of disposing of her property, even by will.—(Later, women were allowed to make a will, provided they were free from family bonds. When the *tutela muliebris* disappeared, they acquired a complete *testamenti factio activa*.)

It was not, as is generally supposed, in the interest of women, with a view to sheltering them from their incompetence or their inexperience, that this inferiority was declared. The guardianship was instituted in the interest of the guardian himself. Gaius, with laudable frankness has made confession of it. "Common opinion," he says, "is that women should be governed by tutors, because they have too scanty wit to govern themselves. This reasoning is more specious than solid. This tutelage has been established in the interest of the tutors themselves, in order that the woman of whom they are heirs presumptive, shall not have the power to deprive them by will, of their inheritance, nor impoverish them by alienation or by debts."—(Gaius, I. 190–192.)

Before Gaius, Cicero had already pronounced against this tutelage. "In place of tutors," he wrote, "in place of officers set apart, as among the Greeks, for the surveillance of women, there should be a censor to teach the men to control their wives."—(Cicero, De Republica, III. 7, nec vero mulieribus praefectus praeponatur qui apud Graecos creari solet; sed sit censor, qui viros doceat moderari uxoribus.)

In spite of the legal inferiority of the Roman woman and her exclusion from the *comitia*, she was not absolutely shut out from the forum. She was admitted into the judicial enclosure. Accompanied by her guardian she could appear in the tribunal, and when her personal interest was not at stake, she could appear alone, as witness for instance, or as representing another.

For a long time, the right to assist a pleader or an accused person was recognized as belonging to women. History has preserved the names of Amesia Sentia and Hortensia, two courageous women who distinguished themselves in the Roman forum.

A law made for a special case, excluded woman from the profession of advocate. A certain Afrania, or Caia Afrania (Juvenal calls her Cafrinia, Juvenal, Sat. II, 69), made herself unendurable in the forum. Continually haranguing in her own cause, she by her loquacity, effrontery and violent behavior, scandalized the judges to such an extent that she was henceforth forbidden to speak in public. Ultimately this prohibition was extended to all women.

Valerius Maximus, in that chapter of his History which is devoted to women who contested their own cases before the magistrates, has left to us a curious and original portrait of this singular woman.

"C. Afrania," he writes, "wife of the senator Licinius Buccio, being extremely litigious, plead continually her own causes before the praetor. This was not for lack of advocates, but from excess of boldness. By reason of making the tribunals resound with howlings uncommon in the forum, she became the most famous example of chicanery ever afforded by her sex. Thus the surname of Afrania was inflicted as a disgrace upon shrewish women. She lived until the year when C. Cæsar became consul for the second time. For in speaking of such a scourge, history should rather record the time of her extinction, than that of her beginning."—(Valerius Maximus, Hist. Lib. VIII, ch. III, 2. C. vero Afrania, prompta ad lites contrahendas, pro se semper apud praetorem verba fecit; non quod advocatis deficiebatur, sed quod impudentia abundabat. Itaque inusitatis foro- latribus assidue tribunalia exerceudo, muliebris calumniæ notissimum evasit exemplum; adeo, ut pro crimine improbis feminarum moribus C. Afraniæ nomen objiciatur. * * * * * Tale enim monstrum magis quo tempore exstinctum, quam quo sit ortum, memoriæ tradendum est.)

In speaking of these "*inusitatis foro latratibus*" in connection with Caphrania, Valerius Maximus falls into error. These howlings were not at all unusual, and did not pertain particularly to Caphrania. For Cicero tells us that the softness of speech which often makes the orator, had in his day become a very rare quality, and that certain advocates in his time howled in place of speaking.—(Et oratorem appellat, et suaviloquentiam tribuit; quæ nunc quidem non tam est in plerisque; latrant enim jam quidam oratores, non loquntur.—(Brutus, XV.) At a later day Quintilian and Martial quoted this saying of Cicero.)

Roman law forbade women to plead, that is to say to argue in court, on behalf of another. It took care to point out that the original reason of this exclusion, pronounced against all women, rested solely on the doings of Caphrania.

The law 1, 5, Dig. III. 1,—(de postulando), contains the following: (Praetor) feminas prohibet pro aliis postulare; et ratio quidem prohibendi, ne contra pudicitiam sexui congruentem alienis causis se immisceant, ne virilibus officiis fungantur mulieres. Origo vero introducta est a' Carfania, improbissima femina, quæ inverecunde postulans et Magistratum inquietans causam dedit Edicto.

The Theodosian Code, (de postulando, II, 10), authorized women to take part in a cause, but only for themselves, and not for others.

Justinian, in his turn, gave a new shape to this legislation by raising to a general and formal command the prohibition against a woman's appearance in matters of justice. He excluded women from all public and civil offices, forbade them to be judges, to plead, to intervene in law on behalf of another, to be procurators, and in this matter, assimilated women to minors.

The text of the law 2, Dig. L. 17, (de diversis regulis juris antiqui), is as follows: Feminæ ab omnibus officiis civilibus, vel publicis remotæ sunt; et ideo nec judices esse possunt, nec magistratum gerere, nec postulare, nec pro alio intervenire, nec procuratores existere. § 1. Item impubes omnibus officiis civilibus debet abstinere.

The Roman law considers the act of undertaking the defense of another to be a masculine duty which the female sex is incapable of performing. The text of the law 18, Cod. II, 13 (12) (de procuratoribus), plainly affirms this principle. Alienam suscipere defensionem virile est officium, et ultra sexum muliebrem esse constat.

If woman cannot be a judge, thus another text points out, this is not for want of the qualities requisite to the proper performance of those functions, but because of custom.

The law 12, § 2, D., de judiciis, tells us: Quidam enim lege impediuntur ne judices sint, quidam natura, quidam moribus; natura, ut surdus, mutus et perpetuo furiosus et impubes quia judicio carent; moribus: feminæ et servi, non quia non habent judicium, sed quia receptum est ut civilibus officiis non fungantur.

This text proclaims it then without circumlocution: woman, like the slave, cannot be a judge nor take part in the administration of justice, not for any reason based on nature, not because she lacks discernment; the cause of her exclusion is solely custom, "because it is admitted that women and slaves cannot fill civil offices." Custom, the proprieties, this is the sole reason for their disability.

Now who, in our time, among even the most ferocious adversaries of the emancipation of woman, would dare to affirm that this reason, drawn from the customs and the proprieties of eighteen centuries ago, has still in our day the least trace of any validity or of any foundation?

We have just seen, in a brief exposition, the different adjudications of the Roman law which excluded women from the administration of justice. In order to comprehend fully the spirit of this exceptional legislation, one must carry one's self back to the period which put it in force, and analyze the surrounding circumstances which furnished an opportunity for its coming to the light.

Women were freed from tutelage and from the *manus*. Too soon emancipated, they were making a scandalous misuse of their independence. In the State, they had usurped a preponderating influence, not in order to play the glorious part of the Fabii, the Cornelii, the Julii, the Terenzii, but to foment conspiracies, excite discords, publish proscriptions. Corruption, under the strangest forms, paraded itself in the most shameful excesses. In the midst of this general dissolution of morals, the Roman law dreamed of restraining the liberty of women with a network of disabilities of a new kind.

Morals had disappeared. In the vain hope of thus restoring the ancient austerity, the legislator, yielding to artless illusions, attempted to create a morality, a hopeless task, for laws have always been powerless to infuse morality into a social body gangrened with licentiousness.

The series of sumptuary laws began with the Oppian law, which forbade women to possess more than a half-ounce of gold, to wear clothing of various colors, to use carriages in Rome, etc. The Voconian law was enacted at about the same period, with intent to prevent women from enriching themselves by will. Let us mention further, among the numerous provisions of the Julian law, that which denied the capacity of adulteresses to testify in a judicial proceeding; finally, a little later, appeared the Velleien decree of the Senate, by virtue of which, in every kind of contract and obligation, woman is incapable of acting as surety, and even of doing any act whatever of intercession which would be as much for the profit of the women as assistance of the men.

In this very time it was that woman was deprived of the right to plead, that she was forbidden to do any judicial act for another, she was even declared incapable of maintaining a banking-house, under the pretext that this was also a masculine occupation.—(Lex 12, Dig. II, 13: Feminæ remotæ videntur ab officio argentarii, quum ea opera virilis est.

The Roman law went further yet. The law Julia de adulteriis, in one of its provisions, had forbidden the reception of the testimony of adulteresses. Under the influence of the anti-feministic tendencies which we have indicated, it was attempted to make general against all women, without exception, this incapacity to testify which in the beginning was pronounced solely against adulteresses.—(Lex 18, Dig. XXII, 5: Ex eo quod prohibet lex Julia de adulteriis testimonium dicere condemnatam mulierem, colligitur etiam mulieres testimonii in judicio dicendi jus habere.)

When, desirous to know the reasons for these astonishing prohibitions, we question the Latin authors, they with one ac_ cord reply that this incapacity results from the weakness of the sex, from its inexperience, its frivolity, its ignorance of the business of the forum.—(Cicero, pro Murena, 12: "propter infirmitatem consilii."—*Ulpian, XI, 1*: "propter sexus infirmitatem et propter forensium rerum ignorantiam.") What vulgar reasons are these!

Unquestionably the object of all this legislation, was to enclose the legal activity of woman in the sphere of her family relations, and, by restraining her faculties as much as possible, to diminish thus her ascendancy over man, and by this means to reduce her influence in society. Furthermore, the intent of the legislator was not concealed. It appears very clearly in a historical reminiscence which I do not think it out of place to recall.

It was several years after the passage of the Oppian law, and the women were demanding its repeal, while Porcius Cato desired to make it perpetual. On the voting day, the women, refusing to allow themselves to be turned aside by any representations, came out from their homes and besieged the streets of the city, and the avenues leading to the Forum. They surrounded the citizens who were going to the *comitia*, and besought them to give them liberty by pronouncing the repeal of the law. Cato, to reach the Forum, had to pass through the crowds of women. It was then, in an explosion of wrath, that he gave utterance to his famous and immortal speech; one of the most incisive and virulent sentences ever pronounced against women. Among other things he said: "Bridle this tyrannical nature and this untamed animal. Our ancestors desired women to be under the power of their fathers, their brothers, their husbands. Remember all those laws by which our fathers restrained the liberty of women, and curbed them under the power of men. And although by these laws your women are enslaved, you can hardly keep them under restraint. * * * Never suffer them to wrest your rights from you one by one, nor to become your equals, for as soon as they have begun but to be your equals, they will be your superiors."
—(Livy, Hist. XXXIV. 2. Date frenos impotenti naturæ et indomito animali. * * * Majores nostri, nullam, ne pri_

vatam quidem, rem agere feminas sine auctóre voluerunt; in manu esse parentum, fratrum, virorum. * * * 3: Recensete omnia muliebria jura, quibus licentiam earum alligaverint · majores nostri, per quæque subjecerint viris, quibus omnibus constrictas vix tamen continere potestis. Quid? Si carpere singula, et extorquere, et exæquari ad extremum viris patiemini, tolerabiles vobis eas fore creditis? Extemplo, simul pares esse cœperint, superiores erunt.)

Lucius Valerius, with manly eloquence, took up the defense of women and declared himself in favor of the repeal. The people were of his opinion, and the defeat of the aged Cáto assured the triumph of the Roman women. The Voconian law was not to endure for any length of time. The Velleian decree of the Senate and the prohibition against pleading alone continued in force down to the present day.

WE HAVE ALREADY SHOWN the system of expansion, or rather the wide sweeping action of the Roman law. The Oppian law against the extravagance of women was enacted at the moment when the cohorts of Hannibal were imperiling the very existence of the Republic. This law which, in the thoughts of its authors, was to be of but a transitory and temporary character, Cato tried to make perpetual. It was the same with the provision of the Lex Julia de adulteriis, relating to the testifying in court of adulteresses, but it was attempted to apply as we have seen to all women, this incapacity pronounced in the first place against the lowest minority of them.

This was also the case as to the prohibition against pleading, introduced into Roman legislation to meet the special case of Caphrania.—(Lex 1, § 5. Dig. III, 1.)

Another provision of this same law, excluded from the profession of advocate all blind persons, and this also was precisely because of a particular circumstance:

One day, after the judge had left the bench, a blind man, a certain Publius, had continued to plead. This act, quite insignificant in itself, provoked an immense deal of hilarity in Rome, which it appeared was of a kind to injure the prestige of justice. The magistrates were incensed at it, and at once the edict of the prætor pronounced the exclusion of all blind persons from the profession of advocate.

Now the laws which took away from women and from blind persons the right to plead, were special laws, exceptional laws, true laws of circumstance. In our humble opinion there is now no more place to invoke against women, the prohibition with which the Roman law smote them because of the act of Caphrania, than there would be to invoke against blind persons the incapacity pronounced against them because of Publius.

But—women have yet the right to tell us—why, O Sir Civilians, who are looking over the dusty shelves of your libraries, to find old enough texts of the *Corpus Juris* which are unfavorable to us, why do you not resuscitate a law eminently more respectable, the law *Cincia de donis et muneribus,* which forbade advocates to receive gifts, recompense or money for their services?—(Claudius, it is true, authorized advocates to take fees.) And since you are in so good a path, you might also exhume and restore a certain law of Leo and Anthemius which prescribed that in order to be received as judge or advocate, one must be imbued with the doctrines of the holy Catholic religion.—(Codex II, 7, Lex 8: Nemo vel in foro magnitudinis tuæ, vel in provinciali judicio, vel apud quemquam judicem accedat ad togatorum consortium, nisi sacrosanctis Catholicæ religionis fuerit imbutus mysteriis.)

Let us no longer trouble ourselves with these Roman laws which, certainly, may have formerly had their importance, and a *raison d'etre,* but which it is assuredly preferable, at the present day, to leave to repose in the silence of oblivion.

(To be continued.)

Department of Medical Jurisprudence.

EDITED BY EDWARD B. WESTON, M. D.

THE MEDICO-LEGAL SOCIETY OF CHICAGO

Held a stated meeting, at the Grand Pacific Hotel, October 6th, 1888, President E. J. Doering, M. D., in the chair.

· The resignation of Dr. Scott Helm, as Secretary, was received and accepted. Dr. Edward B. Weston was elected to fill the vacancy.

A paper on "The Medico-Legal Aspects of Spinal Injuries," by Drs. James Burry and E. Wyllys Andrews, was read by Dr. Burry, and discussed by members of the society.

MEDICO-LEGAL ASPECTS
OF SOME INJURIES OF THE SPINAL CORD.

BY

JAMES BURRY, M. D.,
SURGEON C. S. F. & C. RY., CONSULTING SURGEON
ST. JOSEPH'S HOSPITAL OF JOLIET, ILL.

AND

E. W. ANDREWS, M. D.,
PROF. CLINICAL SURGERY CHICAGO MEDICAL COLLEGE,
SURGEON TO MERCY HOSPITAL, CHICAGO.

Within a period of five years, English railway companies have paid in damages in cases of alleged injury to the spinal cord, the enormous sum of £2,200,000 or $11,000;000.

In our own city, the greatest railway center in the world, and in other parts of our country, large sums have been paid as compensatory damages in similar cases.

$300,000 it is said were paid to the sufferers in the Chatsworth accident, and the largest individual damages were paid in settlement of cases of spinal injury.

Specific instances of the enormous sums which have been awarded in this class of obscure injuries are:

CASE OF WATERMAN V. THE CHICAGO & ALTON R. R.—The plaintiff claimed large damages for spinal concussion said to be produced in an accident. Dr. Clark Gapen and other experts testified that injury was the cause of the patient's symptoms, while Drs. Senn and Whiting testifying as experts for the defense, agreed in stating that the patient had locomotor ataxia. A verdict of $23,000 was awarded.

CASE OF HOLLAND V. THE CHICAGO & EASTERN ILLINOIS R. R.—The plaintiff, an employe of another line, was injured in a collision and afterward reported for work, apparently well. He was not given employment. Shortly after this it was claimed that symptoms of spinal concussion developed, and permanent disability followed. Large damages were claimed and the plaintiff was awarded the sum of $23,000.

CASE OF ROZENZWEIG V. THE LAKE SHORE & MICHIGAN SOUTHERN R. R.—The plaintiff having been put off a train at a place not a regular station, was walking across the tracks and either tripped over some object or was knocked down, he did not know which. Spinal injury of an obscure type was alleged and heavy damages awarded. The case after final appeal to the Supreme Court of the State, was settled by the road paying to the plaintiff $48,500 with interest, or in all, over $50,000 compensation.

CASE OF PHILLIPS V. THE LONDON & SOUTHWESTERN RY.— The plaintiff, a physician, was disabled about two years by a railway injury to the spinal cord. It was proved that he had possessed a practice worth $40,000 per annum, and a verdict of $80,000 was given. Dr. Steele who has met Dr. Phillips during the past summer informs us that he is, except for a slight lameness, quite restored to health.

In examining the expert medical evidence in the above cases, one cannot but see the overshadowing influence of the theories laid down by Erichsen in his work on "Concussion of the Spine." A careful and comparative examination of these theories of Erichsen with those of later investigators in neuro-pathological fields may be of interest.

Erichsen teaches that there are two opposite and distinct conditions produced in the spinal cord by injuries. In one there are all the usual and visible effects of traumatism else-where—laceration of tissue, hemorrhage into the spinal canal or substance of the cord and inflammation of the cord and membranes. In the other there are no definite structural changes, but only that condition which he describes under the term "anæmia of the cord," and which he himself admits can only be inferred and is not a well proved pathological fact.

Cases of the first class, viz., those in which definite structural changes are produced, always give rise in his opinion to definite symptoms and are easily recognizable pathological states. In his ideas of the gross pathology we find nothing essentially different from the views of the older pathologists. Thus we find him describing the condition produced by myelitis as softening of the cord, notwithstanding the fact that modern investigation has shown that inflammation does not always produce softening, and that the latter may exist without myelitis.—(Gowers.)

Grosser structional lesions are not the conditions, however, which have given rise to conflicts of medical evidence. It is upon Erichsen's description of the second class of cases, viz. those in which there are no visible structural alterations, that the greatest and most numerous claims for compensation have been built up. It is well, therefore, in view of the conflicts of opinion which have arisen, carefully to examine the evidence as to the existence of this second class of cases, described under the term "anæmia of the cord."

Accuracy in the use of scientific terms may properly be demanded in a work which is so often quoted in medico-legal contentions. How much evidence is there then of the exist-ence of any such pathological condition as "anæmia of the cord?'' Dana, in his latest writings, asserts "Chronic spinal anæmia can hardly be placed in the category of distinct spinal affections." Gowers, in his work just from the press, embodying the results of original and exhaustive research says, in discussing anæmia and hyperæmia of the cord, "The condition of the vessels of the spinal cord after death affords no indication whatever of their state during life. Local variation occurs only in the local hyperæmia which attends inflammation and the anæmia which results from pressure; hence the occurrence of variations in the state of the vessels of the cord and the effects that such variations may produce, are matters of inference from symptoms observed during life, symptoms that are themselves open to various interpretations. Where the ground is barren of facts, theory is always luxuriant. Anæmia, or congestion of the cord affords a ready explanation of symptoms, the cause of which is unknown and it is scarcely surprising, therefore, that such an explanation has often been given. Some surprise may, however, reasonably be felt at the absolute confidence and precision of detail with which these states have been invoked as morbid processes, when the opinions expressed rest not upon one tittle of definite evidence. Positive assertions always receive some credence, however unwarranted the assertions may be, and positions incapable of proof are also sometimes incapable of disproof. It would be futile and useless to attempt to refute in detail the various statements that have been made regarding anæmia and hyperæmia of the spinal cord. We know nothing of it as an independent condition; nevertheless, volumes might be filled by the collected descriptions of the varieties and symptoms, descriptions in which the unrestricted play of 'scientific' fancy has elaborated a symptomatology for the separate congestion of every part of the spinal cord. It is doubtful if any symptoms can be, with confidence, assigned to mechanical congestion."

In the face of these modern views, what weight shall be attached to the opinions on matters of obscure pathology of a writer, who, not himself a specialist in neurology nor possessed of any of the recent methods of investigation, nevertheless lays down such positive dicta? Views which were published in 1866, twenty-two years ago, remain according to his own statement in the latest edition, "substantially unchanged" to-day. Within recent years the minute and gross pathology of the spinal cord, has been almost entirely re-written. Intelligent discussion of the structural changes which occur in the cord in disease and injury are impossible without reference to the investigations of Charcot, Brown-Sequard, Gowers and Bramwell. Yet, most of these investigations have been made since the publication of Erichsen's treatise and therefore find no place in his system of pathology. This would not be surprising were it not also true that Erichsen held to substantially the same ideas in his latest writings.

What weight should now attach to expert evidence based only upon inference from clinical experience when diametrically opposite testimony rests on the firm basis of post-mortem and microscopic investigation?

That we may not appear in any particular to misrepresent this writer's opportunities for exact knowledge, we may quote his own words in his latest edition:—"No instance (of post-mortem examination) has occurred to me in hospital or in private practice in which I could obtain one. The only case indeed on record with which I am acquainted, in which a *post-mortem* examination has been made in a person who died from the remote effects of concussion of the spine was published by Dr. Lockhart Clark," etc., etc., in 1866.

What is surprising is not so much that these opportunities were wanting, for it is only of late years and in a few hospitals that anything like systematic work has been done in this line, but rather that on such a small basis of known fact so large a structure of inferential pathology has been built, and that it should be stated with the positiveness of well-proven facts and should have carried such weight in the medical world. Even with the same method and from the same observed facts, we find no agreement among those who would dogmatize as to the existence of lesions in preference to discovering them in the dead house and with the microscope. Erichsen has collated a large number of cases from various sources to illustrate certain theories of spinal concussion. Page, on the other hand, pursuing the same clinical method, has drawn largely from the same sources and even from Erichsen's own published cases to support views of a nature directly opposite. Neither writer has utilized modern methods of study, and we are left with the impression that much of this discussion is but threshing old straw, so far as scientific results are concerned. If the conclusions of these older writers are in any measure weakened by being thus at variance, they certainly are still more discredited when it is found that they are at variance with modern ideas.

Nevertheless, the old, not modern views still exert a deciding influence in many cases of alleged spinal injury which assume a medico-legal aspect, and many an expert has testified in court substantially to the ideas of a quarter of a century ago, in seeming ignorance of the revolution which cellular pathology has brought about in the last decade.

Erichsen is in accord with later writers in stating that when there have been actual structural changes in the cord, well-marked symptoms are developed. He loses sight, however, of the additional fact that long continued functional disease produces structural change when he advances his argument in behalf of "railway spine" and claims it is essentially a functional disorder and therefore not accompanied by the usual symptoms following a structural change.

Many months, in the opinion of this writer, may intervene between the time of injury and the beginning of the symptoms of so-called spinal concussion. If, however, the two facts are connected, some functional or structural change must have been going on in the interval. If functional disorder cannot exist except transiently, it follows that the disorder must be or become structural or else cease to exist. But we have seen that structural disease produces definite symptoms and not vague and irregular phenomena. What becomes then of the theories of spinal concussion which, upon the assumed and wholly imaginary pathological state known as "anæmia of the cord," build up a symptomatology equally vague and illusory? In this symptomatology have been included all the mental, psychical and cerebral symptoms which a person who has not met with an accident may suffer, as well as all the minor ills of each and every part of the body which could by any stretch of reasoning be traced to the nerve centers, and all are declared to have their origin in a condition of the cord which modern pathology knows not or recognizes only as transient.

If it be true that Erichsen's theories of pathology are undermined by the results of more modern investigators, what becomes of the vast superstructure of symptomatology which he has reared thereon? It is essential, if we would be scientific, that we refer only those symptoms to the spine which are known to be spinal. This is now very strongly insisted upon by writers too numerous to quote. No proven facts warrant the belief that mental and psychical disturbances, loss of memory, business inaptitude, depression of spirits and the like, have anything to do with the spinal cord. On the contrary, these are truly cerebral symptoms to the best of our present knowledge, and, as such, can be understood and accounted for on plain pathological grounds. Serious they may be, but they are removed from the realm of the mysterious when we recognize their true origin and we can speak rationally of their prognosis and treatment.

But when these cerebral disturbances are referred to that vague state known as "spinal concussion" they seem to take on new terrors and the patient sees in the diagnosis a dreadful portent of hopeless invalidism or gradual progressive decay. If once he has had Erichsen's picture impressed upon his imagination, he certainly will not lack for material out of which to build a gloomy prognosis. To all intents this writer lays down the opinion that any and every bodily ill may find its explanation in "anæmia of the cord" resulting from "spinal concussion." That this invites not only self-deception but corrupt practices, we fear there can be no doubt and such a state of affairs may well be a cause of alarm. Medical men have good reason to fear a condition of things which tends to discredit scientific medicine and the value of expert evidence. Lawyers have good cause to fear a state of affairs which may impose pseudo-scientific doctrine upon the courts in such a way that it cannot be sifted and analyzed. Honest claimants are doubly interested in keeping false claims from being allowed to the prejudice of honest ones. Finally, courts themselves have most of all to fear a state of uncertainty in high expert authority which will invite fraud and defeat the end for which courts of justice exist.

Spinal concussion, when used as Erichsen teaches, is a condition built up almost wholly of subjective symptoms. This renders malingering easy. To illustrate, a man who fears his back has been injured in an accident, consults a lawyer as to the liability of the corporation or individual for the occurrence of the accident. The lawyer, and there is a lawyer to every one hundred men in this city, sends the claimant to a physician, and there is a doctor to every one hundred men in this State, who goes over the ground very carefully with the claimant and asks if he suffers from such and such symptoms, and in order that there may be no mistake about it gives the claimant a written statement of the symptoms usually occurring in well-marked cases of spinal concussion without structural lesion. The claimant, even if he be an honest man, after carefully questioning himself, discovers that he has become the possessor of an inaptitude for business, a mental disquietude, a pain in the back, etc., etc. If he be a dishonest man, he studies his chart and has a stock of symptoms on hand when interrogated as to his condition, and in his business it is "no trouble to show goods." We thus see that the way to imposition is made easy. Avenues of fraud are opened up and capital, lawyers and courts are practically at the mercy of a clever malingerer.

The writers of this paper wish to emphasize the importance of careful and not superficial investigation, and do not believe that the dogmatic precision of an old and inferential pathology which conflicts with modern pathological views, should give answer to the questions arising in alleged injury to the spinal cord.

The paper was listened to with attention, and elicited the following discussion:

DISCUSSION.

DR. HENRY M. LYMAN:—I have listened with a great deal of interest to the valuable paper of Drs. Burry and Andrews, and I must subscribe most heartily to the propositions advanced in it. It is, as the Doctor has well said, true that the minds of the profession have for many' years been too much under the influence of the dogmas laid down in Erichsen's work on Railway Injuries. I am thoroughly satisfied that a great deal of injustice has been done and carried out through the agency of the courts upon the basis of opinions that have been formu-ulated in accordance with that book, and I think it is really a very necessary thing to frequently give a word of caution like this to the profession that they avoid falling into the trap which is unwittingly opened before them by such a work. It has been well said that the pathology of the work is old and the inferences drawn from the cases are many of them strained, and yet it must be acknowledged that there is a sufficiency of truth in a good deal that is advanced in it to make the errors that accompany it doubly dangerous. If I were to speak of books in comparison with one another, I should say a book like Page's, while it may be open in many particulars to the charge made against Erichsen's work, of being old-fashioned and representing somewhat bygone pathology, of the two, is far the superior work. It is written in a much more judicial spirit and I think much more fully and really represents the advanced views of the profession in these matters than does Erichsen's work.

My own observation in cases of this kind leads me to feel that a very large proportion of the cases which have been reported and presented in the courts as cases of spinal concussion are really nothing of the kind; they are cases in which, when there is any real lesion, where any real injury has been sustained, it has fallen more largely upon the brain than the cord. Many of the symptoms presented by these patients can be much more accurately described by supposing that the brain is the organ that has suffered. It is in cases of this class that so many of the numerous and ill-defined symptoms following an injury, occur; patients who suffer with no systematized lesions, with nothing that can be referred to any disorganization proper of the spinal cord, no true paraplegia or hemiplegia; the lesions are those largely of an irregular distribution where the phenomena are largely mental, and possibly, in many cases, intellectual; and we must refer them chiefly to the brain rather than to the spinal cord. It is true of a great many of these cases that the symptoms presented are of this character instead of being symptoms of paralysis either of sensation, motion or nutrition.

We have a large class of cases presenting themselves after these injuries, to which the most convenient term we can apply is hysterical—hysterical conditions following injuries. These occur in males as well as in females. We perhaps have more right to expect the existence of hysteria in females who have suffered injury, but in many cases of males who have suffered injuries they are followed by hysteria, which can only be ascribed to a disorder of the cerebrum. In regard to these so-called hysterical symptoms—how far are they to be allowed weight in judging of the liability of a railroad? For example, in the case of an injury that has been sustained, the courts will hold that it matters not what the form of the disorder is, so long as there is a disorder, for the disorder is the consequence of the injury that has been sustained and the party inflicting the injury is liable for it. There is a certain amount of truth in that proposition; it must be taken into consideration that disorders of this kind are most intensely prone to exaggeration as a consequence of the peculiar conditions which surround patients who have undergone the experience passed through by victims of a railroad accident. The injuries are of a nature to disturb the mental functions of the individual, and the anxieties that grow up, partly through the agency of physicians, and partly through the uneasiness attendant upon lawsuits connected with the railroad company, or parties implicated in the accident, lead to, disturbances of the mind to a great extent, and we should take those things into consideration in our estimate of the probabilities of recovery.

It is a matter of common observation that when patients have been injured in this way and manifest these mental or intellectual symptoms, conjoined with a certain amount of vital innutrition and disorder, when the mental perturbation is removed, there is a great improvement in the symptoms; so that the settlement of a claim against a railroad company is followed by rapid improvement in the condition of the patient. That is a fact which is often laid hold of by a certain class of physicians and surgeons and used as an argument against the genuineness of the conditions experienced by the patient. They say it was a matter of imagination, of self-deception, and sometimes go so far as to claim a form of malingering by the patient. But if you reflect upon the relation which exists between the mind and body, it is easy to understand how a person who is in anxiety of mind will suffer in an aggravated degree bodily symptoms and will improve again on relief from anxiety.

Many of these patients are permanently injured, though they have not received any injuries that are enduring from a surgical point of view. There have been no fractures, perhaps; no permanent strains or sprains or dislocations; no wounds anywhere, no depressions of the cranium, or anything of that kind. Many of these cases, therefore, when they have passed out of the immediate care of the surgeon, are considered cured, and surgically speaking they are cured; but we must remember that a case may be cured surgically, and yet not be cured medically, and therefore a certain class of patients must be recognized as never recovering fully from these injuries; they recover surgically and to a certain degree medically; as in cases of inflammation of the spinal cord, when a patient is suffering from myelitis we get recovery to a certain degree, in the majority of cases, but rarely a complete recovery.

The patients get to walking about with more or less comfort, but never recover the power of locomotion they once had; they have not the power of endurance they once had, and in every respect they are weaker and inferior in their condition to what they were before the injury was sustained. That is something that should be recognized and kept in mind, therefore, that the opinions of physicians and surgeons who are called to examine these cases for injury, should be guarded. I do not know that there is any class of cases in which it is more improper to give a positive prognosis than in cases of severe injury. The probabilities are in favor of partial recovery, that the recovery will be progressive; and yet in every instance the possibility exists that the recovery will be arrested short of complete restoration; and it is impossible, so far as my knowledge extends, to judge in any particular case whether it is going to be a case that is completely curable, or whether it will come to a stand-still before recovery has been completed. There is a class of cases in which the difficulty is principally mental, and those cases may recover completely, I think; and yet it is not possible for the physician to predict positively in those cases, at an early period, that they are going to be of that curable character. And yet, where there is no palpable lesion, no evidence of disorganization of the brain or spinal cord, where the female sex is present, especially in the person of comparative youth, and where there is the possibility of complete change of life and occupation coming in to assist, the prospects of recovery are good.

I remember a case related to me by Dr. Wood, of Philadelphia, where a young woman had sustained an injury in a railroad accident. She had been examined by numerous physicians who had all given an unfavorable prognosis; not less than ten neurologists assuring her she would never recover. That woman came under the care of Dr. Wood, and he assured her there was nothing but hysteria the matter. He put her upon a course of treatment, and finally she engaged in a love match which terminated in marriage, and she was completely cured. I think there is nothing so good as something to absorb the attention of the patient, and turn the current of thought entirely from one's self and maladies, into another channel; it is the very best influence towards the restoration of health to the mind, and in many of these cases it is a mental disorder that exists. I do not wish to take up the time of the society, but would call attention to the fact that there is a class of people who are in such a state of mental instability, that it needs only an excess or injury of some kind to start them upon a course of mental disorder which will have, we know not what termination. In patients of that class, injured by railroad disaster, followed by opinions of men in high standing, and by long litigation, nothing is better calculated to set up a state of ill health, the termination of which can never be predicted.

Dr. L. L. McArthur:—The advances which have been made in the line of nervous diseases, and the advance in the pathology of the spinal cord, have enabled the neurologists to clear up many of the nervous diseases which were classed under the head of spinal concussion. Spinal concussion can be limited to concussion; as in the brain, and yet in concussion of the brain we always expect the symptoms to manifest themselves at or very soon after the injury. But in the class of cases which come under the head of spinal concussion—identically similar in their nature, that is, believed to be without any actual structural lesion of the spinal cord—are cases claimed to occur weeks or months afterward. Hence, I feel inclined to ask the gentleman who closes the discussion, if we have any symptoms which we may rely on as confirming, or being diagnostic of, spinal concussion? If he can in any way enlighten us so as to distinguish those cases in our diagnosis from other troubles of the spinal cord, or if the neurologist has some means of arriving at a positive conclusion, some characteristic symptom which like vertigo, calls our attention to the ear or cerebellum, or the peculiar gait of locomotor ataxia? There seems to be nothing definite conveyed, by the term spinal concussion. . Other names have been suggested, rather than this term which covers up ignorance; and comotio-spinalis might be applied. We know that concussion of the spine is not shock. Moreover, as advances are made in medicine the list of functional diseases are disappearing. Formerly it was satisfactory to make a diagnosis of a case as paralysis; but the diagnosis paralysis being insufficient, has become obsolete. In the same way the functional diseases are, as advances are made, disappearing. We cannot expect to have phenomena take place of a physiological or pathological nature without some textural change; especially if these phenomena persist, and are constantly making themselves evident. Temporarily we might have a functional derangement of the cord in which some symptoms were manifested; but as for weeks, months and years, as in the case of Dr. Phillips, it is unreasonable, in the light of our pathological literature, to expect it without some structural changes.

DR. J. G. KIERNAN:—I did not hear the paper and am not therefore very well prepared to discuss it. With regard to one point raised by Dr. McArthur, I shall have to take issue; first as to the textural question. It seems to me perfectly possible that for a long time there may be very marked symptoms without textural lesions. Cases have been under observation in which no lesion was found and yet in which the symptoms were well marked. I was much pleased to hear Dr. Lyman refer to the fact that many cases could be considered rather as cerebral than as spinal cases. The fact is lost sight of that when the patient recovers from cerebral concussion, he passes out of the surgeon's hands. When I was connected with the institution on Ward's Island, I remember distinctly four cases of supposed recovery from cerebral concussion in which the patients died in two or three years, under my charge in the insane hospital; they did not recover from cerebral concussion. I think if cerebral concussion was as frequently made a matter of litigation and as frequently examined as spinal concussion, a great many more cases might be developed. A large number of the recoveries drift into the insane and poor hospitals and die there.

In regard to the point raised by Dr. Lyman, particularly with respect to the cases classified as mental disorder; the fact that many of these make good recoveries is signally shown in a case of Page's that I have always been suspicious of. Page relates the case of a woman, which he decided, after careful examination, was one entitled to pretty heavy damages; she was incurable, and yet she recovered, married, had children and lived a happy life thereafter. But unfortunately very often those cases do not have such a fortunate outcome. Dr. McElvaine of Peoria, at a meeting of railway surgeons, reported a case in which a woman rallied from the effects of an accident and he believed her to be a malingerer; but finally the woman began to evince all the symptoms of advanced myelitis, and the Doctor was persuaded that her disease had started at the accident to which she traced it.

With regard to mental disturbances always being evidence of microscopic or coarse cerebral pathological lesions, the question is certainly one open to doubt. We all know, who have had experience with locomotor ataxia, that there are very marked temporary mental disturbances which occur in consequence of that disorder; they occur in typical cases, and if they can occur from a spinal disorder of that kind, why not from the condition known as spinal concussion? That there is a great difficulty in diagnosis is shown by an elevated railroad case in Brooklyn. It was a case in which a man pushed a woman down stairs. The question as to whether the case was one of spinal concussion or of hysteria, was debated and evidence given on both sides by very eminent neurologists. I think on the side of the concussion were Drs. Hammond and Spitzka, and that eminent railway expert, John G. Johnson, who has written more on the subject of spinal concussion than any other person. On the other side was Landon Carter Gray. In that case the hysterical symptoms were well marked, and yet there was some spinal disorder, as the woman died with decided myelitic symptoms. An interesting question is that of how far previously existing conditions can be pleaded in mitigation of damages. If a man have syphilis of a passive type, started into activity by an accident, as in a case reported by Dr. Dana, is he not entitled to damages?

Mr. Clark Gapen:—On the very threshold of the subject we find this difficulty; that it is in a more or less chaotic state, and any discussion of it at present must be desultory, a sort of patchwork discussion. A few years ago we thought we were pretty well grounded, and those of us who read Erichsen at that time without any very critical feeling, accepted what he had to say and passed it by as a subject which a master mind had solved apparently for all time to come; but a more critical investigation of Erichsen's work shows that it is a master of expression rather than a masterly statement of fact.

I think Erichsen's work may be criticised, first in the very name which he gives to the injury—concussion of the spine. Concussion of the brain we are accustomed to associate with positive physical and mental manifestations and symptoms developed at the time or immediately following the injury. In his concussion of the spine there are no such symptoms; the symptoms may manifest themselves weeks, months, or even years afterward and he is willing to accept them as evidence of this concussion. I think the symptoms do not bear out the name which he has applied.

With regard to the cases which have been presented; I think that those cases in which there is a positive physical injury to the spinal cord are very rarely passed by; there is very rarely any difficulty that I have noticed. In my observation there is no dispute among surgeons where the spinal cord is injured; we know the symptoms of even a blood clot on the spinal cord is very pronounced and they are unquestionable; yet we are asked to believe that a great injury has been sustained by the cord where there are none of these, even transient, symptoms.

I agree with Dr. Lyman's statement of his arrangement and classification of these injuries, that where these symptoms follow a considerable time afterward, or where they are of a functional nature, that is to say, where there are symptoms that are elusive in their character, which you cannot grasp, they are mental in their quality and in some cases they may all result from the injury. Sometimes, I think, from the tremendous shock of a railroad accident, this disarrangement may occur and the individual be a sufferer for his whole life-time; but such cases are extremely rare and generally marked by present symptoms. The other class of cases are those which arise afterward, and heredity has a great deal to do with these cases; we find some of them are individuals who have inherited imperfect nervous organizations; we find others who have, by dissipation brought themselves into that condition and when they come to sue a railroad company, no matter what their past life has been, what the heredity has been, it is the fault of the railroad company.

Dr. E. W. Andrews:—All authorities, including Erichsen himself, positively assure us that spinal injuries received in railroad accidents are in no essential way different from those received in any other manner. Cases have been cited running back centuries in medical history, of exactly this injury which Erichsen has described as railway spine. In this paper we have not attempted to discuss the pathology; this is well mapped out by pathologists of note.

While it is true, as Dr. Lyman states, that these cases sooner or later cease to be surgical, yet the pathology of injuries is not essentially different from the pathology of disease. In at least one disease, locomotor ataxia, there seems to be very positive testimony that injury may be the exciting, even the predisposing cause. Leyden has asserted this. Petit is strongly of the opinion that locomotor ataxia may be produced directly by injury, and more especially he insists that a case of locomotor ataxia once recovered from, may, as a result of railway injury, be reproduced. Of course if this be the case, if one disease of a special tract may be induced by injury, it would be natural to suppose that others might likewise result from traumatism. Necessarily an understanding of the minute pathology of the cord, and especially the microscopic appearance of the various tracts of degeneration is indispensable to one who would give testimony in a court of justice in cases involving alleged injuries of its substance.

One expert was quite lately trapped in this manner in an important case. A prominent railway surgeon, an expert, went on the witness stand and, with what seems like temerity, acknowledged, in testifying in relation to a case of so-called railway spine, that he was unacquainted with the work of Page. Well meaning surgeons who are willing at the present day to go into a court of justice and give the pathological views of Erichsen, I think are liable to be sadly caught up. In place of such vague terms as spinal concussion, it is perhaps better to use a definite, descriptive terminology. *Intraspinal hemorrhage* is undoubtedly responsible for a large number of spinal symptoms once attributed to "concussion." The *ligamenta subflava* can scarcely be lacerated without producing rupture of the meningo-rachidian veins, and hemorrhages may occur upon the membranes or in the substance of the cord. *Traumatic meningitis* of course exists and can be recognized as a clinical entity. *Traumatic myelitis* is undoubtedly a condition which at certain levels of the cord can exist. Gower speaks of cases of traumatic myelitis in which a post mortem has revealed all the conditions from thickening of the membranes to complete softening and destruction. Slight injury to the bones is another surgical condition determinable from the symptoms and not to be confused with injury to the cord.

And so we may classify the actual states of the cord in injury, and in a very large number of cases specify accurately the lesion. As to *pure concussion*, assuming that there is such a lesion, it may be defined as a stunted condition of the cord, which is inferred to have undergone some form of molecular derangement by which its function is for the time being interfered with. Cases are doubtless on record in which post mortems after spinal injury have failed to reveal any lesion whatever in the tissue. I question, however, whether such cases have been subjected to complete microscopical examination such as is at the present day considered essential. Lidell has related a case in which a post mortem examination was held on a patient who had died as was supposed, from concussion of the cord. At first no sign revealed itself in the appearance of the cord, and yet a more careful subsequent examination showed in the interior of the cord itself, a globular clot which had produced compression and death.

The question of Dr. McArthur, "Does concussion exist?" it is, perhaps impossible to answer dogmatically. My present impression is that transiently it may. Nevertheless, I will add in closing that Sir Joseph Bryant, not a neurologist but as good surgical authority as we have to-day, has recently published a paper in which he claims that even concussion of the brain has no existence as a pathological state. Hilton many years ago denied that any case of death from concussion of the brain, when examined, had failed to reveal structural changes in the gross appearance. The tendency of the present time is to more minute and careful examination of these traumatic troubles of the brain and cord. Much of the symptomatology of "concussion" is inferential, but from the investigations that are being carried on we will undoubtedly be able to define a structural condition corresponding to every symptom which injuries produce.

MEDICAL CHARITIES.

One of the most threatening abuses of medical charity is created by an association organized for charitable purposes, which advertises medical aid and hospital treatment for the payment of a weekly sum, in insurance for this purpose. Dr. L. L. McArthur recently brought this subject before the Chicago Medical Society in a very forcible manner, but no way of meeting the evil was devised by the Society. Judging from the position recently taken in the case of the National Mutual Indemnity Association by Insurance Commissioner Shandrew of Minnesota, the proper method to check this evil is to prevent the incorporation of these bodies. The National Mutual Indemnity Association was a society to "provide suitable medical and surgical attendance for its members in case of sickness or disability." Mr. Shandrew declined to register the certificate of its incorporation, on the ground that "such associations not only fail to protect those for whose benefit they are incorporated, but afford facilities for the organization of insurance schemes whose primary object is profit, regardless of the interest or rights of members."

The State Medical Society, at its coming meeting, should ascertain how far the principles laid down by Mr. Shandrew are legally applicable to Illinois, and then secure, if possible, the vacation of all charters already granted for alleged charitable purposes to bodies used for purposes of gain. It should also take steps to prevent the granting of future charters to such bodies.—*Medical Standard.*

NOTES OF TRAVEL.

CHRISTIANIA AND NORWAY—NORWEGIAN POLITICS AND LITERATURE—
VOYAGE ACROSS THE NORTH SEA—PARIS.

Christiania, like all the principal cities of Norway, is built among the
hills: and from some of the summits of these hills, may be obtained magnificent views of the sea and of the country around.

On a side-hill, in the center of the City, is the castle, where the King re-
sides occasionally, when he visits Norway; the most of his time being
spent in Sweden. Near the castle is the University, a very important institution for the Norwegian. A university in Europe, as is well known,
means something more than in America, and is always more or less under
the control and patronage of the State. For several hundred years, while
Norway was under the dominion of Denmark it had no university, and
the Norwegian who would have a liberal education, must acquire it in
Copenhagen or on the Continent.

In Christiania I formed the acquaintance of Professor Sars of the University, and often visited at the house of himself and his mother, a brilliant
lady, seventy-three years of age.

Political excitement was at that time, (1884), running high. The hoire-
mænd, (men of the right), constituted the King's party, while the opposition were the venstremænd, (men of the left), who were in favor of a
more liberal form of government. In fact, Norway seemed to me to be
fast drifting into republicanism.

One of the most important questions under discussion, relates to the
right of veto claimed by the King, over the Norwegian Legislature (The
Storthing.) This right the left denies entirely. But His Majesty had
scored a point by obtaining the unanimous opinion of the Juridical Faculty in his favor. One could not but notice, however, the ingenious manner
in which the question had been propounded to the Faculty. Not whether

any veto had been provided for in the Constitution, but "how far and
to what extent," "hvorvidt og i hvilken Udstrækning," according to their
opinion. there pertained to the King the right of sanction in respect to
changes of the Constitution? Thus assuming that the right of veto existed,
and only submitting the question as to its extent—whether it was absolute or merely suspensive. It is easy to see that the form of the question
might have much to do with the answer, especially under a monarchical
form of government; since jurists who might doubt the right of the veto,
not being called upon to decide upon the right itself, might give less
attention to the grounds upon which it rested, and confine themselves
principally to the question of its extent, assuming its existence.

Examining the Constitution carefully, it would be difficult for an outsider
to see any veto right expressed with sufficient clearness. in it; but the
history of the country showed that the right had been repeatedly exercised. and acquiesced in by the Storthing. and this was the argument upon
which the royal party mainly depended. 'Another position taken by them
was, that the Constitution of 1814 was in the nature of a contract between the King of Sweden and the people of Norway represented by the
Storthing. and that it could not be changed without the consent of both
contracting parties. This principle, if admitted, would support the veto
power.

On the other hand it was claimed that the King in that very Constitution, acknowledged the independence of Norway, which could only be
maintained by an untrammeled Storthing;—that Norway was attached to
Sweden for certain purposes only, and not for the purpose of a consoli-
dated government.

Those who wish to become more thoroughly acquainted with these questions. should read Professor Sars Historical Introduction to the Constitution:—(Historisk Indledning til Grundloven. tredje Oplag—Kristiania,
1884.)

The Norwegians are a reading and thinking people. The higher class
are well educated, often reading and speaking a number of languages. It
is well known that there are more linguists among the educated classes of
Europe than among those of this country. The reason is apparent; because they so much more frequently come in contact with people speaking
other languages.

The middling and lower classes also in Norway, are in intelligence and
moral standing. above the average of the same classes in other European
countries. and perhaps in this country. In Christiania. there were ten

circulating loan libraries besides the large library in the University. These libraries are extensively patronized by all classes of the people.

The Norwegian literature partakes of the character of the land which has produced it. It is bold and romantic—full of the elements of wild passion, yet softened by the sun of modern civilization. In Holberg they had their Shakspeare—in Bjornson they have their Victor Hugo.—Ibsen, Jonas Lee and others also are shedding brilliancy upon the pathway of Danish-Norwegian literature.

In Christiania, when the bells are heard tolling, it is not for a fire, but to signal the departure of some citizen for the far off country. On one occasion I heard them tolling steadily for nearly an hour. In case of a fire, no public alarm is given, unless the conflagration becomes extensive, in which case the people are notified by the firing of cannon.

The Norwegians, considering them as a whole, are an honest, industrious, intelligent people, and very hospitable to strangers. I was more favorably impressed with the Scandinavians and Russians, and less favorably impressed with some other peoples than I had expected to be.

In Christiania, I heard Miss Thursby, the American, who was singing in eleven languages in Europe, and who was exceedingly popular in Sweden and Norway. Strakosh was with her, and Wolff, the violinist. The son of Ole Bull was the Director.

October 3, 1884. Sailed for Havre, after a pleasant sojourn of two months in Christiania. The North Sea was very rough during most of the voyage. Arrived in Havre on the morning of the 6th, and the same day was in Paris.

Here I spent the months of October and November, months ever to be remembered. It is not my purpose to undertake to describe Paris or Paris life, which has been done so often and so much better than I could do it. My object will be to touch upon some phases of European life less familiar to American readers.   C. B. W.

WILLIAM BLACKSTONE.

WILLIAM BLACKSTONE, * whose name has become, perhaps, more familiar than any other in the mouths of English [and American] lawyers, was the fourth son of Mr. Charles Blackstone, a silkman and citizen of London, by Mary the eldest daughter of Lovelace Bigg, Esquire, of Chilton Foliot, in the county of Wilts. He was born on the 10th of July, 1723, after the death of his father, and he had also the misfortune to lose his mother before he was twelve years of age. His uncle, Mr. Thomas Bigg, an eminent surgeon of London, took charge of his education, and at the age of seven years he was admitted on the foundation of the Charter House. When he attained the age of fifteen he had risen to the head of the school, and was, at that early period of life admitted a commoner of Pembroke College, Oxford. His progress both at the Charter House and at Oxford was distinguished, and he was elected to an exhibition both at the school and at the college. Having selected the law as his profession, he became a member of the Middle Temple on the 20th of November, 1741.

Hitherto he had applied himself exclusively to literary and scientific pursuits; but in entering upon the severer studies of his profession, he conceived it necessary to abandon the more pleasing avocations to which he had devoted himself. The feelings which this change induced he has expressed in some lines, remarkable for elegance both in style and sentiment:

* Abridged from "Roscoe's British Lawyers."

THE LAWYER'S FAREWELL TO HIS MUSE.

"As, by some tyrant's stern command,
A wretch forsakes his native land,
In foreign climes condemn'd to roam,
An endless exile from his home;
Pensive he treads the destined way,
And dreads to go, nor dares to stay;
Till on some neighboring mountain's brow
He stops, and turns his eye below;
There, melting at the well-known view,
Drops a last tear, and bids adieu:
So I, thus doom'd from thee to part,
Gay queen of fancy and of art,
Reluctant move with doubtful mind,
Oft stop, and often look behind.

"Companion of my tender age,
Serenely gay, and sweetly sage,
How blithesome were we wont to rove
By verdant hill, or shady grove,
Where fervent bees with humming voice
Around the honey'd oak rejoice,
And aged elms, with awful bend,
In long cathedral walks extend.
Lull'd by the lapse of gliding floods,
Cheer'd by the warbling of the woods,
How blest my days, my thoughts how free,
In sweet society with thee!
Then all was joyous, all was young,
And years unheeded roll'd along:
But now the pleasing dream is o'er,—
These scenes must charm me now no more:
Lost to the field, and torn from you,
Farewell!—a long, a last adieu!

"The wrangling courts, and stubborn law,
To smoke, and crowds, and cities draw;
There selfish Faction rules the day,
And Pride and Avarice throng the way;
Diseases taint the murky air,
And midnight conflagrations glare;
Loose Revelry and Riot bold,
In frighted streets their orgies hold;
Or when in silence all is drown'd,

Fell Murder walks her lonely round;
No room for peace, no room for you—
Adieu, celestial Nymph, adieu!

"Shakespeare no more, thy sylvan son,
Nor all the art of Addison,
Pope's heaven-strung lyre, nor Waller's ease
Nor Milton's mighty self must please:
Instead of these, a formal band
In furs and coifs around me stand,
With sounds uncouth, and accents dry,
That grate the soul of harmony.
Each pedant sage unlocks his store
Of mystic, dark, discordant lore;
And points with tottering hand the ways
That lead me to the thorny maze.

"There, in a winding, close retreat,
Is Justice doom'd to fix her seat;
There, fenced by bulwarks of the law,
She keeps the wondering world in awe;
And there, from vulgar sight retired,
Like eastern queens, is much admired.

"Oh! let me pierce the secret shade,
Where dwells the venerable maid!
There humbly mark, with reverent awe,
The guardian of Britannia's law;
Unfold with joy her sacred page
(The united boast of many an age,
Where mix'd though uniform appears
The wisdom of a thousand years),
In that pure spring the bottom view,
Clear, deep, and regularly true,
And other doctrines thence imbibe.
Than lurk within the sordid scribe;
Observe how parts with parts unite
In one harmonious rule of right;
See countless wheels distinctly tend,
By various laws, to one great end;
While mighty Alfred's piercing soul
Pervades and regulates the whole.

"Then welcome business, welcome strife,
Welcome the cares, the thorns of life,
The visage wan, the purblind sight,

The toil by day, the lamp by night,
The tedious forms, the solemn prate,
The pert dispute, the dull debate,
The drowsy bench, the babbling hall,
For thee, fair Justice, welcome all!

"Thus, though my noon of life be past,
Yet let my setting sun at last
Find out the still, the rural cell
Where sage Retirement loves to dwell!
There let me taste the home-felt bliss
Of innocence and inward peace;
Untainted by the guilty bribe,
Uncursed amid the harpy tribe;
No orphan's cry to wound my ear,
My honor and my conscience clear;
Thus may I calmly meet my end,
Thus to the grave in peace descend!"

The ease exhibited in these lines betrays a pen accustomed to versification; and a volume of juvenile pieces which Mr. Blackstone had collected, but which were never published, shows, that in his earlier years he devoted no inconsiderable portion of his leisure hours to poetical compositions. An early taste for literature has too often misled the student from the ruder and more rugged paths of his profession; but the taste and genius of Blackstone rendered his literary acquirements subservient to his professional success.

In November, 1743, Mr. Blackstone was elected into the society of All-Souls' College, and in the following year he was admitted actual fellow and spoke the anniversary speech in commemoration of the founder, Archbishop Chichele. From this period he divided his time between Oxford and the Temple, where he had taken chambers with the view of attending the courts. His academical and professional studies were there pursued concurrently. On the 12th of June, 1745, he commenced bachelor of civil law, and on the 28th of November, 1746, he was called to the bar.

For several years Mr. Blackstone made little progress in his profession. Without those powerful connections upon which early success must necessarily depend, and without the advantages which volubility and confidence confer, he possessed no means of forcing himself into notice. He was therefore induced to spend a considerable portion of his time at Oxford, where, having been elected bursar, he employed himself in exploring and arranging the muniments of his college, and in reforming the method of keeping the accounts, a subject which he illustrated by a dissertation now preserved in the archives of the college. He also had the merit of hastening the completion of the Codrington library, which was arranged under his directions. For these services he was rewarded with the appointment of steward of the college manors. On the 26th of April, 1750, he commenced doctor of civil law.

A dispute which arose in All-Souls' College, with regard to the persons who were to be considered as next of kin to the founder, gave rise to Mr. Blackstone's first professional publication. This was the "Essay on collateral Consanquinity," which appeared in 1750, and which was afterward printed in the collection of his law tracts. It excited considerable attention, and when, several years afterward, the Archbishop of Canterbury as visitor, formed a new regulation, he appointed Mr. Justice Blackstone his common law assessor.

The very inconsiderable encouragement which Mr. Blackstone had received in the practice of his profession in London, led him in the year 1753, to the resolution of retiring to his fellowship, and of practising at Oxford as a provincial counsel. At the same time he formed the design of delivering a course of private lectures on the laws of England, which was very numerously and respectably attended. Of these lectures he published an analysis in 1756.

The zeal which he had always displayed in forwarding the interests of his college, and of the university in general, led to various honorable appointments. In the year 1757, he became one of the delegates of the Clarendon press, and applied himself successfully to the reformation of various abuses connected with that institution. He was also elected one of the visitors of Mr. Michel's foundation in Queen's College, where he was equally happy in his efforts to terminate the disputes which had previously existed with regard to this donation.

In the year 1754, he was engaged as counsel in the county election, where a question, arising on the right of certain copyholders to vote, was the origin of his tract published a few years afterward, under the title of "Considerations on Copyholders."

In the year 1756, Mr. Viner, the laborious compiler of the most complete abridgment of the English law that has ever appeared, died, and bequeathed to the university of Oxford the whole profits of his voluminous compilation, for the purpose of promoting the study of the common law of England. This munificent benefaction was employed in the first instance in the institution of a professorship of English law, to which a stipend of two hundred pounds per annum was annexed. The duty assigned to the professor was to deliver one solemn public lecture on the laws of England in every academical term, and also by himself or his deputy to read yearly a complete course of lectures on the same subject, consisting of sixty lectures at the least. On the 20th of October, 1758, Mr. Blackstone was unanimously elected the first Vinerian professor; and on the 25th of the same month he read his introductory lecture, the method, elegance, and learning of which attracted the admiration of every one who heard it. This excellent discourse was afterward prefixed to the first volume of the Commentaries.

The reputation which the first course of the Vinerian lectures obtained was such, that the nobleman who superintended the education of the young Prince, requested Mr. Blackstone to read them to his royal highness; an honor which was respectfully declined by the new professor in consequence of the pressure of his engagements at the university. Copies of the lectures were, however, presented to the Prince, a service for which Mr. Blackstone received a munificent acknowledgment.

The distinction which Mr. Blackstone had acquired by his lectures induced him in the year 1759, to return to London, where he resumed his practice, visiting Oxford at stated periods only, for the delivery of his lectures. The coif was pressed upon him by Lord Chief-Justice Willes and Mr. Justice Bathurst; but he thought proper to decline the honor. In the same year he gave to the world a magnificent edition of Magna Charta and the Charter of the Forest, which issued from the Clarendon press. About this time he also published a small tract on the law of descents in fee simple.

Hitherto, Mr. Blackstone appears to have taken no part whatever in the political discussions of the day; but a dissolution of parliament having taken place, he was returned in 1761 as one of the representatives of Hindon, in Wiltshire. Soon afterward he received a patent of precedence, having declined the office of chief-justice of the common pleas in Ireland.

The rank thus conferred upon him, and the celebrity which he had acquired as a writer, operated very favorably on the professional views of Mr. Blackstone. His practice having considerably increased, he married Sarah, the eldest surviving daughter of James Clitherow, of Boston House, in the county of Middlesex, by whom he had a family of nine children. His fellowship having been vacated by his marriage, he was, in July, 1761, appointed principal of New Inn Hall by the Earl of Westmoreland, at that time chancellor of the university.

In the year 1762, he collected his tracts on legal subjects, and published them in two volumes 8vo.; and in the course of the following year, on the establishment of the Queen's household, he received the appointment of solicitor-general to her majesty, and was elected a bencher of the Middle Temple.

In the year 1765, appeared the first volume of the celebrated *Commentaries on the Laws of England*. The reception of the Commentaries, in regard to the style in which they were written, is all that could have been desired; but in matter they did not escape criticism from the politicians of the day.

In the year 1766, Mr. Blackstone resigned the Vinerian professorship, and the place of principal of New Inn Hall, in consequence of his London business interfering with his duties at the university.

Having been returned for Westbury in Wiltshire, in the parliament of 1768, he took a part in the debates which arose relative to the election of Mr. Wilkes.

Those professional honors to which the talents and acquirements of Mr. Blackstone gave him so just a claim were now opened to him; and on the resignation of Mr. Dunning in 1770, the vacant place of solicitor-general was offered to him. The parliamentary duties incident to this office were probably the ground on which it was declined by Mr. Blackstone. Of a sensitive and retiring disposition, he had been disgusted with the contests into which his parliamentary duties had led him, and he looked anxiously for the shelter from political life which the bench afforded. Very shortly after his refusal of the post of solicitor-general, Mr. Justice Clive, one of the judges of the common pleas, resigned his seat, which was immediately tendered to Mr. Blackstone. The patent for his appointment was about to pass, when Mr. Justice Yates expressed an earnest wish to change his court. In consequence, Mr. Blackstone was, in Hilary term, 1770, appointed to the seat vacated by Sir Joseph Yates in the king's bench. In the ensuing Trinity term, however, on the death of Mr. Justice Yates, he accepted the place originally designed for him in the court of common pleas.

In the latter part of his life, Sir Wm. Blackstone devoted much of his time, in conjunction with Mr. Howard and Mr. Eden, to the subject of prison discipline—a subject with which not merely the welfare of the individuals who are the objects of that discipline, but the virtue and happiness of society at large, are intimately connected. In common with many reflecting men of his day, Sir William Blackstone had remarked the inefficacy of the system which restores prisoners to society, on the expiration of their punishment, more complete adepts in their criminal arts than when they entered the walls of their gaol, and resolutely bent to revenge upon the community the cruelty and harshness they have sustained at its hands. If a scheme had been formed for the propagation of vice, for initiating the uninstructed in its mysteries, and for carrying to their full perfection the talents of the more experienced criminals, no schools could have been instituted better adapted to such ends, than our own prisons toward the middle of the last century. Idleness, drunkenness, debauchery of all kinds, filthiness beyond credibility, an unrestrained communication between the oldest and the youngest offenders, were the distinguishing qualities of almost every county gaol in England. By the exertions of Howard (a name never to be pronounced without feelings of the deepest reverence and the most grateful admiration), the public were roused to a sense of this most disgraceful and injurious system. Among others, Sir William Blackstone exerted himself, in conjunction with Mr. Howard, to procure an act of parliament for the establishment of penitentiary houses near the metropolis, for the reformation of those who had been in confinement:

Sir William Blackstone did not for any long time enjoy the honors to which his learning, his literature, and his diligence had raised him. In his earlier life he had devoted himself but too assiduously to the studies on which his advancement necessarily depended, and his health, which appears never to have been robust, suffered from this injudicious application. He had, unfortunately, also contracted an aversion to exercise, the neglect of which contributed to increase a nervous complaint to which he was occasionally subject, and which produced a distressing giddiness or vertigo. About Christmas, 1779, he was attacked with a shortness of breath, which was thought by his physicians to arise from water on the chest, and the usual remedies were applied, from which he appeared to receive benefit. In Hilary term he came up to town, for the purpose of attending his duties in court, but again became alarmingly ill, with symptoms of drowsiness and stupor. The disorder rapidly increased, and, after lying insensible for some days, he died on the 14th of February, 1780, in the 57th year of his age. He was buried at the parish church of St. Peter, in Wallingford.

The fame of Sir William Blackstone as a commentator on the laws of England, has rendered his character as a judge less conspicuous. His judgments, indeed, are never wanting in learning and good sense; but they would not alone have raised his name to the distinguished station which it now occupies. The notes of his judgments, published with his other reports after his death, are not remarkable for their research or accuracy; and it is probable that his legal acquirements rather declined than advanced after the publication of his Commentaries.

In his political sentiments he was moderate, being esteemed what is usually termed "a firm supporter of the true principles of our happy constitution in church and state." In his views of politics, as well as in those of law, he was inclined rather to extenuate and to justify than to doubt and criticise. A remarkable instance of the caution with which he has avoided offending established opinions or prejudices, may be found in that portion of the Commentaries in which he speaks of the Revolution of 1688. Without venturing to deduce the great and obvious principle which is involved in it, he treats it only as a precedent applicable to a state of things in all circumstances similar; thus divesting one of the noblest moral lessons, which governments were ever taught, of all its salutary warnings. Still, when we remember that Sir William Blackstone had been educated amongst persons professing, for the most part, the principles of high Toryism, that his lectures were addressed to an audience chiefly composed of persons of similar opinions, and when we also take into account the peculiar circumstances of his professional and private life, it would be unjust to accuse him of want of liberality.

The acquirements of Sir William Blackstone as a scholar were, doubtless, very considerable. He had always been in the habit of employing much of his time in reading; and, possessing a powerful memory, with a mind very capable of arranging its stores, he was remarkable for the variety and extent of his information. It is to be regretted that he never applied himself to any undertaking of a purely literary nature, in which there can be little doubt that he would have been eminently successful. Almost the only composition of this kind from the pen of Sir W. Blackstone which has been preserved, is an investigation of the quarrel between Pope and Addison, communicated by its author to Dr. Kippis, the editor of the Biographia Britannica, and by him published in the life of Addison as the production of "a gentleman of considerable rank, to whom the public is obliged for works of much higher importance." In noticing this disquisition, M. D'Israeli has remarked the "masterly force and luminous arrangement of investigation" it displays, "and to which," as he observes, "since the days of Bayle, literary history has been too great a stranger."

The private character of Sir William Blackstone is represented in very favorable colors by his biographer, but seems to have been misunderstood by those who did not enjoy an intimate acquaintance with him. His appearance was not prepossessing. The heaviness of his features and figure, and the contraction of his brow, gave a character of moroseness to his countenance which did not exist in fact. He was not, however, free from occasional irritation of temper, which was increased by the nervous complaints to which he was subject. In his own family he was cheerful, agreeable, and even facetious, and a diligent observer of those economical arrangements upon which so much of the respectability and comfort of life depends. The disposal of his time was so skillfully managed, that, though he was a laborious student, he freely mingled in the amusements and relaxations of society. This he effected by his rigid punctuality. "During the years in which he read his lectures at Oxford," says his biographer, "it could not be remembered that he had ever kept his audience waiting for him even for a few minutes. As he valued his own time, he was extremely careful not to be instrumental in squandering or trifling away that of others, who, he hoped, might have as much regard for theirs as he had for his. Indeed, punctuality was in his opinion so much a virtue, that he could not bring himself to think perfectly well of any who were notoriously defective in it." The diffidence and reserve which characterized his manners were sometimes misconstrued into pride, and the dignity which he preserved on the bench into austerity.

The notes of decisions which he had collected, both at the bar and while on the bench, were published after his death, pursuant to the directions of his will.

THE WOMAN LAWYER.

By Dr. Louis Frank.

(Translated by Mary A. Greene, of the Massachusetts Bar.)

II.

The Catholic Doctrine.—We have shown the minor and secondary part, the actual abjection of woman in Jewish civilization.

While Genesis had condemned woman to pain and suffering —had reduced her to be but a satellite of man, and to live forever dependent upon him,—(Gen. III. 16.)—Christ, the glorious defender of the weak, lowly and oppressed, desired the uplifting again of woman, and proclaimed the equality of the sexes: "There is neither Jew nor Greek, there is neither bond nor free, there is neither male nor female: for ye are all one in Christ Jesus."—(Gal. III. 28.)

Unfortunately, Catholicism was not slow to warp the pure teaching of Christ, and to bend it to wonderful doctrines. The opinion of the Fathers of the church, and the canons of the Councils have consecrated the Pagan theory of the absolute inferiority of woman.

The judgment which the Fathers of the church brought to the subject of woman, is hardly flattering to this pious portion of the human race, upon which the Catholicism of to-day leans, in order to assure its dominion over the world. "Woman," wrote Tertullian, "thou shouldst ever be clothed in rags and in mourning, appearing only as a penitent, drowned in tears, and expiating thus the sin of having caused the fall of the human race. Woman, thou art the gate of the devil; it is thou who hast corrupted those whom Satan dare not attack face to face; it is because of thee that Jesus Christ died."—(*De culta feminarum*, I, 1.)

Another Father of the Latin church, Saint Jerome, is not less extravagant. "Woman given over to herself, is not slow to fall into impurity. A woman without reproach is more rare than the phenix. Woman is the gate of the devil, the road to iniquity, the sting of the scorpion, in a word, a dangerous species." "Woman has no comprehension of goodness," adds Saint Gregory the Great.

Run over the history of the Councils, and analyze their canons. On every page, in each of their surprising decisions, is affirmed, with a sort of misogynistic cynicism, the contempt in which the church held woman. Saint Augustine authorized every husband to slap his wife in the face. The council of Toledo, in the year 400, allowed a married clerk, whose wife had sinned, to confine her in the house, to make her to fast, and to chastise her, without however attempting her life.— [Can. 7.]—(This provision is reproduced in the canon law. *Causa* XXXIII. *quest.* II, ch. X. The canon law also permitted the husband to inflict correction upon his wife. Ill treatment is not a cause for separation unless it exceed the limits of "legitimate correction.")

Then, taking up the famous controversy relative to the question of whether woman should be classed with rational beings or with the brutes, the Council of Macon, in 581, asked of itself whether woman has a soul, and whether she is really a part of humanity: *An mulier sit homo?* Deeply imbued with this idea that woman is a "dangerous species" from whom one must be protected, the Council ordered priests to shun their society, even that of their parents. It forbade bishops, priests and deacons to dwell under the same roof with women, and only allowed them to live with their grandmother, mother, sisters or neices in cases of absolute necessity.—[Can. 1.] Bishops could not allow a woman to come into their rooms except in the presence of two priests or two deacons.—[Can. 3.]

The Council of Metz, in 888, renewed the first of these prescriptions by forbidding priests to receive into their homes even their mother or their sisters.—[Can. 5.]

And in proportion as Catholicism propagated itself, it seemed to desire to emphasize more and more its tendency toward the subjection of women. The principle is, that woman is a "dangerous species," the decrease of which must be accomplished. The Gospel authorized the marriage of ecclesiastics.—(I Tim. III. 2, 12.) The Church declared the humiliation of the part of procreator which the laws of nature assigned to woman. By sanctifying celibacy they lowered the dignity of marriage, and debased the nobility of woman by honoring a perpetual state of virginity.

The Council of Elvira, in 305, Can. 33, that of Neo Cæsarea, in 314, Can. 1, the 5th Council of Carthage, and that of Rome, in 402, Can. 3, interdicted marriage to bishops, priests and deacons, under pain of being deposed.

. Alexander III, in 1159, declared marriage incompatible with benefices, and Innocent III. confirmed this statement. The Council of Trent, ending in 1563, in its 24th session, smote with anathema the opinion that "the conjugal state should be preferred to a state of virginity or celibacy, and that it is neither better nor more *healthful* to live in virginity and celibacy than to contract marriage."

The principles and foundations of the Catholic doctrine being thus defined, it is easy to conceive that the canon law should have excluded women from all spiritual and religious functions.

Starting with the sixth century, from the Council of Epaone, in 527, and the 2nd Council of Orleans, there were no longer deaconesses in France. However, before the Revolution, the Carthusian nuns of Saleth (Dauphiné) performed at the altar the duties of deacon and sub-deacon. Likewise the abbess of St. Pierre de Lyon filled the office of sub-deacon; she intoned the epistle and wore the maniple. A woman could not receive any ecclesiastic order, and however holy and learned she might be, she could neither teach nor baptize,—(Council of Carthage in 398: Mulier quamvis docta et sancta viros in conventu docere non præsumat. [Can. 99.] Mulier baptisare non præsumat. [Can. 100.], nor preach. She was forbidden even to speak in the church. The law for her was to be in submission.—[I Cor. XIV, 34.] ` Id. Council in Trullo, in 692,

Can. 70. Non enim eis loqui permissum est, sed subjici, sicut dicit lex.)

She could not approach the altar, nor touch the sacred vessels, nor wait upon the ministers of the church, nor burn incense:—(Council of Nantes, in 660, Can. 3: Secundum auctoritatem canonum, modis omnibus prohibendum est ut nulla femina ad altare præsumat accedere, aut presbytero subministrare, aut infra cancellos stare, aut sedere. The missal, § 1, de defectibus, reproduces this prohibition.) A woman who might even have the exercise of a jurisdiction, could neither absolve, excommunicate or bless publicly.

By the canon law the following are declared incapable of benefices and offices: those under age, madmen, married clerks, bigamists, heretics, schismatics, simoniacs, sorcerers, outlaws, the sacrilegious, forgers, the excommunicate, those suspended from office, apostates, perjurers, bastards, sodomites, public keepers of concubines, homicides, epileptics, illiterates, the deformed, usurers, usurpers, incendiaries, the incestuous, and finally—one can easily guess the last group—*women.*—(Encycl. Theolog. by the Abbe Migne, Paris, 1846, Vols. 9 and 10, Art. benefices.)

The canon law forbade a woman to become surety for another, or to act as an arbitrator. It however recognized the fact that in France distinguished women exercised the ordinary jurisdiction over their subjects.—(De arbitris, L. I, Tit. XLIII, ch. IV. In partibus Gallicanis feminæ præcellentes in subditos suos ordinariam jurisdictionem habere noscuntur.)

Woman could not bring an accusation, unless it might be in order to pursue the remedy for an injury done to her. Her accusation never had any validity against an ecclesiastic.—(De accusatione mulierum. Causa XV, quest. III, ch. I. Mulieri accusare non permititur; id. ch. II, ch. III. Certis de causis concessa est mulieribus publica accusatio, veluti si mortem exsequantur eorum earumque. Mulier sacerdotem accusare non valet.)

She could neither plead nor act as attorney in a judicial proceeding,—(Causa XV, quest III. Legibus cautum est, ut ob verecundiam sui sexus mulier apud prætorem pro alio non intercedat.) nor be a procurator;—(Decret. Greg. L. II, Tit. XXX, ch. IV, note 41. De confirm. utili vel inutili. But this note informs us of a certain abbess of Gaudersbein who was made, in due form a procurator;) nor testify in court, nor act as judge.—(Causa XXXIII, quest. V, ch. XVII. Mulierem constat subjectam dominio viri esse, et nullam auctoritatem habere: nec docere, enim potest, nec testis esse, neque fidem dare, nec judicare.) In principle, according to the canon law, a woman's deposition is unworthy of credence; nevertheless, in criminal matters the advisability of receiving or not receiving her testimony was left to the discretion of the ecclesiastical authority.—(De test. et attest. L. II, Tit. XX, ch. III. Mulier testificatur, cum de crimine agitur, quatenus ecclesiastica discretione.) But this testimony could never be received in a charge against a priest.—(De accusat. mulierum.—Causa XV, quest. III. Nec sacerdotes accusare, nec in eos testificar valent.)

Finally, if the object was to establish the existence or non existence of cohabitation between husband and wife, the testimony of the husband alone was admissible.—(De frig. et malef. et impotentia coeundi. L. IV, Tit. XV, ch. I, 17. • • • tibi (marito) credendum est, eo, quod caput es mulieris. Id. Causa XXXIII, quest. I, ch. III.)

The reason for this incapacity pronounced against woman, and this humiliating state of subjection and legal inferiority to which she was submitted, we shall find in the following precepts of the church, and the canon law, "Woman was not created in the image of God, hence she ought to veil her face."—(Decret. secunda pars. Causa XXXIII, quest. V, ch. XIII. Mulier non est facta ad imaginem Dei. Vir quidem non debet velare caput suum, quia imago et gloria Dei est, mulier autem ideo velat, quia non est gloria aut imago Dei. Idem, Causa XXVII, qu. I, ch. XXXI.) "It was Adam who was betrayed by Eve, and not Eve by Adam. It is then just that man should be the master of woman that he may not fall again through the wiles of woman."—(Causa XXXIII, quest. V, ch. XVIII. Adam per Evam deceptus est, non Eva per Adam. Quem vocabit ad culpam mulier, justum est, ut eum gubernatorem assumat, ne iterum femina facilitate labatur.) "The law demands that women shall be subject to men, and that they shall be almost as their servants."—(Causa XXXIII, quest. V, ch. XIV. Satis hinc apparet quemadmodum subditas feminas viris, et pene famulas lex esse voluerit.

If it be fostering and professing heresy to affirm that these reasons invoked by the canon law to justify and legalize the inferiority of woman have no legal foundation, no human ground, that they appear to us neither convincing, decisive, nor irrefutable; very well, then, far from being ashamed, truly we are proud to proclaim ourselves heretics.

THE COMMON LAW.—Without taking time to discuss the rudimentary law of the ancient German Colonies, we recall only that institution of Germanic origin, the *vogt* or *advocatus*, whose care it was to represent every woman at the court of the suzerain, in judicial acts and debates.

Under the feudal system, woman was recognized as capable of being enfeoffed.—(Ant. Loysel, Inst. Coutumieres. Ed. Dupin et Ed. Laboulaye, Paris, Durand, 1848, no. 637.)

No legal disability smote the woman of feudal nobility. She enjoyed the feudal rights of suzerainty and justice. Her testimony was received, just as her judgment as arbitrator was made binding on the parties. She could dispense justice and preside over both civil and criminal trials.

The ancient precedents were conceived and established in a spirit which was extremely favorable to woman. There is not a trace in them of the privilege of masculinity. They allowed woman to be a witness, a surety, an attorney, a judge, an arbitrator. Later, under the influence of the canon law, and in the early renaissance of juridical study, under the action of the schools of Roman law, a reaction made itself felt against the rights of woman, and the old disabilities of Roman legislation re-appeared and became a part of the legal institutions.

If we consult one of the oldest legal monuments, the *Book of Justice*, we find formulated there this general principle: "The smallest part of our law applies to women as to men."—(An meins leus de nos droit est peor la condicion as femes que as homes. Li Livre de Jostice et de plet. Ed Rapetti, Paris,

Firmin-Didot, 1850, L. I, VIII, § 2.)

Woman could not be a guarantor. "For it is the same as with the taking away from women the exercise of jurisdiction, because of custom and the weakness of the sex."—(Id. L. XVIII, II, § 1. Feme ne s'entremcte por nul home. Car ausint comme l'en oste as femes office de juridiction, et por lor mors comme por la feblece de lor sen. Id. Boutellicr, L. I, T. CI, p. 577.) However, when the obligation entered into by a woman consisted of a contract to pay in money or in kind, the woman was bound. "A woman should not keep a tavern or a brothel, and if she does, she is in no wise bound. But when a woman carries on an honest business as any man may do, she is bound."—(Liv. de Jost. L. XVIII, II, § 4. L'en deffant que feme ne soit taverniere, ne bordeliere. Et s'ele est, ele n'est obligée de riens. A totes les foiz, que feme fet honeste chose que prodom doit fere, ele est obligée.)

Woman could not be an advocate. Before marriage she could bind herself, and even perform judicial duties, and the married woman could always plead on behalf of her children. It seems indeed that the different texts of the *Book of Justice* contradict each other.—(Ne puet estre avoquaz, ne feme ne orp, por ce qu'il ne puet voir la autece dou juge. Liv. de Jost. L. II, XIX, § 7. Feme ne puet deffendre nului en plet. Mes se ele est sanz seignor, ele puet bien deffendre son pleige, est soi-meisme. Feme qui n'a seignor puet plévir, et puet avoir juridiction, et procuracion, et avocacion. Id. L. XVIII, II, § 3. Feme que pledee est receue por ses enfans. Id. L. X, XVII, § 12.)

According to Philippe de Beaumanoir, a woman is not allowed to hold the position of advocate to plead for another, but she may speak for herself or her children, or any of her relatives, but only under the permission of her husband, if she has a husband.—(Les coutumes du Beauvoisis. Ed. of Count Beugnot, Paris. Renouard, 1842, ch. V, no. 16. Il ne loist pas a feme a estre en office d'avocat por autrui por loier; mais sans loier pot ele parler por li ou por ses enfans ou por aucun de son lignage, mais que ce soit de l'actorité de son baron se ele a baron.)

"Besides," he adds, "she ought not to be a bailiff, advocate, or procurator, or keeper of horses, for all these offices belong especially to men and not to women."—(Id. ch. XXIX, 19. Ne lor doit estre bailliés, ne advocations, ne procurations, ne garde de cevax, car tout cel service apartienent as homes et non par as femes.)

Beaumanoir is strongly imbued with the prejudice of the Roman law against women. He holds that the testimony of women should only be received in certain exceptional cases.— (Neporquant, li cas de crieme en sunt exepté, car en cas ou il a peril de mort ou de mehaing, ne sunt pas femes a ouir en tesmognage, se n'est en fet notoire, li quix fu fes devant tant de prodomes qu'il est apertement seus, si comme devant six de bone renomée ou plus. Id. ch. XXXIX, 31, XXXIX, 54.)

Another author, Boutillier, also tells us that a woman could not hold the office of attorney or of advocate. "For know, that a woman, in whatever state she may be, married or unmarried, cannot be received as procurator for any person whatever. For she was forbidden (to do) any act of procuration because of Calphurnia, who considered herself wiser than any one else; she could not restrain herself, and was continually running to the judge without respect for formalities, in order to influence him against his opinion."—(Item sachez que feme de quelque estat q'elle soit, mariée ou a marier, n'est a recevoir comme prcuratrice, pour quelque personne que ce soit. Car a elle fut défendu, tout faict d'armes et de procuration pour la raison de Calphurnie que jacoit ce q'elle fust femine sage plus que nul autre, si ne sceult elle avoir mesure, et courut au juge sus sans mauiere, pour ce qu'il appoincta contre son opinion." Sommé Rural, Edit. Macé, Paris, 1603. L. I, Tit. X, p. 45.)

Farther on, designating those "who may be advocates in court and who not," Boutillier cites as incapable, minors, the deaf, the blind, clerks, sargeants and women. "For women are excluded because of their forwardness, like Calphurnia, who could never endure that her side should be beaten nor that the judge should decide against her, without speaking forwardly to the judge or to the other party."—(Item sont privées femes par raison de leur hastiveté, si comme fust Calphurnie qui ne pouvait souffrir que en nulle maniére sa partie defendist ne que le juge y donnast appointement sans dire hastiveté au juge ou a partie. Id. L. II, Tit. II, p. 674.)

"The forwardness of Calphurnia" appeared to all the ancient jurists a peremptory reason for excluding woman from the forum. In Germany as in France the inferiority of woman was justified upon the same grounds. "No woman" says the *Miroir de Souabe,* "can be guardian of herself nor plead in court, nor do it for another, nor make complaint against another, without an advocate. They lost this through a gentlewoman named Carfurna, who behaved foolishly in Rome before the ruler."—(Nulle feme ne puet estre tuerriz de soi mesmes, ne porter la parole en justice, ne l'autrui, ne complaindre d'autrui sanz avocat. Ce ont elles perdu par une gentil dame qui eut nom Carfurna qui eut a Rome par devant le roi si folles contenances. Miroir de Souabe, T. II, ch. XXIV, Lassberg, 245.)

I will mention in passing that it was only under Charles VI, in 1394, that the right of women to testify was recognized. The prejudices against the testifying of women were hard to uproot. At the close of the seventeenth century a certain Bruneau, in his Criminal Commentaries, had the audacity to pretend that the deposition of three women was hardly worth that of two men.

The entire system of that ancient legislation which declared the legal inferiority of woman is based on the considerations of the weakness, the *infirmitas,* the *fragilitas,* the *imbecillitas* of the sex. Let us not lose sight of this point, from which we shall later make certain deductions;—the point that if woman had to submit to the odious consequences of an unjustifiable inequality, she reaped on the other hand, certain advantages. The penalties inflicted on women were in most instances, slighter than those imposed on men. "If a woman commits a trespass her punishment is only half that of a man."—(Feme se cle forfet, * * * l'amande n'est que la moitié mendre d'ome. Liv. de Jost. L. XVIII, XXIV, § 64. De toutes amendes

estans en loi, les femes n'en doivent que la moitié. Loysel,
Inst. Cout. No. 853. Cout. d'Orleans.) "Woman shall suffer
but half the punishment, where man suffers the full penalty.
* * * Thus, woman should not be put into irons, nor sent to
the galleys, nor placed in a prison which might enfeeble her
body, or wound her or cause her to lose her memory, for
women are frail by nature."—(La feme ne chet point qu'en
demye amende, ou l'homme cherrait en pleine amende. * * *
Item doit la feme estre emprisonnée ne en fers, ne en busche,
ne de prison qui son corps puisse affoler, ne blesser, ne memoire
perdre, car fresles sont de nature. Boutillier, II, XL.)

In BELGIUM, the legal status of woman was formerly inferior
to that of man. Woman could not be a surety for another.
In Antwerp, however, the Velléian Decree was not in force, at
least the sovereign council of Brabant so decided in May, 1652.
Woman could testify in court. Our ancient courts even had
enough chivalrous gallantry to receive without oath, the testimony of prominent women, their simple affirmation, upon the
faith of Princess or Duchess, being sufficient. There is one
notable decision on this point, of the Grand Council of Mechlin,
in favor of the Countess of Berlaimont.

Our early writers who engaged in the profession of advocate
and held the office of procurator do not speak of the exclusion
of woman from these positions.—(George de Ghewiet, Instit.
de droit belgigue, Bruxelles, 1758, Tome II, p. 205. Méth de
la prof. d'avocat. Sohet, Instit. de droit et de jurisprud. pour
les pays de Liége, Luxembourg et Namur. Bouillon, 1772, L.
I. T. LIII and LIV.) We have no reason, however, to suppose that any woman under the old regime ever did hold either
of these offices in our provinces.

The present state of the question in Europe and the United
States is now to be considered.

In GERMANY, women are not admitted to advanced courses
of study. In Bavaria, a decree made in 1880, by de Lutz,
Minister, formally excluded them from such studies, and at the
same time the Government of Saxony denied to women access
to the Universities, whether as listeners or as students. Then,
in 1886, M. de Gossler, Minister of Public Worship and Public

Instruction, pronounced their exclusion from the Prussian universities.

So, for the time being, the problem of the woman lawyer cannot present itself in Germany. Moreover, by virtue of the German law of the 1st of July, 1878, concerning advocates, the requirements for admission to the bar are the same as those demanded of candidates for the magistracy.—(Art. 1.). The judicial authority has the power to decide as to enrollment as a member of the bar.—(Art. 2.) Finally, in order to be accepted as an advocate in Germany, certain physical conditions must be met. Individuals tainted "with physical infirmities" are not eligible for admission to the bar.—(Art. 5.) Woman might possibly be excluded from the profession of advocate, as physically unfit.

IN AUSTRIA, up to 1868, advocates were true officers appointed by Government. The laws of the 6th of July, 1868, and the 1st of April, 1872, modified this state of affairs. Although these laws imposed no condition of sex for admission to the bar, women could not become advocates, the schools of law being closed against them.

The situation is the same in HUNGARY. The law of December 4, 1874, concerning advocates, did not exclude women from the bar. They, however, being unable to devote themselves to the study of law, have not the power to obtain the diploma required in order to practice it.

IN ENGLAND, as in Ireland, women can attend the university courses, but it is otherwise in Scotland, the House of Commons in its session of March 3, 1875, by a vote of 194 to 151, having refused to allow women to be admitted to the Scottish universities.

The profession of advocate, in ENGLAND, differs essentially from what it is with us. To become a barrister, it is not necessary to possess the degree of Doctor of Laws. It is sufficient to enroll one's self in the Inns of Court, corporations whose object it is to train men to be advocates. There are in London, the Inner Temple, the Middle Temple, Gray's Inn and Lincoln's Inn. These Inns are not only colleges of law, but also a sort of hostelry. The student is obliged to dine there six times each term of three months during the three years he must spend in these colleges. If he belongs to a university, he need dine but three times a term. Then he must pass certain examinations, of not much importance, before a commission designated as *Bencher's*, the managers of these establishments. The organization of these schools is very ancient, going back several centuries.

The Benchers, recruited from the ranks of the barristers, the magistrates and the highest dignitaries, are very conservative, and do not admit women to the Inns of Court.

DENMARK. The Danish law of the 26th of May, 1868, as to the profession of advocate, allows women to defend their own causes before the courts and tribunals. They cannot, however, plead before the Supreme Court, at least, where the affair does not concern their own life or honor, the honor or life of their husbands or of their children.

A royal decree of June 25, 1875, admitted women to the Danish universities. Article 3 of this decree, allows women who have taken the examination in arts to take the full examination in jurisprudence, but the final clause of the article provides that the academic degrees shall not give them any right to a "public nomination." Another royal decree, dated May 12, 1882, authorized women to present themselves for the *partial* examination in jurisprudence, adding that they should not thereby obtain the right to be nominated for advocates, nor the authority to present themselves before the tribunals as if endowed with the powers of advocates.

In these latter days, the question has been raised whether, in spite of these formal enactments, women were not, after all, capable of performing the *duties* of advocate; relying upon these two arguments: that the royal decrees in question did not emanate from the legislative power, but from the King alone; and that the "public nomination," spoken of in the decree of 1875, does not apply to advocates. The Minister of Justice, being interrogated in this matter, replied, by his message of August 23, 1887, that the question should, in his opinion, be solved by maintaining the disability of women.

Almost at the same time a woman who had passed the *par-*

tial examination in jurisprudence, presented herself before the Court of Copenpagen, as if possessing the powers of an advocate. The President refused to admit the procuration, on the ground that the bearer was of the feminine sex. Process was served on the President of the Court in order to compel him to admit the procuration; the President won the case. It was thereupon carried up to the Supreme Court of Denmark, which will not render its decision before the beginning of this winter. (1888-9.)

We are indebted for this official information to the courtesy of M. Buch, Procuror-General of the Supreme Court of Denmark.

IN SPAIN, a royal decree of March 16, 1882, forbade women the access to higher instruction.

IN FRANCE, the matter stands as in Belgium, by force of the decree of the 14th of December, 1810, which governs both countries.

Up to the present time the Faculty of Law in Paris, have only admitted one woman to the degree of Licentiate. This is a young Roumanian, Mlle. Bilcesco, who received her diploma in 1887, after having passed with honor all her examinations. This young girl has continued this year her studies for the Doctorate, and has taken, with honors, the first examination for that degree. Mlle. Bilcesco does not aspire to the title of advocate.

According to information furnished us by M. Colmet de Santerre, Dean of the Faculty of Law at Paris, a young Frenchwoman has just finished successfully, the studies of the first year of the course. At the competitive examination she even received a prize and "honorable mention." She intends, when she becomes a Licentiate, to present herself before a French Court to take the oath as advocate. So it certainly seems that in but two years from the present time, the French tribunals will have to solve the problem of the woman lawyer.

IN HOLLAND, women are admitted to the university courses. Most of the female students are enrolled in the school of medicine or that of letters. Quite a large number of women are practicing as Doctor of Medicine.

There is no law regulating the practice of the profession of advocate. Article 19 of the law of August 18, 1827, concerning the organization of the judiciary, modified by several subsequent laws, declares that every thing which relates to advocates shall be the subject of executive regulation. By virtue of this provision the "regulation of the órder of advocates and their discipline" have been fixed by the royal decree of September 14, 1838, modified by the decrees of December 5, 1844, of December 17, 1875, and of June 1st, 1879.

None of these regulations have foreseen the case of the admission of woman to the bar. It is, however, generally admitted that a woman, Doctor of Law, would be received in Holland to practice the profession of advocate. Such, at least, is the opinion of M. Aug. Philips, Chief of the Order of Advocates of Amsterdam, one of the most eminent advocates in Holland, as expressed in a communication which he has kindly addressed to us.

IN ITALY. We had occasion to raise for the first time in Belgium, the problem of the woman advocate, by making known here the Italian jurisprudence which excluded women from the bar.—(See our Manuel de la profession d'avocat en Italie—Brux. Moens, 1887, pp. 59–64.) A decree of the Court of Appeal at Turin, of November 14, 1883, and another decree of the Court of Cassation of that city, dated May 8, 1884, forbade women to practice as advocates.—(The first of these decrees is cited in the journal "*La Giurisprudenza,*" Dec. No. 1883, Year XX, p. 1076; the second is reproduced in the same journal, of May 17, 1884, Year XXI, pp. 321–324.)

The facts upon which the Court had to decide are worthy of an exposition. As related in the decree of the Court of Cassation, Signora Lidia Poet had submitted the evidence which confers the right to pursue university studies, and had made use of the right accorded to women by Article 8 of the regulation of October 8, 1876, to become a student. She completed her legal studies in the time prescribed by law, passed all her examinations, took the degree of Doctor of Laws, and obtained her enrollment on the "stage."—(The time required to be spent between admission as licentiate and the call to the bar.—Translator.) She applied herself to the study of law practice for two years, and during that period diligently frequented the hearings of the tribunals. Desiring to be inscribed on the list of the Order [of Advocates], she passed successfully the theoretical and practical examination prescribed by law, and the Council of the Order, after consultation, on August 9, 1883, rendered an opinion favorable to her enrollment. The Public Minister, making use of the latitude allowed him by Italian law, opposed this opinion. The Court refused to admit Signora Poet to the bar.

The motives which influenced the Turin Court of Cassation may be thus briefly summarized: "The practice of the profession of advocate cannot be compared with that of any other profession to which the completion of a course of study and the obtaining of a diploma gives a right of access; this practice exacts a concurrence of other conditions prescribed by law. Rights and duties spring from it; the functions of the advocate constitute more than a profession, they are a kind of public and necessary office, according to the saying of Anastasius: laudabile vitæque hominum necessarium officium.

"In fact, every citizen has the choice of resorting or of not resorting to the labor of those who practice a profession. Whilst to have recourse to an advocate is both obligatory and necessary, and whilst those who practice other professions are free to lend the assistance requested of them or to refuse it, advocates cannot refuse theirs, especially in cases where the magistrate orders this assistance to be given. The principle proclaimed by the praetor, Si non habebunt advocatum, ego dabo (Lex I, § 4, de postulando), has been respected by all legislation, and is maintained in full force by the legislation which governs us. The Italian law has also accepted and followed the teachings of the Roman law in the matter of distinctions, favors, privileges and remuneration. It has organized colleges of advocates, having a legal representation; it has granted to them an exceptional jurisdiction and given to them extraordinary means for prosecuting the payment of their fees; it has bestowed a special dignity upon them, that of succeeding to the magistracy after a few years of practice.

"The profession of advocate being a public office, or, at the very least a species of public and civil office, to admit women to the practice thereof, it is not enough to say that in actual legislation no law has pronounced their exclusion; a positive text must be found declaring woman capable of holding all offices and positions as well public as civil. If the Italian Civil Code has extracted women from that species of inferiority (*diminusione di capo*) under which she was placed in the past, and has admitted her to the enjoyment of almost all civil rights on a footing of equality with man; if laws, enacted concerning certain special matters have qualified woman for certain specified offices, it is unquestionable that, in order for women to enjoy certain rights and perform certain duties, a like qualification must be expressly conferred upon them by legislation. In Italian law, there is no enactment which accords to woman the right to practice the profession of advocate, but, weighing the letter and the spirit of the laws bearing on the question, the conclusion is, that, in the mind of the legislator, the profession of advocate ought to be a business reserved for men, and that women ought to remain strangers to it. Articles 39 No. 2, 50 No. 3, 72, 128, of the law concerning the organization of the judiciary, say that those who have carried on the profession of advocate for a certain period of time may be nominated for praetors, judges, and councilors of Appeal and of Cassation. If women were admitted to the bar, they also might perform these judicial duties. Such could not have been the intent of the legislature.

"The qualification of woman for the profession of advocate should be in express terms, for it is an extraordinary thing, outside all usages and even expressly forbidden by the general law The Roman law excluded women from this office, and no modern enactment has abrogated this provision of the general law. The reason for which the praetor forbade women to plead, as a thing contrary to the reserve and modesty befitting the sex, has the same validity to-day that it formerly had.

"It would be unbecoming and villainous (*brutto*)," adds the decree, "to see women descending into the arena of the forum, taking part in the midst of the bustle of public procedure, exciting themselves in discussions which easily carry one beyond bounds, and in which one could not show toward them, all the respeot which it is proper to observe toward the more delicate sex. Moreover, woman might at times be compelled to deal, *ex professo*, with questions which 'the excellent rules of polite society' do not allow to be discussed in the presence of respectable women."

The Turin Court of Appeal has felt itself obliged to terminate its decree by a consideration, which, although it be delicately humorous, hardly seems to us juridical.

"After what has already been said, there is no need even to mention the risk which the gravity of legal proceedings might run, if—to say nothing of other things—one should sometimes see the toga covering the strange and *bizarre* garments which fashion often imposes upon women, or the cap placed upon not less extravagant coiffures; just as there is no further need to mention the very grave danger to which the magistracy would be exposed, of being the object of suspicion and calumny, every time that the scales of justice should turn in favor of the party for whom a woman advocate had pleaded."

The Turin Court of Cassation rejected the application of Signora Lidia Poet. The decree of the Supreme Court involves itself in lengthy disquisitions, philosophical rather than juridical, to demonstrate that the public law and the private law have not established in Italy, the equality of the sexes. One can easily judge of the value of the entire decree, by reading this passage from the strange argument of the Turin Court: "If the legislator had really intended to admit women to practice the profession of advocate, he would not have employed invariably the generic masculine term *avvocato*; he would also have used the expression *avvocata*, which is found in the Italian language and is in use in common speech."—(E di vero, non é poi un argomento tanto lieve quello del trovarvisi sempre adoperato il genere mascolino avvocato, non la parola avvocata, che pur esiste nella lingua italiana e si usa nel comune parlare. Decree Cass. Turin, p. 323. Col. 2 Journ. Ind.)

Truly, the argument against woman which prevails in Italy, must be very weak, for a supreme court to be reduced to invoke in its support such shabby subtilties—we might even say, such pitiful quibbles. [For a full account of Signora Poet's case, with the decrees thereupon, see La Donna e l'Avvocatura, by Signor Santoni-de Sio, Roma, 1884. Translator.]

(A fuller account of this case, with, perhaps, some translations from the Italian, will appear in a subsequent number of the "Law Times."—Ed.)

PORTUGAL has not yet solved the problem of the introduction of women to the universities. The woman lawyer, like the woman physician, is a thing unknown there.

IN RUSSIA, women are excluded from university courses.— (There is, however, a school of medicine, which was founded for women.) This fact reveals nothing surprising for a country where the students are organized as a part of the military, wearing uniforms, and obeying military chiefs. Although exclusion from the universities might be pronounced against women, the Czar rightly judged that they could possibly claim the right to become members of the bar, so long as their incapacity had not been formerly expressed. Hence the Emperor of all the Russias sanctioned the decree of January 7, 1876, which forbade women access to the functions of advocate. As early as 1871, the question of the admission of women to the offices of Russian public administration, was decided in the negative.

IN SWEDEN, women can attend university courses and the schools of law, and obtain there the degree of Doctor.

No Order of Advocates exists in that country. Neither the Civil Code, nor that of Civil and Criminal Procedure of 1734, still in force, compels professional jurists to plead for another before the tribunals. The Code, (Sect. Procedure, ch. XV, 2), expresses itself thus: "Those who demand or defend for another before the tribunals, should be men of good reputation, honest, and endowed with intelligence. In general, the tribunal should in each case, receive the defenders."

As M. the Count K. d'Olivecrona, Counselor of the Supreme Court of Sweden has written to us, the legislature certainly never dreamed, in 1734, that women might present themselves before the tribunals, in the character of advocate.

Up to the present time no woman has appeared before the

Swedish Courts of Appeal, or before the Supreme Court, to fill the office of advocate. Before the *nisi prius* tribunals, especially the provincial ones, women frequently appear, armed with full power from their husbands, and the tribunal allows them to plead.

According to information sent to us from another source, by the Rector of the University of Upsala, a woman who has completed her legal studies and received her diploma, has an incontestable right to practice as advocate before any tribunal whatever in the country.

In TURKEY, the law of January 13, 1876, concerning advocates, evidently does not trouble itself about the woman lawyer. Turkey is the only country in Europe where the women still live in special apartments, and are compelled to veil their faces when they go out. In the country of the harem alone, a court of appeal would be authorized to invoke, against the admission of women to the bar, the text of Lex 21, Cod. II, 13 (12): ne feminæ persequendæ litis obtentu in contumeliam matronalis pudoris irreverenter irruant, et conventibus virorum vel judiciis interesse cogantur.

As to SWITZERLAND, where there is no federal legislation concerning the practice of the profession of advocate, we cannot think of analyzing here all the local laws, whose provisions vary exceedingly from one canton to another. For instance, in the canton of Neufchatel, a woman would be admitted to plead before the tribunals, the profession of advocate being free, but in Geneva, on the contrary it would be otherwise; for the law of June 22, 1878, grants the right to practice as advocate only to Swiss citizens enjoying civil and political rights.

In all Switzerland—we might even say in all the German countries, one woman alone has obtained the diploma of a Doctor of Laws. This is Mme. Emelie Kempin-Spyri of Zurich, concerning whom several judicial decisions have been rendered, which we shall now consider in detail.

In the Canton of Zurich, the profession of advocate is free; the first man who comes, be he shoemaker or stonebreaker, can set up as advocate, though he may not have the least idea of law or of right. The only condition imposed is that of possessing "the right of active citizenship." The advocates of Zurich form a Society (*Advocatenverein*) but not an Order.

On the 24th of November, 1886, before the tribunal of the Second Arrondissement of Zurich appeared Mme. Kempin-Spyri, at the time a candidate in law, who preferred a request, to the end that she might be heard as attorney for, or at least, as assignee of the rights of her husband. Basing itself on Article 174 of the Code of Civil Procedure of the canton of Zurich, by the terms of which the right of active citizenship (*actifburgerrecht*) is essential in order to represent a third party in civil causes, the tribunal rejected Mme. Kempin-Spyri's petition, and refused to recognize her right to represent her husband in court.

As all the magistracy of Zurich was hostile to the admission of women within the bar of the tribunals, Mme. Kempin, without addressing herself to the intermediate jurisdiction of the Court of Appeal (*Obergericht*) adopted the method of redressing public grievances before the Swiss Federal tribunal. The petitioner based her application upon the ground that the cantonal tribunal of Zurich had violated Article 4 of the Federal Constitution.—(This Art. 4 proclaims that there exists in Switzerland no privilege of position, of birth, of family, nor of person.) The contest was against a Swiss citizen of the feminine sex, denying the possession of the right of active citizenship, on the sole ground that this citizen was of the feminine sex.

Article 18 of the Constitution, she further stated, which subjects every Swiss to military service, does not constitute any exception to the fundamental equality of all the citizens, for one cannot but conclude that this Article 18 applies to the male sex only, except that, in time of war, a certain number of women might be called into the sanitary service (*sanitatsdienst*), and the remainder be subjected to a tax for military reimbursement. (*Militarpflichtersatzsteuer.*)

The petitioner, basing her argument further upon Articles 16 and 18 of the cantonal law of Zurich, according to which every person capable of transacting business and having attained his twentieth year, is in possession of the right of active citizenship, so long as this right is not taken away from him by. reason of crime, default, bankruptcy or perpetual poverty, contended that these articles made no distinction as to persons on account of sex; that if women had not up to that time claimed the right of suffrage in the canton of Zurich, they had not thereby lost it; that, even if it be granted that women do not enjoy all political rights, it did not follow that they did not possess the right of active citizenship; that the right of suffrage does not suppose the right of active citizenship, but on the contrary the right of active citizenship is a condition of the existence of the right of suffrage; that, finally, "right of active citizenship" is synonymous with "capacity for civil honor" (*burgerliche Ehrenfahigkeit*), and that this capacity belongs equally to him who has not the right of suffrage.

Lastly, the petitioner maintained, that, contrary to the judgment of the Zurich tribunal, she did possess the right of active citizenship, although she found herself placed, as a wife, under the tutelage of her husband.

Consequently, Mme. Kempin prayed that the Swiss Federal tribunal would reverse the decision of November 24th, 1886,

a. By recognizing her right of active citizenship;

b. By recognizing her right to act, from the time when she' became Doctor of Law, and freed herself from the marital tutelage by carrying on, independently a profession, a business or a trade.—(By force of law in Zurich, the tutelage of the husband ceases at the moment the wife begins to perform independent functions. The tribunal of the canton had held that this provision did not apply to the practice of the profession of advocate.)

(To be continued.)

CONSPIRACY AGAINST THE REPUBLIC.

BLAIR AMENDMENT TO THE FEDERAL CONSTITUTION.

Too many amendments to the Constitution are contemplated, and it is not clear that too many have not already been made. The first eight amendments, which may be called the National Bill of Rights, were of doubtful necessity or utility. Alexander Hamilton who, on account of his consummate wisdom, and because of his tact and skill in carrying the grand work through some of its most difficult stages, has been called "the Father of the Constitution," thought, that as the very purpose of the Constitution was to secure the blessings of liberty, this declaration was a better recognition of popular rights than that contained in the elaborate declaration of rights in every State Constitution. The same idea is embodied in the reason given in "The Federalist," why the Constitution had not given a bill of rights; because the reservation of powers without a bill of rights, was larger than a reservation of powers with a bill of rights.

Several of the States however, were fearful that too much power would be claimed and exercised by the new government which was being formed. They insisted upon amendments, which should guard the rights of the States and of the people against encroachments of federal power. Such amendments were proposed by several of the States, and though they were not made conditional to the ratification of the Constitution, there was a general understanding that those of them which were considered of most importance, would be adopted.

In New York, an effort was made to make the amendments conditional, and was only defeated by a vote of 31 to 27.

After the first eight amendments, constituting the Bill of Rights, had been tacitly agreed upon, it was feared that the very adoption of these might raise an implication that they contained all that the people would insist upon as against the Government; hence a ninth was thought necessary, as follows:

"The enumeration in the Constitution of certain rights shall not be construed to deny or disparage others retained by the people."

To this was added a tenth, as follows:

"The powers not granted to the United States by the Constitution, nor prohibited by it to the States, are reserved to the States respectively or to the people."

These ten amendments were, at various times, from 1789 to 1791 adopted in a body.

The eleventh Amendment was occasioned by the decision of the Supreme Court of the United States in the case of Chisholm, Exr. v. Georgia, 2 Dallas' Rep. p. 419.

This was a suit brought by a citizen of South Carolina against the State of Georgia; and the question was, whether the Supreme Court had jurisdiction in case of a suit brought against a State by a citizen of another State.

The question was argued at the February Term, 1793, and decided by five judges to one, in favor of the jurisdiction.

The decision caused a good deal of excitement. Hence the Eleventh Amendment, as follows:

"The judicial power of the United States shall not be construed to extend to any suit in law or equity, commenced or prosecuted against one of the United States by citizens of another State, or by citizens or subjects of any foreign State."

This was proposed by Congress in 1794, and was declared in force January 8, 1798.

The occasion of the Twelfth Amendment was, the bitter struggle in Congress to determine who should be President, after the presidential election of 1800. The excitement which had been caused by the long contest in the House, resulting in the election of Jefferson, had made apparent the necessity of a change in the mode of electing President.

The Amendment was proposed December 12, 1803, and proclaimed September 25, 1804.

Then came a long period of quiet so far as constitutional changes were concerned; a quiet which lasted over sixty years. Not until about the close of the civil war was there any further amendment.

The Thirteenth Amendment, proclaimed ratified, in December, 1865, declared that neither slavery nor involuntary servitude, except as a punishment for crime, should exist within the United States, or any place subject to their jurisdiction.

The word slave was not in the Constitution, and though slavery existed in this country when the Constitution was formed, it was expected that the Slave States would soon adopt measures looking toward gradual emancipation. The inconsistency of slavery with the fundamental law, was felt and frequently adverted to. By general consent the Constitution was so framed that when slavery should be abolished, the charter of our government would be found perfectly adapted to the new order of things, and posterity would look in vain into the Constitution for any evidence that such a system as slavery had existed.

Such being the case, the Thirteenth Amendment, except as a sanction of the Emancipation Proclamation rendered necessary by the war, and as a guaranty that it should be carried into effect, would not have been necessary.

The suffrage amendments introduced a new departure in the relation of the States to the general government.

The theory of our government in its organization was, that the regulation of the suffrage and the conditions upon which it should be exercised, should, with certain exceptions, be left to the control of the States. In each State the citizen may contend and justly contend that suffrage is a right of citizenship; that as a citizen of the State he is entitled to the suffrage as a matter of right, subject to uniform regulations in common with other citizens. But this contention is between him and the State government; between him and the electors in his own State. As a citizen of the United States, all the right he had, previous to the war, in regard to the suffrage, was, to claim the benefit of the second section of the fourth Article of the Constitution, and the right, under the second section of the first Article, to vote for Congressmen.

The Fourteenth and Fifteenth Amendments, having been adopted as a part of the reconstruction measures rendered necessary by the war, introduced a radical change in this respect in our form of government. The Fourteenth, declared ratified in the summer of 1868, prescribes a penalty for denying the suffrage to certain classes of citizens, while the Fifteenth, proclaimed in March, 1870, substantially guaranties the elective franchise to those classes in all the States, at all general elec-tions, State as well as national.

From this brief history of the amendments made up to the present time, it will sufficiently appear that the first ten were substantially a part of the original Constitution, while the last five have been made to meet certain exigencies in the history and administration of the government.

The civil war rendered necessary the exercise of extraordinary powers on the part of the general government, for its own preservation. But it did not entirely change our form of government, nor did it destroy the autonomy of the Southern States. Their continued existence as States was implied in the very term "reconstruction."

No Republic with a single government—what may be called a centralized republic—has ever endured for any considerable period of time, except San Marino, a Republic of 22 square miles in extent, and containing about eight thousand inhabitants; and no federative or non-centralized republic has endured for any great length of time; those now in existence being all of comparatively recent formation.

The republican form of government is, therefore, still upon trial.

Of the federative republics which have perished, the two most notable examples have been, the Grecian States under the Achaian League, and the Hanseatic Federation. While other things contributed to the downfall of these republics, no candid inquirer can fail to come to the conclusion that one of the most potent causes was the difficulty of maintaining a proper balance of power between the general and local governments.

The Fathers of our Republic studied carefully this balance of power, and guided by the light of history, they placed such safeguards against encroachments of federal jurisdiction on the one hand, and against usurpation of power by the States on the other, that the mixed government thus established has, for a hundred years, commanded the respect and admiration of the world. There is every reason to believe that the perpetuity of the Republic depends largely upon the preservation of this balance of power.

To say that the Federal Government is one of delegated powers, is simply to repeat what every student well understands. But the powers of the State Government are inherent in the people of the State, and in the State Legislature, as representing the people. There are certain limitations placed upon the exercise of that power. Some of these limitations have been established by the people of the United States in the Federal Constitution—some by the people of the State in the State Constitution—others necessarily result from a republican form of government. But within these limitations the States are sovereign. They possess what has been well designated by jurists as quasi-sovereignty; while as to foreign States or communities, the people of the United States, represented by the Federal Government, constitute the State.

This State sovereignty, except as limited in the manner described, should be sacredly respected. It is just as dangerous for the Federal Government to encroach upon the rights of the States as it would be for the States to usurp the power of the general Government. Every disturbance of this balance of power is fraught with danger to our institutions.

The motto of Illinois is, "State Sovereignty—National Union." But the States can maintain their sovereignty only by acting in concert. Let, therefore. the motto of Kentucky be added, "United we stand—divided we fall."

Every amendment to the Constitution is a change in our form of government; and every change tending to the centralization of power, is a blow at the liberties of the people. Under our form of government, the rights and liberties of the citizens can only be preserved by maintaining the rights of the States. Let the people once become habituated to surrendering the rights of their States to the general Government, and they will soon reconcile themselves to the surrender to the same power, of their rights as individuals.

The Fourteenth and Fifteenth Amendments, taking jurisdiction over subjects which, under our system of government, were, with the exceptions stated, under the control of the States, could only be justified by the condition of the country after the war, and should not be regarded as precedents for the still further derangement of our federative system.

The Blair Amendment, proposed in a time of profound peace, is a plain encroachment upon the rights of the States, and is not called for by any such emergency as gave rise to the other amendments. The right to legislate upon the subject of education, is in that vast reservoir of rights which are reserved to the States, not only by the 10th Amendment but by our very form of government.

The original Constitution gave to Congress no power over the subject of religion or of education. The Blair Amendment proposes for the first time to give Congress such power. Where is this encroachment upon the rights of the States to stop?

The joint resolution introduced by Senator Blair, proposing his Amendment, provides, that

"Each State in this Union shall establish and maintain a system of free public schools adequate for the education of all the children living therein, between the ages of six and sixteen years, inclusive, in the common branches of knowledge, and in virtue, morality, and the principles of the Christian religion."

What are the principles of the Christian religion? If the question could be determined by reference to the teachings of Christ. there would be less difficulty attending the matter. But Jesus had far less to do in establishing the Christian religion than Paul; and Paul said, "If any one preach any other gospel unto you than that ye have received, let him be accursed." Is this one of the principles of the Christian religion? It was the hypocrites whom Jesus denounced; but Paul denounced also those who honestly differed with him in opinion.

In some respects Paul was one of the most remarkable men that ever lived. In his moments of enthusiasm and of spiritual exaltation, he gave forth some of the grandest utterances recorded in the pages of history. Nevertheless he was a persecutor, by temperament and practice. Before his conversion he had persecuted the Christians, making havoc of the church, entering into every house, haling men and women, and committing them to prison, (Acts 8. 3), pursuing them relentlessly, even unto death. (Acts 26. 10.)

There is sufficient reason to believe that in this respect his nature, after conversion, was essentially the same as before. He hurls his anathema at heretics, not only in the passage cited, (Gal. 1. 8, 9), but in various others. In 1 Cor. 16. 22, he says, "If any man love not the Lord Jesus Christ, let him be anathema maran-atha." In 2 Thess. 1. 8, he pictures the Lord Jesus as "taking vengeance" on those who obey not his gospel. In 1 Tim. 1. 20, he says that Hymeneus and Alexander, who had departed from the faith, he had "delivered unto Satan." In 2 Tim. 4. 14: "Alexander the coppersmith did me much evil; the Lord reward him according to his works." In Titus 1. 11, referring to those in the church who were unruly, and vain talkers and deceivers, he declares that their "mouths must be stopped," and in Galatians, 5. 12, he says, "*I would they were even cut off*, who trouble you."

An attempt has been made to break the force of this passage, by claiming that the apostle meant only that the offenders should be cut off from the church; but that he had power to direct. This is something which he "would" could be done. The Greek verb is apokopsontai, from kopto, "to strike, smite, cut." Apokopto, "to cut off, to hew off." It is manifest that the words "I would, that they were even cut off," had a deeper significance than mere expulsion from the church, coming as they did, from one who had been accustomed to persecute even unto death, those holding a different religious faith from his own.

This disposition of Paul must have been well understood by the author of the story related in Acts 13. 8–11, where the apostle is represented as punishing with blindness that "child of the devil," Elymas, who withstood Paul, seeking to turn away the deputy from the faith.

The inquisition, which did its bloody work for so many hundred years, like every thing else, had a cause. It found at least some excuse in the fierce denunciations of heretics by Paul, and in the reported killing of Ananias and Sapphira at the word of Peter. As late as the middle of the present century, an approved Catholic historian commented upon this transaction in the following terms:

"The sudden death with which they [Ananias and Sapphira] were smitten at the feet of the prince of the apostles, demonstrated to the faithful, that they could not with impunity deceive the ministers of the Lord."—(Darras, Hist. Cath. Ch. vol. 1, p. 31.)

The History of the Church by Darras, was indorsed by Pope Pius IX, August 8, 1855.

The inquisition found still further support in a document in general circulation in the early ages of the church, and then considered of high authority. It was called the Epistle of Clement to James; and a translation of it may be found in the 17th volume of the Ante-Nicene Christian Library.

In this epistle Clement describes his ordination. He says when Peter was about to die, the brethren being assembled, (at Rome), he laid his hands on Clement, as the Bishop, and communicated to him the power of binding and loosing, etc., and as to him who should grieve the President of the truth, after declaring that such a one sins against Christ, and offends the Father of all, Peter proceeded as follows:

"Wherefore, he shall not live; and therefore it becomes him who presides, to hold the place of a physician; and not to cherish the rage of an irrational beast."

When, afterward, the Church, having grown strong and dominant, found itself possessed of civil power, or safe from interference, what more natural than that it should undertake to rid itself of those making trouble in the church by employing the means for which it found such sanction?

The Spanish inquisition of the 15th century was the successor of the Dominican inquisition of the 13th century. This in its turn was the legitimate outgrowth of the papal and episcopal persecutions of the preceding ages, which had been continued, with but little interruption from the edict of Constantine in 316, against the Donatists, and that of Theodosius, in 382, against the Manichæans, who were punished with confiscation and death. Thus has persecution been a handmaid of the Church for fourteen hundred years, commencing at a period but little removed from the time of the apostles. No other religion, in the history of the world, has been attended with so much persecution.

Nor has it been confined to the Roman Catholic Church. Nearly every sect of the Christian religion has sought to defend and strengthen itself by persecution, whenever it has found itself armed with the sword of civil authority. The bloody persecutions of the Catholics by Protestants in Great Britain and elsewhere, are well known to every student of history. Equally well known are the persecutions of the Baptists, Quakers and others in this country.

Among the laws of Connecticut of 1650, are the following:

"If any man or woman be a Witch, that is, hath or consulteth with, a familiar spiritt, they shall be put to death."—(Exodus 22. 18, Levit. 20. 27. Deut. 18. 10, 11.)

"If any man after legal conviction, shall have or worship any other God than the Lord God, hee shall bee put, to death."—(Deut. 13. 6—17. 2, Ex. 22. 20.)

Among the laws of Massachusetts (General Laws of Plymouth, published in 1658), is one reciting that "of late time the Quakers have bine furnished with horses, and therby they have not onely the more speedy passage from place to place, to the poisoning of the inhabitants with theire cursed tenetts, but alsoe therby have escaped the hands of the officers that might otherwise have apprehended them;" it was therefore enacted that the horses furnished them or which were brought into the country by them should be forfeited to the Government. —(Brigham's Compact etc. of New Plymouth, Boston, 1836, p. 127.)

If any person should permit a meeting of Quakers in nis house, he was to be publicly whipped, or pay £5.—(Ibid. p. 131.)

The ministry were supported by taxation.—(Ibid. p. 186.)

The following may be taken as a specimen of the laws enacted under a religious rule:

If any man had a stubborn or rebellious son 16 years or more of age, he or the mother could bring him before the magistrates, and "such a son shall be put to death."—(Deut. 21. 20, 21.) See Conn. Blue Laws of 1650.

Here was a cruel and inhuman enactment of a distant land, thousands of years old, brought to this country and put into the form of law, because it was found within the lids of a religious book. Could any thing more vividly illustrate the danger of religious legislation? And having once accomplished the divorce of Church and State, shall we now take the back track, with such beacon warnings before us?

In the "Establishment of Civil Government by the free planters of the Colony of New Haven," June 4, 1639, it was enacted,

"That Church Members only shall be free Burgesses, and they only shall chuse magistrates," etc.—(Conn. Code of 1650, p. 18.)

What guaranty have we that this law of suffrage will not be re-enacted, if the Church gets control of the State?

That we have no such guaranty is manifest. Listen to an exponent of the national reform religion, writing in the Christian Statesman of November 1, 1883:

"What effect would the adoption of the Christian Amendment, together with the proposed changes in the Constitution, have upon those who deny that God is the Sovereign, Christ the Ruler, and the Bible the law? This brings up the conscience question at once. * * The classes who would object are, as 'Truth Seeker' has said, Jews, infidels, atheists and others. These classes are perfectly satisfied with the Constitution as it is. How would they stand toward it, if it recognized the authority of our Lord Jesus Christ? To be perfectly plain, I believe that the existence of a Christian Constitution would disfranchise every logically consistent infidel."

In the Statesman of February 21, 1884, Mr. J. C. K. Milligan, writing upon the same subject said: "The worst result will be to disfranchise them."

Those who are endeavoring to establish a National religion, do not admit that they are working for a union of Church and State, but at the same time they advocate the supremacy of the Church over the State. They avow their purpose to bring the whole land under the control of a religion the principles of which would have to be authoritatively determined.

President Seelye, of Amherst College, in an article published in the "Forum," for July, 1886, entitled, "Should the State teach Religion?" (a question which he answers in the affirmative), after stating that religious instruction of a people is indispensable, and that the family would not and could not provide it, also that "the Church is confessedly not doing this work, and unless you give it the ubiquity and power of the State, the Church neither will nor can do it," said:

"The State should provide for instruction in the Gospels for its own preservation; if the conscience of its subjects approve, well; if not. the State will be cautious, but courageous also, and if it is wise, it will not falter."

The word "subjects" was well chosen by President Seelye to designate the citizens of a free country, whom he proposes to bring under his religio-political despotism.

In a speech in Kansas City, Sam Small, a prominent worker in this movement, said:

"I want to see the day come when the Church shall be the arbiter of all legislation, State, National and municipal; when the great churches of the country can come together harmoniously and issue their edict, and the legislative powers will respect it and enact it into laws."

In March, 1884, Rev. J. W. Foster, in the columns of the Christian Statesman, said:

"According to the Scriptures, the State and its sphere exist for the sake of and to serve the interests of the Church. * * The expenses of the Church in carrying on her public aggressive work, it meets in whole or in part out of the public treasury."

What is this in fact but a union of Church and State, except that the Church instead of the State is to be in the ascendency? The change of conditions would be far from being an improvement.

The editor of the Statesman does not advocate union of Church and State; but says:

"It is the duty of the State, as such, to enter into alliance with the Church of Christ, and to profess, adhere to, defend and maintain the true religion."

The spirit of the inquisition is not yet extinct, nor are its methods entirely foreign to the purposes of many of those engaged in this religious crusade against the Constitution. Their hearts are filled with bitterness and hatred toward those who differ with them in opinion in religious matters. They would fain strike them to the earth as Peter was supposed to have struck Ananias and Sapphira.

Rev. E. B. Graham, one of the Vice Presidents of the National Reform Association, an organization whose special object is to secure an amendment to the Constitution, making Christianity the national religion, said in an address delivered at York, Nebraska, reported in the Christian Statesman of May 21, 1885:

"If the opponents of the bible do not like our government and its Christian features, let them go to some wild, desolate land; and in the name of the devil, and for the sake of the devil, subdue it, and set up a government of their own on infidel and atheistic ideas; and then if they can stand it, stay there till they die."

At Lake Side, Ohio, in August, 1887, Dr. McAllister said:

"Those who oppose this work now will discover, when the religious amendment is made to the Constitution, that if they do not see fit to fall in with the majority, they must abide the consequences, or seek some more congenial clime."

In a speech in a Convention of the same National Reform Association, held in New York, in February, 1873, Rev. Jonathan Edwards, D. D., said:

"We want State and religion—and we are going to have it. It shall be that so far as the affairs of State require religion, it shall be revealed religion, the religion of Jesus Christ. * * * The atheist is a dangerous man. * * Tolerate atheism, Sir! There is nothing out of hell I would not tolerate as soon. * * Atheism and Christianity are contradictory terms. They are incompatible systems. They cannot dwell together on the same continent."

The spirit here exhibited is the same as that which left its footprints in the "Blue Laws" of several of the American Colonies. It is inherited from the inquisition, and turns for its justification or excuse to the teachings of those who founded the Christian religion.

Those animated by this spirit, can even coolly contemplate the contingency of a war, to be prosecuted for the establishment of the Christian Religion. Said Rev. M. A. Gault, in the Statesman of April 1, 1886, "It cost us all our civil war to blot slavery out of our Constitution, and it may cost us another war to blot out its infidelity."

In reference to this phase of the subject, a timely warning was given by Mr. Abbott, editor of the Index, in a protest against the movement, which he was permitted to present at the National Convention of the National Reform Association, held in Cincinnati in 1872: He said:

"I make no threat whatever, but I state a truth fixed as the hills when I say, that before you can carry this measure and trample on the freedom of the people, you will have to wade through seas of blood. Every man who favors it votes to precipitate the most frightful war of modern times."

To accomplish their purpose, the fanatics who are engaged in this enterprise, are willing to unite with those whom they and their ancestors have been abusing for centuries—the Roman Catholics.

"Whenever" said the Christian Statesman of Dec. 11, 1884, "they [the Roman Catholics] are willing to co-operate in resisting the political progress of atheism, we will gladly join hands with them."

In the Statesman of August 31, 1881, Rev. Sylvester F. Scovel said:

"We may be subjected to some rebuffs in our first proffers, and the time has not yet come when the Roman Church will consent to strike hands with other churches as such; but the time has come to make repeated advances, and gladly to accept co-operation in any form in which they may be willing to exhibit it. It is one of the necessities of the situation."

Said Dr. A. A. Hodge, of Princeton, in an article in the Princeton Review, for January, 1887:

"All we have to do is for Catholics and Protestants—disciples of a common master—to come to a common understanding with respect to a common basis of what is received as general Christianity; a practical quantity of truth belonging equally to both sides, to be recognized in general legislation, and especially in the literature and teaching of our public schools."

Said the Christian Union, of the 26th of January, 1888:

"It is quite possible that the time may come when the real issue will be between the theist and the atheist. * * Whenever that time comes, the Protestant and the Catholic will stand side by side in a common defense of those common beliefs which have been their mutual possession these many centuries."

At the Saratoga National Reform meeting, August 15-17,

1887, a motion was adopted requesting the.National Reform Association to undertake to secure a basis of agreement with the Roman Catholic authorities. And these newly made friends are already working together in Washington, to forward the religious legislation there pending.

Now who are the atheists, who, by this grand religio-political combination of orthodox Protestants and Roman Catholics, are to be driven from the country?

Cousin, the eclectic philosopher, maintains, with a good deal of force, that properly speaking, there cannot be, in the last analysis, any such thing as atheism. He says:

"It is sufficient for you to have the idea of the imperfect and the finite in order to have the idea of the infinite and the perfect, that is of God; though you may not thus name him; though you may be able to express in words the spontaneous convictions of your intelligence, or for want of language and analysis, they may remain obscure and indistinct in the depths of your soul."—(Hist. Mod. Philosophy, vol. 2, p. 420.)

This simple and beautiful explanation of Cousin, who, imbued with the spirit of charity, would deny the possibility of atheism, is not acceptable to the religionists of the day. They must have atheists, and they must have the privilege of defining an atheist. An atheist is one whose idea of the Infinite is different from theirs. Or, an atheist is one who does not believe in a personal God. Or, an atheist is one who does not accept "Our Christ." Whatever may be the definition finally agreed upon—and it would have to be settled eventually by a Supreme Court chosen in the interests of the national religion—an atheist, thus defined, is to be placed outside the Constitution; is to be no longer entitled to the benefit of its provisions. He is to be disfranchised and outlawed, and driven from the country. Even those who did the most in founding our government, would not, if living, be permitted to participate in its blessings.

It is time the people arouse to a sense of the danger which is menaced to their free institutions, and realize the attempt which is being made against their liberties.

Some of the religious journals oppose the movement; among others, the ably conducted *American Sentinel*, published at Oakland, California. The only considerable national organization which is effectually making opposition; is the American Secular Union.

It is a question that interests the so-called atheists not only —it interests all classes. For no sooner will the Constitution be placed under the control of the Christian religion by the combined forces of Protestants and Catholics—and it can be done in no other way—than the question will immediately arise, which of the allied armies best represents the Christian religion? The Catholics have the older title, having themselves made the bible, and it may turn out that they will vindicate their right to control the Constitution. In that case those who originated the movement may find themselves called upon to drink of the cup which they had prepared for the atheists.

If, on the other hand, the Protestants should prevail, the next question will be, which branch of them, or which denomination, or sect, or combination of sects, is best entitled to speak for the Christian religion, and therefore best entitled to say what shall be taught in the public schools under the amended Constitution?

It is no answer to say that the Blair Amendment provides that no public money shall be expended for instruction or training in the doctrines of any religious sect, and that such peculiar doctrines shall not be taught. The fact would still remain, that one sect or combination of sects might say what should be taught, and with such power in their hands, this provision of the Amendment would be of but little practical value.

Nor does it essentially detract from the dangerous character of the proposed Amendment, that the author has the inconsistency to declare, in the first Section, that "No State shall ever make or maintain any law respecting an establishment of religion, or prohibiting the free exercise thereof." This is a mere subterfuge. What more efficacious law respecting the establishment of a religion could its votaries desire, than an Act requiring the principles or doctrines of that religion to be taught at the public expense; thus compelling those who do not believe in such religion to pay for promulgating its doctrines to the youth of the country?

The ecclesiastical power has already lost its hold upon the reason and conscience of the masses. This attempt to get control of the Constitution, is a desperate effort to bring the aid of the civil power to the support of a "lost cause."

The attempt should meet with a prompt and merited rebuke. Let Church and State remain forever separate. Let us heed the maxims and warnings of the founders, the defenders, and the preservers of the Republic—of Madison and Hamilton, of Washington and Paine, of Jefferson, of Lincoln and of Grant. Let not a spirit of persecution worthy only of the middle ages, find sanction and encouragement under the stars and stripes, which have been dedicated to liberty. Let the Constitution remain what our fathers intended it to be, the common heritage of a great, a generous and a free people.

Charles B. Waite.

THE DEATH OF YOUNG HARRY VANE.

Among the perfidious acts which characterized the restoration to power of Charles II., was the arrest and imprisonment of young Harry Vane, and his final trial, condemnation and execution.

No man of his time had had a more varied experience, or had given more thought to the great problems of government which were then presented to the age, than Vane. He had in his youth received a most careful training from his father, who occupied a most exalted position in the State, and he had spent some years in America, where he had been elected the chief executive of Massachusetts Bay. He was a leader in the Long Parliament and up to the time when Pride's Purge took place, had generally coincided with the opinions of Cromwell, although he hesitated to give him absolute power, or follow implicitly in his wake. Had he co-operated cordially with Cromwell, whom we regard not only the most far seeing statesmen of his age, but possessed of matchless courage, and could he have laid aside for a single hour his mystic views of religion, which seemed to confuse and cloud his judgment in the management of the State, we believe that Cromwell would have been able to establish not only a constitutional but a representative government for all time, instead of giving over the management of affairs to the perfidious House of the Stuarts, who not only disregarded all forms of popular government, but debauched public morals and ruined the Commonwealth. But however this may be, when Cromwell died, and confusion and weakness and indecision manifested themselves, Monk led back Charles II., and Vane retired to private life.

After Charles had wreaked vengeance on the regicides, it was suggested that Vane had not been arraigned for the part that he took, although he did not sit in judgment on the martyr King, and that he deserved to be punished. The advisors of Charles II. called to mind what Vane said during the closing hours of Richard Cromwell's reign, in regard to the Stuarts; and Charles became exasperated. Said Vane: "Among all the people of the universe, I know of none who have shown so much zeal for the liberty of their country as the English, at this time have done; they have by the help of divine providence, overcome all obstacles, and have made themselves free. We have driven away the hereditary tyranny of the house of Stuart at the expense of much blood and treasure, in hopes of enjoying *hereditary liberty*, after having shaken off the yoke of kingship; and there is not a man among us who could have imagined that any person would be so bold as to dare to attempt the ravishing from us of that freedom, which cost so much blood and so much labor. But it so happens, I know not by what misfortune, we are fallen into the error of those who poisoned the Emperor Titus, to make room for Domitian; who made away with Augustus that they might have Tiberius and changed Claudius for Nero."

These sentiments were too much for Charles Stuart, and it was resolved that he should die.

He was accordingly on this bare suggestion arrested and thrown into the tower, the common receptacle for all state prisoners. After remaining there for some time, he was transferred to one of the fortresses that occupy a conspicuous position on Scilly Island, off from the extreme point of Lands End. Here, after the lapse of some two years, he was brought to trial in the Kings Bench, at Westminster Hall, on the 2d of June, 1662. His indictment charged him with much verbosity and circumlocution, of being a "false traitor" "and of traitorously imagining the death of Charles II., and of *keeping him out* of the kingdom, and of trying to overturn the ancient government of England."

The indictment was in Latin, but Vane was not permitted to either read it or to hear it read in that language, which he thoroughly understood; but it was declared that the averments in the same were broad enough to permit any species of evidence which bore upon the subject, whether manifested by acts or deeds or not. The judges who presided were the willing tools of the King, and they hesitated at nothing. They neither regarded the laws of God nor man. Vane's case was not a solitary one, for in that "frightful record" of the State trials, there are many instances where all that was necessary to convict was to indict. But not in that age had one stood at the bar who possessed such transcendent abilities, or who could, single-handed and alone, without the aid of counsel or without a witness, cope with court and counsel in such a manner as he could and did. The court was organized to convict, and he was prosecuted not only by the court but by the attorney general, the solicitor general and four other lawyers, among whom were Glyn and Maynard, who had taken part against Strafford when he fought for his life.

In answer to the indictment, he urged that as the offences charged in it were committed by him as a member of Parliament, or as acting in obedience to it, no inferior court, according to long established usage, was qualified to sit in judgment upon him, and that the only tribunal that he was amenable to was Parliament itself. He therefore objected to pleading either guilty or not guilty, as that would be recognizing the jurisdiction of the tribunal. "It may be better," he said, "to be immediately destroyed by special command, without any form of law. It is very visible beforehand, that all possible means of defense are taken and withheld. Far be it from me to have knowingly, maliciously or wittingly offended the law, rightly understood and asserted; much less to have done anything that is morally evil." He protested against the arbitrary action of the court which he more than intimated had already prejudged his case, and refused for some time to plead to the indictment in any shape. He did however at length plead "not guilty" and was then returned to the tower. His trial commenced four days later.

He claimed the right to be represented by counsel, but it was denied him, the judges saying in bitter irony that "they would be his counsel." The attorney general, Sir Geoffrey Palmer, began by specifying the overt acts upon which the indictment was based. Almost every one of these acts related to his course and conduct while a member of Parliament, and Vane suggested that if they were to take his life for these things they might as well slay the whole Parliament at once, and be done with it. The journals of Parliament were produced to show what he had said and done, and every thing was claimed to be evidence against him, while nothing was allowed in his favor.

Vane demanded delay that he might summon witnesses on his part and prepare for his defense, but this was denied him and he was hurried onward to his doom. Vane's defense has been handed down by himself. It was written out immediately after his condemnation and is overwhelming in argument and in vindication of his course. He fought for his life for ten hours, without refreshment, but it was of no avail. The jury were packed against him. He was found guilty and sentenced to death.

He claimed the right to take exceptions to the rulings of the court but this was denied him, and when called up for sentence, he staggered the judges by tendering to them a bill of exceptions, and cited the statute of Edward I., which the judges confessed they had overlooked, by which it was among other things provided: "That if any man find himself aggrieved by the proceedings against him before any justices, let him write his exceptions, and desire justices to set their seals to it;" but the infamous wretches denied him the right. Vane caused each judge to put himself individually upon record as denying him this right, which caused them much embarrassment and confusion.

At last he reminded the court that before they could pass judgment upon him he desired them to determine

1. Whether a Parliament were accountable to any inferior court?

2. Whether the King being out of possession—Here the

court broke in impatiently, "that the King was never out of possession."—Whereupon Vane instantly rejoined that if that was the case, the indictment must inevitably fall to the ground, for the charge against him was that "he endeavored to *keep out* his majesty, and how could he keep him out if he were not out?" He felt however that all was useless and at length accepted his fate.

The reporter of "The State Trials," in referring to this incident, says, that "when he saw they would overrule him in all, and were bent upon his condemnation, he put up his papers appealing to the righteous judgment of God, who would judge them as well as him."

The execution was appointed to take place the 14th of June. The sentence was that he should be hanged, cut down while living, his body cut open and his bowels burnt before his face; that his head should be severed from his body and his body then quartered. It was finally agreed "out of mercy" that he should undergo the milder and less barbarous punishment of being beheaded, but this was granted simply as a favor.

The bill of exceptions that he prepared has been carefully preserved, and would be at the present day considered a most interesting relic.

While awaiting his doom he wrote out in prison his "Reasons for an Arrest of judgment, writ by the Prisoner but refused to be heard by the Court;" in which he arraigns his persecutors in the most vigorous manner. He shows that every principle of law and justice was violated in his case, and it will remain for all time a monument to his intrepidity and a lasting disgrace to those who so cruelly treated him.

Among his memoranda is an abridged account or substance of what he said when defending himself at his trial, in which he says: "The causes that did happen to move his late Majesty to depart from his Parliament and continue for many years, not only at a distance and in disjunction from them, but at last in a declared posture of enmity and war against them, are so well known and fully stated in print, not to say written in characters of blood on both parts, that I shall only mention it and refer to it. This matter was not done in a corner. The appeals were solemn, and the decision by the sword, was given by that God who, being the judge of the whole world, does right and cannot do otherwise. By occasion of these unhappy differences, most great and unusual changes, like an irresistible torrent did break in upon us, not only to the disjointing that parliamentary assembly among themselves, but to the creating such formed divisions among the people, and to producing such a general state of disorder, that hardly any were able to know their duty and with certainty to discern who were to command and who to obey. All things seemed to be reduced, and in a manner resolved into their first elements and principles."

This gives a very clear presentation of the condition of things at the time when Charles I. was called to account for his misdeeds. Vane shows distinctly that he never acted as one of the Judges of the High Court of Justice, and even disapproved many of the measures resorted to both before and after that time. He shows, further, that when he had voluntarily retired to private life, he was willfully and wickedly drawn forth from that retreat and put on trial for no crime whatever, either in thought or deed. His untimely end was indeed the work of fiends. Charles II. had not wit enough to discern or comprehend it.

On the 13th of June, he took leave of his children, but the parting scene is too painful to be narrated. On the 14th of June, 1662, in the full glory of ripened manhood, Vane was brought forth to die, on Tower Hill.

Of his associates who had striven with him for the rights of the people, many had passed peacefully from earth in the due course of nature, and many had suffered terrible deaths, as cruelly and unjustly as he was about to suffer, while others had bowed themselves ignobly before the monster that now occupied the throne, and had been left with life. Fairfax had thus bowed and retired to private life, and Lambert, who had been tried with him (Vane), had submitted and was then cultivating flowers and working embroidery. The heads of Cromwell, Ireton, and Bradshawe grinned from the gables of Westminster Hall. Pym and Hampden had died in the morning

of the strife, and Blake had fallen somewhat later, but all of
their bodies had been flung into dishonored graves.   Harrison
and Scot, and many others had been torn limb from limb.
The immortal Milton, now old and blind, had been long in
hiding, but was kept informed of all passing events, while Algernon Sidney was reserved for a later day, but for a like fate
with himself.

Of those who are known as the regicides, four and twenty
had died natural deaths.   Ten had been hanged, drawn and
quartered.   The prison walls had closed around twenty five
more, some of whom were never to leave it alive—while twenty, who had made their escape to foreign lands, were followed
by hue and cry.   Some fell by the dagger of the assassin,
and three, Goff, Whalley and Dixwell, had fled to the wilds of
America.   They roved the woods with the savage denizens of
the forests, and slept in caves and amid the rocks, watched
over, however by a kind Providence, and ministered to by
sympathizing friends.

Downes, Garland, Harvey, Hevingham, Millington, Potter,
Challoner, Harrington, Phelps, Smyth, James Temple, Peter
Temple, Tichbourne, Wayte, Sir Hardress Waller, and Mayne
and Haselrig all died in the Tower.   Silburne perished in
Jersey, and Henry Morten at Chepstow Castle, whither they
had respectively been transferred, while Fleetwood and Helvlet
were ultimately released, and died in America; at least Fleetwood did.   Lambert died in Guernsey.   Hutchinson perished
after years of imprisonment in Deal Castle.   They died in exile,
in prison, by the hand of the assassin, on the battle field and
on the scaffold.   Their generation was not worthy of them; but
no cause has ever been maintained by more steadfast striving,
or possessed a nobler line of martyrs.

According to the custom of the times, Vane was expected to
address the multitude who had assembled to see him die, but
the King had notified him in advance that he would "not be
permitted to say anything reflecting upon his majesty or the
government."   His response to the message was made on the
scaffold, where at the very opening of his address he said: "I
shall do nothing but what becomes a good Christian and an

Englishman;" but he insisted that he had not had a fair and impartial trial, and then added: "When I was before them (the judges), I could not have the liberty and privilege of an Englishman, the grounds, reasons and causes of the actings I was charged with duly considered. I therefore desired the judges that they would set their seals to my bill of exceptions; I pressed hard for it again and again, as the right of myself and every free born Englishman by the law of the land, but was finally denied it"—Here Sir John Robinson, the lieutenant of the tower, interrupted him, told him it was a lie and commanded him to stop. Vane reiterated his statement, but Robinson commanded the trumpets to sound and a tumult was raised, so that he could not be heard. When silence was at length partially restored, he said: "God will judge between me and you in this matter." He then undertook to go on, and after referring with some pathos to the rectitude of his life, lifted up his eyes to Heaven and spread out his hands and said: "I do here appeal to the Great God of Heaven and all this assembly, or any other persons to show wherein I have defiled my hands with any man's blood or estate, or that I have sought myself in any public capacity or place I have been in." The effect upon the multitude was electric. His attitude was so dramatic that the sheriff and lieutenant of the tower became somewhat alarmed, and snatched a paper which he held in his hands, away from him. They commanded all those who were taking notes of his speech to deliver the same up, and when they remonstrated with the wretches, Vane said; "My usage from man is no harder than was my Lord and Master's;" but the noise and trumpets broke in again, and he was not permitted to finish what he had to say. Having anticipated this, he had carefully made a memoranda of his address and given it to a friend before he reached the place of execution, and it has come down to us in that shape. Having thus been roughly and brutally interfered with, he was then compelled to lay his head upon the block, and it was severed at a blow. The cry of anguish which went up was never forgotten, and resounded throughout the world.

He died a martyr for the cause of representative government

—a "government of the people, by the people and for the people."

We visited the spot but a few weeks ago, where this fore-runner of American liberty laid down his life. There rise, as they have risen for almost a thousand years, the cold gray walls of the tower, with the clouds lowering dark and threatning above them—and there, shrouded in gloom are the grated windows that look forth on the narrow space 'which so many have trod never more to return—and there is the spot where the forlorn mother stood whom Shakspeare has immortalized in that touching apostrophe to her babes that were about to be smothered:

> "Pity, you ancient stones, those tender babes,
>   Whom envy hath immured within your walls;
> Rude cradle for such little pretty ones.
> Rough rugged nurse, old sullen playfellow
> For tender princes, use my babes well."

No one with the least sensibility can visit Tower Hill and study its surroundings, without being overwhelmed with sadness as he thinks of the bloody deeds that have here taken place. Harry Vane had in his youth, as we have shown, spent several years in America, and had become thoroughly imbued with the spirit of freedom. We look upon him as almost one of us. "His name is the most appropriate link to bind us to the land of our fathers. It presents, more, perhaps, than any that could be mentioned in one character, those features and traits by which it is our pride to prove our lineage and descent from the British Isles."

Elliott Anthony.

DISTRICT COURTS IN ILLINOIS.

During the last few years, through the public press, and in other ways, the attention of the public has been often called to the admitted evils prevalent in justice of the peace courts in Chicago. Frequent, and often well founded complaints are made both of the justices and of the constables.

The causes of the evils complained of, may be perhaps briefly summarized as follows:

1st:—The fee system under which both justices and constables are paid fees, and not salaries, for their services.

2nd:—The low grade of many justices and constables, both as regards ability and character.

3rd:—The system under which justices are appointed, and constables elected.

4th:—The extension of the jurisdiction of country justices over the City of Chicago, which leads to suits being brought against citizens of Chicago in remote and inaccessible portions of Cook County.

How best to remedy these evils is an open question, and one beset with many difficulties.

It has been proposed by some, to enact a law under the present constitution, by which justices in municipal corporations of a stated population, can be paid by salaries instead of by fees.

This plan is beset by constitutional difficulties, and at best is but a partial remedy.

Sections 21 and 29, Article 6, of the Constitution of 1870, of the State of Illinois, require the organization, jurisdiction, powers, proceedings and practice, of all courts of the same class or grade to be uniform.

The 22d Section of Article 4 of the Constitution provides that the general assembly shall not pass local or special laws in reference to a large number of subjects, amongst which are these: "Regulating the practice in courts of justice," and "Regulating the jurisdiction and duties of justices of the peace, police magistrates, and constables;" the closing clause of the section reading as follows:

"In all other cases where a general law can be made applicable, no special law shall be enacted."

These provisions make it difficult to frame laws under the existing Constitution which will remedy the evils complained of.

Hon. H. B. Hurd, when engaged some years since upon the revision of the statutes of the State, drew a proposed act, by which it was in substance provided, that all justices of the peace in Chicago should be paid by fixed salaries, leaving the present fee system in full force, so far as regards other portions of the State.

Able constitutional lawyers, among them, the Hon. Milton Hay of Springfield, and the Hon. Clark Upton of Waukegan, now Circuit Court Judge of Lake County, feared that any such measure would violate the provisions of the Constitution above cited, and Mr. Hurd was reluctantly compelled to abandon his proposed change in the law.

It requires no argument to show that changes deemed necessary in Chicago would neither be desirable nor practicable outside of large municipal corporations. Justices of the peace in county districts, where the litigation brought before them is but slight, and of little importance, should be paid by fees and not by salaries. It is far otherwise in cities of such a population as Chicago.

It is a foregone conclusion that no system of paying justices throughout the State by salaries would meet with favorable consideration in the Legislature.

All admit that the fee system is pernicious in the extreme. As long as a justice is paid by fees, he is constantly tempted to decide in favor of a plaintiff, who brings suits before him, in order to gain continued patronage, thereby increasing his business and compensation.

Much useless and needless litigation is fomented by both justices and constables, the constables often acting as purveyors to the justices. This will continue to be more or less the case while the the fee system continues, for justices and constables are but human.

It is truthfully said that a justice court is the "poor man's court." Many suitors therein are too poor to retain counsel, and when this is otherwise, the small amounts involved in the majority of cases, prevent generally the employment of counsel of a high grade of ability and character, and render it impossible for lawyers as a rule to spend much time in preparing cases or trial.

Yet the limited jurisdiction of a justice of the peace, is no bar to questions being raised before him as difficult as any coming before courts of record.

The absence of the aid afforded by counsel to both judge and litigants, renders it all the more important that the State should furnish judicial ability and character in police and justice courts of as high an order as is practicable. The rich can care for themselves; the poor and friendless must be protected as far as possible from ignorance, wrong, and oppression.

It is a well recognized fact that the judges of Cook County find it difficult under the present method of appointment, to find suitable candidates to recommend to the governor for appointment as justices in the North and West Divisions of Chicago, owing to the unwillingness of good lawyers to accept such positions.

A large proportion of the population of a crowded city gains its only idea of the administration of justice, from impressions gathered at trials in police and justice of the peace courts. It is scarcely therefore to be wondered at, that anarchy and socialism flourish in Chicago.

That the present method of appointing justices of the peace in Cook County is a vast improvement over the old method of election, cannot with truth be denied, but the present method is far from being perfect or satisfactory. The recommendations to the Governor, of persons for appointment as justices by the judges, are often to say the least, unsatisfactory, and discreditable to the good sense and discretion of the judiciary of Cook County.

The present provision of the Constitution requiring the judges of Cook County to recommend persons to the Governor, for appointment, is wrong in governmental theory, and hurtful in its influence on the bench making such recommendations. It confers on the judiciary, power which properly belongs to the executive portion of the government.

Any attempt to combine judicial with executive or legislative functions must necessarily be disastrous in its effects. Such attempt exposes the judicial portion of the government to the corrupting and festering influences of political life, and makes politicians of judges.

The judiciary should never be exposed to influences of this character, and should be free even from the suspicion of undue influence. The people, for a slight benefit or a benefit which can be attained by other methods, cannot afford to lower the tone of its judiciary.

Once destroy in a people belief in the purity of its judges, and anarchy surely follows.

It is now generally admitted that the conferring of what is virtually political power upon the county courts of Illinois is a mistake, and a bill is pending in the Illinois Legislature, which if passed, will take away from these courts the existing supervisory and appointive power in elections.

It would be wise and no doubt extremely acceptable to the circuit court judges of Cook County, to take away from them the power to appoint South Park Commissioners. Judges should have no political patronage to bestow, and be thus relieved from the pressure and influence of political cabals and rings. It is an open secret that the often unsatisfactory recommendations of the judges of Cook County to the Governor, of persons for appointment as justices, is frequently owing to the pressure of such influences.

To any one at all conversant with Chicago politics, it is well known that under the elective system, few if any fit persons can be chosen as constables,. With the numerous justice and constable offices scattered throughout the County, it seems well nigh impossible to regulate them, and properly and promptly punish malfeasance in office.

The case of the People v. Meech, 101, Ill. p. 200, would seem to make it impossible, without an amendment to the Constitution, to abate the crying evil of compelling citizens of Chicago to attend suits before justices of the peace in remote and inaccessible portions of Cook County, instituted mainly not to attain justice, but for the purposes of blackmail and oppression.

It was held in said case, that "the act of 1881, to amend certain sections of the act relating to the election of justices of the peace, creating each county in the State, except Cook County, a district, and making two districts of Cook County, and limiting the jurisdiction of such officers within such districts, is in contravention of that part of the Constitution which requires that the jurisdiction of the justices of the peace shall be uniform, and also that part which prohibits the passage of any local or special laws regulating the jurisdiction of justices of the peace, such amendment operating to change the pre-existing law on the subject only in Cook County."

A grievous disease requires a severe remedy.

An amendment to the Constitution would seem imperative, not only as regards constables but justices. The Chicago Bar Association has formulated and sent to Springfield, a proposed amendment to the Constitution of the State reading as follows:

"RESOLVED by the House of Representatives, the Senate concurring therein:. That there shall be submitted to the voters of this State at the next election for members of the General Assembly, a proposition to so amend section twenty-eight of Article six of the Constitution that the same shall read as follows:

"Instead of justices of the peace and police magistrates in cities, villages and incorporated towns containing fifty thousand or more inhabitants, there shall be established a convenient number of district courts. Such courts and the judges thereof shall have the same jurisdiction and powers as justices of the peace, and such further jurisdiction and powers as may be prescribed by the General Assembly. The judges and the clerks of such courts shall be appointed or elected in such manner and for such term as shall be provided by the General Assembly. All fees shall be accounted for by the respective clerks receiving the same, and paid into their respective city or village treasuries monthly.

"The salaries of the judges, clerks and deputy clerks shall be fixed by the General Assembly, and paid out of the respective city, village or town treasuries. No salary shall be increased or diminished during the term of office of the officer to whom it is payable. Instead of constables, there shall be a high constable of such city, village or incorporated town, who shall have the right to appoint deputies. Such high constable shall be appointed or elected, as shall be provided by the General Assembly. He and his deputies shall have the same powers and perform the same duties as constables, with such further powers and duties as shall be prescribed by such General Assembly. No summons, attachment, replevin, or other first process, except in criminal cases, issued by any justice of the peace, or police magistrate, shall run within the jurisdiction of any such district court.

"Until such courts are organized, the justices of the peace, police magistrates and constables heretofore provided for, shall be continued the same as if this article had not been amended."

The committee of the Bar Association in reporting to that body a resolution identical wi+h the one sent to Springfield, except as to the provision above cited, allowing justices to be elected, said, "the following features are included in the proposed amendment:

"1. The abolition of the fee system in the compensation of justices and the substitution of salaries.

"2. The abolition of constables paid by fees, the direct fomenters of much needless litigation, and a source of much wrong and oppression, and the substitution of a high constable with power to appoint deputies. A high constable can be placed under bonds and held liable for the misconduct of his deputies.

"3. The appointment of a chief clerk, who can also be held responsible for the misconduct of his deputies by being required to give bonds.

"4. The appointment of judges by the Governor with the advice and consent of the Senate. This method of appointment is precisely the same as that by which the justices of the Supreme Court of the United States, the judges of the circuit and district courts of the United States, and the judges of the Supreme Courts of many of the United States, having a judiciary of a very high order of talent, are appointed.

"5. The extension of this system of district courts to all cities, towns, and villages, of fifty thousand inhabitants and upwards, enabling other municipal corporations in Cook County and elsewhere, to rid themselves of the well recognized evils of justice courts in large municipal corporations.

"6. The abolition of the service of summons and other first process of justice courts, within the confines of any municipal corporation for which district courts are created. This will eliminate the evil of bringing suits before country justices in remote portions of Cook County, against residents of Chicago.

"District courts in New York, Massachusetts, New Jersey, and perhaps other States, have for years been in successful operation."

This resolution, at the request of the Association, has been introduced in the General Assembly by Mr. Whitehead, a member of the lower house, who is also a member of the Chicago Bar Association.

The committee's provision in regard to the appointment of the justices, was as follows:

"The judges shall be appointed by the Governor with the advice and consent of the Senate, and shall hold their offices for four years and until their successors are appointed and qualified."

Personally, the writer prefers the provision just cited, recommended by the committee (of which he was a member), as he believes that all judges should be appointed either for life, or for a long term of years, and never elected. The change made by the Bar Association leaves the question of appointment, or election, open.

Whether it will seem best to the members of the Legislature to submit this proposed amendment to the people for adoption, time alone can tell. Continued agitation generally seems necessary to effect reforms. The presentation of such a measure must necessarily again direct attention to the grievous evils, which it is sought thereby to remove. That eventually something will be done to remedy the evils complained of, there can be little, if any, doubt. If effective measures are taken, it matters little by whom proposed, or what shape they take. It has been suggested by one of the judges of the Circuit Court of Cook County, that this proposed amendment should be so framed as to render it optional with a municipal corporation of fifty thousand inhabitants or more, as to whether district courts should be created within its boundaries. There can be no objection. it would seem, to incorporating such suggestion in any proposed amendment, and it would probably make the measure more popular and increase its chance of adoption.

If district courts should ever be created in Chicago, one court in each division of the City, three in all, with three or four judges in each court, would probably be sufficient to transact all necessary business. All the judges of any such court should be compelled to hold sessions in the same building, though it would probably be necessary for one court to be located in each division of the City. In this way the one or more dockets kept by each court would be accessible, and misconduct in either judges, clerks, or constables, would easily be detected. Much of the litigation would be dispensed with, which is now prevalent in justice courts. The efforts of the judges would be exerted to discourage litigation, instead of encouraging it. Petty neighborhood quarrels would cease to occupy the time of magistrates. The present abominable practice of holding persons to await the action of grand juries, upon trivial and insufficient reasons, would largely cease to exist.

Any amendment to the Constitution must necessarily largely leave to the Legislature the arrangement of details, as it is poor policy to hamper constitutional provisions with minutiæ.

It is believed that if district courts can be established in Chicago, and fair salaries paid, say from $2500 to $3500 per annum, a class of able, conscientious lawyers, of good social standing, can be induced to accept positions on the district court benches, as is the case in the Eastern States. In Massachusetts, some years ago, a judge of a district court was appointed to the Supreme bench, while still acting as district judge; and the district judges in the Eastern States are able lawyers. and refined, educated gentlemen.

A position on the district bench will be, as it should be, re garded, as the stepping stone to a position on the circuit bench. It is to be hoped that this, with other needed legislative reforms, now proposed in Illinois, will receive the warm approval and support of the legal profession. Lawyers as educated men, owe a duty to the community which cannot be evaded, to suggest and carry out by voice, pen and influence, necessary changes in the laws of the State. The profession cannot escape such responsibility, if it would command respect and influence. The selfish, money making spirit of the day, should not be suffered to contaminate and destroy the legal profession.

The profession of law is not a mere means of acquiring money. When such an idea prevails, the profession is doomed. New problems are now confronting us at every stage of our progress, and it is certain that unless lawyers direct and guide legislative work, others less fitted to do the work, will.

Charles E. Pope.

ELIJAH B. SHERMAN.

Mr. Sherman is of Anglo-Welsh ancestry, his father being Elias H. and his mother Clarissa Wilmarth Sherman, who were residents of Fairfield, Vermont. There he was born, June 18, 1832. He remained upon the ancestral farm, engaged in farm avocations during the summer months, and attending school and teaching during the winter, until about twenty-two years of age. In 1854, he removed to Brandon, Vermont, where he was for awhile employed as clerk in a drug store. During the following year, he entered the academy at Manchester, where he began a course of study preparatory to entering college. Upon leaving the academy, he entered Middlebury College, at Middlebury, Vermont, from which institution he graduated in 1860. From the first he took a high rank in college, and was selected as poet for the junior exhibition, as well as for the graduating exercises of his class. Since graduation, he has been several times invited to address the associated alumni of his college.

After graduation, Mr. Sherman spent a year in teaching at South Woodstock, Vermont, at the expiration of which time he took charge of the Brandon Seminary, where he continued until May, 1862. He then enlisted as a private in the 9th Vermont Infantry, and was soon after elected lieutenant of Company C. He served with his regiment until January, 1863, when he resigned, his regiment then being on duty at Camp Douglas, Chicago.

He immediately entered upon the study of law, and attended the full course of lectures, at the law department of the University of Chicago, graduating in 1864. He was admitted to the bar upon graduation, and at once engaged in the practice of his profession in this City. From that time he has been in continuous and successful practice.

He was for several years solicitor for the State Auditor, and in that capacity had charge of many important litigations. As such solicitor he instituted the proceedings for closing the affairs of the Republic Life Insurance Company, the Chicago Life Insurance Company, and the Protection Life Insurance Company. In all these cases important constitutional questions were involved, and Mr. Sherman's interpretation of the general insurance laws, under which the proceedings were commenced was sustained by the higher courts, and the cases have thus become precedents. He had also other important cases involving kindred questions, some of which have gone to the Supreme Court of the United States.

In 1876, he represented the fourth senatorial district in the Illinois Legislature, and was re-elected in 1878. In the Legislative Assembly he occupied a high position, and his name is identified with all the more important legislation of those years. He served as chairman of the committee on judicial department, and was chiefly instrumental in establishing the system of appellate courts in this State. He also served on various other committees.

In 1879, Mr. Sherman was appointed one of the masters in chancery of the United States Circuit Court for the Northern District of Illinois, by Judges Harlan, Drummond and Blodgett. The duties of this important office he has discharged to the complete satisfaction of the bench and bar. For several years, about this time, the writer was in the habit of meeting him in the Philosophical Society. Mr. Sherman frequently engaged in its discussions, and was always listened to with marked attention. He has ever been an active member of the various law associations of the City, and was in 1881-2 President of the State Bar Association. He has also been Vice President of the American Bar Association. He delivered the annual address before the State Bar Association in 1882. This address was published ·by the Association and was largely circulated. It attracted much attention, not only for its merit as a brilliant literary production, but because of its effective blows at existing faults in our jurisprudence, coupled with admirable suggestions for their reform.

He is prominent in Grand Army and masonic circles, and is a member of the Ill. Commandery of the Loyal Legion, and of the Union League Club. He has been for many years an active member of several literary societies, and is now President of "Saracen Club" which numbers among its members, many men and women of literary culture and scientific attainments.

In 1884, Mr. Sherman received the honorary degree of LL.D. from Middlebury College, in recognition of his literary ability, his eminence as a lawyer and jurist, and his valuable public services.

His address delivered on the death of Gen. Grant, is one of the most finished and eloquent of the many tributes to the memory of that distinguished citizen, statesman and soldier. He pronounced an eulogy upon ·Gen. Logan, in which eloquence and pathos are deftly mingled. He has delivered many public addresses, several of which have been to the Sons of Vermont, of which society he has been President, all of which have displayed ripe scholarship and high literary excellence.

In 1884, he was appointed chief supervisor of elections by Judge Drummond, a position which he has filled to the satisfaction of both political parties.

Since his appointment as master in chancery of the Federal Court, Mr. Sherman has been chiefly employed in the discharge of the duties pertaining to that important position, in which he has been called upon to hear and decide many difficult chancery causes. He has found the work of a jurist much more congenial and satisfactory than that of an advocate, and his admirable analyses of facts in complicated cases and his clear exegesis of the law has won him the esteem of the federal judges, and the admiration of those members of .the bar who have had occasion to bring to him their cases for examination.

In private and in social life, he is one of the most agreeable of gentlemen. He is an interesting conversationalist, is well read in current literature, and is a close and accurate thinker.

In 1866, he was married to Hattie G. Lovering, of Iowa Falls, Iowa, an intelligent and estimable woman.

WILLIAM C. GOUDY

Has attained a high and enviable position at the bar, and is well known outside of this City. He is a native of Indiana, and was born in 1824. He came to Illinois when but eight years of age. He graduated from Illinois College, at Jacksonville, in 1845. He read law in the office of Hon. Stephen T. Logan, at Springfield, and in 1848, commenced practice in Fulton County, Illinois. He soon made for himself an excellent reputation.

From 1852 to 1855, he was State's Attorney for the tenth judicial district, and from 1857 to 1861, was a member of the State Senate from the Counties of Fulton and McDonough. In 1863, he received a number of votes in the democratic caucus for United States Senator. In 1862, he was a candidate for the constitutional convention, and was a delegate to the national convention of 1868.

In the early years of his life, he was considered one of the prominent and promising leaders of the Illinois democracy, and was an adroit manager in political affairs. He has always been considered a prudent and thoughtful counselor in public affairs.

As State Senator he was distinguished for his watchful care of the interests of his constituents, and of the State at large, as well as for the prudence and skill with which he framed all measures committed to his charge, and conducted them to final issue.

In 1859, he moved to Chicago, where was formed soon after, the partnership of Goudy and Waite, C. B. Waite being his partner. He has since been connected with two or three other firms.

The firm now is Goudy, Green & Goudy, and consists of Wm.

C. and Wm. J. Goudy, and A. W. Green, 65 —161 Lasalle St.

Mr. Goudy is now general solicitor for the Chicago and North Western Railway Company.

Though not ostensibly an active politician, his influence is widely felt in the politics of the democratic party of the City and State, and even of the nation. He is very often consulted in the preliminary caucussing, and in the arrangement of the primaries and conventions of the party. The political arrangements are often made in accordance with his advice, and there is a devoted following of his friends who always endeavor to have them so arranged. He is thus naturally accredited with various ambitions of a political character, which may or may not have any foundation in fact.

Neither any notice of the democratic party nor any sketch of the representative members of the Chicago bar would be complete without the name of Mr. Goudy.

As a lawyer, he occupies a high place in the Supreme State and Federal Courts. In the Supreme Court of this State, he has for many years had a large practice. More than a quarter of a century ago, he had a high position before that tribunal, a position which he has ever since maintained.

LEONARD SWETT

Was born near the Village of Turner, Oxford County, in Maine, on what was and still is known as the Albine Richer farm. At the age of twelve years, having previously attended the schools of his neighborhood, he began the study of Latin and Greek with the Rev. Thomas R. Curtis. The boy had been, by his parents and their neighbors, already chosen for the ministry.

When fifteen years of age, he went to North Yarmouth Academy, where he remained two years. He then entered Waterville College (now known as Colby University), where he remained three years. He now read law two years with Howard and Shepley, of Portland, when he left to seek his fortune, and to take his chances in the battle of life.

He intended to settle in the south, but after traveling through the southern States for a time, he came west. This was in 1847. At that time we were in the midst of the war with Mexico, and young Swett enlisted as a private in the 5th Indiana Infantry, commanded by General James H. Lane, afterward United States Senator from Kansas. Though not commissioned as an officer, he had practical command as captain of the company, of which he was orderly sergeant. Having entered the City of Mexico after its capture, the company was detailed to guard trains from Vera Cruz to Jalapa, Pueblo and Cordova and return. In May, 1848, he was taken sick at Vera Cruz, and lay for a month in the hospital. When peace was declared, he returned to the north, but with shattered health.

Upon regaining his health, he applied himself to the continued study of the law, and in 1849, was admitted to the bar at Bloomington, in this State. He there commenced practice, and rode the circuit with Abraham Lincoln, Stephen T. Logan, John T. Stewart, U. F. Linder, Edward D. Baker, and other prominent lawyers of that day, and while being trained in this school, was recognized as the peer of those with whom he was associating. From that time on, he spent several months of each year in the courts with Lincoln, until the latter was elected President. In Lincoln he always found a warm friend, a safe counselor and a congenial companion. The intimacy continued up to the time of Lincoln's death. In Judge David Davis, Mr. Swett found also a life-long friend. These two (Davis and Swett), had exercised a very strong influence in procuring the nomination of Mr. Lincoln for the presidency. The nomination was effected by a combination of the Illinois, Indiana and Pennsylvania delegations; a combination which Messrs. Davis and Swett did much to bring about.

During the war, Mr. Swett was in the employ of the Quicksilver Mining Company. This corporation owned the Almaden or quicksilver mine in California, and was involved in litigation for twelve years, of the last four of which Mr. Swett had full control. This kept him in Washington the greater part of the time. Not being an applicant for office, having already a lucrative employment, and being in the confidence of Mr. Lincoln, he was often consulted in the administration of the affairs of the nation, during those trying times.

In 1865, he came to remain permanently in Chicago. With the exception of State Senator for one term, he' has held no public office, nor does he appear to have aspired to official position. He has devoted himself assiduously to the practice, and occupies a very high place in the profession, especially as a criminal lawyer. In a score or more of murder cases which he has defended, he has been almost invariably successful.

He is an active politician, upon the republican side. His voice has often been heard upon the platform and in the conventions of his party.

When he settled in Chicago, in 1865, he formed, with Van H. Higgins and David Quigg, a partnership which continued for several years. His previous reputation and well known ability brought him at once into prominence, and insured him a lucrative practice, which he has since retained. The present firm is Swett and Grosscup, consisting of Leonard Swett, P. S. Grosscup and Frank L. Wean. Office, 48 Montauk Block.

He is a clear reasoner, and applies his strong logic to every subject he considers, his appeals to court or jury often presenting fine specimens of effective oratory.

A similarity between Mr. Swett and Lincoln has often been suggested among those who knew them both. That such a resemblance, both physical and mental, exists, there can be no doubt. The same plainness and directness, both in speech and action—the same disregard for form and ceremony, and disposition to get at once to the very heart and core of whatever is to be done or investigated—the same appreciation of a good thing, whether it be something said or something done —the same direct, forcible and attractive, though often grotesque, way of putting things.

An instance may be given. One day the writer of this, happened to enter one of the courts just as Mr. Swett was in the midst of an argument before the judge. He had just stated, with great clearness, a proposition maintained by his opponent. He then stated another proposition, also maintained by his opponent, but which was manifestly incongruous.   "Now this," said Mr. Swett, at the same time bringing his right forefinger down upon the palm of his left hand, "*is mixing things.*"   We can imagine Abraham Lincoln, under the same circumstances, saying and doing precisely the same thing.

Mr. Swett may still be considered in the prime of life and in the zenith of his intellectual powers.   He has a commanding influence among his professional brethren and before the courts, and is in the best and highest sense representative of the Chicago Bar.

,DAVID B. LYMAN.

The winter of 1872–3, was passed by the writer in the Sandwich Islands, and while there he became acquainted with the relatives of David B. Lyman, of this City, who was born in that country.   Various members of his family there occupy high official positions, one of them, being at the time spoken of, Governor of the Island of Hawaii, the largest of the group.

David B. was born March 27, 1840, at Hilo, in the said Island of Hawaii.   His father, Rev. David B. Lyman, was formerly of New Hartford, Connecticut.   Having graduated at Williams College and studied theology at the Andover Theological Seminary, Mr. Lyman sen. married and sailed, in November, 1831, for the Sandwich Islands, as a missionary of the American Board of Commissioners for Foreign Missions.

Young Lyman acquired his education by his own efforts. having maintained himself since early boyhood, and applied his leisure hours to study.   At a very early age he held several important positions under the government of the Sandwich Islands, thereby obtaining means to procure a university education.

In the year 1859, he left Honolulu, sailed around Cape Horn, and arrived in New Bedford, Connecticut, in May, 1860.   He entered Yale College in September, of that year, and graduated in 1864.   After leaving Yale, Mr. Lyman attended Harvard Law School, from which he graduated in 1866. While enrolled as a student at Harvard Law School, in the years 1864 and 1865, he was connected with the sanitary commission as hospital visitor. He was then in charge of the 5th corps hospital of the Army of the Potomac, and the Point of Rocks hospital in Virginia, and for the last few weeks of his service was in charge of the sanitary commission connected with the forces around Washington.

In 1866, after finishing his course at the law school, Mr. Lyman, having been admitted to the bar in Boston, removed to Chicago, and entered the office of Messrs. Waite and Clark, as a clerk, where he remained two years. On the first of July, 1869, he formed a partnership with Huntington W. Jackson, under the firm name of Lyman and Jackson. This firm is still the same, having continued twenty years. The office is at 107 Dearborn St. (Portland Block.)

Mr. Lyman is a good classical scholar, and has fine literary attainments. He has been highly successful in the practice of his profession. He has devoted most of his time to real estate and commercial law, but is well versed in every department of general practice. He is a careful and prudent manager, and a safe counselor. He has the confidence of his clients, because they know he will not advise them to commence a suit unless the law as well as justice is on their side, and even then, when there is no remedy save litigation.

Mr. Lyman is noted for his indefatigable industry, for his painstaking preparation of his cases, for his unvarying courtesy toward every one with whom he comes in contact, and for the thorough and conscientious discharge of his duty to his clients. These qualities, added to his well known ability and learning, have given him a high standing in the profession.

He was married October 5, 1870, to Miss Mary E. Cossitt, daughter of F. D. Cossitt, of Chicago.

JEREMIAH LEAMING.

Mr. Leaming may be considered as a representative of the "solid" element of the bar of Chicago.

He was born at Dennisville, Cape May County, New Jersey, January 20, 1831. He studied law at Bordentown, Burlington County, New Jersey, and in June, 1856, was admitted to practice in the Supreme Court of New Jersey. In August, 1856, he was, on certificate, admitted to the Supreme Court of Illinois, and about that time commenced practice in this City.

It will be seen that Mr. Leaming is one of the oldest practitioners at our bar. For many years the firm was Leaming and Thompson, the partner being our well known townsman, Col. Richard L. Thompson. Office, 142 Dearborn St.

Fully thirty years ago, we knew Mr. Leaming well, and often met him in business relations. What he was then, in mental and moral characteristics, he is now; the only difference is in intellectual caliber and acquirements, and in the position which he holds in the profession, a position which he has attained, not by any sudden flight, nor by any combination of fortuitous circumstances, but by constant, steady labor, by holding every advanced position, and making it a stepping stone to one still higher.

Mr. Leaming has paid particular attention to the law of real estate, and to the examination of titles. Probably no attorney's opinion upon an abstract of title would be considered more reliable.

In preparing his cases for trial, he leaves no point uncovered, no position unguarded.

The story is told, that a young advocate, traveling in England once with an experienced barrister, famous for winning his cases in court, offered him £5 to tell him the secret of his success. The offer was accepted, and the secret was imparted in a confidential tone, thus: "Good witnesses." When, as

hey were drawing to their journey's end, the barrister asked
is young friend for the £5, he was met by the reply, "Where
e your witnesses?"

Mr. Leaming always has his witnesses. If he has not got
hem, he keeps out of court.

He enjoys the most unlimited confidence of his associates and
ends. He was a candidate of the democratic party for Cir-
uit Judge in 1886, but was defeated by a certain combination
f the labor and other elements inside and outside of his party;
combination made with reference to other candidates, but
ith whose defeat he became involved. He is considered by
e bar available for still higher judicial position, having been
uently mentioned as candidate for the Supreme Court.

Department of Medical Jurisprudence.

SOME MEDICO-LEGAL ASPECTS OF ANÆSTHESIA.

READ BEFORE THE MEDICO-LEGAL SOCIETY OF CHICAGO, DEC., 1888,
BY EDWARD B. WESTON, M. D., CHICAGO.

The introduction of ether and chloroform for artificial anæsthesia, added a new class of cases to legal medicine.

At first there was not only a want of more than superficial knowledge of the action of the drugs, of the proper methods of administering them, and of the patients to whom they might be obnoxious, but the criminal classes at once saw in them the means for, or aids in, the commission of crime.

In the early days of their use, the surgeon and physician must have employed them with fear and trembling, both for the safety of the patient, and for his own safety in case of accident to the former. But now the anæsthetizer in using the common agents, ether, chloroform, nitrous oxide or the a. c. e. mixture, begins his work almost with temerity. The action of the drugs being well known, and the physical condition of the patient having been ascertained, the physician must use, as in all his work, "ordinary skill."

If suits for damages have become less frequent, in consequence of the knowledge of anæsthetics, gained from years of experience, and by a knowledge of the extent to which they can be used for criminal purposes, they have not disappeared; and still are of great interest in medical jurisprudence.

The subject may be considered in two general divisions:

1. Those cases in which an anæsthetic has been used in medicine, lawfully.

2. Those cases in which an anæsthetic has been used criminally.

The second division may be again divided: (*a*), cases in medicine where it was used criminally; (*b*), cases where it was used as a means for suicide; (*c*), cases where it was used for the purpose of robbery, rape, murder, or other crime.

There may also be other cases, in which medico-legal questions might arise; for instance, where a person had administered an anæsthetic to himself for its intoxicating effects; and where it had been administered for the detection of crime.

We will first briefly consider that division of the subject including those cases in which the anæsthetic has been used in medicine lawfully.

It cannot be expected that agents with qualities which render a person so completely insensible, mentally and physically, to all external impressions, can be used incautiously; or that the person using, or administering them, does not assume the most serious responsibility.

The physician administering an anæsthetic, or responsible for the same, runs the same risk of a suit for malpractice that the doctor does in prescribing, or the surgeon in operating.

In case an operation is to be performed, the person giving the anæsthetic should be legally and actually as well qualified for his duty as the operator himself. Often, however, in an emergency, and especially in the country, a skilled anæsthetist cannot be got, and the physician has to trust the sponge to the most intelligent layman at hand. In such case the physician in charge would not be liable, to the same degree, should accident occur. But if possible, a responsible assistant should always be obtained to give the anæsthetic.

If injury or death follow the administration of an anæsthetic by a legally qualified physician, or by a person not legally qualified, while giving an anæsthetic by invitation of, and under the direction of a qualified physician, the first question to be decided would be, what was the cause of death? Was it the anæsthetic, or some coincident cause? If by careful inquiry, by post-mortem examination and otherwise, it should be decided that the anæsthetic was the cause, the question would then be asked, Did the administrator use "ordinary skill?"

What do we here mean by "ordinary skill?" The person using the anæsthetic agent, being legally qualified, must know the action to be expected from the agent employed, on a person both in a state of health and of disease. He must be competent to decide whether it be safe to administer *any* anæsthetic to the person presented for anæsthesia, and if so, *which* is the suitable agent to use. He must know how to give it in the manner recognized as correct, and so give it. In case of accident, he must know and have at hand, and skillfully apply, the proper remedies. In case of accident he will be interrogated on these points, and the law will hold him responsible for the use of "ordinary skill."

The question may come up, as to whether a given operation was of sufficient gravity to justify the use of the particular anæsthetic administered. As when death had resulted from chloroform, given for tooth extraction, when the nitrous oxide might have been used.

In case of a person found dead, under circumstances which prove that he died from chloroform, or other anæsthetic, administered to himself, the question—and an important one it is—would arise, did he take it with suicidal intent, or to relieve pain, or to produce sleep, or for the silly purpose of producing intoxication or exhilaration from partial anæsthesia?

It is possible that anæsthesia may sometimes be produced to aid In criminal abortion, or to conceal the same. The woman might testify that the anæsthetic was given for a different purpose, and she would not be able to swear as to what was done; or possibly even to identify the operator. Of course her wish would be to conceal the crime, and shield the criminal.

If she die under suspicious circumstances, an inquest and thorough investigation would disclose the cause of death, even though the criminal might not be brought to justice.

It is now known that an anæsthetic cannot be used as an aid in the commission of crime, to the extent formerly believed.

Chloroform is the anæsthetic generally used for criminal pur- , poses, as it can be given without any special apparatus, and being quicker in its action and less disturbing to the victim, than ether. But it is not the instantly overpowering agent which it was once popularly thought to be. A criminal would now hardly attempt to anæsthetize a person by waving a chloroform saturated handkerchief before his face. Nor would a person dare to claim he had been rendered insensible in such a way. Nor would one attempt to chloroform a waking person of nearly equal strength, for the crime could probably be committed as easily as the chloroform given.

It was once a much debated question whether a person could be anæsthetized while asleep. But it was long since settled in the affirmative. Yet, it is not always, or often, easy to do this, unless the administrator is an expert, and then the attempt often fails. But if the person is sleeping very soundly, and the criminal is an adept, the victim may be anæsthetized, and robbery, rape or any crime committed.

The crime most often declared to have been committed by the aid of an anæsthetic is, undoubtedly, rape. It is a question of the greatest interest both legally and medically. But having nothing new to present it is unnecessary to consider the subject at length.

It may however be safely asserted, that it is hardly within the bounds of possibility that a woman should have sufficient consciousness to have knowledge of the crime at the time of its commission and at the same time be unable to resist or make outcry.

The following summary from Wharton and Stillé's "Medical Jurisprudence," 1884, may well be quoted here:

"1. That the consciousness or perception of external objects and impressions is impaired in the early and lost in the final stage of etherization.

"2. That during the time the mind remains susceptible to external impressions at all, these reach it in a feeble or perverted manner.

"3. That the emotions, and especially those of an erotic character, are excited by the inhalation of ether.

"4. That voluntary muscular movement is not paralyzed

until the state of perfect narcotism is produced, at which time, however, all outward consciousness is extinct.

"5. That the memory of what has passed during the state of etherization is either of events wholly unreal, or of real occurrences. perverted from their actual nature.

"6. That there is reason to believe that the impressions left by the dreams occasioned by ether may remain permanently fixed in the memory with all the vividness of real events."

That a woman often has erotic sensations while anæsthetized, and caused by the anæsthetic is without doubt true. And the impressions left are so vivid, so real, that only the strongest proof can dispel them. For this reason the invariable rule should be, never to give a woman an anæsthetic unless the most trustworthy witnesses are present. Charges of this nature are often brought against the physician or dentist by women who are perfectly honest and respected by all.

The question of the propriety of diagnosis of feigned or hysterical disease by means of anæsthesia is an important one. If the patient willingly consents to take the anæsthetic, it would be lawful to give it, provided there was a necessity for a more. certain diagnosis. But in cases where the parties decline to take the anæsthetic, each case would have to be settled by itself.

In regard to insanity following anæsthesia, we quote the following, written by Dr. Lyman of Chicago, from the "Annual of the Universal Medical Sciences:" "Insanity following the use of anæsthetics has been noticed. Bull mentions such a case. The well known alienist, Savage, of London, read a valuable paper on this subject, at the fifty-fifth annual meeting of the British Medical Association. He calls attention to the fact that, in persons who are predisposed to insanity, intoxication with vegetable, mineral, or organic poisons, and the use of alcholic or anæsthetic inhalations, may be followed by acute delirious mania, from which the patient may recover, or lapse into dementia, or even into the progressive paralysis of the insane.

"These conclusions are based upon a number of interesting observations which agree with the facts recorded by Crothers and others who have written upon inebriety. Savage utters a word of caution against the use of chloroform during childbirth, when a predisposition to insanity exists, for in this way puerperal insanity may be excited. He also records a case of mania, followed by dementia, after nitrous oxide, thus agreeing with the opinions of Bropley, previously noted."

AN IMPORTANT COURT DECISION.—Some time ago, a man liv- in West Virginia, was convicted in the supreme court of the State for practicing medicine in violation of the Medical Practice Act of the State.

The case was appealed to the Supreme Court of the United States, which gave the following important decision, rendered by Justice Field:

"The power of the State to provide for the general welfare of its people, authorizes it to prescribe all such regulations as in its judgment will secure, or tend to secure them against the consequences of ignorance and incapacity, as well as deception and fraud. Few professions require more careful preparation than that of medicine, and no one has a right to practice it without the necessary qualifications. The Statute only requires that whoever assumes, by offering his services to the community, that he possesses the requisite qualifications, shall present evidences of them from a body designated by the State as competent to judge of his fitness to practice medicine."

NATIONAL HYGIENE.

BY LUCY WAITE, M. D.

What is hygiene and what are its possibilities? What evidence have we that we are not under as perfect hygienic and sanitary regulations as possible? Is there a real necessity for a national system of hygiene? How can such a system be established and what would be its limits? Hygiene is that branch of science which evolves rules for the perfect culture of mind and body. How to preserve a sound mind in a sound body is the secret which the study of the laws reveals to us. It is a system of principles and rules for the preservation of health and the avoidance of disease.

National hygiene comprises all rules and regulations which promote the public or general health. Health is the result of the equal development of the mental, moral and physical powers. When the equilibrium between these factors is in any way destroyed, the result is abnormal. The same law holds good in excess of mental and moral, as in excess of physical activity. When the mental predominates, the place of the physical is supplied by excess of mental—the equilibrium is destroyed, the result, insanity or death.

It is as impossible to separate rules for purely moral health from those for physical health, or moral from mental, as it is to separate the head from the body, and still have a living human being. A great physician once said: "Sanitary surroundings will not compensate for social transgressions against the laws of morality; for public virtue is essential to public health, and both to national prosperity." Dr. Richardson, in

(102)

his most instructive work on "Diseases of Modern Life," has a chapter on diseases from the effects of the passions, with sub-headings, Effects of Anger—Hatred—Fear—Grief—and the Reel of the Passions. Fully realizing the indestructible link between mind and matter, and knowing well the necessity for mental and moral culture, we claim that the physical is equally important, and unless these three are developed in equal proportions, the result can never be a perfect being. It is one of the strangest features of our social life that this law is recognized by so few and has so small a part in our social laws and customs. The farmer, for instance, makes a thorough study of the feeding of his horses, cows and pigs, but his children can eat anything.

If a man owns a fine horse, he gives the most careful attention to his eating, exercising, rest, etc., but will himself start out after a hearty meal, on a long walk, when he would not think of allowing his horse to do the same. In the vegetable world no one expects a rose to grow from a pumpkin seed—but a child is expected to grow strong and healthy on pork, pie crust and pickles. "Science does its duty," says Max Mueller, "not in telling us the causes of spots on the sun, but in explaining to us the laws of our own being and the consequences of their violation." This sentence from Max Mueller defines the possibilities of a scientific hygiene—to explain to us the laws of our own being and the consequences of their violation. What evidence have we that we are not under as perfect hygienic and sanitary regulations as possible? All branches of science have made great strides in the last few centuries, and it is true that the frequency and fatality of contagious diseases, due to crowding and filth, have much decreased since the days of the black death and the great plague of Athens. To the credit of the medical profession be it said, that great advance has been made in the treatment of curable diseases, but corresponding advance has not been made in the prevention of preventable diseases. The black death of the ancients is now malignant typhus; the great plague of Athens, now malignant scarlet fever; small-pox is the same dread disease which depopulated hundreds of cities in the 9th century, and cancer is as fatal to-day as it was in the time of our fathers in medicine.

In the 6th century, the physicians of Constantinople were greatly troubled at what they called the plague of drowsiness and distraction, and to-day we are seized with equal horror at seeing the same manifestions of symptoms, the only difference being that we call it by a more scientific name, and have the satisfaction of writing cerebro-spinal-meningitis in the death certificate. The late scourge of yellow fever in the South, and the prevalence of typhoid fever in our northern suburb, is a disgrace to an enlightened people.

But it is in regard to brain and nervous affections that we find the most appalling state of things. The statistics in regard to idiocy and insanity are truly startling. In the Medical Press, Dr. Downs gives some very interesting facts in regard to idiocy. There are at present in the United States, nearly as many idiots as insane, and the rate of increase nearly as rapid. In 1850, there were 15,787; in 1880, 76,895. He says that in periods of great excitement, as war or political intrigue, the per cent. of the feeble-minded has been greatly increased and is sometimes capable of being demonstrated with mathematical accuracy. Alcoholism is held responsible for much of the mental and consequent physical degeneracy. It was found that in Norway, after the removal of the spirit duty, insanity increased 50 per cent., and congenital idiocy 150 per cent. In regard to idiocy as influenced by the trades and professions of the parents, Dr. Downs found among four hundred cases with fair social condtions, 25 per cent. children of the three learned professions, 3 per cent. were children of lawyers, 4 per cent. of physicians, and 18 per cent. children of ministers. Of the men of eminence, he found that the legal profession gives birth to 11 per cent., the medical to 9 per cent. and the clergy to 4 per cent.

It is estimated that there are now in the United States, 168,900 insane. In 1850, the ratio of insane in our population was one in 1,500—in 1860, one in 1,300—in 1870, one in 1,000, and in 1880, one in 550—an enormous increase in ten years. In comparing the statistics of our own country with England, France and Germany, we lead with a horrible majority. England has within 15 millions, as large a population as our own country, and not half the number of insane. France has a population by 13 millions less than the United States and only a trifle over half the number of insane. Germany has only 5 millions less in population, and 50 thousand less insane. Late statistics from New York State show an increase during the year '87–'88, of 710 over the last year, there being in 1888, 14,772 insane in the State of New York alone. This was the greatest increase in a year in the history of the State. The asylums are full, many over crowded. In our own State the public asylums are taxed to the utmost to care for all who apply.

These statistics show beyond a doubt that idiocy and insanity in our own country are alarmingly on the increase. The following statistics in regard to the use of narcotics, may throw some light on the cause. Dr. Hammond, in a lecture before the N. Y. Medical Society in 1885, said that in 1840, about 20 thousand pounds of opium were consumed in the United States. In 1880, 533,450 pounds were bought and used. In 1868, there were about 90,000 habitual opium eaters in the United States; now they number over 500,000, and the majority of these are women. The statistics in regard to some of the principal diseases of modern life, are almost beyond belief. In Massachusetts, for instance, the increase of death from Bright's diseases. In 1850, the mortality was 1.1 in 1,000 deaths; in 1860, 2.9; in 1870, 10.5; in 1880, 19.7, and in 1886, 30.5. The points here given are sufficient to show that we are not as a nation under the most favorable hygienic conditions, and that as regards the prevention and cure of mental diseases at least, we are far behind the principal European nations. The cause is not so easily found. Many factors combine to produce the state of things these statistics reveal. But one potent factor is clearly the demoralized condition of the medical profession in our country, and of public opinion in relation to it.

The medical profession is fast loosing the confidence of the people. The result is a rapidly increasing use of all sorts of patent medicines, full of narcotics and poisonous drugs of every description. Our drug stores are thrown open to the people—

medicine is dispensed by the 5 cts. worth, without a physician's prescription, and the country is flooded with patent medicines. Fourteen million dollars worth of patent medicines is sold annually in the United States, and it is said that ten millions more are spent in advertising these drugs. Dr. Emlen Painter, says, in the "American Druggist," that there are 36,500 proprietary medicines in the market. He claims that they are totally unworthy the distinction of being prescribed by medical gentlemen, that they are directly at variance with scientific progress; and had they never existed, both medicine and pharmacy would have this day reached a higher place in the development of science. Our medical journals are full of advertisements of patent medicines.

Do not doctors read enough to support the journals without the aid of proprietary medicine advertisements? Our religious and literary journals are also full of these advertisements. It is stated in some of the eastern medical journals that the Open Court of this City, is the only literary paper which, to their knowledge, refuses to publish them. Sample copies of the New Ideal, another liberal journal published in Boston, show none of these advertisements. Prof. Chandler, in a strong appeal to physicians to take some steps toward remedying this evil, said: "These firms of manufacturers of patent medicines, nine out of ten, live solely by the newspapers, and sometimes are admirably managed. I know some establishments," he says, "in which there is a regular staff employed. There is the literary man who writes the letters giving marvelous accounts of marvelous cures; there is the artist who shows the patient before and after taking 22 bottles of the medicine; there is the poet, who composes poems upon the subject; there is the liar who swears to what he knows is not true, and the forger who produces testimonials from his own imagination. The real business is advertising for dupes, the medical part is a side issue."

What is the explanation of this state of things in a country claiming to be civilized? Statistics may again help us to a solution. By the latest census there were 65,000 physicians in the United States—an excess over any of the European countries, of 50,000. Our land is flooded with an army of half educated physicians, disputing among themselves until they have lost the confidence of the people. The profession is divided into so many schools and "pathies," that there is no opportunity for concerted action on a scientific basis. So much time is consumed in trying to prove each other fools and knaves, that very little is left to instruct the people in hygiene and sanitary regulations. Our colleges are to a great extent financial enterprises. Competition runs high, and students must be obtained, no matter how unfit or unprepared for entering the profession. In cities with a population which does not warrant them in supporting two colleges, are found ten and twelve, thereby so dividing the clinical material that only a very small per cent. of the students can obtain practical hospital work.

The prevailing fashion of having every idea in medicine represented by a separate college, is unique to our country. We have our allopathic and homeopathic colleges, Eclectic Schools, and Christian Science Institutes, and not long ago there was unearthed in Cincinnati a vitapathic college, whatever that may mean, with a course of instruction of four months. The citizens of Cincinnati, to their credit, were indignant at this discovery and investigated; but found the institution chartered and were helpless. In a recent address before the Chicago Medico-Legal Society, the President, Dr. Doering, said: "I question which is the greater public calamity, an occasional epidemic of cholera, or the regular recurring annual epidemic of some 4,000 doctors let loose on an innocent and unsuspecting public." During the year '86-'87, the twenty universities of Germany, graduated 847 students. In the same year the 117 colleges of the United States graduated 4,000. Truly we are a great people. What is the result of this division of medical education, this half educating principle in vogue in our country? Each physician chooses what he will learn. He studies that system of therapeutics to which he is inclined by his previous education, and in favor of which he is prejudiced by his surroundings—remains totally ignorant of any other, and wrapped in his mantle of ignorance, sits comfortably down —easily satisfies himself that in his system of therapeutics is comprised the whole of medical knowledge, and calmly denounces all who differ with him, as either fools or knaves.

It is time that a scientific spirit be infused into the medical profession, and if it cannot come in any other way, it must come through the law of supply and demand. Many physicians object to the popular discussion of these subjects, claiming that such a reform should come from within the profession and not from without. Very true; but they have had time enough. The subject has long been agitated by individual members of the profession, and by some of our more independent medical journals. The doctors show no encouraging symptoms of being willing to mix their own medicine, and indeed after all these centuries of drugging, it would seem but fair that the people should have a chance to mix the doctors a dose.

The "Medical Record" said not long ago in an editorial on this subject: "The discussion of this question in conventions on social topics and similar gatherings, shows the inevitable trend of public opinion. An impartial observer of the progress of medical education in this State (N. Y.), must admit that it has been retarded by the financial plan on which our colleges have been managed. The whole matter of raising the standard of medical education is in the hands of a small minority of the profession, and this minority must be influenced by public opinion." Is there any way out of this lawless state of things? How can justice be done to both the profession and the public? Clearly by establishing one standard of medical education. The public should insist that a physician should be a physician —not a "pathist" of any description. That he should understand all known systems of cure, and be intelligent enough to use what is best in all or to choose from all the best. Not until medical education is under the control of the State and the public demand from their medical advisers one standard, can there be any great advance in medical and sanitary science.

This brings us to the last question. How can a national system of hygiene be established and what would be its limits? In seeking for a solution of this question, we cannot begin better than by noting the systems in vogue in other countries, and what is being done in our own. England has a Central Board of Health which stands in the relation of an advisory board to the local boards. All England and Wales is divided 'into rural sanitary districts, with sub local boards. This arrangement exists also somewhat in France, but there the power of the Central Board is limited to the prevention of outbreaks of contagious diseases. In Munich, Leipsic and Copenhagen, there are institutions for the teaching of hygiene to the people. The Hungarian Minister of Education, M. Trefort, has been making great efforts to have hygiene taught in all high schools by medically trained hygienists, and has created in the University of Prague a special course to teach hygiene to physicians. Stockholm has a fully equipped institution of hygiene.

In our own country, a National Board of Health was appointed in 1878 by the Federal government, but no record of any work done can be found. The Encyclopedia says: "Little practical work has been done, the 'board being very much hindered by political intrigue." Some good work has been done by individual State Boards. Nearly every State has a board of health, but their powers are very limited. New York has made State enactments under which action can be taken, but as a rule work must be done under municipal by-laws, which are neither thorough nor effective. Our own State Board is almost entirely limited to the control of the practice of medicine. Michigan is the first State to start a scientific systematic hygiene. A laboratory has been established at Ann Arbor, and a course of lectures begun under a paid professor and assistants. Nearly all the general work done in the United States has been done by the American Public Health Association, which has headquarters at Concord, New Hampshire.

This Association was organized in 1872 by a few prominent physicians, and is now a flourishing society, accomplishing as much good as possible, unsupported by legal authority. The Society published in 1886, at great expense, four essays on sanitary topics, which should be in every school and private library. They are called the Lomb prize essays. Prizes of three and five hundred dollars having been given by Mr. Henry Lomb, of Rochester, New York, to the writers of the accepted essays on the following subjects: Healthy Homes and Foods for the working classes—the Sanitary Conditions and Necessities of School Houses and School Life—Disinfection and Individual Prophylaxis against Infectious Diseases—the Preventable Causes of Diseases—Injury and Death in American Manufactories and Workshops, and the best means and appliances for preventing and avoiding them. These private societies are doing an immense amount of good, but such an important .subject as the regulation of the public health should be under the control of the State.

It is an acknowledged principle in our government that "it is the business of the government to do for the mass of individuals those things which cannot be done or cannot be so well done by individual action." A system somewhat similar to that existing in England would be well suited to our country. There should be in each State a State Board of Health, working in concert and suggesting to each other methods and means through a Central Committee formed from members of all the State Boards. The Central Committee would act as an advisory board, suggesting measures and regulations to be passed upon by the several State Boards; all measures originating with the State Boards being referred before the final decision to the Central Committee for suggestions and corrections. What would be the duties of the State Boards? Within the bounds of sanitary and hygienic legislation they would be almost limitless. It is manifestly impossible in the limits of this article, to go into the details of such a subject. First and foremost they would turn their attention to the medical profession—to reform the profession itself, so that it be worthy the confidence and respect of the public, and so reform the people through education and wise legislation on the subject, that they shall appreciate the profession, and give to physicians the confidence necessary in order that they may do good work for the people.

Place the licensing power to practice medicine in the hands of the State Board, and take it away entirely from the colleges. This alone would weed out at least half of them. Oblige every physician practicing in the same State to pass the same examination, and let it cover at least all the known systems of therapeutics recognized by the people. Gradually concentrate the medical education of the State in one city and in one college; discourage the building of free dispensaries, except in connection with the hospital and college, and there is no reason why we should not be able to obtain in our own country as thorough an education in medicine as in any country in Europe. Having reformed the doctors, they would turn their attention to the people. They would discourage in every way the manufacture and sale of patent medicines, and under no conditions should these be sold without a physician's prescription. If a physician who knows the ingredients and the effect upon the system, chooses to use them he should be allowed to do so. But drugs in the hands of the people are fast making us a nation of invalids, and materially aiding in filling our insane asylums and homes for the feeble-minded.

Not a drop of medicine should pass into the hands of the people except through a physician's prescription. Give the people the broadest possible education in public and private hygiene. Give them every aid in preserving health and prolonging life, but let drugs be dealt to them sparingly and by a thoroughly trained hand. It behooves every physician who honestly loves his profession and who hopes to see it hold again the place in the minds and hearts of the people which legitimately belongs to such a high calling, to take up this reform in an earnest and bold spirit which must lead to success. It should further be the duty of the State Board, to follow the example of the American Public Health Association, and circulate literature on all sanitary topics; to introduce bills into the Legislature to prohibit the marriage of idiots, lunatics, paupers and those affected by incurable diseases; to suggest to Congress measures regulating the quarantine systems, public water supplies, sewerage systems, and construction of public buildings. They would establish sanitary engineering and laboratories for scientific investigation into the cause and prevention of disease; especially of idiocy and insanity. They would introduce the rules of right living into all our schools and universities.

It would further be their duty to instruct the people in private hygiene. Teach them the necessity of pure air and sunlight in their homes—the importance of cleanliness, exercise, rest; of good food and proper clothing; how to avoid in particular, lung, throat and heart troubles. They would organize public baths and gymnasiums, and in every way, public and private, place the people under sanitary conditions. They would explain to women scientifically, philosophically, if need be, why they cannot with impunity, squeeze their lungs into half the space allotted them by nature, and their liver into the other half. They would explain to men why they cannot smoke eleven cigars a day and then sleep soundly at night— why they cannot eat highly spiced foods and drink many kinds of wine late into the night, and wake in the morning with a clear brain and a pure heart. They would educate—educate. I am convinced that it is not because of willful carelessness on the part of either men or women, that we are becoming practically a nation of invalids, but because of real ignorance of the laws of health, and of the means to be taken to insure a long life and a natural death.

A physician of large knowledge, once said: "In all my experience I have never known but one man who really died a natural death." The fearful mortality among children should alone open the eyes of the people to the need of some more systematic effort for the promotion of sanitary conditions. Our latest statistics show that one third of the entire mortality occurs among children under five years of age. The little ones come already weak and tired—bearing on their innocent shoulders the sins of many ancestors—make a brief struggle against all the adverse conditions which surround them, only to fall on the threshold of life, victims to heredity and ignorance. In the days when medicine was left to the schoolmen and the clergy, surely the people were excusable for dying off by the thousands from all sorts of diseases and plagues. But are they to-day, when medicine is becoming to a great extent a popular science? So long as every accident, every death was attributed to some power outside of ourselves, and for which we could not be held responsible, progress in social and sanitary science was impossible. But science has taught us there can be no effect without a cause.

We see whole cities depopulated by some terrible disease—we see crime running rampant in a land blest with an army of good and intelligent men and women. We see starvation in the midst of plenty—sickness, misery and death in a world where there should be perfect health, happiness and life, and we no longer rest satisfied with the assurance that as an enlightened people we are in no way responsible. Surely these evils are no law of nature. There must be a cause, and we cannot shirk the responsibility. Reason tells us we are directly responsible, and the cause must be found.

If we aspire as we should to once more having upon the earth a race of healthy men and women, we must begin with the children. Teach them that it is their sacred duty to care for their bodies, that a sound mind in a sound body is the best gift of the gods, and that this is in their power to obtain. Teach them that death from disease is unnatural and the direct result of a broken law; that the young should never die; that only the old die well. Make the rules of hygiene and of right living part of the curriculum of every school and college in our land. Let physiology be taught on a scientific basis. Let the children learn the structure and functions of their own bodies, as openly and as plainly as they learn their problems in mathematics. Ignorance is not innocence, and knowledge is a powerful weapon against temptation. Let them know and realize the interdependence of mental, moral and physical health. Surround them with every hygienic condition and teach them the fear of nature's laws. Then and then only, may we hope for a race of beings who will one day be worthy to commune with nature, and who, after a wise and useful life spent in harmony with her laws, will deserve their long rest on her bosom.

REVENUE LAWS OF ILLINOIS.

The Revenue Reform League of this City, of which Francis B. Peabody is President, appointed a Committee on Measures, which, at the Annual Meeting of the League, held January 16, 1889, made a report, recommending "a limitation of the percentage of taxation allowed the different taxing bodies to about one-fourth the amount now allowed by law, with an additional limitation covering the total amount of taxes that can be levied for all purposes; also a limitation on the amount of corporate indebtedness, to 2 per cent. on the assessed value.

"This limitation of taxing power will necessitate raising the assessment rate, and will result in breaking up the present iniquitous system of assessing at a percentage ununiform and varying with the varying judgment and conscience of the different assessors, and will secure an assessment at a fair cash value as provided by law and as honesty requires.

"At the same time the assessment is increased it becomes necessary to correspondingly decrease the limit of power to create indebtedness."

The committee recommend, also, a reduction in the present exorbitant percentage allowed on tax sales.

The League passed a resolution, urging upon the General Assembly the calling of a convention for the revision of the Constitution of the State.

At an adjourned meeting of the League, on January 30, bills prepared by the Committee were adopted, making important changes in the revenue laws, especially in reference to tax liens, which, if the bills pass, are to be foreclosed in chancery.

Editorial Department.

WHERE WOMEN VOTE.

Hamilton Willcox of New York has recently published a pamphlet, showing the extent of woman suffrage at the present time. From this it appears that some form of suffrage for women prevails in 110 States, territories and provinces, with an extent of over 15,000,000 square miles and a population of nearly 300,000,000.

In the province of Ontario, women vote (unless married) for all elective officers save two. In the adjoining province of Quebec, women are voters in the cities of Quebec and Montreal, and in various other cities, by provincial law. In British Columbia, women vote for all elective officers but member of Parliament. In England, Scotland and Wales, women (unless married) vote for all elective officers but members of Parliament. In Ireland, women vote every-where for poor-law guardians; in Dundalk and other seaports, for harbor boards; and in Belfast, for all municipal officers. In Sweden, their suffrage is about the same as in Britain, and they vote, too, indirectly for members of the House of Lords. In Russia, women, heads of households, vote for all elective officers and on all local questions.

In Austria-Hungary, they vote (by proxy) at all elections, including members of provincial and imperial parliaments. In Croatia and Dalmatia, they vote at local elections in person. In Italy, widows vote for members of Parliament. In Finland, women vote for all elective officers. In Africa, in the colony of Good Hope, the women have municipal suffrage. In British Burma, women tax payers vote in the rural districts. In Madras Presidency, Hindostan, they can do so in all municipalities. In Bombay Presidency they likewise can. In all the countries of Russian Asia they can do so wherever a Russian colony settles. The Russians are colonizing the whole of their vast Asian possessions, and carry with them every-where the "mir," or self-governing village, wherein women, heads of households, vote. In New Zealand, municipal suffrage exists and the Legislature has resolved that women shall vote for members of Parliament. It also exists in Victoria, New South Wales, Queensland and South Australia. In a large number of islands also, some form of woman suffrage prevails.

In our own country we have municipal suffrage in Kansas, and in Wyoming Territory women vote for every office on the same terms with men. Indeed, some form of woman suffrage has been introduced in twenty-four of the forty-five States and Territories.

From every quarter comes the same report that women's partaking in elections brings purer politics, better government and fairer play for women. But this is under great disadvantages.; for in large regions woman's political freedom is still limited to school or village elections; in many it is confined to mere municipal elections; only in Wyoming is it equal in extent to masculine suffrage. In many of these communities the mass of men are still disfranchised, as are the mass of women. In America alone has the grand idea of universal suffrage been put in full practice for men. But the idea that womanhood necessitates life-long, exceptionless disfranchisement has been abandoned. The day cannot be far distant when women will vote to the same extent as men.

GIRARD'S WILL
AND THE GIRARD COLLEGE.

On the 16th of February, 1830, Stephen Girard, of Philadelphia, made in his will a munificent provision for the foundation of a college for the education of orphan children.

The college building was commenced in 1833, and completed in 1847, at an expense of about two millions. Besides the main college hall there are now some fifteen or twenty other buildings connected with the institution. The cost of the college grounds and buildings has been over three millions of dollars, while the present value of the same is estimated at about ten millions, and the entire Girard College estate at twenty millions.

The City of Philadelphia was made trustee for carrying out the purposes of the founder, and in return for such a splendid bequest, one would suppose the City would be not only willing but eager to carry out, completely, and even punctiliously, the views and wishes of the benevolent testator, especially after that provision of the will which was considered the most objectionable, had been sustained as legal and valid by the Supreme Court of the United States.

But what are the facts? Mr. Girard in his will thus states the reasons and motives which influenced him in making the bequest:

"XX. And, whereas, I have been for a long time impressed with the importance of educating the poor, and of placing them, by the early cultivation of their minds and the development of their moral principles, above the many temptations to which, through poverty and ignorance they are exposed; and I am particularly desirous to provide for such a number of poor male white orphan children as can be trained in one institution, a better education, as well as a more comfortable maintenance, than they usually receive from the application of the public funds; and whereas, together with the object just adverted to, I have sincerely at heart the welfare of the City of Philadelphia, and as a part of it, am desirous to improve the neighborhood of the river Delaware, so that the health of the citizens may be promoted and preserved, and that the eastern part of the City may be made to correspond with the interior:

"Now I do give, devise and bequeath all the residue and remainder of my real and personal estate of every sort and kind wheresoever situate, unto" the Mayor, Aldermen and citizens of Philadelphia, "their successors and assigns, in trust, to and for the several uses, intents and purposes hereinafter mentioned and declared of and concerning the same, that is to say: (Here follow certain directions in reference to certain portions of his estate.)

"XXI. And so far as regards the residue of my personal estate, in trust, as to two millions of dollars, part thereof, to apply and expend so much of that sum as may be necessary, in erecting, as soon as practicably may be, in the center of my square of ground between High and Chestnut streets, and Eleventh and Twelfth streets, in the City of Philadelphia, (which square of ground I hereby devote for the purposes hereinafter stated, and for no other forever), a permanent college, with suitable out-buildings, sufficiently spacious for the residence and accommodation of at least three hundred scholars, and the requisite teachers and other persons necessary in such an institution as I direct to be established, and in supplying the said college and out-buildings with decent and suitable furniture, as well as books and all things needful to carry into effect my general design.

(Here follow specific details for the construction of the college building, for supplying the college with books, apparatus, etc., for organizing the institution, supplying it with teachers, etc., for admission of students, etc.)

"Due regard shall be paid to their health, and to this end their persons and clothes shall be kept clean, and they shall have suitable and rational exercise and recreation. They shall be instructed in the various branches of a sound education, comprehending reading, writing, grammar, arithmetic, geography, navigation, surveying, practical mathematics, astronomy; natural, chemical and experimental philosophy, the French and Spanish languages, (I do not forbid, but I do not recommend the Greek and Latin languages), and such other learning and science as the capacities of the several scholars may merit or warrant.

"I would have them taught facts and things, rather than words or signs: and especially I desire that by every proper means a pure attachment to our republican institutions and to the sacred rights of conscience, as guarantied by our happy constitutions, shall be formed and fostered in the minds of the scholars.   * * * *

"In relation to the organization of the college and its appendages, I leave necessarily, many details to the Mayor, Aldermen and Citizens of Philadelphia, and their successors; and I do so with the more confidence, as, from the nature of my bequests and the benefit to result from them, I trust that my fellow-citizens of Philadelphia will observe and evince especial care and anxiety in selecting members for their City Councils and other agents.

"There are, however, some restrictions which I consider it my duty to prescribe, and to be, amongst others, conditions on which my bequest for said college is made, and to be enjoyed, namely: First, (surplus income to be added to principal, and principal to be preserved intact, only interest, income and dividends being devoted to the current expenses of the institution.)

"Secondly, I enjoin and require that no ecclesiastic, missionary, or minister of any sect whatsoever, shall ever hold or exercise any station or duty whatever in the said college; nor shall any such person be admitted for any purpose, or as a visitor, within the premises appropriated to the purposes of the said college.

"In making this restriction I do not mean to cast any reflection upon any sect or person whatsoever, but, as there is such a multitude of sects, and such a diversity of opinion amongst them, I desire to keep the tender minds of the orphans, who are to derive advantage from this bequest, free from the excitement which clashing doctrines and sectarian controversy are so apt to produce. My desire is that all the instructors and teachers in the college shall take pains to instill into the minds of the scholars the purest principles of morality, so that on their entrance into active life, they may from inclination and habit evince benevolence toward their fellow-creatures, and a love of truth, sobriety and industry, adopting at the same time such religious tenets as their matured reason may enable them to prefer."

Nothing appears to be known as to the views of Girard concerning religious subjects, except from the provisions of the will, and from the fact that four of his ships were named, respectively, "Voltaire," "Helvetius," "Montesquieu," and "Rousseau," and the writings of some of these authors were in his library.

As to what should or should not be taught in the college, it must be conceded, that nothing could be made clearer than the testator's intent in that regard. And how has that intent been carried out?

In the first place, there has been erected, within the college grounds, an imposing chapel, of most elaborate ecclesiastical architecture. Such a building was never contemplated in the will, and had the testator supposed it necessary it would have been expressly forbidden.

Entering the chapel, there may be found in the pews a book called "a Manual for the Chapel of Girard College." In it are liturgical selections for morning and afternoon of every day in the month, besides special services for Sundays, Christmas, Good Friday, Easter and other holy days. The manual contains numerous forms of prayer, consisting principally of extracts from the Book of Common Prayer of the Protestant Episcopal Church.

In a petition for the sick and dying (p. 20), the orphans are taught to pray that departing souls "may be cleansed in the blood of Christ." On p. 23, in a responsive hymn which "may be said or sung" according to the rubric, is an address to "the everlasting Son of the Father," in which are used these words: "When thou tookest upon thee to deliver man, thou didst humble thyself to be born of a virgin."

In the Manual are nearly two hundred hymns. The following may be taken as specimens:

Hymn 4, the following line:

"The God incarnate! Man divine!"

In hymn 8, in answer to the question how came the thousands of children in heaven, the answer is:

"Because the Saviour shed his blood
To wash away their sin:
Bathed in that pure and precious flood,
Behold them white and clean."

Not only blood atonement but the doctrine of the trinity is taught in these hymns.

Hymn 69, verse 1:

"Holy, holy, holy, Lord God Almighty,
Early in the morning our song shall rise to thee; --
Holy, holy, holy, merciful and mighty,
God in three Persons, blessed Trinity."

Hymn 74:

"Wash me, cleanse me in the blood
That flowed on Calvary."

Hymn 134:

"Buried in sorrow and in sin,
At Hell's dark door we lay," etc., etc., etc.

It would be an insult to the intelligence of our readers to assume that it is necessary to go into argument to show that the inculcation of these doctrines is a flagrant violation of the will.

But this is not all. While the injunction in regard to ministers is technically observed, lay preachers, of various sorts, are permitted to hold forth on Sunday, in this chapel, and expound the scriptures according to their own views. In a recent discourse, one of these lay preachers, while preaching an orthodox sermon, took occasion to ridicule Thomas Paine, one of our noblest revolutionary patriots, and a man whom Girard held, no doubt, in the highest respect. The lay minister held the character of Paine up to contempt, and characterized those who had met to celebrate his birthday, as "fanatics, long haired men and short haired women.".

It will be noticed, it was not only ecclesiastics and ministers who were to be excluded from the college grounds, but "missionaries" as well. What are these lay preachers but missionaries? They are home missionaries detailed to operate upon the "tender minds" which Girard desired should be kept free from their influence until those minds could adopt "such religious tenets as their matured reason might prefer." Possibly if left alone their matured reason might reject the doctrines of the trinity, blood atonement of Christ, hell fire, etc., and they might by the light of history look upon Thomas Paine as a man as worthy of respect as Moody or Sankey.

The orthodox protestants congratulate themselves upon having outwitted Girard. One of the lay preachers, in his opening remarks, unwittingly admitted, that "the founder of the College never contemplated or intended such a service as then and there engaged their attention." In explanation of the manner in which it had been brought about to the glory of God, he quoted several times the lines:

> "God moves in a mysterious way
> His wonders to perform."

Never was there so shameless a perversion of a great trust. If the American people, outside of Philadelphia, have any sense of honor and propriety, they will in some way combine to cause the City of Brotherly Love to be cited before the courts, to show cause why it should not be required to carry out in good faith the trust confided to it by Stephen Girard.

Those who may have an inclination to examine this matter further, are recommended to procure a small volume, written by Richard B. Westbrook, D.D., LL.D., and published by the author at 1707 Oxford St., Philadelphia, in which will be found these and other facts, and the whole subject fully and ably discussed.

NOTES OF TRAVEL.

PARIS—BJÖRNSTJERNE BJÖRNSON.

On the 7th of October, 1884, in Paris, I first met Bjornson. He had just returned from Tyrol where he had been spending a couple of months. He received me very cordially, and invited me to dine with him next day. After dinner, we took a walk in the Bois de Bologne. We had been corresponding for some months, and the conversation turned very naturally upon the political affairs of Norway, which had been discussed in the letters.

He is a large, broad chested man, with dark, bushy hair. He was then 53 years of age. Had a wife and five children. He has a frank, open countenance—is very interesting in conversation—at times becomes very brilliant.

During the two months that I now spent in Paris, I had frequent opportunities of seeing and studying this distinguished man, than whom probably no one, since the death of Victor Hugo, stands higher in continental literature. Besides meeting him often on other occasions, I was a regular attendant at his Sunday evening receptions, where a brillant coterie of personal friends held conversation in four languages; French, German, Norwegian and English; and not a few of his guests could converse in either of the four.

One evening, I found him engaged in replying to a letter which he had received from Ingersoll; of whom he was a great admirer. The same evening he read to me his new poem, "Bonder de Kommer." "The Peasants are coming."

Bjornson prefers to reside in Paris, on account of its literary advantages, but he is a constant power in Norwegian politics. He represents the radical element—being in favor of bringing his native country as fast as possible to a Republican form of government.

One of Bjornson's characteristics is, the remarkable versatility of his genius. He is at the same time great as a novelist, a poet, an essayist, a dramatist, an orator, and a philosopher. One of his earlier writings, "The Republic," is pervaded by a deep and profound political philosophy.

One day Bjornson asked me if I had heard the music at the Theatre du Chateau d'Eau, near the Place de la Republique. I said I had not and asked him if it was good. He replied "I suppose it is the best in the world." When I reflected that this had not come from a Frenchman, I resolved to go. If it was not the best, it would be difficult to say where it could be excelled. The music was entirely instrumental. There were 100 instruments, one of which was played by a lady.

The first piece was the Symphonie en la majeur, by Beethoven. It lasted three-fourths of an hour. Before the first part was finished, many of the audience were in tears.

I do not purpose to describe any of the sights of Paris—its public buildings—its parks—its fountains—its churches—its cemeteries—its museums and collections of paintings, statuary and antiquities—its many and varied places of entertainment and amusement—its theaters or the grand opera. This I attended with Strakosch and the American singer, Miss Thursby, who had just returned from an engagement in the Scandinavian countries. There she had been accompanied by Wolff, the violinist, under the management of the son of the famous Ole Bull.

The American minister, Mr. Morton, was absent from Paris, but from the accomplished and gentlemanly Secretary of Legation, Mr. Henry Vignaud, of Louisiana, I obtained a ticket to attend the opening of the Chamber of Deputies, on the 14th of October. There was nothing on this occasion to particularly distinguish it from other legislative bodies.

On the evening of October 21, in company with Fernando Jones, of Chicago, I attended the "Ramblers' Club." It was composed of American travelers and sojourners in Paris, and part of the exercises consisted in the relation by the members, of their experiences and adventures in traveling. Some of these were very amusing. One of the members had invented a new balloon, for taking observations in time of war, and this invention he elaborated at considerable length. It was connected with a new system of explosive projectiles.

When an American has become adjusted to his surroundings, he may feel almost as much at home here, as in New York or Chicago. When one contemplates the quiet, orderly and industrious inhabitants of the Paris of to-day, he wonders where the excited people came from who have repeatedly carried destruction through the City.

The first week in November was an exciting one to Americans in Paris, who were eagerly watching the returns of the presidential election. It was not until Saturday, the 8th, that the matter was looked upon as decided.

Perhaps the most interesting thing I saw in Paris was the Hotel and Museum de Cluny, especially the great hall and roof of the ancient castle of Therme. This hall must be from 60 to 70 feet across, each way, and about the same in height, with a self-supporting roof of solid masonry. The roof appears to have stood in its present condition 1500 years. According to the chroniclers, it was here that Julian the Apostate was proclaimed Emperor, in the year 360. It appears to be as old as the reign of Constance Chlore. When one observes the signs of the great antiquity of this stone, and reflects upon the distance across, and the quantity of stone overhead, it is impossible not to have a feeling of danger; especially when the eye is directed to some ominous fissures.

Having seen something of Paris, but having a vivid consciousness of how much there was that I had not seen, I took the cars, on the 8th of December, for Berlin.

C. B. W.

BOOK REVIEWS.

A TREATISE ON PRIVATE CORPORATIONS. The effect of the clause of the Constitution of the United States that forbids a State to pass a "Law impairing the obligation of Contracts," upon the police control of a State over Private Corporations. BY WM. WHARTON SMITH. PHILADELPHIA BAR. PHILADELPHIA: REES, WELSH & CO., LAW PUBLISHERS, 19 SOUTH NINTH STREET, 1889.

This book comes recommended by its size, provided the subject is properly handled and judiciously condensed, for in that case it must be "multum in parvo," consisting as it does, of only about 50 octavo pages.

That this method has been pursued soon becomes evident from an examination of the contents.

The titles of the chapters will give an outline of the work:

Ch. I. General nature of Police Power.

II. Article I, Section 10, of the Constitution of the United States, the decision in the Dartmouth College case, and the questions following that decision.

III. Principle of Providence Bank v. Billings.

IV. The remedy exercised by, or against a corporation is no part of its franchise, and is within legislative control.

V. Police control over railroad companies.

VI. Control of charges of corporations other than railroads.

VII. Regulations over corporations not demanded by public safety.

VIII. A State cannot violate an express provision contained in the charter of a corporation, provided same be constitutional.

IX. Cases illustrating the extreme exercise of Police Power.

X. Limitation on Police Power, even in these cases.

XI. The effect of a reservation to a State of the power to alter, amend or repeal a charter.

XII. Conclusion.

In regard to the general nature of police power, the author gives the definition of Chief-Justice Shaw in Commonwealth v. Alger, 7 Cush. 53:

"We think it a settled principle, growing out of the nature of well ordered civil society, that every holder of property, however absolute and unqualified may be his title, holds it under the implied liability that his use of it may be so regulated that it shall not be injurious to the equal enjoyment of others having an equal right to the enjoyment of their property, nor injurious to the rights of the community."

To which the author adds:

"While this definition of the police power of a State is not broad enough to cover all the cases that have arisen since it was decided, it yet shows with great clearness and force the foundation of the power."

He comments on the Dartmouth College case, 4 Wheaton, 518, in which it was held that the charter of a private corporation is a contract within the meaning of Article I, Section 10, of the Constitution of the United States. Also upon subsequent cases, defining the limits of the principle announced by Chief-Justice Marshall in the Dartmouth College case.

The author then comes to the legislation and adjudications under it, in reference to railroad companies. The first of these cases was Chicago, Burlington and Quincy R. R. Co. v. Iowa, decided in 1876. (94 U. S. 155.) In this case it was held that the Company was subject to legislative regulation, in its rates of charges, applying the principle laid down in Providence Bank v. Billings, that any privileges which may exempt a corporation from the burdens common to individuals, do not flow necessarily from the charter. They must be expressed in it or they do not exist.

"Railroad companies," says Waite, C. J., in the opinion of the court, p. 161, "are carriers for hire. They are incorporated as such, and given extraordinary powers, in order that they may better serve the public in that capacity. They are, therefore, engaged in a public employment, effecting the public interest, and under the decision in Munn v. Illinois, subject to legislative control as to their rates of fare and freight, unless protected by their charters."

The question then arose, what constituted such an exemption? which gave rise to various decisions:

Peik v. C. & N. W. Ry. Co., 94 U. S. 164; Ruggles v. Ill., 108 U. S. 526; Stone v. Farmers' Loan & Trust Co., 116 U. S. 307; the Granger cases, Stone v. Wisconsin, 94 U. S. 180; and others.

Some cases go so far as to hold that a State can still regulate the charges, after granting the company express exemption from such control. The question, the author says, has not yet come before the Supreme Court of the United States, but he gives the weight of authority as decidedly the other way.

The bar will find this a very convenient manual of reference, containing, as it does, a clear statement of elementary principles and of points decided, with a condensed but sufficiently complete review of the cases, which have now become authority upon the subject.

GENERAL DIGEST OF THE DECISIONS OF THE PRINCIPAL COURTS IN THE UNITED STATES. Refers to all Reports official and unofficial published during the Year ending September, 1888. ANNUAL, BEING VOLUME III OF THE SERIES. Prepared and published by THE LAWYERS' CO-OPERATIVE PUBLISHING COMPANY, ROCHESTER, N. Y. 1888.

A volume of over 1500 pages. It combines under one classification thoroughly revised, the entire work of the year, with added-citations of every later publication of the cases—both official reports and unofficial—forming a comprehensive epitome of the case law for the year, in the most convenient possible form for quick reference. The Annual Digest reaches the attorney at just the time he needs it for work in the fall and winter terms of court.

The Digest work is in charge of Mr. Burdett A. Rich, editor-in-chief of the U. S. Supreme Court Digest, which has received high commendation. This in no respect falls below the standard there set. Price $6.00.

Not being in active practice, we cannot speak of the merits of this as compared with the United States Digest, but will give what the publishers say in their prefatory note:

"The large size of this volume is not due to padding or superfluous matter of any sort. The paragraphs are intended to be digest matter in the true sense, making every point express the case and the principle upon which it is decided, with its exact modification or application, and with no immaterial matters or unnecessary verbiage.

"By careful attention to the arrangement and relation of clauses, the exclusion of redundant language and irrelevant facts, an effort has been made to render paragraphs concise and clear as well as correct.

"The aim of the classification is to make the arrangement of the matter in titles and sub-titles sufficiently simple to enable one familiar with any classification, easily and quickly to find what he seeks. Abundant cross-references are used for this purpose, and each general title is made as complete as possible, except where a distinct branch of it is referred to as a division of some other title, to save duplication, which, to economize space, has been studiously avoided. In respect to this completeness of each subject in one title, the classification differs somewhat from that of the preceding two volumes of the series, especially in reference to matters of practice, such as Appeal and Error, Evidence, Pleading, Trial and Witnesses.

"Heavy faced words in paragraphs are also used to bring out the distinctive elements in each, as a further aid to rapid examination.

"As the table of cases came last, it contains references to official reports not published when the body of the work was printed. All possible references have been given.

"The work has been prepared under the general supervision of Burdett A. Rich, who has been ably assisted by E. H. Smith, C. A. Ray, E. W. Haviland, D. L. Covill, H. P. Farnham, and others."

If the work is as good in other respects, the advantage of having it placed so early in the hands of practitioners, is too manifest to require comment.

The same Company publishes, four times per annum, a book, entitled "Lawyers' Reports, Annotated," at $5 per book.

Both the Reports and the Digest are published in the form of a semi-monthy magazine; the former at $20 and the latter at $5 per annum.

Combined subscription to both Semi-Monthy and Annual Digest, $8.50; combined subscription to entire series—Lawyers' Reports annotated, Semi-Monthly and Annual Digest per year, $25.00.

MASSACHUSETTS IN THE WOMAN SUFFRAGE MOVEMENT. A GENERAL, POLITICAL, LEGAL AND LEGISLATIVE HISTORY FROM THE YEAR 1774. BY HARRIET H. ROBINSON. BOSTON: ROBERTS BROTHERS. 12 vo. pp. 280.

The author of this work was the wife of the celebrated writer of the Springfield Republican, William S. Robinson, known as "Warrington." She is herself a good writer, author of various works, among others, a play, written in a pleasing and sprightly manner, entitled "Captain Mary Miller."

She is the woman for the removal of whose political disabilities, Senator Dawes lately introduced a Bill in Congress.

The book before us is full of interesting information.

The author, Mrs. Robinson, published, in 1877, "Warrington Pen-Portraits:" consisting of Personal and Political Reminiscences, from 1848 to 1876, from the writings of her deceased husband; a book which has entertained many who were his personal friends and admirers.

NEW LAW MAGAZINE.

THE GREEN BAG. A USELESS BUT ENTERTAINING MAGAZINE FOR LAWYERS. EDITED BY HORACE W. FULLER. PUBLISHED MONTHLY. $3 PER ANNUM. SINGLE NUMBERS, 35 CENTS.

There is much in a title. This title is very captivating. Here is something useless. How restful to the wearied practitioner to know, that he can throw himself back in his chair, with his feet upon the table, and take up this magazine, with the blissful consciousness that it contains nothing which promises to be of any practical value—nothing which he is under obligation to pay particular attention to or to try to remember.

Still he is not absolutely prohibited from being instructed or benefically impressed by something which he may chance to find within its covers. And then the audacity of supposing that people will pay money for that which is of no use, is of itself attractive. The title alone will probably secure a fair sale for the magazine.

And yet we are not sure but the promise held out is broken in the very first number. Among other articles, not altogether useless, is one by Professor J. B. Ames, on the Specific Performance of Contracts. It is not, however, so long as to be tiresome.

The leading article is a sketch of our distinguished townsman, Chief Justice Fuller, with a fine portrait and autograph. This is sufficient to make the first number attractive to the Chicago Bar.

SIR EDWARD COKE, Knt.

Lord Chief Justice of England, in the Reign of James 1st.

THE CHICAGO LAW TIMES.

VOL. III.]   JULY, 1889.   [No. 3.

EDWARD COKE.

Sir Edward Coke * lived in an eventful period in the history of England. His life, which commenced under Edward VI., included the short but sanguinary reign of Queen Mary, the entire reign of Elizabeth, that of James I., and the early part of the reign of Charles I. Born to comfort, if not to affluence, he nevertheless formed and maintained habits of untiring industry, and these, with his indomitable energy and perseverance, enabled him tó achieve greatness as a lawyer and a jurist. He had great influence at court, and at the same time, maintained, especially in the latter part of his life, his independence and love of liberty.

He was born February 1, 1551, at his father's seat in the parish of Milcham, near East Dereham, in Norfolk.

His father, Robert Coke, was a bencher of Lincoln's Inn, and a barrister of very extensive practice. His mother, Winifred Knightley, was daughter and co-heiress of William Knightley, of Morgrave Knightley, in Norfolk, and a very estimable woman. Coke, in after life, always spoke of her with much gratitude and reverence.

His father died in 1561, leaving his only son, then in his eleventh year, and seven daughters. Edward had been scarcely two years at Cambridge when he lost his mother. He erected a monument to her memory in the church at Titleshall.

* This sketch is condensed from the Life of Sir Edward Coke, in two volumes, by Cuthbert William Johnson, of Gray's Inn, Barrister-at-Law, London, Henry Colburn, Publisher, 1845.

In 1560, being then nine years of age, he was sent to the grammar school at Norwich, where it is said by the editors of the Biographia Britannica, he displayed great diligence and application.

After remaining at this school seven years, he was removed to Trinity College, Cambridge. This was in 1567. He was matriculated as a pensioner of the college, but it does not appear from the University books, that he ever took a degree.

He remained at the University four years. There is no account of his studies to be found at Cambridge; there exist no traditions concerning his sayings and doings. Being intended for the profession of the law, it is supposed he paid more attention to the study of Norman French and to the year books, than to mathematics or classic lore.

Young Coke now began to read such books as would serve him in his future professional pursuits. Among the books at Holkham Hall, there are many law authorities containing his autographs and notes, dated at a very early period of his life. He must have possessed in his early youth, the power of intense application, in a remarkable degree. The books which he studied so steadily and so perseveringly, were of a nature which almost defy the mental digestion of a modern student.

There were then no law books written with the elegance of Blackstone's Commentaries, or Fearne's Contingent Remainders. Every law authority was composed in the barbarous law French of the age, and Coke had to struggle to obtain knowledge from such authors as Fleta, Britton, Hengham and Littleton; from the year books, and the reports of Plowden and Dyer.

In his twenty-first year, Coke was removed from Cambridge to Clifford's Inn, in London, and in the following year, 1572, entered himself a student of the Inner Temple. As a student he was speedily noticed for a very close application to his studies; and more publicly by a very clear statement to the benchers, of the Cook's case, which had caused among these lawyers no little embarrassment. They very much admired the way in which Coke had unraveled the story.

He was admitted to the bar in his twenty-seventh year, when

he had been a member of the Middle Temple only six years, which at his age was thought to be a very extraordinary circumstance; the students then being accustomed to remain eight or nine years.

The rules prevailing among the benchers were rather strict. Long beards were prohibited. The treasurers of all the inns of court conferred together in full parliament, on this important matter, and decreed, in 1st and 2d Philip and Mary, "That no fellow of this house should wear his beard above three weeks growth." Gambling was prohibited. "None of the society shall within this house exercise the play of shoffe-grotte, or slyp-grotte, upon pain of six shillings and eight pence." The use of wine and tobacco was also prohibited.

The inns of court were frequented by a great multitude; many gentlemen's sons attending who had no intention of practicing the law as a profession.

In Trinity term, 1578, Coke, who was then in his twenty-eighth year, pleaded his first cause. His practice speedily became considerable, and soon after, he received the appointment of reader of Lyon's Inn.

The estates left him by his father had increased in his hands, and his practice having become lucrative, he added to them by various purchases. These became so numerous that they finally attracted the attention of the government. There is a tradition in the Coke family, that when he was in treaty for the family estate of Castle Acre Priory, in Norfolk, James I. told him that he had already as much land as it was proper a subject should possess. To this Sir Edward replied, "Then, please your Majesty, I will add only one *acre* more to the estate."

Thirty years Coke spent at the bar; first as a barrister, then solicitor-general to Queen Elizabeth, and lastly as attorney-general. These were the happiest years of his life. The court had not then entangled him; parliamentary affairs and family broils had not yet rendered him notoriously uncomfortable and ridiculous.

Coke had for his contemporaries at the bar, some of the ablest lawyers whom England has produced; men alike distinguished for their learning and their probity. Among the foremost of these were Plowden, Bacon, Egerton, Croke and Yelverton. There were, besides these, Hobart and Tanfield, Heath and Dodderidge.

In 1582, Sir Edward Coke married his first wife, Bridget Paston, daughter and co-heiress of John Paston, Esq., of Huntingfield Hall, in Suffolk, with whom he received then and at her father's death, a fortune very large for those days, amounting to thirty thousand pounds. Coke thus became connected with several of the first families of the kingdom. By this wife he had ten children.

At this period he was rapidly rising in his profession. Incessantly and happily employed, he returned from his chambers in the Temple to an elegant and well regulated house. Thus engaged, his name is not connected with the state prosecutions of those days; for he had not yet become a political character.

From 1585 to 1610, he held various offices; recorder of Coventry, and afterward of Norwich—bencher of the Inner Temple—recorder of London—solicitor-general. Also reader or law lecturer to the Inner Temple. In this capacity he had delivered five lectures on the statute of uses to a large and learned audience, when the plague broke out in the Temple. He then left London for his house at Huntingfield, in Suffolk, on which occasion, to do him honor, nine benchers of the Temple and forty other templers accompanied him on his journey as far as Romford.

In 1592, Coke entered political life, being that year elected as the representative of Norfolk in the House of Commons.

In his political career he was devotedly loyal to the Queen—was what was called a high prerogative lawyer. But during the reign of King James, he appeared as a patriot and a reformer, which has occasioned charges of political inconsistency. This apparent inconsistency is by his friends accounted for by the difference in the characters of the reigning sovereigns, and by the advance of the commons in their demands in behalf of liberty.

The first parliament in which Coke appeared, was speedily prorogued, and it did not meet again for four years. Its duration was then short, and it met again in 1601.

In the parliament which met at Westminster, on the 19th of February, 1593, he was unanimously elected speaker. This honorable body was commanded by the Queen not to interfere with matters of Church or State. This injunction was by her communicated to the speaker, in person, and by him loyally delivered to the assembled parliament.

Sir Edward held the speakership but for one session; it being then not usual to hold it longer.

Almost immediately after the dissolution of the parliament of 1592, Sir Edward Coke was appointed the Queen's attorney-general; and he held that office during the rest of her reign.

In the year 1598, he lost his first wife, which may be regarded as the commencement of a series of misfortunes.

He soon again turned his thoughts to matrimony, prosecuting a successful treaty with Lady Elizabeth Hatton, the beautiful, young and wealthy widow of Sir William Hatton, the daughter of Thomas Cecil, first earl of Exeter, and granddaughter of the great Burleigh. This rash and ill-considered union commenced, continued, and terminated most disastrously. Both parties were ill-tempered, talented and haughty, with too much obstinacy to give way to each other. Moreover, the ordinances of the church were not duly observed, in the solemnization of the marriage. For this they were prosecuted in the Archbishop's court.

In 1606, Coke became Lord Chief-Justice of the Court of Common Pleas, and soon after was removed to the King's Bench.

Space cannot be here given to the causes and progress of the rivalry between Coke and Bacon. This contributed to his embarrassments. Coke managed, however, to surpass Bacon in the favor of the Queen.

On the 22d of May, 1603, Coke received the honor of knighthood, from the hands of King James I.

In the trial of Sir Walter Raleigh, which took place soon after, Coke appeared to little advantage. Such was his zeal in the service of his royal master, that he indulged in coarse language, brutal observations and a savage temper.

Nor was he less guilty of religious bigotry. His zeal for the established religion far outran his sense of justice.

The last important trial, in which he appeared as pleader, was the trial of the conspiracy case, growing out of the celebrated gunpowder plot.

Soon afterward, Coke somewhat redeemed himself from the reputation of being a mere courtier, by the bold and courageous stand which he took in favor of the rights and liberties of the judiciary, against certain prerogatives claimed in the royal behalf. It was in this contest that he acquired the reputation of being a reformer, and an advocate of liberty.

In 1614, Coke was elected high steward of the University of Cambridge. The next year he participated in a new series of state trials, of which there were so many during the reign of King James. These were the Overbury murder trials. About this time also he came in conflict with Bacon, in regard to the King's prerogative in interfering with the proceedings of the courts; the prerogative being sustained by Bacon and denied by Coke. Whether this resistance upon his part was based upon principle or is to be attributed to the natural obstinacy of his character, we are not called upon to decide. It is but fair to credit him with valuable service in the cause of liberty.

His opposition was so strong, that he was finally summoned to the King's council chamber, and after being reproved for his obstinacy, he was sentenced to be sequestered the council chamber until his Majesty's pleasure be farther known—was forbidden to ride his summer circuit as justice of assize, and it was ordered, that during the vacation, while he had time to live privately, and dispose himself at home, he take into consideration and review his book of reports, "wherein, as his Majesty is informed, be many extravagant and exorbitant opinions, set down and published for positive and good law." This sentence must be looked upon as the most honorable incident in the life of Sir Edward Coke.

On the 16th of November, 1616, not have made such changes in his reports as were satisfactory, Coke was, for this and for his obstinacy generally, dismissed from the Court of King's Bench. Six years afterward, he was even sent to the tower. When Lord Arundel was sent by the King to the prisoner to inform him that he would be allowed "eight of the best learned in the law to advise him for his cause," Coke, while thanking the King, sent for answer, "that he knew himself to be accounted to have as much skill in the law as any man in England, and therefore needed no such help, nor feared to be judged by the law." The real crime was, objecting to the illegal and arbitrary imposition of ship-money. It is said he owed the loss of his place to Villiers, Duke of Buckingham.

In 1616, we find Coke, at the age of 67, intriguing to be restored to the favor of the Court, and conspiring with Secretary Winwood against Chancellor Bacon, who had so long stood in his way. About the same time, he was involved in difficulty with his wife, Lady Hatton, in regard to the marriage of their daughter. It appears that Coke, in order to recover his interest at court, proposed to marry his daughter to Buckingham, then a royal favorite, and that, too, without consulting either mother or daughter. The opposition he encountered was to have been expected, and the whole affair places him in a very unfavorable light.

Lady Hatton carried off and secreted the daughter—Lord Coke, having discovered the place of her retreat, proceeded to the place and carried her away by force, he and his sons breaking through several doors, in order to obtain her. Lady Hatton complained to the privy council. But not long afterward a reconciliation was effected. This quarrel gave rise on the part of Coke's enemies to many sarcastic observations. Thus it was said of him:

"Cum pari certare dubium; cum rege stultum;
Cum puero clamor; cum muliere pudor."

Coke parted with a large portion of his estate for the endowment of his daughter, but did not thereby succeed in the accomplishment of his main object. Lady Hatton finally withdrew her opposition, and the marriage took place.

Coke's public life was not yet terminated, for though deprived of the Chief-Justiceship, he was again elected to the House of Commons; in which body he of course occupied a very high position.

In the trial of Chancellor Bacon, Coke was one of the accusers. But he appears to have refrained from taking a very prominent part in the prosecution, actuated, as is supposed, by feelings of forbearance towards his old and talented, though fallen competitor.

A parliament was summoned to meet on the 12th of February, 1624. Coke was returned to it from Coventry, of which city he still continued Recorder. About this time, having exposed himself to the vengeance of the King, having been, as a member of parliament, one of those who were alluded to in the royal proclamation, as "ill-tempered spirits" who had "sowed tares among the corn," he was, in company with Sir Robert Phillips, arrested and committed to the tower. He was about seventy-five years of age when this outrage was committed. The severity of the proceeding was somewhat mitigated by the consideration shown him in searching among his papers; special instruction having been given not to interfere with his valuable private papers. His imprisonment appears to have been of short duration; its object being to search for documents of a political character.

In 1624, Coke represented the House of Commons in the impeachment of the Earl of Middlesex. The Earl was defended by the King, but he was nevertheless convicted.

At the age of seventy-five, Coke was now leading in the work of parliamentary reform, and withstanding the encroachments of the crown, with all the vigor of his earlier years. In the first parliament of Charles I., we find him maintaining the struggle in which he had been so prominent in preceding parliaments. A specimen of this resistance to the royal prerogative, may be given:

On the 10th of April, 1627, the King sent a message to the House of Commons, desiring the members, in order to expedite the public business, not to make any recess as usual during the Easter holidays. Coke spoke of the King's message with dissatisfaction:

"I am as tender" said he, "of the privileges of this House as of my life, for they are the heart-strings of the commonwealth. The King makes a prorogation, but this House adjourns itself; the commission of adjournment we never read, but say, 'This

House adjourns itself.'"—(Parl. Hist. vol. 7, p. 436.)

The malice of his enemies pursued Coke in his old age. While yet on his death bed, Sir Francis Windebank came to his house at Stoke, by virtue of an order from the Privy Council, in search of certain seditious papers—at least such was the pretense. In his search for these papers he seized and carried away Coke's will, his life of Judge Littleton in his own handwriting, his commentary upon Littleton's Book of Tenures, and upon Magna Charta, Pleas of the Crown, and Jurisdiction of Courts, besides fifty-one other manuscripts. Seven years afterward, upon the motion of Sir Edward Coke's son, the King was requested by the House of Commons to restore these valuable papers to his family. His will was never recovered, but the remainder were, in consequence of this address, principally returned.

Coke had for a neighbor in his old age, the great Hampden, who made so successfully the resistance to ship-money.

Sir Edward Coke died on the 3d of September, 1633, in the eighty-third year of his age. He was a very remarkable man, of a most pronounced character. He has been called the glory of the English law.

His faults, which were very serious, were of a political and religious character. Though in middle life and in his old age he was a strenuous advocate of the rights of the people as represented in parliament, and fought nobly against the encroachments of the royal prerogative, in earlier life he pandered to the arrogance and cruelty of the crown, and prosecuted patriots without the slightest compunction.

So, too, as an advocate of protestantism—as defender of the royal faith, he could write letters and treatises upon the burning of catholics, without the slightest sign of disapprobation. Though great in some respects, he was not sufficiently great to free himself from the shackles of religious bigotry.

But Sir Edward Coke was never accused or even suspected of bribery or corruption. No orphan denounced him—no widow execrated his name for a betrayal of trust. He had the reputation, not only of being the greatest jurist of his age, but of acting uprightly and fearlessly in the administration of justice.

COKE'S REPORTS IN VERSE.

The following are some of the attempts which have been made to reduce the reports of each case to a verse of two lines:

HUBBARD. If lord impose excessive fine,
The tenant safely payment may decline.

4 Rep. 27.

SNAGG. If a person says, "he killed my wife,"
No action lies, if she be yet alive.

4 Rep. 16.

GAUDEY. 'Gainst common prayer if parson say
In sermon aught, bishop deprive him may.

5 Rep. 1.

Also a law report converted into song:

A woman having a settlement,
Married a man with none.
The question was, he being dead,
If that she had was gone.

Quoth Sir John Pratt, her settlement
Suspended did remain,
Living her husband, but him dead,
It doth revive again.

Here, also, is a rendering in verse of Coke's Littleton, sec. 1:
"Tenant in fee simple, is he which hath lands or tenements to hold to him and his heirs for ever," etc.

Tenant in fee
Simple, is he,
And need neither quake or quiver,
Who hath his lands,
Free from demands,
For him and his heirs forever.

JOSEPH STORY.

AN ADDITIONAL WORD.

Of all those who have honored the legal profession, no one has more truly honored woman than Judge Joseph Story. Hence, as a woman, I would like to add a few words to the biographical sketch of him found in the January number of the CHICAGO LAW TIMES.

Josiah Quincy in some reminiscences of him (Figures of the Past), said he felt safe in saying that Judge Story was above the prominent men of his day in the adoption of views respecting women very similar to those afterward proclaimed by Mr. Mill. He would not admit that sex or temperament assigned them an inferior part in the intellectual development of the race. It was all a matter of training. Give them opportunities of physical and mental education equal to those enjoyed by men, and there was nothing to disqualify them from attaining an equal success in any field of mental effort. This was the conclusion Mr. Quincy gained from an inimitable stage-coach conversation which passed between Judge Story and himself, while journeying from Boston to Washington, in January, 1826.

Mr. Quincy's acquaintance with him had begun when, as an undergraduate, he had dined with him in Salem, Mass., during a visit to that town. He was then fascinated with the brilliancy of his conversation. Now, as at the "base of the profession which Judge Story adorned," he regarded him with peculiar reverence, and felt highly honored to be invited to join him on his annual journey to Washington, where, as Associate Justice of the United States Supreme Court, he spent the winter months.

Judge Story, on this occasion, was unusually brilliant, although he was noted as one of the most brilliant conversationalists of the day.   Having spent a part of the previous summer in traveling with Daniel Webster, he had fresh subjects for conversation.   There was one thing, however, he did not talk about, and that was law.   He recited original poetry with evident pleasure.   This, however, was before he had bought up and burned all the copies he could find of his *Power of Solitude.*

On this journey—(They were only four days going to New York, upon which they congratulated themselves, when thinking of the week's time their ancestors needed), he discussed literary matters; but it was the conversation on novels, in its appreciative knowledge of woman's work which makes the journey worthy of notice here.   After speaking of Mrs. Radcliffe in terms of admiration, he wished she could have had "some of the weird legends of Marblehead upon which to display her wealth of lurid imagery."   Those who not only know the legends of Marblehead but who have visited the old town, best appreciate what this wish implied.

Continuing his criticism of novels, he thought Miss Burney's *Evelina* was very "bright and fascinating," while the conversations of Maria Edgeworth were "nature itself and yet full of point—the duller speeches of her characters being simply omitted as was proper in a work of art."   He showed that natural chivalry and broad mind which so impressed Mr. Quincy when he said: "It is only the nature of their education which puts women at such disadvantages and keeps up the notion that they are our inferiors in ability..   What would a man be without his profession or business which compels him to learn something new every day?   The best sources of knowledge are shut off from women. and the surprise is that they manage to keep so nearly abreast of men as they do."   I never visit any of our now established colleges for women that I am not reminded of these words of Judge Story, spoken over sixty years ago, and I think how he would have enjoyed the society of the young women whose minds are enlarged by the "best sources of knowledge."   He had glimpses, however, of this joy in woman's development, in his friendship with Harriet Martineau, with whom he had a charmingly frank correspondence.

The summer following this memorable stage ride, Judge Story in the closing words of a discourse delivered at the anniversary of the Phi Beta Kappa Society, in Cambridge, Massachusetts, in August, 1826, more fully proclaimed his knowledge and appreciation of woman's work. "Who is there," he asked, "that does not contemplate with enthusiasm the precious fragments of Elizabeth Smith, the venerable learning of Elizabeth Carter, the devoted piety of Hannah More, the persuasive sense of Mrs. Barbauld, the eloquent memoirs of her accomplished niece, the bewitching fictions of Mme. D'Arblay, the vivid, picturesque and terrific imagery of Mrs. Radcliffe, the glowing poetry of Mrs. Hemans, the matchless wit, the inexhaustible conversations, the fine character painting, the practical instructions of Miss Edgeworth—the great *known* standing in her own department by the side of the great *unknown?*"

How such a soul would have enjoyed and complimented the work of Mrs. Browning, George Eliot, or the New England tales of our own Miss Jewett, had they then existed! But why was not Jane Austen mentioned? It is certain Chief-Justice Marshall thus wondered, for, after having read the address, he sent his friend the following letter, which, as revealing another chivalrous friend to woman's work in the legal profession, deserves a place here: "I have read it (the address) with real pleasure, and am particularly gratified with your eulogy on the ladies. It is a matter of great satisfaction to me to find another judge, who, though not as old as myself, thinks justly of the fair sex and commits his sentiments to print. I was a little mortified, however, to find that you had not admitted the name of Miss Austen into your list of favorites. I had just finished reading her novels when I received your discourse and was so much pleased with them that I looked in it for her name and was rather disappointed at not finding it. Her flights are not lofty; she does not soar on eagle's wings, but she is pleasing, interesting, equable and yet amusing. I count on your making some apology for this omission."

As there seems to be no apology, it is possible that this letter introduced Jane Austen to Judge Story. He did not speak of her in the stage ride, but, in a much later conversation Mr. Quincy says he talked freely of her, placing her much above Miss Burney and Maria Edgeworth, and complimenting her with a "panegyric quite equal to those bestowed by Scott and Macauley." His son, Wm. W. Story, also tells in his biography of his father, that when he was engaged in making a bust of him in marble, to beguile the time he had his daughter read to him Jane Austen's *Emma.* Scarcely a year passed, he said, that his father did not read more than one of her works and with an interest that never flagged.

A study of Judge Story's life reveals several causes for this innate deference to woman, manifested not only in his home life, but in every relation where woman enters man's career. Only those cognizant of the laxity in this direction, especially among the old English barristers, can realize the value of the legacy thus left to the American bar by the learned Joseph Story. One of these causes was the deference his father ever paid to his mother's judgment. She took great interest in passing events, and in politics, which her grandson says, she read with avidity and strong personal feeling even to her death. It is a significant fact, to be particularly pondered at this time, that the mothers of John Quincy Adams, Josiah Quincy, the great Boston mayor, and other notable men of that day were deeply interested in public events, especially politics, even to the time of old age and death.

Another influence upon the young mind of Joseph Story, was his attendance, until he was fifteen years of age, at the Marblehead Academy, where girls went the same hours and studied the same books as the boys. This experience was in his mind when, in later life, he said he was early struck with the "flexibility, activity and power of the female mind. Girls of the same age were on an average of numbers quite our equals in their studies and acquirements, (See in *Education* for March, 1889, an article on the Mental Capacity of the Sexes, proving this by statistics) and had much greater quickness of perception and delicacy of feeling than the boys." His impression was that the principal difference in intellectual power resulted not so much from "original inferiority of mind as from the fact that education stops with women almost at the time it effectively begins with men."

A later influence was that of the small societies in Salem, composed of both sexes, one or more of which he joined while settled there as a young lawyer. These, under such fantastic names as the *Moscheto Fleet, the Antediluvians, the Sans Souci, the Social Group*, were formed to promote social intercourse. One of his lady friends said of him at this time: "He was a very handsome young man, with the air and manners of a gentleman. He was a great and general favorite with young ladies, who always felt flattered by his attentions. Perfect propriety was one of his distinguishing traits."

Out of this circle he married the young woman of whom he wrote after her death six months later: "In losing my wife, I have lost the companion of my studies, the participator of my ambition, the consoler of my sorrows, and the defender of my frailties."

The new domestic life, which, after several years of grief and bitter loneliness, came to him, also proved the capacity of the learned lawyer to fully assimilate affection's blessings. The pictures of the peaceful home life linger like a benediction. He left all his law in his library, and, his son tells us, spent his evenings, when at home, in receiving his friends, listening to music, talking with his family, and what was very common, in playing a game of backgammon. This was the only game of the kind he liked, cards and chess never claiming his attention. He brought to the home a sunny temperament and that certain purity of atmosphere which ever delights the woman heart; for he was one of the comparatively few who had passed through the dangerous period of college life and early manhood without a stain or reproach. His son tells us he never used tobacco in any form, and never tasted wine or spirituous liquors, until he was thirty-two years of age—the year he began his duties as United States Judge—when he was advised by a physician to take a little wine for his stomach's sake; for hard, protracted study had told on his physical nature.

As the years roll on, developing the ideas involved in the

great moral movements of this century, especially the woman movement, such well rounded, balanced men as Joseph Story will more and more receive the respect of men as well as women; for purity of life is more and more to be demanded as a necessary accompaniment of great mental and legal attainments.   In the realization of a larger, a better civilization, the purely one-sided genius will disappear.

A few years since, I was visiting the quaint old town of Marblehead.   While viewing the Town House—a building in its prime in the days of George III.—a house nearly opposite, was pointed out to me as the birthplace of Judge Joseph Story. While gazing upon it, many things came back to me which I had read and heard concerning the eminent jurist, whose loyalty to woman in all the relations of life equaled his great legal abilities and his high judicial honors.

Elizabeth Porter Gould.

SPRINGER AMENDMENT
TO THE FEDERAL CONSTITUTION.

The following amendment to the Constitution of the United States is proposed by Congressman Springer, of Illinois:

ARTICLE XV*

The Congress shall have power to make a uniform law of marriage and divorce.

Appended hereto are the causes of divorce, in this country, compiled from the Revised Statutes and subsequent session laws of the various States.

From this summary it will be seen that there is less real diversity in the divorce laws of the different States than many suppose.

Leaving out of the account South Carolina, in which State, though for certain causes the marriage is void or may be declared void, there is no law of divorce, we find that adultery is a cause for divorce, in every State. In three only, is there any difference in this respect, whether the adultery is committed by wife or husband. In Kentucky, adultery by the wife is sufficient, but it is necessary that the husband should be living in adultery. So in North Carolina and Texas, the act on the part of the wife is sufficient, while the husband must be separated and living in adultery. In Texas, he must have abandoned his wife.

Again, in all the States but two, Connecticut and Louisiana, impotency is cause for divorce, or for declaring the marriage void. In many of the States, it must have existed at the time of the marriage, and in some, it must be continuing at the time of application for divorce.

In all the States, abandonment is cause for divorce. The difference is in time of absence. But that may be considered matter of evidence; the question being the intent to abandon. In Virginia and Louisiana, that intent will not be considered sufficiently proved, until there has been an absence of five years. In Rhode Island it may be five years or less in the discretion of the Court. In Connecticut, Delaware, Georgia, Maryland, Maine, Massachusetts, Minnesota, New Jersey, Texas, West Virginia, Vermont and Ohio, the time specified is three years. In Alabama, Illinois; Indiana, Michigan, Mississippi, Iowa, Nebraska and Pennsylvania, two years will suffice, while in Arkansas, Colorado, Florida, Kansas, Kentucky, Missouri, Nevada, Oregon, Wisconsin, Washington and Montana, one year is deemed sufficient. In California, New Hampshire, Tennessee, North and South Dakota, New York and North Carolina, the abandonment may be proven by any competent evidence, without reference to the time of absence. But in New York and North Carolina the divorce from this cause can only be from bed and board.

In some States divorce can be obtained for absence a certain number of years without being heard from—willful absence a certain number of years, etc.

Again, cruelty is cause for divorce in all the States; though in Michigan, New York, New Jersey, North Carolina, Virginia, West Virginia, Georgia and Maryland, only separation from bed and board can be obtained for this cause. In Nebraska, the divorce may be complete, or from bed and board only; so also in Tennessee, at the discretion of the Court. The degree and nature of the cruelty are differently characterized in different States. Thus, in Virginia, Washington, Georgia and Maryland, it is simply cruelty, or cruel treatment; in California, Colorado, Delaware, Florida, Kansas, Nebraska, Maine, Massachusetts, Rhode Island, New Hampshire, Nevada, Michigan, Ohio, Montana and New Jersey, it is extreme cruelty; Illinois, extreme and repeated cruelty; Connecticut, intolerable cruelty; in Indiana, Minnesota, New York, Oregon, Tennessee,

Wisconsin, and West Virginia, cruel and inhuman treatment; in Vermont, intolerable severity; etc., etc. In Alabama, Arkansas, Iowa, Missouri, Pennsylvania and North Carolina, it must endanger life. In Kentucky only is any time specified. In that State, the statute requires cruel and inhuman behavior for six months. But cruel beating or injury, or attempt to commit such personal violence, is made a special cause, without reference to duration of time.

Habitual drunkenness is a cause for divorce in thirty-three States. In Arkansas, Colorado, Kentucky, Minnesota, Missouri, Oregon and Montana, it must have continued one year; in Illinois, two years; in New Hampshire and Ohio three years. In Wisconsin, if the wife is given to intoxication, it is cause of divorce in favor of the husband, but on his part, the habit must have been of one year's continuance. In Kentucky, it must be accompanied by a failure to provide for the family.

In Georgia, North Carolina and West Virginia, drunkenness is cause for divorce from bed and board only.

In twenty-eight States, having former husband or wife living, is either cause for divorce, or, as in most cases, the marriage is on that account, void or voidable.

In thirty-five States, imprisonment for, or conviction of felony or other infamous crime is cause for divorce; in Alabama, Kansas, New Hampshire, Ohio, Texas, Vermont and Washington, actual imprisonment is required; in the others, conviction is sufficient. In New Hampshire, the imprisonment must be for more than a year; in Vermont, under sentence for three years or more; in Alabama, two years, under sentence for seven years or more. In Maine, sentence to imprisonment for life and confinement under it, render the marriage void. In some of the States, which require conviction and sentence only, the sentence must be for life or a term of years.

Here are the seven principal causes of divorce. Adultery, abandonment or cruelty is sufficient in all the States; impotency in all but two, while habitual drunkenness, crime, or having former husband or wife living, is sufficient in a large majority of them.

Thus there is a consensus of the States upon the subject,

growing out of a common understanding as to the mutual obligations of husband and wife. These obligations are well summed up in the Ohio statute:

"Husband and wife contract toward each other obligations of mutual respect, fidelity and support."

It will be noticed that there are in some of the States special causes of divorce, which do not prevail in the others. And in Maryland and Rhode Island, divorce may be obtained when the marriage was void; in the latter State also when it is voidable merely. In the absence of any statutory provision upon the subject, the courts would refuse to grant a divorce for cause which rendered the marriage void; there not being. in that case, any binding marriage, such as would be necessary to sustain the decree.—(See Finn v. Finn, 62 How. [N. Y.] Pr. 83.)

In South Carolina, the marriage is void when there was a former husband or wife living, with certain exceptions specified. Also marriages between whites and colored people, are declared by statute null and void. Marriages are voidable also for want of consent, or when for other cause not valid.

There is, however, as before stated, no law of divorce in South Carolina. By Act of 1878, all divorce laws in that State were repealed. The State Constitution gives the Courts of Common Pleas jurisdiction in cases of divorce. But Art. XIV requires a judgment of a court "as shall be pronounced by law;" and in Grant v. Grant, 12 S. C. 31, it was held that in the absence of a law authorizing such a judgment, none could be pronounced.

In order to decide upon the merits of the Springer Amendment, it is necessary to consider, first, whether a uniform divorce law is desirable; and secondly, whether if it is desirable, this is the proper way to bring it about.

First, is a uniform divorce law desirable? Its utility and desirability are not so great as might at first sight appear. It is those who favor more stringent divorce laws who are the most urgent in this movement, but they overlook the fact that the result would be directly the opposite of that for which they are working. The majority must prevail, and the majority are in favor of liberal divorce.

If, therefore, a general divorce law should be established by national authority, it would be a law of a liberal character. The result would be, that those who might desire a divorce, and who would be entitled to it according to the present law in most of the States, but who now are unable to obtain it in their own States, would, instead of going as they are now obliged to do, into another State to reside for that purpose, retain their residence, and get the divorce at home. The few States which are conservative upon the subject, would surrender their preferences and their independence of action, without receiving any corresponding benefit. If a liberal system of divorce is an advantage, we have it now. What matters it, whether it be by State or federal authority? If, on the other hand, the object be to reverse the policy of the country, by placing the legislation where it would naturally be more conservative, and where, being somewhat more removed from the people, it would less faithfully reflect their views and wishes, then that object is of itself sufficient to condemn the measure, since it is an attack upon the republican character of our institutions.

Secondly, conceding, for the sake of the argument, that a uniform divorce law is desirable, is this the proper mode to obtain it?

Why resort to an amendment of the federal Constitution? Or what necessity for national interference? How do we know the State Legislatures would not pass uniform laws if appealed to? Not the slightest attempt has been made to induce them to do so. Let a committee be appointed, consisting of one prominent citizen of each State, to consult and adopt a draft of a uniform law, and let that law be submitted to the Legislature of each State, with a memorial setting forth the advantages of the proposed law. We have no right to assume that the States would not all pass such an act; and if they should once pass it, the same considerations that induced them to enact the law, would prevail to preserve it afterward from material amendment.

Let the principle of comity be first invoked. If that fails, it will then be time enough to contemplate the system of force implied in a constitutional amendment. Such an amendment means that the policy prevailing in three- fourths of the States, shall be forced upon the other fourth, whether they wish it or no; since three-fourths of the States, by ratifying the amendment, can say that the power shall be transferred from the States to the general government, and afterward the same three-fourths can decide upon the character of the law.

Even should the principle of comity fail altogether, there will still remain very serious objections to the proposed amendment.

It is an unnecessary transfer of power from the States to the general government, and thus an unnecessary disturbing of the balance of power between the States and the nation, the maintenance of which is so essential to the preservation of our liberties.

All that was urged upon this ground against the Blair Amendment [See Law Times for April], is equally applicable here.

It is strange that such a proposition should have been introduced into Congress by a democrat; being as it is, so palpably in violation of the principle of popular sovereignty, so ably advocated by Stephen A. Douglas.

When Mr. Springer introduces his joint resolution, he virtually says: "Illinois is unable properly to regulate her own domestic affairs, and asks the aid of the other States." Or else, assuming that the other States are incapable of enacting such laws as the good of the people requires, in matters of purely domestic concern, he offers the aid of Illinois. Nay, more; he is willing that three-fourths of the States, including Illinois, should coerce the other fourth into the adoption of their views concerning the marriage relation. Or else, he is willing that Illinois should be forced, by three-fourths of the States, to change her domestic policy.

Chicago being a great divorce center, there is an idea, more or less prevalent, that the divorce laws of Illinois are very liberal. But this is a mistake. They are more conservative than the average, outside of New York. While divorce can be obtained in nearly all the States for extreme cruelty, in Illinois, "extreme and repeated cruelty" is required. While in thirty

States, habitual drunkenness is sufficient, continued for one year in some States, and in others with no time specified, in Illinois, it must be continued two years. In regard to abandonment, it is about on an average. In seven States, no time is specified; in eleven, one year; in two, five years; in twelve, three years; while in eight, Illinois included, it is two years.

The number of divorces in Chicago, is to be accounted for by the rapid growth and metropolitan character of the City, and the desire which seizes upon every one who goes there to reside, to better his or her condition as soon as possible. This state of affairs will gradually change as the City becomes older. The cause is too deep seated to be effected by constitutional changes.

There is a mania in some quarters, for changing the Constitution. Some of the ablest jurists of the country have lately expressed the opinion, that it requires no amendment. None of those proposed should be adopted, unless it be the one upon the suffrage question; and even that, meritorious as it is—fully justified as it would be by the fact that the general government had already taken jurisdiction of the suffrage question—affecting as it does, the rights of half the citizens—even that it would be better to waive, and leave the whole question of suffrage to State action, if that amendment is to open the door for all sorts of amendments upon every conceivable subject.

It has hitherto been supposed that the federal government was for national purposes; and that domestic affairs were to be left to the States. But now it is proposed that the general government take jurisdiction over the relations between husband and wife. Why not over all other subjects of legislation? What is there peculiar in this relation, to throw it into the hands of Congress? Why call upon the States to surrender their power to legislate upon the subject? Why should a State in favor of liberal divorce laws be forced to have stringent ones? or vice versa? Why should South Carolina, which does not want divorce laws, be forced to have them? Why should the people of the great State of New York, who do not believe in divorce except for adultery, be forced to grant divorces for other causes?

A federal divorce law must be executed through the federal courts. It has been suggested in some of the newspapers that the law would be carried out by the agency of the State courts. But it may be safely assumed that such a suggestion did not come from a member of the bar. Every lawyer knows that it would be necessary at once for the federal judiciary to take control over the whole subject. What kind of a national law would that be which should depend for its execution upon the voluntary action of State officers, or upon the voluntary action of a State, compelling its officers to carry it into effect?

It is too manifest for argument that the whole adjudication of that class of cases would be transferred from the State to the federal courts, and behold what a change that would involve. If the State courts are to surrender such an extensive part of their jurisdiction, why not surrender it all? Why keep up the expense of State governments and of a State judiciary, if the federal government and the federal courts are to make such extensive inroads upon their jurisdiction?

The conclusion is, that the Springer Amendment is not a matter of national necessity or of national concern; and that no amendment of any other character can be justified, except by some emergency in the administration of the government, which, in this case, does not exist.

Charles B. Waite.

CAUSES OF DIVORCE.

[Unless the husband or the wife is expressly or by necessary implication separately referred to, the cause of divorce is common to both parties.]

ALABAMA.—Divorce, for incapacity; adultery; abandonment for 2 years; imprisonment in the penitentiary for 2 years under sentence for 7 years or more; crime against nature; habitual drunkenness; pregnancy of the wife at the time of the marriage, by another person, without the knowledge of the husband; actual violence by husband attended with danger to life or health. or reasonable apprehension of such violence.—(Code of Ala. 1886, vol. 1, pp. 523-4, secs. 2322, 2324.)

ARKANSAS.—For impotency; desertion for one year; former husband or wife living at the time of the marriage; conviction of felony or other infamous crime; habitual drunkenness for one year; cruel and barbarous treatment, endangering life; indignities rendering condition intolerable; adultery; permanent or incurable insanity, occurring subsequent to marriage.—(Dig. of Ark. St. 1884, p. 580; sec. 2556.)

CALIFORNIA.—Annullment of Marriage, for want of legal consent; former husband or wife living; being of unsound mind; consent obtained by fraud or force; continuing incapacity.

Divorce, for adultery; extreme cruelty; desertion; willful neglect; habitual intemperance; conviction of felony.—(Deering's Annotated Code of 1885, pp. 28, 32; secs. 82, 92.)

COLORADO.—Impotency continued, (see condition in Act of April 9, 1885, Session Laws, p. 189); former wife or husband living; adultery; desertion for one year, or desertion and absence from the State with no intention of returning; failure of husband for one year, to make any provision for support of his family; habitual drunkenness for one year; extreme cruelty; conviction of felony or other infamous crime.—(Gen. St. of Col. 1883, p. 397, § 1093.)

CONNECTICUT.—Adultery; fraudulent contract; desertion for 3 years; absence 7 years without being heard from; habitual intemperance; intolerable cruelty; sentence to imprisonment for life; infamous crime involving violation of conjugal duty, and punishable by imprisonment in State prison.—(Gen. St. of Conn. 1888, p. 612, sec. 2802.)

DELAWARE.—Divorce, for adultery; desertion for three years; habitual drunkenness; impotency; extreme cruelty; conviction after marriage, of a felony.

Divorce from bonds, etc., or from bed and board, at the discretion of the Court; for procurement of marriage by fraud for want of age; willful neglect by husband for 3 years to provide necessaries for wife.—(Rev. Code of Del. 1874, p. 475.)

FLORIDA.—Being within the prohibited degrees; impotence; adultery; former husband or wife living; extreme cruelty; violent and ungovernable temper; habitual intemperance; desertion for one year; when the other party has obtained divorce in another State or territory.—(McClellan's Dig. Laws of Flor. 1881, pp. 472, 473; ch. 93, secs. 4, 5, 7.)

GEORGIA.—Intermarriage within the prohibited degrees; mental incapacity or impotency; force, menaces, duress or fraud in obtaining the marriage; pregnancy of the wife. etc.. as in Alabama; adultery; desertion for 3 years; conviction and sentence to imprisonment in the penitentiary for 2 years or longer.

Partial Divorce (Bed and Board).—Cruel treatment; habitual intoxication; any ground which was held sufficient in the English courts prior to May 4, 1784.—(Code of Geo. 1882, secs. 1712-13-14.)

ILLINOIS.—Impotency; former wife or husband living; adultery; desertion for 2 years; habitual drunkenness for 2 years; malicious attempt to take the life of husband or wife; extreme and repeated cruelty; conviction of an infamous crime.—(Starr and Curtis' Annot. St. Ill. p. 885.) [By Act of June 15, 1887, Session Laws, p. 225, various marriages, including those between cousins of first degree, were declared void.]

INDIANA.—Adultery; impotency; abandonment for 2 years; cruel and inhuman treatment; habitual drunkenness; failure of husband for 2 years to make provision for his family; conviction subsequent to the marriage, of an infamous crime.—(Rev. St. of Ind. 1888, sec. 1032.)

IOWA.—Adultery; desertion 2 years; conviction of felony after marriage; habitual drunkenness; inhuman treatment endangering life; when the wife at the time of the marriage was pregnant by another, unless the husband have an illegitimate child or children then living, which was unknown to the wife.—(McClains' Annot. St. 1888, vol. 1, pp. 891, 893, secs. 3414, 3415.)
Marriage voidable for impotency, insanity or idiocy, or having former husband or wife living. Also, when prohibited by law.—(Ibid. p. 897, sec. 3422.)

KANSAS.—Former husband or wife living; abandonment for one year; adultery; impotency; wife pregnant, etc., as in Alabama; extreme cruelty; fraudulent contract; habitual drunkenness; gross neglect of duty; conviction of felony and imprisonment in the penitentiary therefor.—(Dassler's Laws of Kan. 1885. p. 687, sec. 4457.)

KENTUCKY.—Impotency; living apart 5 years; abandonment for one year; living in adultery; condemnation for felony; concealment of any loathsome disease existing at the time of marriage, or contracting such afterward; marriage induced by force, duress or fraud; uniting with any religious society whose creed and rules are inconsistent with the marriage relation; habitual drunkenness for one year, without provision for maintenance of family; cruel and inhuman behavior for 6 months; cruel beating or injury or attempt; pregnancy of wife, etc., as in Alabama; adultery or lewd, lascivious behavior by wife.—(Gen. St. Ky. 1887, pp. 727, 728.)

LOUISIANA.—Adultery; habitual intemperance; excess, cruel treatment or outrages, rendering the marriage relation insupportable; condemnation to an ignominious punishment; abandonment for 5 years; being guilty of an infamous offense and fleeing from justice.—(Voorhies' Rev. St. 1876, sec, 1190, p. 312.) [By Act of April 8, 1884, Session Laws, p. 365, marriages between whites and negroes to 3d generation, declared void.]

MAINE.—Prohibited marriages, void. Marriages are also void on account of sentence to imprisonment for life and confinement under it.

Divorce.—Adultery; impotence; extreme cruelty; desertion for 3 years; gross and confirmed habits of intoxication; cruel and abusive treatment; gross, wanton and cruel refusal or neglect to provide maintenance.—(Rev. St. 1883, pp. 520, 521.)

MARYLAND.—Impotence; adultery; abandonment for 3 years; previous illicit intercourse with another man. Also when marriage is void, ab initio.

A Mensa et Thoro.—Cruelty; excessively vicious conduct; abandonment and desertion.—(Rev. Code, 1878, pp. 480, 481.)

Marriage within the prohibited degrees is void.—(Ibid. p. 478.)

MASSACHUSETTS.—Adultery; impotency; extreme cruelty; desertion for 3 years; gross and confirmed habits of intoxication; cruel and abusive treatment; failure to provide maintenance, as above; separating and uniting with a religious sect, etc., (see Ky.), continued 3 years; sentence to confinement at hard labor for 5 years or more.—(Pub. St. Mass. 1882-7, p. 813.)

MICHIGAN.—Marriage void.—Within the prohibited degrees; former husband or wife living; one of the parties insane or idiot, (Act of April 11, 1883, Session Laws, p. 17); also want of legal consent: consent obtained by force or fraud.

Divorce.—Adultery; incompetency; sentence to imprisonment for 3 years or more; desertion 2 years; habitual drunkenness; divorce by the other party in another State.

From Bed and Board.—Extreme cruelty; desertion for 2 years; gross, or wanton and cruel neglect by husband to provide maintenance.—(Howell's Annot. St. 1882, secs. 6223-6229.)

MINNESOTA.—Marriage void.—Within the degrees; former husband or wife living. Voidable.—Absence 5 years; want of age; force or fraud.—(St. 1878-1888, vol 1, p. 626, secs. 1, 2.)

Divorce.—Adultery; impotency; cruel and inhuman treatment; sentence to imprisonment in State prison; desertion 3 years; habitual drunkenness one year.—(Ibid. p. 626, sec. 6.)

Limited Divorce. (From Bed and Board.)—Cruel and inhuman treatment; such conduct by husband as may render it unsafe and improper for wife to cohabit: abandonment by husband; his refusal or neglect to provide.—(Ibid. p. 630, sec. 31.)

MISSISSIPPI.—Being within the degrees; impotence; adultery; sentence to the penitentiary; desertion 2 years; habitual drunkenness; habitual cruel and inhuman treatment, marked by personal violence; pregnancy of the wife, etc., as in Alabama; former husband or wife living; insanity; idiocy.—(Rev. Code, Miss. 1880, p. 337, secs. 1155–1157.)

MISSOURI.—Impotency, continued; former husband or wife living; adultery; absence without reasonable cause for one year; conviction of felony or infamous crime; habitual drunkenness for one year; cruel or barbarous treatment endangering life; indignities rendering the condition of the other intolerable; husband becoming a vagrant; pregnancy of wife, etc., as in Alabama.—(Rev. St. Mo. 1879, vol. 1, p. 360, sec 2174.)

MONTANA.—Impotence; former husband or wife living; adultery; absence without reasonable cause one year; desertion and absence of husband from the State without intention of returning; habitual drunkenness for one year; extreme cruelty; conviction of felony or other infamous crime.—(Compiled St. Mont. 1887, p. 919, sec. 999.)

NEBRASKA.—Marriage voidable when under the age of legal consent, or when obtained by force or fraud.—(Annot. St. Neb. 1887, p. 381, sec. 2.)
Divorce.—Adultery; incompetency; sentence to imprisonment for 3 years or more; abandonment for 2 years; habitual drunkenness.—(Ibid. p. 382, sec. 6.)
Divorce from Bonds of Matrimony or from Bed and Board.—Extreme cruelty; desertion for 2 years; gross or wanton and cruel refusal or neglect of husband to provide maintenance.—(Ibid. p. 382, sec. 7.)

NEVADA.—Marriages within prohibited degrees, and when former husband or wife was living, are void.—(Gen. St. Nev. 1885, p. 139, sec. 487.)
Voidable, for want of age or understanding, or for fraud.—(Ibid. p. 140, sec. 488.)
Divorce.—Impotency; adultery; desertion for one year; conviction of felony or infamous crime; habitual, gross drunkenness; extreme cruelty; neglect of husband for one year, to provide, when not the result of poverty.—(Ibid. p. 488, sec. 491.)

NEW HAMPSHIRE.—Marriages within the prohibited degrees, or when former husband or wife was living, are void.—(Gen. Laws N. H. 1878, p. 431, sec. 1.)
Divorce.—Impotency; adultery; extreme cruelty; imprisonment under conviction for more than a year; such treatment as seriously to injure health or endanger reason; absence without being heard from for 3 years; habitual drunkenness for 3 years; joining any religious sect whose teachings are inconsistent with the marriage relation and refusal to cohabit for 6 months; abandonment; absence of either for 3 years, the husband, when

absent, not providing for maintenance; absence of wife from the State 10 years without the husband's consent; husband having left the United States with intention of becoming a citizen of some foreign country, without making provision for maintenance.—(Ibid. p. 432, sec. 3.)

NEW JERSEY.—Former wife or husband living, [marriage also void;] being within prohibited degrees; adultery; desertion for 3 years, [construed by Act of April 1, 1887, Session Laws, p. 132]; impotency.

Divorce from Bed and Board, for extreme cruelty.—(Rev'n of N. J. 1709-1877, vol. 1, p. 315, secs. 2–5.) [No change in Supplement, 1877–1886.]

NEW YORK.—Marriage voidable when the woman was under 14 years of age, (Made 16 by Act of Feb. 21, 1887); for want of consent of father, mother, guardian or legal custodian; also when either party was under the age of legal consent; when former husband or wife was living; for idiocy or lunacy; for force, duress or fraud; for continuing incapacity.—(Throop's Annot. Code. 1885, Pt. 2, p. 116, secs. 1742, 1743.)

Divorce, for adultery.—(Ibid. p. 122, sec. 1756.)

Separation from Bed and Board.—Cruel and inhuman treatment; conduct rendering it unsafe or improper to cohabit; abandonment; refusal of husband to provide.—(Ibid. p. 126, sec. 1762.)

NORTH CAROLINA.—Voidable.—Marriage within the prohibited degrees; marriage of a male under 16, or a female under 14; when former husband or wife was living; for impotency or incapacity of contracting.—. (Code of N. C. 1883, vol 1, p. 688, sec. 1810.)

Marriage between a white person and negro or Indian to 3d generation, void.—(Ibid. p. 513, sec. 1284.)

Dissolution of Marriage, and Divorce.—Separation and living in adultery; adultery by the wife; impotency continued; pregnancy of the wife, etc., as in Alabama.

Divorce from Bed and Board.—Abandonment; malicious turning out of doors; cruel or barbarous treatment, endangering life; indignities to person, rendering condition intolerable and life burdensome; habitual drunkenness.—(Ibid. p. 514, secs. 1285, 1286.)

NORTH DAKOTA.—Marriages within prohibited degrees, or when former husband or wife was living, are void.

Voidable, for incapacity; consent obtained by force or fraud; want of legal consent, or of sound mind.—(Comp. Laws of Dak. 1887, p. 545, secs. 2537, 2538, 2539, 2553.)

Divorce.—Adultery; extreme cruelty; desertion; willful neglect; habitual intemperance; conviction of felony.—(Ibid. sec. 2559.)

OHIO.—Former husband or wife living; willful absence 3 years; adultery; impotency; extreme cruelty; fraudulent contract; gross neglect of duty: habitual drunkenness for 3 years: imprisonment in a penitentiary under sentence; procurement of divorce by the other party without the State.—(Rev. St. 1886, vol. 2, p. 1197, sec. 5689.)

OREGON.—Marriage within the prohibited degrees, or when former husband or wife was living, or either party being qne-fourth or more of negro blood, are void.

Voidable, for want of assent, or when obtained by force or fraud.—(Hill's Annot. Laws, 1887, vol. 1, p. 451, secs. 490, 491. Act of Feb. 21, 1887, Session Laws, p. 52.)

Dissolution or Divorce.—Impotency continued; adultery; conviction of felony; habitual, gross drunkenness for one year: desertion for one year; cruel and inhuman treatment, or personal indignities rendering life burdensome.—(Ibid. p. 452, sec. 495.)

PENNSYLVANIA.—Impotency continued; former husband or wife living; adultery; desertion and absence without reasonable cause 2 years; barbarous treatment endangering life of the wife, or indignities to her person rendering her condition intolerable and life burdensome; marriage within the prohibited degrees, or procured by fraud, force or coercion: conviction of felony and sentence for more than 2 years: condition of husband rendered intolerable or life burdensome from cruel and barbarous treatment by the wife.—(Brightly's Purdon's Dig. 1700–1883, vol. 1, pp. 611, 613, secs. 1, 2, 7.)

From Bed and Board.—Adultery: abandonment by husband: turning wife out of doors.—(Ibid. p. 616, sec. 25.)

RHODE ISLAND.—Divorce may be obtained when marriage is void or voidable; in case either party is for crime deemed to be civilly dead, or may be presumed to be naturally dead; for impotency: adultery: extreme cruelty; desertion for 5 years, or desertion for a shorter period in discretion of the court; continued drunkenness: neglect or refusal of husband to provide: any gross misbehavior and wickedness, repugnant to and in violation of the marriage contract.—(Pub. St. R. I. 1882, p. 426, secs. 1 and 2.)

Divorce from Bed and Board, for any of above and for such other causes as may seem to require the same.—(Ibid. p. 427, sec. 11.)

SOUTH CAROLINA.—Marriage voidable for want of consent. or when for other cause not valid. Void when former husband or wife was living, [with certain exceptions]. Marriage of whites with colored people. null and void.—(Gen. St. of S. C. 1882, pp. 589, 590, secs. 2028, 2029, 2032.)

No law of divorce, since 1878.

SOUTH DAKOTA. Same as North Dakota.

TENNESSEE.—Impotence continued: previous marriage still subsisting; adultery; desertion or absence for 2 years without reasonable cause:

conviction of infamous crime; conviction of felony and sentence to penitentiary; maliciously attempting the life of the other party; refusal by wife to remove with husband to the State without reasonable cause, and willful absence from him 2 years; pregnancy of the woman, etc., as in Alabama; habitual drunkenness.—(Code of Tenn. 1884, sec. 3306, p. 611.)

Divorce from Bonds of Matrimony or from Bed and Board, at the discretion of the Court. Cruel and inhuman treatment; indignities to person of wife, rendering her condition intolerable; abandonment by husband, or turning wife out of doors, or refusal or neglect to provide for her.—(Ibid. sec. 3307, pp. 611, 612.)

TEXAS.—Marriage voidable, for impotency, or any other impediment rendering contract void.—(Sayles' Tex. Civ. St. 1888, vol. 1, p. 885, Art. 2860.)

Divorce.—Excesses, cruel treatment or outrages, rendering living together insupportable; when wife has been taken in adultery; absence of either, 3 years, with intention of abandonment, or abandonment by husband and living in adultery with another woman; conviction of felony and imprisonment in State prison.—(Ibid. Art. 2861.)

VERMONT.—Marriages within prohibited degrees, or when former husband or wife was living, are void.—(Rev. Laws Vt. 1880, p. 476, sec. 2346.)

Voidable, for want of sufficient age; for idiocy or lunacy; physical incapacity; consent obtained by force or fraud.—(Ibid. sec. 2349.)

Divorce.—Adultery; sentence to hard labor 3 years or more, and actual confinement; intolerable severity; desertion for 3 years; absence 7 years without being heard from; gross or wanton and cruel refusal or neglect by husband to provide.—(Ibid. p. 477, sec. 2362.)

VIRGINIA.—Marriages between whites and colored persons, marriages when former husband or wife is living, and marriages under the age of consent, are void.

Voidable, when within the prohibited degrees; also for insanity or incapacity.—(Code of Va. 1887, p. 560, secs. 2252, 2254.)

Divorce.—Adultery; impotency; indictment or sentence to death or confinement in penitentiary; conviction, prior to marriage, of an infamous offense; being a fugitive from justice, or having been absent for 2 years; abandonment for 5 years; pregnancy, etc., as in Alabama; when the wife had been a prostitute.—(Ibid. p. 561, sec. 2257.)

Divorce from Bed and Board.—Cruelty; reasonable apprehension of bodily hurt; abandonment.—(Ibid. sec. 2258.)

WASHINGTON.—Consent obtained by force or fraud; adultery; impotency; abandonment for one year; cruel treatment, or personal iniquities, rendering life burdensome; habitual drunkenness; neglect or refusal of husband to provide; imprisonment in penitentiary. Also, "for any other cause deemed by the Court sufficient, and the Court shall be satisfied that the parties can no longer live together."—(Wash. Code, 1881, p. 340, sec. 2000.)

Marriage voidable for want of legal age or sufficient understanding, or for consent obtained by force or fraud.—(Ibid. p. 411, sec. 2381.)

WEST VIRGINIA.—Voidable.—Marriages between whites and negroes; marriages when former husband or wife was living, and those within prohibited degrees. Also, for insanity or incapacity, or for want of consent. —(Amended Code of W. Va. 1887, p. 597, sec. 1.)

Divorce.—Adultery; impotency; sentence to confinement in penitentiary; conviction prior to marriage, of an infamous offense; abandonment for 3 years; pregnancy of the wife, etc., as in Alabama; when the wife had previously been without the knowledge of the husband, notoriously a prostitute; when the husband, without the knowledge of the wife, had been notoriously a licentious person.—(Ibid. p. 598, sec. 5.)

Divorce from Bed and Board.—Cruel and inhuman treatment; reasonable apprehension of bodily hurt; abandonment; habitual drunkenness.—(Ibid. sec. 6.)

WISCONSIN.—Marriages within prohibited degrees, or when former husband or wife was living, are void.—(Rev. St. Wis. 1878, p. 661, sec. 2349.)

Voidable, for want of age or understanding, or when obtained by force or fraud.* Also void when either party is sentenced to imprisonment for life. —(Ibid. secs. 2350. 2355.)

Divorce.—(1) Adultery; (2) impotency; (3) sentence to imprisonment for 3 years or more; (4) desertion for one year; (5) cruel and inhuman treatment, or wife being given to intoxication; (6) habitual drunkenness for one year; (7) voluntarily living separate for 5 years.—(Ibid. sec. 2356.)

Divorce from Bed and Board.—For 4th, 5th and 6th causes above specified; extreme cruelty; refusal or neglect of husband to provide. Also when it is unsafe and improper for wife to live with her husband.—(Ibid. sec. 2357.)

* Marriages are void or voidable for these causes, and when within the prohibited degrees, in nearly all the States. Some of the statutes upon this subject (as distinguished from divorce) may not have been specifically mentioned.

THE WOMAN LAWYER.

By Dr. Louis Frank.

Translated from the French, by Mary A. Greene, LL.B., of the Suffolk. [Mass.] Bar.

III.

The Swiss Federal tribunal, by a decree setting forth at length its motives, dated January 29, 1887, rejected the appeal of the petitioner. (Madame Kempin-Spyri.)—(Entscheidungen des Schweizerischen Bundesgerichtes. J. 1887, Band XIII, Helft. I, 1.)

The decree is divided into three heads. The tribunal recalls, in the first place, that the right to regulate the representation of parties before the tribunals; that is to say, the profession of advocate, belongs to the cantons. Since this matter belongs to the domain of judicial procedure, and the regulation of it is reserved to the cantons, there can be no question in the case, of a violation of the right to act, nor of a violation of the public right.

In the second place, the tribunal declares that the only question is, whether the decision appealed from violates a provision of the Federal or the cantonal Constitution. It concludes in this manner: "That from the present legal point of view, the difference in the regulation of the rights of men and of women, and notably as concerning their right to participate in public life, does seem to have some foundation; that a cantonal decision which excludes women from the right to represent parties before the tribunals, cannot be considered as contradicting Article 4 of the Federal Constitution.

Finally, in the third place, the federal tribunal considers how the expression "right of active citizenship," should be interpreted, adding that the sole question is as to the interpretation of a cantonal law, which obtains its authority from the Federal tribunal, and that there cannot be therefore, in this case, a violation of the Federal Constitution; that the Federal Constitution contains no provision pointing out in what sense the right of active citizenship presupposes the ability to represent third parties before the tribunals; that it results with certainty, from the interpretation of the law of the Canton of Zurich, that this law takes the expression "right of active citizenship," in the sense of right of suffrage. That if the cantonal tribunal of Zurich decides that the right of active citizenship, taken in the sense above indicated, is not to be acquired by women, there is no violation thereby of the Constitution; that it is true that neither the Federal Constitution nor the laws of the Canton of Zurich take away from women the right of suffrage, but, given the historical evolution of Swiss law, one must admit that, by those citizens to whom the right of suffrage belongs, citizens of the masculine sex exclusively, are understood. and not those of the feminine sex. By these arguments, the Federal tribunal rejected the appeal of Mme. Kempin-Spyri as without foundation.

Madame Kempin-Spyri has kindly communicated to us a series of facts relative to her case. Here are some of the most interesting of them.

Mme. Kempin has tried, in several other Swiss cantons, to be admitted to the bar. In the Canton of Berne, in order to practice as advocate, one must pass certain special examinations. The President of the Court of Appeal of Berne refused to Mme. Kempin the authority to present herself for these examinations. After having conferred with the principal authorities of the Canton, the honorable President informed this lady that the principal condition requisite to submit proofs for the examinations, is the possession of "the capacity for civil honor," (burgerliche Ehrenfahigkeit) which women do not enjoy in the Canton of Berne. Elsewhere the responses of the legal authorities have been the same.

Mme. Kempin-Spyri has opened a consultation office in Zurich, and already has quite a large clientage. She writes us that she has now become convinced that advocates of the feminine sex would be especially acceptable to women, and so this consideration alone would suffice to explain the hostility shown them by the advocates of Zurich.

However, little by little, thanks to the recommendation of her patron, the advocates and magistrates have consented to enter into fraternal relations with "Die Rechtsgelehrte." As no alteration in the legislation of Zurich can be expected from henceforth for many years, Mme. Kempin, being a woman of quick intelligence, and of uncommon will and energy, has resolved to emigrate to America. In a few weeks she will leave Switzerland and Europe, to establish herself in the United States. She hopes to be able to practice her profession there, without feeling hampered by absurd restrictions.

Professor Maili, the foremost advocate in Zurich, and one of the best known of Swiss jurists, has sent us the following testimonial:

"Mme. E. Kempin, Doctor of Law, has been an occupant of my office from the beginning of August, 1887, up to the present day. She has always distinguished herself by her intelligent and assiduous work.

Zurich, August 15, 1888. Prof. Maili."

[Note by the Translator. Mme. Kempin arrived in New York in the early autumn of 1888, and applied to the Columbia Law School for admission. The Faculty has the matter now under consideration.]

In the UNITED STATES, the oldest traces of the movement in favor of the woman lawyer, go back to 1867. Mrs. Arabella A. Mansfield was the first woman to be admitted to the bar, in June, 1869, in the State of Iowa. Other woman lawyers made their appearance in Utah and in Maine, in 1872; then, very quietly, women began to be members of the bar in most of the States.

In the United States the distinction does not exist, as it does with us, between advocates and attorneys, or, as in England, between barristers and solicitors. The American lawyers practice as advocates and attorneys. They are designated by the term, "attorneys and counselors at law," and women, when admitted to the bar, plead, and take upon themselves the whole procedure.

By a liberal interpretation of the regulations in force concerning attorneys, and without the intervention of any new law, the States of Iowa, Missouri, Michigan, North Carolina, Maine, Indiana, Kansas. Connecticut, Nebraska, [the Territory of] Utah, the District of Columbia, the Territory of Washington and some other States, have admitted women to the bar.

Illinois, California, Minnesota, Massachusetts, Oregon, Wisconsin, Ohio and New York have passed special statutes authorizing women to practice as advocates, almost immediately following the rendering of decisions by the courts of these States, which did not consent to recognize the right of women to become attorneys at law.

Pennsylvania has very recently admitted to the bar a woman, Mrs. Carrie Burnham Kilgore, after having for ten years refused her access thereto. The court has finally yielded to her claim without making the intervention of the legislature necessary.

Of the forty-nine States and Territories of the Union, there are but few that do not possess woman lawyers. In 1880, according to the last national census, the United States could count 64,062 male lawyers and 75 female lawyers. These latter were thus divided among the different States: California, 2; Dakota, 1; District of Columbia. 3; Florida, 1; Georgia, 2; Illinois, 9; Indiana, 1; Iowa, 5; Kansas, 1; Louisiana, 3; Maryland, 1; Massachusetts, 4; Michigan, 7; Missouri, 2; Nebraska, 1; New Hampshire, 3; New York, 7; New Jersey, 2; North Carolina, 3; Ohio, 5; Pennsylvania, 8; Tennessee, 1; Texas, 2; Virginia, 1.—(Tenth Census, U. S., Dept. of the Interior, Washington, 1883, Vol. I, Table XXXI. p. 733.)

[Translator's Note. This table, although correctly cited here, appears to be of absolutely no value. The "lawyers" enumerated could not all have been members of the bar, for Pennsylvania, Massachusetts and New York at least, did not admit women to the bar until some years after the taking of this census, while New Jersey, New Hampshire and some others cited in the table have not even yet (1888) admitted women. Moreover, Maine, which does not appear by the table to have a woman lawyer at all, admitted Mrs. Clara H. Nash, in 1872, who has remained a resident of that State ever since, and Wisconsin certainly had women members of its bar in 1880. That the term "lawyers" in this table is not synonymous with "members of the bar," is proved by the "Remarks upon the List of Occupations," where the compiler says that the term "lawyer" may include "law scrivener, collector of debts, prosecutor of claims, counselor, attorney, possibly also judge." See Tenth Census, U. S., Vol. I, p. 708.]

Since 1880, the number of woman lawyers has increased considerably; the numerous States which have been hostile or indifferent to the emancipation of women, have been converted, little by little to new ideas.

In 1886, the number of woman lawyers had risen to more than a hundred, and at the present time, according to official information sent to us, more than a hundred and fifty women are pleading before the American tribunals.

In most of the States, it might even be said in all, women can practice as attorneys in all the courts, and wherever they practice, they are admitted to the Circuit and District Courts of the United States. Moreover, the Federal Congress of the United States passed a law, February 15, 1879, which declares that any woman who shall have practiced at the bar of the highest court of a State or Territory for the space of three years, and who shall have merited by her ability and character, the good opinion of the Court, may be admitted to practice in the Supreme Court of the United States. This law is of very great importance. It gives, in some sort, to women, access to the highest political functions of the nation. Indeed, according to the Federal Constitution of the United States of 1787, by a provision never subsequently modified, the Supreme Court has not only purely judicial attributes, but is also invested with political attributes, which are, to enforce respect for the Constitution—to uphold the acts of Congress as against the special laws of the States—to keep treaties inviolate—to maintain harmony among the different States, and to interpose in controversies between citizens and foreigners.—(In 1787, the principles of private international law not yet being established, the judgment upon controversies between citizens and foreigners was held to be a political attribute.)

By force of the Act of February 15, 1879, several women have been received as advocates at the Supreme Court of the United States. The best known of these attorneys of the feminine sex is Mrs. Belva A. Lockwood.

In the Eastern States, which are more conservative than the Western, woman lawyers are not so numerous. At present there is one only in each of the following States: Maine, Connecticut, New York, Pennsylvania and Massachusetts; and four in the City of Washington, D. C.—[There are now two in Massachusetts, Miss Robinson, admitted in 1882, and Miss Greene, admitted in 1888.] Miss Lelia Josephine Robinson, member of the Suffolk Bar (Boston) to whom we have written, has kindly furnished us some information for which we are much indebted to her. We asked her to communicate to us her personal sentiments on the subject of the privilege enjoyed by woman lawyers in the United States. Here is a part of her reply, which we think will be interesting to transcribe:

"Woman lawyers are nowhere unpopular so far as I know. They are popular just in proportion to the individual qualities which make popularity, the same as it is with men." [The foregoing was a reply to a direct question put by Dr. Frank, asking if woman lawyers are popular in the United States.] "The general opinion seems to be that it is well to give women a chance to show what they can do, and let the result prove either their skill or their incapacity. I think from what information I have, that women who have seriously devoted themselves to practice, and who have practiced long enough to make the proof of any value, have succeeded at the bar as well as men. Some have done better; others have not done as well. One must not lose sight of the fact that in our country, business comes very slowly to a lawyer, at least, except in rare cases, and that women have only been at the bar a very short

time, so it is not possible to express a definite opinion as to
the chance of success they may have in practice.

"During the two years following my admission (in 1882),
business came to me so slowly that I became somewhat im-
patient, although I was more favored than some of my classmates. I went West, where I did better. Since my return to
the East, my work leaves me little leisure and business comes
in very encouragingly. I can even predict that, in the near
future, I may have a very good practice. Before my departure
for the West, I hesitated about going into court, and confined
myself to office work. That was a mistake. I now take court
business, and I enjoy it. ⁂ It may perhaps interest you
to know that I have always been treated with the most perfect
courtesy and the greatest kindness by my colleagues in the Law
School and at the bar, as well in the East as in the West."

Women may, in some of the States, become public officers
and justices of the peace. In Massachusetts, the office of
special commissioner has been recently created, the holder of
which has powers answering to those of a justice of the peace.
Women lawyers are qualified to discharge these functions.—
[Translator's Note. Dr. Frank has not quite understood the
facts concerning the office of special commissioner. The act
reads thus: "The governor, with the advice and consent of
the council is hereby authorized to appoint women, who are
attorneys at law, to administer oaths, to take depositions and
to take acknowledgments of deeds, and women so appointed
shall be designated in their commissions as special commissioners."—Laws and Resolves, Mass., 1883, ch. 252, sec. 1. It
will be seen that the office can only be held by "women who
are attorneys at law," and that but three powers are given
them. Upon a strict contemporaneous construction of the
Constitution and Laws of Massachusetts, the Supreme Court,
before the passage of this act, decided that a woman could not
be a justice of the peace.]

In a large number of States, women are notaries public.

In Wyoming, women were at one time admitted to jury
duty. This reform, which several other States have adopted,
and which will perhaps cause some grave magistrates of old

Europe to smile, has produced happy and remarkable results, which are summarized in a learned report addressed to the governor of Massachusetts, by Judge John Kingman, counselor of the Supreme Court of the United States.

"When men," writes Mr. Kingman, among other things, "alone composed the jury, the tribunals were always powerless to execute the laws against drunkenness, gambling, licentiousness and lewdness in all its forms. Neither the petit nor the grand jury could be counted upon for that; but several ladies at each session very soon put an end to that state of things.

"There have been comparatively few women among us, and they are generally too busy at home, for the courts to succeed in getting a sufficient number among the jurors. But those who have taken part have always acquitted themselves of their duties with credit. An amended verdict, either civil or penal, has not been seen when women have formed a part of the jury. It could not be otherwise, for they pay the greatest attention to the course of the proceedings, they confine themselves better to the evidence, they weigh more the documents presented, they allow themselves to be less influenced by their business relations and by outside considerations; lastly, they bring a more scrupulous conscience to the loyal accomplishment of their duty.

"There has never been an instance of a woman juror who has drawn odium upon herself, or toward whom respect has been lacking; on the contrary, they were invariably much esteemed and appreciated. And the mere presence of women in the court-room has produced another good effect in the order, the decorum, and the more decent and respectful bearing which the men have preserved towards them. From every point of view, the trials have taken on a more serious aspect, and the course of justice has been more rapid.

"Certainly, the experiment of the participation of women in the application of our laws has succeeded excellently in the courts, and it seems to me particularly just that those persons who suffer the most from the consequences of crime and vice, should be called upon to take part in their repression.

"In conclusion, I ought to say, that in the widest possible

sense, with all the advantages and benefits which I have observed to flow from the change accomplished in our laws, I have not remarked any of the inconveniences so warmly asserted by those who opposed the admission of women to public life."—(It is impossible to deal further with the question of mixed juries. We reserve for analysis later, the article on "Women Jurors," which Miss Lelia Robinson has recently published.—See Chicago Law Times, Vol. I, p. 22.)

In Europe, we should be almost tempted to consider as revolutionary, or to treat as Utopian the honorable Counselor Kingman, who, however, is far from being alone in his opinions. The prominent position of woman in the United States has not escaped the attention of M. de Tocqueville. In his celebrated analysis of American manners and institutions, the eminent French writer made this declaration: "If any one should ask me to what I think the singular prosperity and growing strength of the American people should be attributed, I should answer that it is due to the superiority of their women."—(De la démocratie en Amérique, T. III.)

We have collected some facts concerning the women who have distinguished themselves by their legal study and labor, or by the remarkable pleas made by themselves before the tribunals. We mentioned previously the Jewish women versed in juridical science, and need say nothing further on that point.

In Athens, the eloquent Aspasia was accused of having outraged religion by her discourses, and morals by her conduct. She plead her cause herself, and the people acquitted her.—(Diodorus Siculus Hist., Lib. XII.)

In the Roman Forum, two women made themselves famous. Amesia Sentia, as Valerius Maximus tells us, being brought to justice, defended herself before the judges, the praetor, L. Titius presiding, and in the midst of an immense concourse of people. She unfolded all her points, all the heads of her defense with talent and even with much force. (Non solum diligenter sed etiam fortiter.) She was acquitted at the first hearing, almost by a unanimous vote. As she bore under the guise of a woman the soul of a man, the name of Androgynus was given to her.—(Valerius Maximus, Hist. Lib. VIII, ch.

III; De mulieribus quae causas apud magistratus egerunt.)

The other famous female orator of Rome, whose name history has preserved to us, was Hortensia, daughter of the illustrious L. Hortensius, the most renowned of the orators who were the rivals of Cicero. These are the circumstances which brought about the appearance of this woman in court. The triumvirs had laid a heavy impost upon Roman women, and no man had deigned to lift his voice in their favor, nor to lend them his assistance. Hortensia decided to assume the delicate mission of defending the cause of the women before the tribunal of the triumvirs. According to the testimony of Valerius Maximus, she acquitted herself of the task with as much intrepidity as success. (Constanter et feliciter.) The eulogy which the Latin historian has pronounced upon her is worthy to be transcribed:

"Faithful image of the eloquence of her father, she obtained the remission of the greater part of the tax imposed upon her sex. L. Hortensius seemed to live again in this woman, and to breathe once more in the words of his daughter. (Revixit tum muliebri stirpe L. Hortensius, verbisque filiæ adspiravit.) If the masculine branch of his posterity had seen fit to follow this vigorous impulse, the eloquence of Hortensius, that great inheritance, would not have come to an end with this one plea, the work of a woman."—(Valerius Maximus, Hist. Lib. VIII., ch. III.)

At the time of the Renaissance, several women in Italy distinguished themselves by their aptitude for legal study. In the twelfth century, Dotta, daughter of Accorso, one of the most famous glossologists, was a reader of law at Bologna.— (In the ancient Italian universities, the rectors took charge of the most distinguished students, in private courses, which were called by the name of Lecturæ Universitatis. The student *readers*, really private instructors, received a salary.)

In the fourteenth century, two women of Bologna, Bettina and Novella Andrea were readers of canonical law at the University of Civil Law at Bologna. They were both the daughters of Giovanni Andrea, 1270–1348, the most celebrated canonist of the Middle Ages. Novella was her father's substitute in giving instruction. Christinus of Pisa relates how, when the old professor was unable to give his lesson, his daughter took his place. Since Novella's physical beauty was as great as her learning, she delivered her lectures from behind a curtain, so as not to distract the attention of her pupils. It is, however, probable that the legend is exaggerated, and that Novella contented herself with veiling her face. This superior woman ·was born at Padua in 1312, and died at Bologna in 1350. In the fourteenth century there were two more women who were distinguished in the study of juridical science, Joanna Bianchetti and Magdalena Buonsignori, reader of law at Bologna, to whom we owe a little treatise of some reputation, *De legibus connubialibus.*

In the eighteenth century, Bettina Calderini of Florence, and Bettisia Gozzadini of Bologna were professors at Bologna, the one of civil, the other of canonical law. At the same period Novella of Bologna was teaching law at the University of Padua.

Four women who were very learned jurisprudents of a more recent time must be mentioned, Maria Pizzelli of Rome, Maria Delfini Dosi of Bologna, Maria Pelegrini Amoretti in the eighteenth century, and in the nineteenth, Madalena Noe Canedi. Maria Pelegrini Amoretti was received as Doctor of Law at Padua in 1777. The dissertation, *De jure dotium,* presented by her won a considerable reputation which the poet, Parini, celebrated in an ode entitled *Il pericolo.*

The seventeenth century could count four famous woman orators in Italy, Elizabeth Mastola, Laura Corgna, Isicratea Monti and Emilia Brembati.

In France, in the eighteenth century, a woman, Mlle. de Lézardiere, produced a legal work which is held in the highest estimation, La Théorie des Lois Politiques de la Monarchie Francaise. Guizot considers this work the most instructive in existence upon the early French law. Monseigneur Dupanloup has pronounced, moreover, a well merited eulogy upon this writer, in the lines which I here reproduce: "Thus," wrote the Bishop of Orléans, "it is a woman who has consecrated a life, in which austere toil and works of charity alone had place, to produce the first work which should open the way to the new discoveries of modern science, a work of prodigious erudition. This *savante*, for indeed one must decide to call her thus, has left a memory to be venerated among her compatriots."—(Dupanloup, Femmes savantes et Femmes studieuses, p. 20.) The complete work of Mlle. Lézardiere, in four volumes, was published in 1844, under the auspices of the French government.

Under the old régime, a woman of great wit, the Marchioness de Créqui, requested and received the authority to present her defense in person. In 1807, Mlle. Legracieux de Lacoste obtained a like favor in the Court of Cassation of France. "The time to come will be grateful to us for having noted," wrote M. Denevers,—(Quoted in Dalloz, Defense, No. 195) "as a historical fact in procedure, that the Supreme Court admitted the young gentlewoman Legracieux de Lacoste to plead solemnly her own case in a civil action, against M. Justin Blanchet. A pure and measured utterance, a beautiful voice, a heartfelt accent, a care for all the proprieties of the sex and the cause, such are the oratorical means by which Mlle. Lacoste excited, throughout an entire hearing, the kindly attention of the Supreme Court and of an immense concourse of hearers, even of those who were the least disposed to applaud her. * * This success and the charms of speech which are noticeable in the case of so many women, would perhaps make us regret that, imitating an ancient people, a career at the bar is not accessible to them, if on the one hand, perfect propriety did not throw a serious obstacle in the way, and if, on the other hand, one could forget, that in society one must never determine according to the exceptional cases."

In 1817, before the Court of Appeal of Brussels, a woman asked to be empowered to present a defense for her husband. The court refused to authorize her. "Wherefore," reads the decree, "the Lady Cauchois-Lemaire cannot be admitted, as spouse and friend, to plead in an appeal from the public suit instituted at the expense of her husband."—(Dalloz, Défense, No. 72.)

As to the United States, where the number of woman lawyers is daily increasing, it appears impossible for us to accord special mention to each one who practices there.

Mrs. Arabella A. Mansfield was the earliest woman lawyer in the United States. The first woman to become a member of the Chicago bar, was Mrs. Myra Bradwell. The feminine world points with pride to the case of Miss Hulett, who, after having finished her studies at the age of nineteen, had, at twenty-three, an income of more than three thousand dollars a year. Miss Lavinia Goodell, advocate in New York, enjoyed a considerable reputation in America, which was acquired by her integrity, knowledge and skill. It was owing to her persevering and meritorious efforts that the legislature of the State of New York passed a law giving women the right to practice at the bar.—[Translator's Note. Miss Goodell did not practice in New York, but in Janesville, Wisconsin, and she died in 1880, six years before the New York statute admitting women to the bar, was passed. Miss Kate Stoneman, of Albany, whose petition for admission to the bar was rejected by the New York court in 1886, secured the passage of the act referred to.]

For the first time, in December, 1880, a woman lawyer, Mrs. Laura de Force Gordon, presented herself before a California jury, in defense of an individual accused of murder. Here is the account given by the American newspapers of this début: "Mrs. Gordon was dressed in black. She wore, as her sole ornament, a rose on her corsage. Her appearance caused a general stir in the court room, which Mrs. Gordon feigned not to notice. During her argument, applause broke forth several times, in spite of the severe reprimands of the presiding judge. At last the jury rendered a verdict of "not guilty," which caused a fresh outburst of enthusiasm. Mrs. Gordon is young and pretty, as well as eloquent."

Another woman, Miss Lelia Josephine Robinson, still quite young, has acquired a brilliant reputation. Having passed the examinations at the Boston University Law School with success, and obtained the degree of Bachelor of Laws, *cum laude*, Miss Robinson wished to practice in Massachusetts. The court refused to admit her. Almost immediately the legislature passed unanimously the Act of April 10, 1882, granting to women the same right that a man has to practice the profession of the law. At present Miss Robinson, after having been admitted to the bar of Suffolk County, practices in Boston. Miss Robinson is a very excellent writer. She has recently published a most important work, "Law Made Easy." In a volume of six hundred pages, divided into forty-two chapters, she has made a summary of the public and private law of the United States. The style of the work is very pure. The method reveals, in Miss Robinson, a logician of the first order. The matter is not inferior to the style, and the author has treated her subject with the knowledge of a skilled jurist. We have drawn this praise of Miss Robinson's work from the testimonials of Messrs. E. H. Bennett of Boston University, William F. Warren, President of that University, Roger S. Greene, Chief-Justice of Washington Territory, T. Wentworth Higginson, the celebrated American historian, and of many other prominent persons in American scientific circles.

Mrs. Belva A. Lockwood practices at Washington as counselor of the Supreme Court of the United States. It was owing to her unceasing exertions before the two Houses of Congress, that the federal law of February 15, 1879, was enacted, which we have already considered.

She was admitted to the bar of the Supreme Court of the United States, in March, 1879. For a number of years she had been in active practice before the Supreme Court of the District of Columbia. She is one of the most remarkable women of the Union. She was a candidate for the Presidency of the United States in 1884, and again in 1888.

Mrs. Lockwood has sent us some further information. Mrs. Laura de Force Gordon, whose success before a California jury we have recorded, was received as a counselor of the Supreme Court of the United States, by a decision of that court, dated February 3, 1886.

Mrs. Ada M. Bittenbender, of Nebraska, was nominated last year, for judge of a county court in that State.

Mr. Justice Miller, of the Supreme Court of the United States, appointed, last year, Miss Phebe Couzens, to fill the place of her deceased father, who performed the duties of United States Marshal in the District of Saint Louis. Miss Couzens discharged with ability the duties of her office, until the nomination of her successor. She had previously been Assistant Marshal, under the direction of her father.

A curious and truly original innovation has just been introduced into the police system of the United States. A short time since, the office of "Police Matron" was established there, a special police duty confided to women.

Women in the United States, are admitted to the committees or commissions of Congress, and even to the public assemblies of the Legislatures, and they can present their petitions and grievances there.

[Translator's Note. It seems that Dr. Frank may have supposed that women can appear on the floor of Congress, or of the legislatures, to address them. This, of course we know is not done, unless by special courtesy, although they may address committees at their hearings.]

In India, the Vice-Judge of Nayada, sometime since, authorized Ethira Julu, a native woman, to plead causes of secondary importance before him.

To complete and close this chapter devoted to woman jurists, let us recall the name of Signora Lidia Poet, which has called forth the strange Italian decisions we have analyzed. Signora Poet is now in the office of her brother, an advocate at Turin. Let us recall also the names of Mme. Kempin-Spyri at Zurich, of Mlle. Bilcesco, and of Mlle. Marie Popelin.

We should not overlook the name of Mme. de l' Arenal, a contemporaneous Spaniard, who has devoted herself to criminal law, and has written several works upon the penitentiary system. Two English women must also be mentioned: Miss Mary Carpenter, who has made a study of the prison system, and Miss Elizabeth Fry, who labored for the reform of the penitentiary system.

Furthermore, let us note the fact that in most of these countries, the right of woman to present her own defense is recognized; that frequently in France, England, and especially in Sweden, they make use of this opportunity, without the occurrence of any irregular or abnormal incident in connection with the exercise of the right.

Without doubt, a woman of a rancorous disposition, of a peevish and excitable character, a shrewish and vulgar woman, would be a disastrous calamity at the bar. If we desire that the tribunals may for all time, be unhampered by that Caphrania of the Roman Judgment-hall, we might, nevertheless, view with satisfaction a woman as a member of our Order, who should bring to the practice of our profession the charms and advantages of her sex. The quarrelsome woman, the execrable and infernal, Roman Caphrania, we repudiate; to her as to her fellows, let us with one accord forbid the access to the bar. But to one Caphrania of shameful memory, we can oppose a hundred woman jurisprudents, endowed with the most brilliant qualities, the most noble characters. A like proportion is not found among the ranks of men.

Taking account of the surprising success which every where greets, in all the universities, these emulators of man, are we not warranted in predicting that women by reason of their activity and their peculiar disposition, are called to become at the bar, what they have been upon the throne, where, to use a comparison borrowed from Fourier, from Semiramis to Victoria, down the ages, one may count seven great queens for one mediocre, whilst one constantly sees seven mediocre kings for one great king.

To be continued.

THE ROYAL COURTS OF JUSTICE.

With the changes which have taken place in the reorganization and consolidation of the great historic courts of England, under the judicature acts of 1873 and 1875, has come a change in the location of the courts and buildings themselves, as wonderful as that which added to the title of the Queen, that of Empress of India.

For more than fifty years the British public had felt that the arrangement of the courts at Westminster Hall was entirely inadequate for the transaction of the public business, and that it had been entirely outgrown by the courts themselves and their constantly increasing business.

The necessity of adopting some plan by which all the courts could be assembled under one roof, and provided with all of the modern conveniences; was felt by all who had studied the subject, and accordingly a royal commission was appointed by an act of Parliament in 1863, after years of discussion and agitation, to whom the whole subject was committed, who were required to employ an architect, select a location for the erection of new buildings for the Courts of Law, and recommend a plan for the same.

After several years spent in deliberating upon the subject, a site was selected and the plans of the buildings submitted to public competition. The plans of Mr. J. E. Street, R. A., one of the most renowned architects in Europe, were adopted, and the work entered upon in 1868. The buildings were finished in 1882, and formally dedicated, Dec. 4, 1882, by Her Majesty,

with the most imposing ceremonies, and all the business of
the several courts of justice was transferred hither from Westminster Hall, the first day of Hilary term, Jan. 11, 1883.

This vast and handsome structure is on the north side of the
Strand, a little beyond the line of Temple Bar and of Old Shire
Lane (so called "because it divideth the city from the Shire"),
and extends back to Carey Street and Lincoln's Inn.   It is of
a composite form of architecture, chiefly resembling the ancient
halls of the Flemish style, and was planned so as to allow
of all the divisions of the High Court of Justice and branches of
the Supreme Court being assembled under one roof.

The eastern part of the building contains the wing for masters, registrars and other officials, and the whole structure occupies five acres.

The Strand front is of Portland stone, 500 feet in length and
about 80 feet in height, pierced with Gothic windows and set
off by gables and pinnacles.   On the City side of the site of
Temple Bar, stands a great campanile or bell tower, 160 feet
high.

In the center of the main building, the gable reaches a
height of 130 feet, and contains a great rose window above the
main window of the Central Hall, which is 230 feet long, 40
feet wide and 80 feet high.

At each end of this new *salle des pas perdus*, appears a marble gallery, like the wooden galleries at the end of the halls of
Trinity College, Cambridge.   At the north end of the Central
Hall, a corridor runs east and west, the whole length of the
building; while another corridor, continuing in the direction of
the Central Hall, leads out into Carey Street, past two jury
halls as large as courts, and a refreshment room for the members of the bar, with kitchen, cellar, larder, and robing room.

The chief entrance from the Strand opens under an arch of
50 feet, on either side of which are Gothic traced windows
with Lancet arches, and above the windows are recesses for
sculpture.

Through the central arch is an entrance porch. . A second
porch succeeds to this, from which rise steps leading to the
south gallery of Central Hall, and to the level of the courts;

for the eight round the Central Hall are above its level, while the floor of the hall is 4 or 5 feet higher than the Strand. The long Strand and Carey Street fronts are formed by two buildings, of which the westernmost, called the main building, contains the courts and the Central Hall.

The eastern building is joined to the main building by a narrow front on the Strand, and by a like erection, without depth at the Carey Street end; but except for these two communications, the two wings are separated from each other by an open space called the Quadrangle, which is more than twice as large as the Central Hall.

The carriage entrance sweeps into it, from the Strand between two smaller arches for pedestrians. From the Quadrangle, which gives light and air to both buildings, many entrances lead into each.

The eastern building differs in style from the other, and the brown Portland stone, which in the western part of the building, holds all the prominent positions, is here largely relieved by red brick. From the tower in Fleet Street, a Janus clock, facing two ways, shows conspicuously from the east and from the west, in the style (well suited to London) of the clock of St. Mary-le-Bow in Cheapside. Including staircase, corridors, halls and rooms, there are 800 apartments in the main edifice and 300 in the eastern building.

As a specimen of the modern style of architecture, and planned with the special design to accommodate the public business and in administering the law, this structure is worthy of the most minute study, and possesses many conveniences in the way of retiring rooms, reception rooms for ladies, and rooms for parties and witnesses who are compelled to attend the various courts, that seem never yet to have been thought of or provided for at all in this country.

We will, however, first turn our attention to the site of this great structure, and will then describe in detail the internal arrangement of the building and court rooms.

SITE OF THE NEW LAW COURTS.—The location of the new courts and the historical associations connected with the same, are worthy of remembrance.

Twenty years ago, says the Law Times, the site of the new law courts was one of the worst parts of the metropolis; and it is quite true that when the seven acres of fetid grounds, muddy lanes and dirty alleys, were cleared away, there was nothing worth preserving of the many miserable houses and other erections which were then demolished. But there was a time when this locality was the abode of fashion, and the resort of the learned. From the time of Charles II. to the reign of "Good Queen Anne," a fashionable promenade stretched along what is now the western front of the new courts. This was called Clement's Lane, and in it there dwelt Sir John Trevor, sometime speaker of the House of Commons and Master of the Rolls, who was subsequently buried in the Roll's Chapel. Oliver Cromwell spent some years of his life in this lane, and the site of a mansion occupied by Lord Paget may be seen from the windows of the Lord Chancellor's room in the eastern wing of the new building. Boswell Court, a little to the northeast, was a private resort of lawyers in the time of Johnson; and not far from the new rooms allotted to the Lord Chief-Justice, there lived in 1639, Sir Thomas Lyttleton.

The locality is also memorable as having been the residence of the widow of Sir Walter Raleigh; while in new Boswell Court, as recently as 1850, might have been seen a watchman's box, such as was used by the precursors of the present police.

Boswell Court opened into Carey Street, the south side of which was pulled down and is now occupied by the north front or Lincoln's Inn side of the new courts. In one of the houses in this street resided Sir William Blackstone, and Benjamin Franklin is said to have lodged there when serving his time as a printer's apprentice, while at the old Plough tavern, John Gully, the notorious prize fighter, made the money which enabled him to secure a seat in the House of Commons as a member of Pontefract.

A little further eastward is the boundary line of the City of London and the city and Liberty of Westminster. Along this line there ran a broad alley called Shire Lane, and afterward Serles Place.

On the right was "Smashers Corner," so called because the

houses were occupied by coiners of bad money. The spot is now occupied, singularly enough, by the Royal Courts of Justice branch of the Bank of England. The next noticeable place was the Anti Gallican, a public house near the Strand frequented by sporting men. Close by was Cadger's Hall, a rendezvous of beggars, and near it was a famous sponging house, in which in 1823, Theodore Hook was detained as a crown debtor, for £12,000.

James Perry, the proprietor of tho Morning Chronicle, lodged in the same Lane for many years. But Shire Lane will be chiefly remembered in connection with the Kit Kat Club, which met at the Trumpet Tavern; and here in the reign of Queen Anne the leading wits of the day were in the habit of spending their evenings together, including Addison, Steele, Congreve, Dryden, the Duke of Marlborough and Sir William Walpole.

In 1725, the neighborhood became notorious in connection with the doings of Jack Sheppard. He was a constant visitor of a tavern called "The Bible," which was a house used by printers. On the western side of Bell Yard, which was almost parallel, resided Pope's friend, Fortescue, who in 1777, was Master of the Rolls. He it was who induced Pope to write the facetious law report of Stardling v. Styles.

In addition to the above there are many other details of interest, connected with the site of the new law courts. From being the Belgravia of the Stuarts, it became worse than the Seven Dials. It was in every sense a den of iniquity; therefore, nothing more fitting could have happened than that it should have been entirely swept away by the majesty of the law, and its place occupied by the palatial Royal Courts of Justice.

PALACE OF JUSTICE.—The first sight of that immense pile composing tho Royal Courts of Justice which fronts tbe Strand and runs through to Carey Street, is disappointing.

We had expected to see a structure of great height, of immense size and of surpassing grandeur. The outline is impressive, presenting to the eye an oblong pile of buildings, some 500 feet long and 280 broad, and from their central position the courts can be readily reached from almost any point, but the proportions are not good, and to our eye, the height is not sufficient, and the consequence is that the whole structure has a squatty appearance. The ground plan of the building is in the form of a rectangular parallelogram, measuring about 500 feet on two of the sides, and a little less on the others.

· Roughly speaking, the space inclosed within this boundary is occupied by an outer row of buildings and two interior quadrangles, one of which contains the Central Hall; or perhaps, it gives a more correct idea to say that the plan consists of two quadrangles, round one of which are grouped the offices, and round the other the courts; this last quadrangle being roofed over and forming the Central Hall. As compared with Westminster Hall this hall is disappointing. It strikes one as being, in proportion to its height—some 70 or 80 feet—very narrow, indeed.

The roof, too, will of course not compare with that of Westminster, and the hall, which is, roughly speaking, 220 feet long and 50 feet broad, seems altogether of a character out of place in any but an ecclesiastical building.

This hall of the new law courts does indeed present a different appearance to that at Westminster during term time, as it is only intended that it should be used by jurors and the parties to causes, and witnesses. The public have no occasion to go into it and are mostly excluded. It is not necessary for the bar to use it, either in getting to a court or in going from one to another.

For this purpose barristers are provided with a corridor which passes outside of the whole of the courts, between them and the walls of the Central Hall. This corridor, which is designed to be cool in summer and warm in winter, is most useful, and as it is exclusively used by barristers, gives them the greatest facilities in passing from court to court.

Immediately above this corridor is found another for the public, access to which is obtained by two entrances out of the Strand, just outside the main entrance to the building, that is, just east and west of the entrance to Central Hall. Into the latter, solicitors, or their clients, witnesses and jurors, will pass to reach the six different short flights of steps leading to their waiting rooms and lavatories, and thence by a staircase either to the jurors' galleries or to the courts. They too, are provided with their corridor, and with all the modern conveniences which indicate the abode of civilized man.

The ground on which the building is erected, slopes from north to south with a steep incline towards the river, so that the level of the Strand on the south is eighteen feet below the level of Carey Street on the north.

The courts are on the Carey Street level, so that as one stands on the floor of the Central Hall which is three or four feet above the Strand, the courts on the first floor are some fifteen feet higher. Taking each row of courts as it runs alongside of the Central Hall, we find a corridor for the bar on one side and a corridor for the judges on the other side. That for the bar admits direct to each court; that for the judges is so arranged that on one side of it there are the private rooms occupied by the judges and their personal officers, and on the other are doors giving immediate access to the bench in each court, so that each judge can communicate with every other judge without more trouble than that of sending a message or making a short excursion along a private way. There are entrances to the building on the Carey Street front which are set apart for the judges and which afford a direct and private entrance to their own special corridor. Every court is, as far as possible, removed from the noise of the street traffic outside, and no window giving light to a court looks out on the street.

The courts receive light principally through the roof, and where there are windows they look out on a "well" lined with white glazed bricks; and by this means, not only is the greatest amount of light possible obtained, but air for the purpose of ventilation is also afforded.

INTERNAL ARRANGEMENT.—The arrangements of the courts differ considerably. Taking first of all the court which is understood to have been originally intended for the Master of the Rolls, the scheme is as follows:

The judge's seat is on a high platform, under a graceful oak canopy, and on either side are two oak stalls, probably intended for distinguished visitors to the bench of the Chancery Division.

On a lower platform is a long table, destined for the registrar and judge's officers. Below this are the solicitors seats, facing the counsel and provided with a long table furnished with inkstands. There is room on shelves behind the seat, for hats, books and papers. The Queen's Counsel seats are immediately in front, within about fourteen feet of the judge, and extremely convenient for addressing him. The desks in front of these seats are sloping and slide forward. They appear to present rare facilities for papers slipping down among the leader's feet. But the worst arrangement in this part of the court is that of the queen's counsel seats, which lift up like the seats of stalls in cathedrals.

"It is not, however," said a barrister to us, "the lifting up but the coming down of the seat which is the point of difficulty." The seats are very heavy and they are apt to come down with a crash which will have a fearful effect upon a nervous judge or counsel. One witty correspondent in writing upon this subject some years ago before the courts were occupied, said: "It will be necessary to put the learned leaders through a course of seat drill, training them to use the utmost caution in the descent of their seats."

The first row of seats for the outer bar in this court is precisely similar to the leader's seat, and behind this are four seats for the bar, ascending by steps, and behind them is the gallery for spectators. The short-hand writers' seats are on the right and left of the registrar's platform on the level of the floor.

The walls are lined with book-shelves, and the court is lighted by three two-light windows on either side and from the roof. The ventilation is secured by open panels in the roof.

Taking next a court intended for one of the courts of the other divisions, we find different arrangements as regards the solicitors seats. Here the solicitors sit with their backs to the counsel and facing the judge. In front of them are two tables. The jury box is on the left of the judge. It contains three rows of seats and there is a separate entrance for the jurymen. The witness box is on the right of the judge, immediately facing the jury. The arrangements as to seats for counsel are similar to those in the court last described, but there are eight rows of seats. The court is lighted from a cupola in the roof.

The general effect of the courts is admirable. The proportions are good, although much smaller than the ordinary court rooms in the United States, and the fittings are all of solid oak, frequently carved and ornamented very elaborately. The acoustic properties are good, but the great distance which some of the counsel are from the jury box, makes it difficult for them to hear. In England it is not thought necessary for counsel to be so near the jury that they can touch them with their hands, or wink at them as they make telling points.

The western portion of the building takes up two thirds of the whole space. The great quadrangle round which the eastern portion stands, measures about 300 feet in length by about 100 feet in breadth. In this portion of the building, which begins on the south side of the Strand, and starting from the clock tower which forms so conspicuous a feature in the building, runs up the whole length of Bell Yard and some distance along Carey Street on the north, are grouped on four floors some of the most important offices in connection with the courts. Facing Bell Yard we find the whole of the top floor occupied by the chancery taxing masters.

At the south end of the same portion of the building are placed the offices of the Masters of the Queen's Bench Division on the court floor and the floor next above it, and the central office is placed on the ground floor.

At the north, on the court floor and the floor next above are the offices of the chancery registrars, and on the ground floor those of the chancery paymaster and the branch office of the Bank of England.

At the north side of the great quadrangle and on its western side, and also on the western side of the Central Hall on the two uppermost floors, are the offices of the chief clerk of the judges of the chancery divisions. At the north end of the great quadrangle is the bar room (not tap room), on which the late Mr. Street, the renowned architect, expended ornamentation with a profusion not to be found elsewhere in a building by no means deficient in ornament. Above the bar room are the lunacy rooms.

The original project for the building comprised more than nine hundred apartments, including twenty-two court rooms, but parliament modified that scheme, and the estimate was reduced and the amount of room restricted.

Great difficulty was found in providing for all of the officers of the probate, divorce and admiralty division, and for several others; and many rooms originally designed for waiting and consultation rooms have, we are informed, been taken possession of in order to accommodate the demands of the public.

COURT ROOMS AND ACCOMMODATIONS FOR THE BAR.—The first feeling that one experiences in going into the court rooms, is one of surprise at their modest proportions, and this is not materially diminished when one passes into the three larger ones, two of which are at the south and the third at the north end of the Central Hall. It was at first intended that there should be four such larger courts, but the original plans in this respect have been modified, and what would have been the fourth one has principally been converted into a broad vaulted chamber, which is no doubt intended to give a means of communicating with some additional buildings. These, our informant said, it may surprise some to hear, will be built at the northwest corner of the present buildings, and plans for them have, indeed, already long ago been prepared.

The whole of the present nineteen courts are on the same floor, and are built, so to speak, in pairs.

Facing the judge's seat in each court, is the gallery for the public, and in the smaller courts, there is certainly not room for more than forty persons in these galleries. This is much to be regretted, as there are cases in which we cannot but think that it is a matter of the highest importance that there should be room for at least two or three times that number. However this may be, the design of all courts is to accommodate the parties who have business to transact, and not the public in general. On a line with the galleries for the public are the galleries for jurors, in one court to the right of the judge's seat, and in another to the left.

The judges' seats are somewhat peculiar, and as we should think, likely to prove uncomfortable; they resemble such as are found in college chapels for heads of houses, but are much narrower.

On a line with the seats for the judges in the smaller courts will be found on either side of·them four or five seats petitioned off. These again, though they have no canopy over them as the judges' seats have, have a quasi ecclesiastical look that seems much out of place. Immediately in front of the bench, are the seats for the officers of the courts.

In the common law courts, the tables for solicitors are placed so that they face the judge, but in the chancery, the solicitors appear to sit with their backs to the bench and turn around in order to address the court.

The bar have but little reason to complain of the amount of space allotted to them, as the whole body of the courts seems to be absolutely given up to them. By the relegation of the public and the jurors to galleries, counsel are able to pass in and out of all the courts with the greatest freedom.

The short-hand reporters and the reporters of the daily papers have not been forgotten. Their seats are at the sides of the courts, between those of the Masters and the Queen's Counsel, but at right angles to them. They are, therefore, exceedingly well placed-for hearing. The fittings of the interior of the courts are all oak, presenting a very solid and handsome appearance, the oak wainscoting going all around them to the height of some ten feet.

VENTILATING AND LIGHTING.—Great attention has been paid to the ventilation and lighting of the courts, and the arrangements appear to be excellent. The royal courts of Cook County may well pattern after them.

We counted sixteen small courts all arranged alike except that those on the east side are wider than those on the west by some two feet. The three larger ones would appear about half as large again. There are book cases in all of them, in which many of the later acts of Parliament and recent decisions of the courts of last resort are kept for the use of the court and bar.

CONSULTATION ROOMS.—Outside the courts but on the same floor, there are some ten consultation rooms, and robing rooms for the bar are found at the north and south ends of the buildings. Those at the north are on the floor on which counsel enter, but owing to the descent from Carey Street to the Strand, those on the south are on the first floor.

Just at the entrance on the south or Strand, are two good sized arbitration rooms; they are on a level with the ground, and to an outsider seem to be dark and cold.

HEATING APPARATUS.—Underneath the Central Hall are six large boilers and a steam engine, which are used in warming the building by means of hot water pipes, whose ramifications extend throughout the passages, and as regards the engine, in supplying power for lighting by etectricity the entire building.

While the corridors are warmed by means of hot water pipes, the rooms are all provided with open fire places, and the consumption of coal must necessarily be enormous.

It will scarcely be credited that the space originally provided by the architect, was not sufficient for a fortnight's consumption. "Fresh cellerage" as the Englishmen say, or as we say, "additional cellerage," had to be provided. In the west end of the building are "lifts" [elevators], for raising coal to the several floors.

The sanitary arrangements are ample, and in the roof are large tanks of water for the service of the building, and to supply the numerous hydrants set in every corridor for the protection of the building from fire.

Among the minor defects noticeable in this large and admirable building, may be noted that much of the stone with which the staircases are constructed and the passages paved, is already wearing out.

It must, like most of the stone used in the erection of our Chicago Court House, have been originally soft and unfit for use.

There is another similarity to our Court House, and that is, th. t many of the stairways, staircases, corridors and passages are exceedingly dark, and have to be constantly lighted, policed and protected in order to avoid danger, to those who are not prepared for steps, descents and pitfalls.

This structure is among the grandest and most complete of

its kind ever devised, and surpasses in its design and details anything before attempted in ancient or modern times. The Royal Assize Courts of Manchester just completed, is modeled after the Royal Courts of Justice, and contains many conveniences that they do not.

St. George's Hall in Liverpool, we regard as one of the finest structures of the kind in the world, and yet it did not cost as much to erect as the Cook County Court House, in the City of Chicago. The science of court house architecture appears to be yet in its infancy in this country, and until it becomes understood that these buildings are to be designed to transact the public business and not to furnish lounging places for the idle and those seeking to be amused, we can hope for but little improvement in their internal arrangements. Most of our court rooms are too large, and in most of them there are not accommodations for ladies, or for witnesses or jurors, but all are permitted to huddle together promiscuously and vitiate the air with their presence, without any adequate means of ventilating the rooms, to the death and destruction of the judges, the attorneys and officers of the court. The acoustic properties of many of our court rooms, are as bad as anything can possibly be. This could be remedied by placing over the judge's seat a canopy to hold the sound, such as is provided in every court room in Europe, and not making the rooms so high as they are now.

The Central Criminal Court rooms at the Old Bailey, where all of the important criminal cases are now tried, are not much larger than the small court rooms recently erected in the rotunda of our court house, but they have several rooms attached-- for witnesses, for jurors, for ladies, with lavatories and other conveniences, which render them very complete in all of their appointments.

There is not a court room in Europe that is as large as the common law court rooms on the 2d and 3d story of our court house in Chicago occupied by Judges Gary and ourselves. Indeed these court rooms are almost as large as the House of Commons.

In the Royal Courts of Justice, the witnesses and their friends are not allowed to crowd into the court rooms, but are retained in a witness room and are called in as they are wanted. Here, the counsel in the case, the parties, the witnesses and all of their friends think it necessary not only to crowd into the court room, but to crowd on to the jury, and they seem to take it as an affront if they are prevented from so doing.

The very fact that the court houses in England have been designed to transact business and not to enable counsel to play "star engagements" has its effect, and while as some contend it has produced a decline of eloquence, it has served to facilitate the administration of the law, and thereby saved much valuable time and a great amount of money.

There people do not go to gossip and hear the lawyers spar, because they are not furnished any facilities for so doing. Here, lawyers, especially in criminal cases, take control of the court, consume days and weeks in obtaining juries, and then an equal amount of time in trying the cases, and courts are by our laws powerless to check them.

In England, lawyers stand up when impaneling juries or when examining witnesses, or making objections to the introduction of testimony. In Illinois, they are permitted to sit or lie down, and resent it as an innovation if requested to assume an upright posture.

We want new court houses designed with special reference to the accomplishment of the objects of their erection, with all of the modern appliances and modern conveniences, and a bar willing to co-operate with the courts in all of their efforts to administer the laws and execute justice, and then over the entrance to the Temple of Justice should be inscribed in letters of gold, the words found in our Bill of Rights which supplement the great charter of King John:

"Every person ought to find a certain remedy in the laws for all injuries and wrongs which he may receive in his person, property or reputation; he ought to obtain by law, right and justice freely and without being obliged to purchase it, completely and without denial, promptly and without delay."

Elliott Anthony.

A CENTURY OF REPUBLICANISM.

Following our Centennial celebration, when the public mind has been called to our constitutional government, it may not be unprofitable to calmly glance over our history and gather what lessons we may from our experience of a hundred years. When our fathers set out with their somewhat doubtful experiment of a republic, it was generally predicted that they would fail, and that in a few years they would return, if not to the subjection of England, at least to the refuge of a monarchy. It was then a question whether a republic was, under any circumstances, possible, and especially under the difficulties with which we had to contend—a great war on our hands disputing the existence of the nation itself, a great number of disconnected States with little community of interest, a wild region with almost no arts or industries, and a perpetual enemy of savages in our midst and on our borders.

It was doubtful, I say, whether, under such circumstances, a people could govern themselves, if, indeed, they could do so at all. It was apprehended, in particular, that, as republicans, we should be theoretical and visionary; that, with wild and impracticable ideals, we would not attempt the merely possible in government, or be content with anything we might realize; and that, in consequence, we should be revolutionary and unstable, always changing for something unattainable. It was thought, too, that in the variety of our individual opinions, in which every man would think himself supreme, we should be irreconcilable as a whole, and unmanageable as a body politic;

that, in our inexperience in government, and our impatience of moderation, the minority would not submit to the majority, or one department work harmoniously with another. In consequence of all this, it was thought that we should be beset with internal dissensions and insubordination, and be the prey of civil wars and anarchy, so that we would ultimately welcome a monarchy or even despotism, as a happy deliverance.

In the absence of that peace which was thought to belong only to an empire or strong personal government, it was believed, too, that there would be no adequate encouragement to industry; that in the insecurity of person and property which would follow our failures, we should not try to become rich. Depending on spoils and political preferments instead of labor (as republicans and liberals were then thought to do), it was contended that we would, instead of developing our resources, idly try to get what is our neighbor's by political reform. In brief, it was predicted that, instead of a great and prosperous career, we should not be able to maintain the status with which we set out.

Such was the prospect with which, in the eyes of the world, our fathers commenced their career a hundred years ago—a prospect which was shared also by many of our friends whose forebodings shadowed a dark future for us. For, with the exception of a few visionary Frenchmen, who were on the eve of their great revolution, there were few anywhere who were not convinced of the impossibility of a republic, and some of our own wisest statesmen thought our experiment of questionable expediency.

Now, in answer to these forbidding prophecies and forebodings, as well as to the unfavorable criticisms of to-day, we adduce the facts of our history for the past hundred years. The record which we as a republic have made in this time is full of significance to the statesman and historian.

And first, with regard to the apprehension that we should be beset with wars, and so be rendered incapable of realizing the advantages of peace. During all this time—that is, in the first century of our existence—we have had but two foreign wars, one with England in 1812, and one with Mexico in 1845; this being the greatest example of protracted peace and comparative immunity from bloodshed known in history. Not to compare it with the almost perpetual and interminable war history of the ancient civilizations, or of the governments of the Middle Ages, which were founded and carried on in blood, or even with the ceaseless wars of modern Europe prior to our independence, in which, since the Reformation, all the States, from Sweden to Turkey, have been involved (once for a period of thirty, and once for a period of seven years), when peace was only an armistice, and new wars could not commence because old ones never ceased; not, I say, to compare our history with those times, when, certainly, it cannot be said that monarchies were a preventive. of war, or that empires meant peace; but to confine ourselves to the last hundred years, and to the parallel courses of other nations with ours, we find that we, inexperienced as we were in government and diplomacy, and having new principles to establish and illustrate, have given the noblest peace example of them all. For, in this same period, while we have had but two wars, England has had eight foreign wars, besides her Indian, Persian and China wars, France has had nine wars, Prussia six, Russia fourteen, Austria five, Spain four, and Italy five.

Comparing more at length our history with that of England in this respect, we find that, while we have been enjoying a hundred years of peace (or 113 since our Declaration of Independence), broken only in 1812 and in 1845 with wars, which together aggregate but six years, England at the same time has had twenty-eight years of war. From 1778 to 1783, she had a war with France. From 1780 to 1783, she had a war with Spain. During the same time she had a war also with Holland. In 1793, she commenced the war of the Revolution, which lasted till 1802, or nine years, and in 1801 the war against the Confederation of the North, all of which wars were had before our peace was once broken. Then, in 1803, she began the war against Bonaparte, which lasted twelve years. From 1812 to 1815, she carried on a war with the United States, and from 1854 to 1856, she carried on the Crimean War with Russia. During the same period she has also had nine wars with India, two with China and one with Persia. Accordingly, while our first century has been a century of peace, England's, with which more than any other we are unfavorably compared, has been a century of war.

Comparing, again, our history with that of France, we find that, in the period in which we have had but two short wars, France has been almost perpetually at war, aggregating forty years out of the hundred. For, in this time, she engaged in 1778, in a war with England, rendering aid to the American colonies in their efforts for independence; in 1792, she entered the field against the allied powers of Europe, continuing the struggle for twenty-three years, till 1815. In 1793, she declared war against England; in 1812, she declared war also against Russia, and in 1813 against Austria, Russia and Prussia.

In 1854, she engaged in the Crimean War; in 1857, she, with Sardinia, aided Victor Emanuel against Austria. In 1862 she fought with Mexico, to enthrone Maximilian, and in 1870, commenced her fatal war with Prussia. In short, while we have pursued a policy of peace, France has pursued one of glory and conquest, the result of which, compared with our prosperity, has been humiliation and defeat.

Comparing, in the next place, our history with that of Prussia, we find that the strongest of monarchies while professing a traditional peace policy, has had three times as many wars as we. In 1792, she commenced a war with France, which she carried on through the whole revolutionary period. In 1803, she renewed it, as a member of the Holy Alliance, and continued therein till the fall of Napoleon in 1815. In 1848, she assisted the duchies against Denmark, fighting till 1850. In 1866, she again fought against Denmark in the Schleswig-Holstein War. In 1866, she commenced the war against Austria and the South-German States, and finally, in 1870, entered into the Franco-Prussian War. Thus, monarchical Prussia, as compared with republican America, has had a career of war, and established her monarchy in blood rather than in sweat.

Comparing, again, our history with that of Russia, we get a similar result. Instead of an almost uniform reign of peace, as in the United States, Russia has in this time had war as the rule, with only short intervals of peace. In 1795, she had war with Poland, entered into to complete her subjugation of that country. In 1784, she completed her war with Turkey, and her invasions of the Crimea, which were begun as far back as 1769. In 1796, she fought with Persia. In 1799, she took part against the French revolutionists. In 1805, and again in 1812, she took part against Napoleon. In 1809, she fought with the Turks; in 1826, with Persia again, as also in 1840. In 1849, she fought against Hungary; in 1853, against Turkey; in 1854, against France and England in the Crimean War, and in 1877 against Turkey. In short, Russia's history, as compared with ours, shows that we are far less inclined to war than she, and that republicanism is more peaceful than absolute monarchy.

Comparing, next, our history with that of Austria, we have a similar showing. Though more inclined to peace than most European countries, and though suffering frequent dishonor and loss of territory for the sake of peace, Austria has yet had a large number of wars. In 1805, she fought against France in the Holy Alliance, and, until the fall of Napoleon, was fighting in one capacity or another for her Italian possessions. In 1848, she had the memorable war with Hungary and its allies. In 1849, she fought with Sardinia and France for her Italian interests. In 1864, she engaged with Prussia in the Schleswig-Holstein War against Denmark, and in 1866, she fought against Prussia and Italy in the disastrous war which decided her fate at Sadowa, and compelled her to withdraw from participation in German affairs.

Our history, when compared with that of Spain, shows a like result. For, in this time of comparative peace with us, Spain has had a comparative season of war. In 1796, she had a war with England; in 1807 she had a war with France, as also in 1823; and in 1859 one with Morocco. In short, that most monarchical of countries, with unlimited loyalty to king and pope, knowing nothing but submission and obedience, has, besides her endless rebellions, had twice as many foreign wars as our independent and individualized Americans who have acknowledged no authority but themselves.

And, comparing finally our history with that of Italy, we have still the invariable result—peace in America and war abroad. For, in this time, Italy has engaged in the following wars: First, those growing out of the French Revolution and of the intervention of Napoleon in Italian affairs, which lasted till 1814; secondly, that of the Milanese and Venetians against Austria in 1848, for their independence and supremacy; thirdly, the wars of independence between Piedmont and Austria, into which the rest of the Italians were largely drawn; and finally, the wars of Garibaldi for the Union of Italy, conducted against Austria and the Pope. In short, Italy has, as far as it can in this period be considered a nation or people in itself, had a history of war, while most of its individual states have been separately at war, or been drawn into the wars of their dependencies.

Such, therefore, is our record as compared with that of England, France, Prussia, Russia, Austria, Spain and Italy, in regard to war. And yet these constitute all the great powers of of Europe, so that the comparison is exhaustive, and can be said to be with the whole world. It is a record of peace compared with seven records of war; so that, when compared with the other great countries, our showing, notwithstanding the patronizing forebodings of war which others indulged in at our beginning, is the best of all. As far, therefore, as eight examples of history running through a hundred years can prove anything, they prove that a free republican government is more calculated to keep at peace than a monarchy, and in so far to keep the peace of the world and promote the happiness of mankind.

And here we may pause to observe that in both of our wars we have been successful; so that never yet, as a nation, have we been conquered. In the same period, however, all the other nations mentioned have been once or oftener conquered. England was overcome in the first war of the French revolution, as well as in the American war. France was finally overcome in the wars of the Empire, and again in the war with Prussia in 1870. Prussia was overcome in the first war of the Revo-

,lution. Russia was badly conquered in the Crimean War. Austria was conquered in her wars with Napoleon, with Italy, and with Prussia. Italy was conquered in the Napoleonic wars, and in the war with Austria, in 1864, until she was rescued by Prussia. And Spain was conquered in her war with Napoleon and her first mentioned war with England. All this comparison proves, not only that a republic is as good as any other government in keeping at peace, but also as good, if forced into war, in raising armies and fighting its battles.

So much, then, for foreign wars, which comprise generally a great part of the faults and failures of governments, as well as of the misery of mankind; all of which have been so signally avoided by our republic.

I shall speak next of rebellions and civil wars. In this respect, it was thought, at the beginning of our career, that we, as a nation, would particularly suffer. It was believed in the first place, that, as a republic, with all the people free, and alike entitled to rule, we should be more exposed and inclined to civil dissensions; and in the second place, that, without a monarchical government, we should not be able to quell our rebellions when they should arise, and so to preserve the internal peace with force.

In comparing ourselves with other great powers, however, we find that our history in this respect is not only creditable, but vastly better than theirs. For, during all this time, we have had but one great rebellion or civil war; while in the same time England has had two, France eight, Prussia two, Russia four, Austria six, Spain six, and Italy three.

To compare more minutely, we observe that, in our long reign of internal peace, broken only once in the year 1861, England has had her Irish rebellion in 1798, and her Sepoy rebellion in 1857. I do not here speak of our bloodless whisky rebellion in 1786, or of Shea's rebellion in 1793. These will be mentioned hereafter in comparing our insurrections and riots with those of Europe, when speaking of the so called rebellion against England of Robert Emmett and his followers in 1803, and of the Chartists at Newport in 1839.

In France, in the same period, there have been the rebellions

and civil wars of 1789, together with the revolutions immediately following; the rebellion in La Vendée in 1793; the rebellions and revolutions of 1830 and 1848; the *coup d'etat* and
civil war in 1851; and, finally, the rebellion and commune in
1870.

In Prussia, in this time, there have been the rebellion of the
Liberals in 1848, which extended throughout the whole continent of Europe, and engaged particularly the students of the
universities, and to some extent, the soldiers of the army, and
also the war of 1866, which was largely with parts of its own
present territory, as Hanover and Frankfort.

In Russia, which was struggling with a rebellion in the Crimea at the commencement of our career, and which had just
closed the great Cossack Rebellion, there have been, during
our existence as a nation, the rebellions of the Poles in 1795
and 1830, and rebellions in her Asiatic provinces in 1840 and
1872, resulting in the severe Khiva campaigns.

In Austria, there have been, in this period, rebellions in Lom-
bardy in 1797, resulting in the loss of that province to Austria;
in Milan, Venice and Sardinia, in 1848; in Vienna in the
same year, when Prince Metternich took his flight, and the
emperor was soon after compelled to fly; and, finally, in Hungary, under Kossuth, in 1848.

In Spain, in this time, there have been the uprising of the
Asturias in 1808; the wars of the Revolution in 1820; the
movement of Don Carlos in 1834; of O'Donnell and Concha
in favor of Christina in 1841; the revolutionary wars of 1843;
the revolt of Cuba in 1851; the military insurrection under
Espartero in 1854; the later war against Cuba, commenced
in 1868, and the recent Carlist war, which was commenced
about the same time.

And, finally, in Italy, in this same period, there have been
the wars following the French revolution, which have been
largely civil; also the internal revolutions of 1848 and 1849,
which resulted in the independence of several of the States;
and the succeeding wars of Garibaldi and Victor Emanuel for
the union of the Peninsula.

Thus, it appears that in all the great nations during the

last hundred years, there have been more civil wars and rebellions than in ours, our republic making the best showing in the very respect in which it was predicted that we should fail altogether. As far, therefore, as the examples of all the great nations, taken for a hundred years, can prove anything, they prove that a republic is less inclined to civil wars and rebellions than a monarchy. This ought to be enough to settle forever the objections to republican institutions on the ground that they expose the people to lawlessness and civil strife.

I have, in this comparison, not included our wars with the Indians, or the wars of the other nations with their respective savages—the wars of England, for example, with the uncivilized tribes of Africa, Central Asia, Ashantee, etc.; those of France with the Arabs in Algiers; those of Russia with the northern Asiatic tribes; those of Spain with the South American and Mexican Indians, etc. There is nothing in these wars of a civil, diplomatic or international character, which bears on the question now in discussion. It will be conceded, no doubt, that, having had in this respect as great a difficulty as any of the nations to deal with, we have solved it quite as well as they have solved their relations with savages.

Let us next look at insurrections, riots, and other uprisings and lawlessness of a smaller kind. In this respect our government compares favorably with any or all of the others. Without attempting to enumerate all the lawless uprisings, either of our own or other countries, it may be observed that about our only insurrections of any consequence have been the Whisky rebellion, Shea's rebellion, the Kansas riots, John Brown's insurrection, the riot in New York to resist the draft, and the recent labor riots. That is, in all our history we have had only about seven insurrections of any consequence.

In the same time, however, the riots in other countries have been almost without number. Hardly a month passes but the cable brings us news of a riot in some part of Europe. In Great Britain it is generally in the coal mines, or at the great strikes among mechanics, or else between the Orangemen and Catholics, or between the Home Rulers and royal police. In France and Spain the riots are generally of a political character, preceding elections and great events in the legislative assemblies. In Prussia, they are generally socialistic, or on account of the price of beer or bread, of which there have been a great many. In Russia, they are by Poles and Liberals, of whom great numbers have to be annually sent to Siberia; and in Italy they are either of a political or religious character, sometimes aiming at the independence of a State, and sometimes at a restriction of some privilege of the Pope or Church.

In most European countries riots are so numerous, and the tendency to them so great, that it is deemed necessary to maintain great armies to keep down the people, and also to support much larger bodies of police than we do. Many of the streets and public buildings are permanently guarded; the houses of the people are carefully watched and often searched; the people themselves are generally kept under police surveillance by a system of registration and passports; and, in various other ways, precautions are taken against lawless uprisings, all because of this tendency to riot. In short, without specifying the cases, it is obvious that riots in other countries have been more numerous during the last hundred years than in ours, and that we, instead of being exceptionally plagued with them, enjoy an exceptional immunity from them.

There is, therefore, no justification in our history of the adverse prophesies and forebodings which were indulged in at the beginning of our career, about lawlessness and dissensions, which, it was thought, would prove so numerous as to render a republican government impossible; but, on the other hand, our history as compared with that of other countries, shows that a republic is no more inclined to riots and disorders than other forms of government, but rather that it is less exposed to them.

I shall speak next of revolutions, or governmental overthrows. For it was predicted at the beginning of our career that we should be the prey of revolutionists, and that the republican government with which we began would not long endure, but be overthrown for something else, and finally end in anarchy or a monarchy.

We find, however, that in all our history there has not only not been any revolution, but not an attempt at any. For even the great rebellion did not aim at the overthrow of our government, but only at the withdrawal of some of the States from the Union, (with the view of forming a similar government.) Our government has stood not only unmoved, but even unattacked, during all this time. In the same period, however, all the other great powers, except Great Britain and Russia, have been overthrown, and these only barely escaped. For, in the last hundred years, France has had ten revolutions, Prussia one, Austria one, Spain fifteen, and Italy five.

To particularize, during our first century, we have not only not had one overthrow of our government, or of any one of our governments, but we have made no radical change in our government. The same constitution, the same general basis of laws, the same free institutions all stand as they stood at the beginning. The changes that we have made have been only for the perfecting of our system. We have, if possible, become more republican than ever, or more nearly a perfect republic.

If in England there has not, in this time, been any revolution in the full sense of the term, there has been almost the same thing in the changes that have been forced on the government through the enemies of that government. There was, in 1801, a general reconstruction of the whole empire, by which Ireland was incorporated, and a new name given to the empire. The title of "King of France" was dropped by the British ruler, and his realm called "The United Kingdom of Great Britian and Ireland." At the same time, a series of reformatory and liberalizing measures have been adopted by Parliament, through which an almost entirely new character has been given to the empire. England has been peaceably revolutionized. This last remark applies also, in part, to Russia. But if there have been no violent revolutions in England and Russia during the last hundred years, they are the only exceptions, and the only powers that can compare with the United States as examples of governmental stability.

For, in Prussia, in this period, besides the revolutions which it has been compelled to undergo as part of Germany (in the several overthrows of the German Empire), her government was forcibly overthrown in 1848, when the regent was compelled to fly for his life, and a new constitution was forced by the revolutionists on the State, a circumstance similar to what occurred in many other States of the Continent, when Prague, Copenhagen, Munich and Athens were all besieged by their own citizens, and the kings of the two latter capitals compelled to abdicate.

In Austria, in this time, besides the revolution which overthrew the king, as the Emperor of Germany, and compelled him to withdraw his power from the German states, and besides the change of the kingdom into the Austrian-Hungarian Empire, there was, in 1848, an overthrow of the government similar to that just described in Prussia. The capital was stormed, and the Emperor Ferdinand compelled to abdicate, and Francis Joseph was installed in his place with a new constitution and new dynastic principles.

In France, in this time, there have been in succession the Revolution of 1792 and the establishment of the republic; the overthrow in 1795 of the Directory and Council of Five Hundred and the establishment of the Consulate; the overthrow of this in 1804 and the establishment of the Empire; the overthrow of this in 1814 and the restoration of the Bourbon monarchy; the restoration of the Empire again in 1815; the restoration of the Bourbons the same year; the overthrow of these and the enthronement of Louis Philippe in 1830; the overthrow of the Orleanist dynasty and establishment of the republic in 1848; the overthrow of this and the re-establishment of the empire by Napoleon III. in 1853; and, finally, the overthrow of Napoleon III. and the establishment of the republic in 1870.

In Spain, in this time, there have been the following revolutions: In 1808, Charles IV. abdicated in favor of Ferdinand. The same year Joseph Bonaparte was made King of Spain; he was almost immediately ousted, and again restored. In 1814, his government was overthrown, and Ferdinand again restored. In 1820 a popular revolution was successful, which put a new constitution and a new Cortes in power. In 1823, this Cortes and constitution were overthrown, and there was a return to despotism. In 1833, on the death of Ferdinand, the Infanta Isabella seized the throne. In 1840, another revolution compelled the dissolution of the Cortes, and the forming of a new ministry. In 1843, the regency of Espartero was overthrown by a revolution, commencing at Barcelona. The same year there was a reaction against the new government, and Isabella, then thirteen years old, was declared of age and made queen. By a new insurrection Espartero next gets control and forms a new ministry under himself. Next, in 1868, we have Isabella expelled, and soon after an Italian, Amadeus, made king. Then, in 1872, the republic is declared, and finally, in 1874, Alfonso is made king.

And, finally, in Italy, in this time, which was largely under Austria at the beginning of our career, there have been the following revolutions: In 1798. the complexion of the government was wholly changed by the wars following the French revolution, the old Germanic-Italian Empire being entirely destroyed. In 1802, the Italian republic was formed, with Bonaparte for president. In 1805, this was made a kingdom under Bonaparte. In 1814, Austrian rule was re-established. Next, we have revolts and overthrows of particular states, until Garibaldi restores the unity of all Italy under Victor Emanuel.

Such is the history of the great nations in regard to revolutions; a history in general of overthrows and governmental insecurity. At the same time all the small German and Italian States, and the smaller monarchies and principalities of Europe generally, have, in this period, been many times overthrown, or merged in larger States and empires, so that, in most cases, the thrones of Europe, even, have not stood the century through, much less the dynasties. The map of Europe has been changed over and over again, and European history, instead of being fixed like the mountains, is changeable like the sea. While, therefore, our republic has stood like a house founded upon a rock, without so much as being shaken by the storms of surrounding wars and revolutions, the European monarchies have yielded to every popular wave, and have been often swept away by the slightest gusts. Surely the history of the last hundred years proves, as far as the example of all the nations for a hundred years can prove anything, that republics are no more exposed to revolutions than monarchies, but, on the contrary, are even more secure than they.

And here let us observe that, in all this period in which our republic has stood so securely and peacefully, all the great imperial confederacies or empires, which alone correspond in magnitude and difficulty of management with our union of States, have been overturned. For, after all, the comparison should be made more properly with those confederacies than with the single States. For ours is a nation of nations, embracing as many States as all of Europe combined, and bound up in one great union of the whole. We have not merely a nation and a nation's difficulties to deal with, but a cluster of nations, our republic embracing the most numerous and extensive alliance of States that has been known in history. And yet, while the little European confederacies could scarcely keep united long enough to effect the purposes of a campaign, and while, when they were united, they were but short-lived and full of dissension, we have not only stood as a whole during all this time, preserving our great central republic in entirety and security, but have carried on, with equal success, and without internal or inter-state difficulties or dangers, some forty-two independent republics.

The great wheel and the wheels within the wheel have all been running without jars or breakage, and they promise, for the next century, to run as smoothly as ever. We have done this, while all the similar confederacies of a monarchical character have been revolutionized or entirely destroyed. For, in this same period, the German Empire or confederation has been four times overthrown, the federacy of the Italian States likewise four times, and the Austrian Empire three times; and all the single States composing each of those empires have likewise been overthrown, most of them many times, in the last hundred years.

The German Empire was broken up in 1804, by Napoleon, who formed in its stead the Confederation of the Rhine. Eleven years later this confederation was destroyed, and the German

Confederation formed. In 1866, this was again destroyed, and the North-German Confederation took its place. And finally, in 1870, this gave way to the present German Empire. The Austrian Empire, or at least its relation with the German Empire—a vital part of itself—was revolutionized in 1804, 1815 and 1866, as already explained; and the Italian federation of States, under whatever name, was overturned in 1802, 1805, 1814 and 1856, not to count the partial revolutions at other times.

Thus a comparison of our federal success with that of European confederacies proves that a republican confederation can stand and preserve its parts better than a kingly one. The nearest approach to our federal success is in that of the similar republican confederation of Switzerland.

In the next place, we may observe that in all this period of a hundred years there has been no change in our territory by conquest, division or cession, except a constant increase. No foot of land has ever been wrested from us by force, none ever awarded by arbitration to another power against us, none ever sold by us from fear that it would be taken by an enemy, none ever parted with for any cause whatever. There has been no division of our territory by the withdrawal of any State or section, no disunion or releasing of our power in any degree over one acre of land. The land, and the government over it all, has been maintained, so that it is altogether ours. No part over which we have been in conflict have we yielded, and no rights that we have ever had over neutral ground or the sea coast, have we given up. On the contrary, we have in this time added the immense tracts of Louisiana (including the greater part of the Mississippi valley), Florida, Texas, New Mexico, California and Alaska—as much, almost, as the entire territory of Europe.

In the same period, however, the territory of all the great European states, or their power over it, has been materially changed, nearly every nation, at one time or another, losing a material part of itself. Spain has lost Mexico and nearly all her South American and West India possessions. England, besides losing, at the beginning of this period, her American colonies, has lost her title and claim as King of France and all her pretensions to equibalance the Continent. France has lost, besides Hayti, her beautiful provinces of Alsace and Lorraine, and her entire claim to the west bank of the Rhine. Prussia has lost all control over Denmark, Luxemburg, Bohemia and the other German states now under Austria, which she formerly held as part of the German Empire. Russia has lost her claims on the south and east, which she was compelled to forego in the Crimean War. Italy has lost (for much of this time), Savoy, Piedmont, Nice, and all right to a control in the German Empire; and Austria has lost not only its Italian possessions, but its supremacy and entire control in Germany.

In short, a comparison of our government in its acquisitions with those of Europe, which have had all these losses, and, at the same time, had no gains to compare with our enormous acquisitions just mentioned, proves, as far as a comparison of all the great powers of the civilized world can prove anything, that a republic can preserve its territory and aggrandize itself quite as well as a monarchy.

On the whole, I think we can safely conclude, from this exhaustive comparison of our nation with the other nations in all that constitute the general objects and evidences of good government, that we have, during our century of existence with our republican institutions, had more peace, stability and security than any monarchy of Europe. Our people have, in general, felt just as safe in their lives and property, whether against their fellow-citizens or against an enemy, as any others in the world, and they have, in every way, had just as effective governmental protection.

I might close here, as having already given a sufficient answer to the inquiries so frequently made about the success of republics, and of ours in particular, and also to the prophecies and forebodings that were indulged in about our certain failure as our fathers set out a hundred years ago. But I shall add, without attempting to elaborate or specify (which I hope to do at another time), that not only have we, under our republican government, enjoyed the negative advantages of peace and security equal to any other people, but we have also been able, under the same government, to develop our resources quite as well, and to advance the happiness of our people in as great a degree. Our agriculture has advanced with such improvements in implements and success in method, that we are able, with less labor than any European country, to support ourselves, and, to an extent, to feed the whole world besides. Our mining operations have been the most extensive and successful on record, so that we are in a condition to largely supply Europe, at a cheaper rate than she can produce at home, with the more important minerals, such as coal, iron, petroleum and gold.

Our manufacturers are fast coming to compete in nearly all, departments (and not in a few only, as in France, Italy and Germany respectively), with those of any part of the world; rivaling England in her specialty of hardware and cotton goods, Germany in woolens and earthenwares, France in wines and fineries, and Italy in silks and marbles. Our commerce is larger than that of any other nation, except England, and embraces, as few others do, all the civilized and half-civilized peoples. In the fine arts we have made a proud beginning, having done more in architecture during the last century than any nation of Europe. In short, our success has been such that never in the course of a hundred years has there been so much done in any other country, nor has there been a nation which has grown so rich or great. Certainly, our industrial and commercial history proves that a monarchy is not necessary to develop a country well.

As for the apprehension so often expressed that, being theoretical and impractical, as republicans are generally charged with being, we could not carry out our ideals, we are famed for being the most practical people in the world, and are distinctively known as "the practical nation." And as for the apprehension that, being republicans, and enthusiastically devoted to an idea, we would not care sufficiently for money and material interests, but only for politics and pettifoggery, we have the reputation in Europe of caring more for money than any other people; as also, we may add, of having more money.

Our people, moreover, are just as moral as any other, notwithstanding the old apprehensions that we would run to licentiousness, infidelity, and everything that is tentative and revolutionary. We have more churches than any country in Europe, and the people take a greater interest in religion. In fact, it has been often remarked by foreigners, that we are the most religious nation in the world, and this, notwithstanding we have no state religion or religious laws. The benevolence of our people, and their care for the poor and unfortunate, are quite as great as in any other land, and our benevolent institutions quite as numerous and well supported. Crime is no more common than in other lands, the greater part of our criminals being foreigners. In short, our history abundantly illustrates the fact, that a republic, without any state church or army, or great body of police, can develop and maintain as moral a class of citizens as any other.

With regard to education, our people are, as a whole, as intelligent as any other. If Prussia has men more learned than we, we have a greater number of learned men. Our common school system is quite as good as any in Europe, and is, perhaps, better calculated than any other to substantially elevate the whole people. Our colleges are more numerous than in any other country, and the number of students greater, and the best of the colleges are fast taking rank in wealth and facilities for culture with the best European universities which have stood for centuries. The education of our women, in particular, is of a higher grade than that of any other land; and, in general, there are not so many who cannot read and write, or who are ignorant of the common branches as in other countries. The North-German states alone are our rival in universal elementary education.

While, moreover, our institutions of whatever kind, and for whatever purpose, are in general of the best, showing that republican government is compatible with the best social and political appliances that have hitherto been known, we have also developed some new ones of special excellence, which were hitherto unknown, or else existed as mere doubtful problems in the heads of impractical theorists. One of these is the separation of church and state, without detriment either to the state or to religion. Another is the absolute freedom of all religions and anti-religions without any deleterious effect on our customs or morals. Another is the complete secularization of the schools. with similar harmlessness to both religion and education. Another is dispensing with a standing army without exposing ourselves to either internal or external assaults. And another is the equality of the people, which refuses to recognize any ranks, titles or special privileges, without detriment to anybody. In short, our republic has introduced additional guarantees for intellectual, religious and personal freedom. There is now scarcely any degree of liberty or equality conceivable, even in the most extravagant ideas, that we have not embodied in our system, and proven to be henceforth possible.

And finally, as a general result, our people are, on the whole, as comfortable as any in the world, which is, after all, the most adequate test of a government's success. More of them are wealthy and living in good houses with plenty to do and to eat than in any other country. They more generally marry and live in families than elsewhere, everybody having a home, and every family, as a rule, a whole house to itself. The people are thrifty and hopeful, nearly every one expecting that either he himself or his children will one day be rich or influential.

On the whole, therefore, we think that we can safely conclude that our history and our present condition abundantly prove the success of our government, and that the old prejudices and uncertainties as to the practicability of a republic may be set aside as forever exploded. It can no longer be said that republicanism has no experience in its favor. Side by side with the most successful monarchies that have ever existed, and in the most successful period of their existence, it has established its superiority by the most exact and minute tests that are possible. And now after one century, in which our free experiment has been such a trancendent success, and in no respect a failure, we have as good a prospect for the next hundred years as any nation in the world.

Austin Bierbower.

Department of Medical Jurisprudence.

EXPERT TESTIMONY.

At the meeting of the Medico-Legal Society of Chicago, held December 1st, 1888, the attention of the society was given to the consideration of a suit for malpractice in which one of the members of the society had recently been a successful defendant.

We do not care to report the meeting, nor the case considered; but the following extracts will be of interest:

Dr. F. C. Hotz said: "From a medical point of view I think we may disagree with some applications Dr. G. made, but I am sure on the whole the case was managed well. We all have our individual views in regard to treating a case: I may use one medicine and another person another medicine for the same purpose, but that does not make the other treatment unjustifiable. We are none of us infallible: one may use corrosive sublimate and another something else, for conjunctivitis; and if one makes a mild application of nitrate of silver (5 grains to the ounce), and my views are opposed to the use of nitrate of silver, I should not be justified to condemn the treatment of the other as long as the majority of oculists consider it a valuable remedy.

"But this meeting, I believe, was called for the purpose of bringing out the medico-legal aspects of the case. There was one point that interested me. I was surprised by being informed by the court that whatever occurs at a consultation is not a privileged communication; that we are obliged to give a full statement of whatever the doctor who has called us in consultation said, and what our answer was. That was surprising to me as I thought such matters were confidential.

"I should like to hear from legal lights present how it is that the statements of the client to the lawyer are considered privileged, while those of a patient to his physician or of one physician to another are not, and the physician may be forced on the stand to give away that confidential statement if he is called as a witness. This may place the consultant in an awkward position. For, as I said before, medical men may disagree in regard to a certain application and so express themselves to each other without intending to condemn the treatment of the brother physician or to make it appear in any way wrong; while the same remarks repeated on the stand before a jury of laymen may prejudice the case considerably against the defendant.

"Another medico-legal point is this: I became thoroughly convinced of the utter uselessness of expert testimony. All it can do is to muddle the heads of the jury. The expert is not allowed to give his opinion upon the merits of the case, from a medical point of view. Oh, no, that is for the jury to decide. He is given a hypothetical case. Those of you who have been there and heard all that was put in a hypothetical case by the one side first, and then by the other side, will certainly agree that it is the easiest thing in the world to prove anything with these hypothetical cases. The prosecution will put it in the strongest way against the defense. They make it appear that the doctor has been as cruel as a butcher at the stockyards, handling the poor woman worse than an animal, and showing ignorance in everything; they put all this into a hypothetical case to the expert, and of course he has to answer that such treatment is all wrong. Then comes the defense and puts another hypothetical case. In the light of their evidence of course the expert will say, 'he could not treat it any differently; that was elegantly done.' And there sit the twelve wise men, unfamiliar with medical technicalities, and they are to form an opinion out of this chaos of hypothetical cases'

"I am sure no jury has ever gone into the jury room and paid any attention to the expert evidence in the case. The best illustration of the uselessness of expert evidence was furnished by the case of Dr. B. two years ago, where the prosecution was smart enough not to call any experts at all, and the doctor made the mistake of calling in a great many. The prosecuting lawyer, pointing to the mountain of expert evidence said: 'What does it amount to; the doctors all stick together;' and made it clear to the jury that every doctor went on the stand for the express purpose of perjuring himself in order to protect the defendant; and that made such a deep impression on the jury that in spite of all the expert evidence brought forward for the defense, the jury gave a verdict of $4,500 against Dr. B. I think expert evidence is of no use before a jury."

Judge Oliver H. Horton: "I had not the slightest idea of participating in the discussion this evening. I came to learn. As the case is presented here, I see very little in the nature of law points; it was simply a question of fact. Was the Doctor's treatment proper or improper? Almost absolutely a question of fact. The mode of handling it is a question of the capacity, ability and experience of the lawyer. The mode of presenting these facts, whether admitted upon one side or exaggerated upon the other, is not a question of law but of the practice of particular attorneys.

"With regard to the question of privileged communications: It is not a privilege that applies to the lawyer but to the client, and the lawyer cannot claim the privilege. That is upon the theory, as I understand it, as distinguished from the rule applied to medical men and religious confessors, that if it were otherwise the client could not present to the lawyer, fully and fairly not only the strength but the weak points of his case if his statement of them was to be brought as evidence against him; otherwise he could not go fairly into the case; he could not have full consultation with his counsel. But in the case of the physician it is not that he is consulted with regard to a particular lawsuit, where he has to state the things that are against him as well as for him—if he is a judicious client he will always state the things against him so the lawyer can prepare for it—but it is the statement of facts without regard to whether it is to result in a lawsuit, and the theory is that the facts as they occur at the time, without thought or preparation for a lawsuit, ought not to harm anybody. I suppose that would be a sufficient distinction, or reason for the difference.

"As to expert testimony, I do not think as a rule that lawyers have the highest appreciation of or place the highest value upon it.

"In the matter to which Dr. Hotz referred, of hypothetical questions as being so misleading to laymen—in any profession, for instance in your profession, to a jury who are utterly inexperienced, a hypothetical question is so misleading as to oftentimes result in injustice, but until somebody is sagacious enough to give us a better mode I know of no way to stop the present.

"Counsel for the plaintiff cannot be required to put a hypothetical question upon the defendant's case, but a suggestion from the doctor, it seems to me, would be very valuable. Instead of putting a hypothetical case, where the doctor had seen and examined the patient, the question should be, 'You saw the patient, what is your judgment?' and I think the question would have influence, from the doctor as an expert. 'When you saw this case, what was your opinion as to the defendant's treatment?' That, however, is not a legal aspect of this particular case, but only the mode of trying it by the lawyers; it is not in the law but in the mode of trying the case. I think the gentleman spoke here, if I caught the name correctly, who treated the case following Dr. Gradle's treatment. He could speak from what he saw. 'You saw the patient, what is your judgment from seeing her?' not from the hypothetical question. But if he had not seen the patient, how are you going to ask him his opinion as an expert? In no mode that I know of except in a hypothetical case. Presumably the hypothetical question states the case as presented by the evidence. If it does not the question is erroneous, but if it states the facts in the hypothetical question as developed in the evidence, then it is proper, and how else will you get the opinion of experts who have not seen the case?"

Dr. Hotz: "My point is, not that the hypothetical case is

put by the prosecuting lawyer on the evidence of the prosecution alone, but that it is so one sided. It is put on the evidence so far as presented, that is true, but the defendant's—for instance, Dr. Gradle's statement, was not in the evidence when they put the hypothetical question. It is true it was presented on the evidence, but it was so one sided that it did not make a case."

Judge Horton: "If it was a jury of experts that could see the weakness of that it ought not to do much harm. But if it is not a correct statement of the evidence, and the question be objected to, the objection would be sustained. If it was a correct putting of the one side before the evidence of the defendant had appeared, then an expert witness who had had some experience, and saw how it would come out on the other side presently, would say, 'If your supposed case comes out on the evidence then my views would be so and so, but if other facts enter into the question my judgment might be entirely different.' Another thing I have observed somewhat as a rule, that the lawyer is seriously at a disadvantage when examining an expert where he is not thoroughly conversant with the subject himself, for the expert in nine cases out of ten will down him. Unless he is thoroughly posted, crammed for that particular case, if you please, he is apt to come out second best.

"I think the case you stated to-night is a good illustration of the fact that expert testimony often does more harm than good. It is a good deal in the general view of the jury, like a case against a corporation. Expert testimony does not weigh as a rule. It is my belief that I could take medical experts and prove that any man in America was insane, and I ask you doctors if that is not pretty nearly true? And if that is true, how can you expect it to have weight against the truth, for we all know there are some sane people in America. The thought is in the air and it has an effect upon expert testimony of all kinds."

Dr. Hotz: "I would like to ask if it is the fault of the expert testmony or the fault of the lawyer in not being able to bring it out?"

Dr. Henry Gradle: "What Dr. Hotz said concerning ex-

pert testimony in general, was certainly true of this case, viz:
that there are always enough different opinions among different
experts to get the jury decidedly perplexed, and that a skillful
lawyer will have no difficulty in drawing out these differences
of opinion. Dr. Hotz was asked by Mr. Brand, whether he, as
consulting physician, saw anything in the case that indicated
injudicious treatment or improper violence. He answered,
'no.' The attorney on the other side asked him whether he
or any one else could in a case of that kind swear to their best
knowledge and belief, on seeing the patient a single time, that
no harm could have been done. Of course the case was put
in so vague a manner, that he said no. It is one of the difficulties in expert witnesses that no matter how definite a stand
they make take, the attorney on the other side can introduce
testimony from the same man that may at least render the
thing shaky in the eyes of a technically unintellectual jury.

"Judge Horton referred to the fact that members of the
Medico-Legal Society might injure each other by serving in
each other's behalf. I think this was attempted in the present
case, but it had escaped me until it was commented on to-night.
I remember that when I was on the stand I was asked if I
was a member of the Medico-Legal Society? And the same
question was put to some of the experts, but as some of them
did not happen to be members, the prosecuting attorneys made
no use of that point in their speech."

Judge Horton: "My thought was that there is a sort of
general prejudice in the public mind that gets into the jury
box, against expert testimony, a sort of feeling, as one of the
gentlemen here put it, that the doctors will help one another.
Just as you will find it with lawyers; you try to prove a lawyer's bill by lawyers as experts, testifying to the value of
the services, and the doubt as to the fairness of the testimony
will go through the jury instantly. They say, well, those lawyers will help one another. And the same thought obtains
that the doctors will help one another as experts. It may
be the fault of our system of jurisprudence; it may be a weakness of human nature; but the fact exists; hence it requires
cautious and careful handling to win a case upon expert testi-

mony where there is a complication of facts, or disputed facts. It is very difficult.

"I think it quite possible, as I suggested to your President, that in case a member of this society was prosecuted and witnesses were called who were members of the same society, it might add to that feeling and weaken the expert testimony of co-members of the society.

"To criticise the handling of any case in court, not having heard the trial of the case, would be like one physician criticising another without knowing anything about the case or the treatment. It is a thing that is impracticable—impossible to do and do properly.

"Allow me to suggest a word as to experts, called out by the remarks of the two last speakers. It is the custom of experts to answer a question literally and stop, because counsel says, 'That is all; you have answered the question.' A witness has always the right to explain his answer, and I think the experienced expert will demand his rights and explain his answer, and then he will not be caught in that 'vise' the doctor spoke of.

THE USE OF THE TITLE 'HOMEOPATHIST.'

Judge George C. Barrett, of the Supreme Court of New York City, in reply to the question: "Has a physician, designating himself an 'Homeopathist' and called as such to a patient, any legal or moral right to adopt other than homeopathic means in the treatment of the case?" sends the following answer to the New York Medical Times:

"I have your note of the 11th inst. asking my opinion upon a question of professional ethics. In my judgment there can be but one answer to your question, and that is in the negative. If I call in a medical man who designates himself an 'homeopathic physician,' it is because I do not wish to be treated allopathically, or eclectically or otherwise than homeopathically.

There is an implied understanding between myself and the homeopathist that I shall receive the treatment which, by tradition and a general consensus of opinion, means small doses of a single drug administered upon the principle of *similia similibus curantur*.

"If there is to be any variation from that method I have a right to be informed of it and to be given an opportunity to decide. Common honesty demands that before a confiding patient is to be drugged with quinine, iron, morphine or other medicaments, either singly or in combination, he should be told that the 'homeopathist' has failed, and that relief can only be afforded by a change of system. An honest homeopathist, who has not succeeded, after doing his best with the appropriate homeopathic remedies administered on homeopathic principles, should undoubtedly try anything else which he believes may save or relieve his patient. But when he reaches that point, the duty of taking his patient into his confidence becomes imperative. The patient may refuse to submit to the other system, or he may agree, but prefer a physician whose life has been specially devoted to practice under that other system. He may say to the homeopathist: 'You have failed, but I prefer to try another gentleman of your own school, before resorting to a system that I have long since turned my back upon.' Or he may say, 'Well, if homeopathy cannot save me, I prefer to go to headquarters for allopathic treatment.' All this, gentlemen, is the logical sequence of the particular designation, 'homeopathist.'"

FEES FOR MEDICAL SERVICES.

A decision was recently rendered by Judge Brady of the New York City Supreme Court, in a suit brought by Dr. Srange for payment for professional services.

The judge decided that in a case of this kind the plaintiff had a right to show that his standing in the profession was high, as bearing upon the question of the amount of compensation. The judge also said:

"There is also evidence tending to establish a custom or rule of guidance as to the charges of physicians for services rendered, and which makes the amount dependent on the means of the patient—his financial ability or condition. This is a benevolent practice, which does not effect the abstract question of value, nor impose any legal obligation to adopt, and cannot be said to be universal. Indeed, there does not seem to be any standard by which, in the application of the rule, the amount to be paid can be ascertained. Each case is under the special disposition of the surgeon or physician attending, and he is to decide as to the reduction to be made on account of the circumstances of his patient; and therefore, when the amount is in dispute, it follows that it is to be determined by proofs to be given on either side. The measure of compensation must be controlled more or less by ability in all the professions, and the service rendered by its responsibilities and success.'

(From the Scottish Law Magazine.)
ELECTRICITY AND THE DEATH PENALTY.

We have been favored by Mr. Clark Bell, President of the Medico-Legal Society of New York, with the advance sheets of an article upon this subject, in which he gives an account of the movement in America, and the inquiries which have there been made into the matter.

"There has been," he says, "for more than a quarter of a century in this State a prejudice against the scaffold and the hangman.

"Those who have yielded to the stern exactions of the law, which demands a 'life for a life,' have felt an almost insurmountable repugnance to the rope.

"The bungling of sheriffs' assistants, the negligent or ignorant adjustment of the noose, have often caused such revolting scenes at public executions as to fill the beholders with horror, and add to that ever-increasing number, now close to a majority, who demand the entire abolition of the death penalty as a punishment for crime.

"The removal of the scaffold as a factor in the civilization of our century, has engaged the attention of the Medico-Legal Society for many years."

We do not think that the above remarks apply with much truth to the state of feeling in this country. There is much irritation at times at the bungling of hangmen, and there is a party—though not, we think, a growing party—in favor of the abolition of the death penalty; but there is no demand for the substitution of any other form of capital punishment for hanging. That there is an "almost insurmountable repugnance to the rope" on the part of those who are compelled to "yield (in quite another sense than our author) to the stern exaction of the law, which demands 'a life for a life,'" undoubtedly holds good here, and to many this will appear one of the strongest arguments in favor of maintaining the old form of punishment. Mr. Bell then proceeds to give an account of the action of the authorities which led to the new enactment:

"The Legislature of the State, upon the recommendation of Governor Hill, in his messages of 1885 and 1886, named a Commission to examine the subject and report their conclusions, composed of Hon. Elbridge T. Gerry, a member of the Medico-Legal Society, Mathew Hale, Esq., of the Albany Bar, and Dr. Alfred P. Southwick, of Buffalo.

"On January 17th, 1888, this Committee submitted their report to the Legislature of New York. It is a very exhaustive and elaborate document, and it gives the history of human punishments for crimes in earliest times and in all countries.

"It enumerates and describes thirty-four different methods in which the death penalty has been hitherto inflicted.

"The guillotine is in vogue in nineteen civilized countries, the sword in nineteen, the gallows in three, the axe in one, the cord in one, while executions are public in twenty-nine countries and private in seven.

"The Committee claim and enumerate the following as facts

demonstrated by their inquiry:

"1. That the effort to diminish the increase of crime by the indiscriminate application of capital punishment to various offenses involving different grades of moral turpitude, or, in other words, by enlarging the number of capital offenses, has proved a failure.

"2. That any undue or peculiar severity in the mode of inflicting the death penalty neither operates to lesson the occurrence of the offense nor to produce a deterrent effect.

"3. That from the long catalogue of various methods of punishment adopted by various nations at different times, only five are now practically resorted to by the civilized world. These five are—(1) the guillotine; (2) the garrote; (3) shooting; (4) the sword; (5) the gallows.

"In recommending a change from the present barbarous and inhuman system of hanging, four substitutes are considered—(1) electricity; (2) prussic acid or other poison; (3) guillotine; (4) garrote.

"This Committee do not seem to have considered the proposal made by Professor Packard of a painless death by inhaling sulphuric oxide gas in a small room in each jail, nor the lethal chamber suggested by Dr. B. Ward Richardson, of London; and they discard the use of the hypodermic injection of prussic acid or other deadly poison, as 'hardly advisable, because against the almost universal protest of the medical profession.'

"Their conclusions are as follows:

"1. That death produced by a sufficiently powerful electric current is the most rapid and humane produced by any agent at our command.

"2. That resuscitation after the passage of such a current through the body and functional centers of the brain is impossible.

"3. That the apparatus to be used should be managed to permit the current to pass through the centers of function and intelligence in the brain.

"The Commission suggested other considerations of great public interest, which may be stated as propositions:

"1. That the State, by the present universal sentiment of

mankind, can only justify itself in taking human life as a punishment for violation of laws; inflicting the death penalty, where necessary, for the safety of society, and to deter others from the commission of crime.

"2. That the State has not the right to torture the criminal, nor to inflict any punishment whatever in any vindictive spirit, or by way of retaliation for the crime.

"The Committee submitted a draft of a Bill, and recommend:

"(*a*) That executions should be private;

"(*b*) That the details of the execution should not be furnished to the public press; and

"(*c*) That the bodies should be delivered to medical schools for dissection in aid of science, or be buried in the prison yard.

"The idea of punishment for crime has colored all human laws.

"Such legislation has been called *punitive* for centuries.

"These statutes are denominated *penal* in all the codes.

"It is little more than half a century since hanging was the penalty in England for more than one hundred statutory offenses, many of which are now regarded as trivial.

"Nearly all of these are abolished; but we still call the measure of punishment *penalties*, and we even say, 'the death penalty' when we discuss it, and use the term '*capital punishment*' for judicial killing.

"The report of the Legislative Commission, considered in its broadest and ablest aspect, outside the abolition of hanging and substituting the electric current, lies in claiming that the universal public judgment and opinion of mankind should be recognized by the law-making power, declaring:

"That the penalty for the violations of the law in what are called 'capital cases' should not hereafter be regarded or treated as punitory.

"That the State does not claim the right of inflicting any punishment upon the homicide in a vindictive or retaliatory sense, or in any degree or view as 'punitory' or compensatory for the act committed.

"That beyond the protection of society, the rights of men, and what is called the 'deterrent effect' of human punishment, the State has neither the right nor wish to go."

We are not sure that we follow our learned author here, or the Committee of whose report he so much approves. If he means that we do not execute criminals for their own good, or for the sake of abstract justice, or to feed our revenge, but simply to "deter others in all time coming from the like offense," we do not think that there is any discrepancy between the law-making power and "the universal public judgment and opinion of mankind." Nor do we appreciate the objection to the use of the word punishment or penalty as applied to a capital sentence. We do not inquire too closely into the signification and the Greek root of these two words, but we think that both the words, in accordance with the ordinary meaning attached to them by those who use the English language, are quite appropriately used of capital sentences. In most cases sentences are inflicted upon offenders solely for the sake of their deterrent effect. We sentence a man to the cat or to penal servitude not for his own sake or for the sake of abstract justice, but for the good of society; and if that consideration in the case of hanging renders the word *punish* inappropriate, it does so equally in the case of flogging and imprisonment.

The Legislature consulted the Medico-Legal Society of New York, and that body appointed a committee, which prepared a report, which was adopted by the Society and transmitted to the Legislature. The leading recommendations in that report were as follows:

"4. That hanging should be abolished as cruel and contrary to the public sense of our civilization.

"5. That as a substitute for the present death penalty we would recommend:

"(1) Death by the electric current, or—

"(2) Death by hypodermic or other injection of poison, or—

"(3) Death by carbonic oxide gas injected into a small room in each jail, as recommended by Professor John H. Packard (*Medico-Legal Papers*, vol. iii. p. 521), giving our preference to the first, or death by electric current.

"6. That in our judgment executions should be private, and not public.

"7. That if it were possible to prevent the publication of details of executions in the public press, it would be a public good.

"8. That the bodies of criminals should be delivered to the medical schools, after execution, for dissection."

Thereafter the Legislature of New York passed a law, which received the approval of Governor Hill, and of which the following are the most important provisions:

"§ 505. The punishment of death must, in every case, be inflicted by causing to pass through the body of the convict a current of electricity of sufficient intensity to cause death, and the application of such current must be continued until such convict is dead.

"§ 507. It is the duty of the agent and warden to be present at the execution, and to invite the presence, by at least three days' previous notice, of a Justice of the Supreme Court, the district attorney, and the sheriff of the county wherein the conviction was had, together with two physicians and twelve reputable citizens of full age, to be selected by said agent and warden. Such agent and warden must, at the request of the criminal, permit ministers of the gospel, priests or clergymen of any religious denomination, not exceeding two, to be present at the execution; and, in addition to the persons designated above, he may also appoint seven assistants or deputy-sheriffs who may attend the execution. He shall permit no other person to be present at such execution, except those designated in this section. Immediately after the execution, a *post-mortem* examination of the body of the convict shall be made by the physicians present at the execution, and their report in writing, stating the nature of the examination so made by them, shall be annexed to the certificate hereinafter mentioned, and filed therewith. After such *post-mortem* examination, the body, unless claimed by some relative or relatives of the person so executed, shall be interred in the graveyard or cemetery attached to the prison, with a sufficient quantity of quick-lime to consume such body without delay; and no religious or other services shall be held over the remains after such execution, except within the walls of the prison where said execution took place, and only in the presence of the officers of said prison, the person conducting said services, and the immediate family and relatives of said deceased prisoner. No account of the details of any such execution, beyond the statement of the fact that such convict was on the day in question, duly executed according to law at the prison, shall be published in any newspaper. Any person who shall violate or omit to comply with any provision of this section shall be guilty of a misdemeanor.".

As soon as the law was passed, the indefatigable President of the Medico-Legal Society again addressed himself to the matter:

"This statute going into effect January 1, 1889, the writer felt it the duty of the body to consider, for the benefit of public officials, 'what was the best method of carrying the same into effect,' and recommended to the Society the appointment of a committee to consider the subject and report.

"That Committee made a detailed report, which was, after discussion, unanimously adopted by the body."

The report is an elaborate document, and sets forth the results of a number of experiments upon dogs, calves and a horse. The result at which the Society arrive as to the best means in which to apply the fatal current, is as follows:

"After mature deliberation we recommend that the death current be administered to the criminal in the following manner:

"A stout table, covered with rubber cloth and having holes along its borders for binding, or a strong chair, should be procured. The prisoner lying on his back, or sitting, should be firmly bound on this table, or in the chair. One electrode should be so inserted into the table, or into the back of the chair, that it will impinge upon the spine between the shoulders. The head should be secured by means of a sort of helmet fastened to the table or back of the chair, and to this helmet the other pole should be so joined as to press firmly with its end upon the top of the head. We think a chair is preferable to a table. The rheophores can be led off to the dynamo through the floor or to another room, and the instrument for closing the circuit can be attached to the wall.

"The electrodes should be of metal, between one and four inches in diameter, covered with a thick layer of sponge or chamois skin.

"The poles and the skin and hair at the points of contact should be thoroughly wet with a warm aqueous solution of common salt. The hair should be cut short. Provision should be made for preventing any moisture reaching from one electrode to the other.

"A dynamo capable of generating an electro-motive force of at least 3000 volts should be employed, and a current used with a potential between 1000 and 1500 volts, according to the resistance of the criminal.

"The alternating current should be made use of, with alternations not fewer than 300 per second. Such a current allowed to passed for from fifteen to thirty seconds will insure death."

When one considers that these sentences set forth the means to be employed in deliberately taking a human life, it is hardly possible to imagine anything more gruesome than the scientific precision of the details. The objection that it is dangerous to argue from the effects of electricity upon animals to its action upon man, is met in the report in this wise:

"If any doubt should exist in the minds of some that electricity would not necessarily be fatal to man, because it has been successfully applied to lower animals, we have but to call attention to the fact that since 1883, some 200 persons have been killed, as we are credibly informed, by the handling of electric lighting wires."

We disapprove of the change which has been effected in the mode of executing the capital sentence by the New York Legislature. That change, and the whole argument upon which it rests, seem based upon the conception that the destruction of life, is the object of capital punishment. The matter is treated as though the criminal were a dangerous animal, or a homicidal maniac, or a being smitten with an incurable and contagious malady, whom it was desirable to remove from the world. In such circumstances the arguments in favor of an orderly, painless departure would be irresistible. But capital punishment is a measure of a wholly different character. The object of capital punishment is not to destroy a noxious life, but to inflict such a punishment as will strike the popular imagination with the greatest terror without exciting such sympathy for the victim as will outweigh popular indignation against his offense. So far from the taking of life being the object aimed at, it is a regrettable circumstance that the destruction of life should be one of the incidents of the punishment. The life is taken only because no punishment which spared the life, and excited no overwhelming pity, would impress the popular mind with an equal sense of terror.

Perhaps no other form of death is invested with such a sense of horror and degradation as death by hanging. It is this fact which gives its value to the gallows. In substituting death by electricity for hanging, the effort is made—we do not know whether it be successfully made—to eliminate everything from the severest penalty of the law except the one thing, which, as we have pointed out, is not the real end, but only a regrettable, albeit an inevitable, incident of the punishment—the destruction of the life of the condemned. In examining the proceedings which led to the enactment of the law, it is hard to avoid two conclusions in regard to the authors of this measure.

1. They appear to be at heart opponents of capital punishment, and would gladly see it abolished altogether. If so, we think they are wise in their generation. If executions must be carried out by scientific apparatus, public sentiment will not, we think, endure the maintenance of capital punishment. We have already pointed out how death by electricity secures the maximum of mischief with the minimum of benefit. It is the tremendous responsibility of taking a life, not any repugnance to the manner in which life is taken, that makes people squeamish about capital punishment. If the life is taken by machinery, popular attention will be centered upon the one circumstance that occasions qualms in the public conscience — that human life is irrevocably taken.

2. The authors of this measure seem to regard the con-

demned as a patient rather than as a miscreant. It is necessary, in the public interest, that the homicide should be not punished—Mr. Clark Bell objects to that word—but rather should have something disagreeable inflicted upon him, which will deter others from doing the like; and law, sanctioned by public opinion, declares that the something disagreeable must be death. But the death must be made as little unpleasant as possible. When a child has to take a nauseous dose there is no help for it, but the humane man of medicine makes the ordeal as little disagreeable as he can by mixing a syrup with the draught. Even so, if the homicide must be executed, there is no help for it; but the humane medical jurist makes the passage as dignified and comfortable as possible, by killing him instantaneously in his chair by an electric shock. Mr. Clark Bell treats the homicide in the same spirit as he treated the convulsed child (see a case referred to in the article ''Murder from the best Motives'' in ''The Month''.) Both are *cases*. The homicide is no more to be execrated for his crime than is the child for its agony—the one has to be slain for the good of society, the other for its own comfort. Let both be disposed of according to the most approved scientific methods. Be it trusted that when the homicide's turn comes, science will prove more unerring than it appears to have been in the case of the child.

Here, in Edinburgh, we read with sad indifference of accidents and catastrophes by land and sea, of cities destroyed by earthquakes and floods, of provinces ravaged by plague and famine. We listen with equanimity to the clash of contending armies. We know that every minute a member of our race passes out into the night; and we study with feeble interest the weekly mortality statistics of our own town, in relation to the weather of the preceding week. But the whole city goes with blanched cheek and bated breath when, as on the other morning, the black flag waving over the Calton prison, tells that on the scaffold the hangman has done his ghastly duty.

The gallows and the rope, through long centuries of use, have taken a strong hold of the imag ation of the Anglo-

Saxon race. "To be hanged by the neck, what a death!" exclaimed a wretched murderess, the other day, as the judge pronounced the terrible sentence. Is not the horror which these words express a most powerful plea for the maintenance of a form of punishment the terror of which is a most formidable preventive against the darkest crime of which humanity is capable?

(The foregoing article from the Scottish Law Magazine we have published in connection with the proceedings of the Medico-Legal Society of New York, in order to give both sides of the question.

We are not in favor of the death penalty in any form. If the penalty is to be retained, the form of enforcing it should be freed from all elements of barbarity.—EDITOR LAW TIMES.)

MOTLEY'S CORRESPONDENCE.

In the correspondence of John Lothrop Motley, author of "Rise of the Dutch Republic," recently published, there are some interesting descriptions of English public men. Motley, it may be remarked, was educated for the law, but found other occupations more congenial, and probably more useful to mankind. In 1851, the historian met Lyndhurst and Brougham at dinner. Here is what he writes of the latter :.

"Brougham is exactly like the pictures in *Punch*, only *Punch* flatters him. The common pictures of Palmerston and Lord John are not like at all to my mind, but Brougham is always hit exactly. His face, like his tongue and his mind, is shrewd, sharp, humorous. There certainly never was a great statesman and author who so irresistibly suggested the man who does the comic business at a small theatre. You are compelled to laugh when you see him as much as at Keeley or Warren. Yet, there is absolutely nothing comic in his mind. But there is no resisting his nose. It is not merely the configuration of that wonderful feature which surprises you, but its mobility. It has the litheness and almost the length of the elephant's proboscis, and I have no doubt he can pick up pins or scratch his back with it as easily as he could take a pinch of snuff. He is always twisting it about in quite a fabulous manner.

"His hair is thick and snow-white and shiny; his head is large and knobby and bumpy, with all kinds of phrenological developments, which I did not have a chance fairly to study. The rugged outlines or headlands of his face are wild and bleak,

(321)

but not forbidding.   Deep furrows of age and thought and toil, perhaps of sorrow, run all over it, while his vast mouth, with a ripple of humor ever playing around it, expands like a placid bay, under the huge promontory of his fantastic and incredible nose.   His eye is dim and could never have been brilliant, but his voice is rather shrill, with an unmistakable northern intonation; his manner of speech is fluent, not garrulous, but obviously touched by time; his figure is tall, slender, shambling, awkward, but of course perfectly self-possessed.   Such is what remains at eighty of the famous Henry Brougham."

The table talk of these two veterans of the law was not particularly interesting or brilliant.   Motley says he does not repeat it because it is worth recording, but because he "tries to Boswellize a little" for the entertainment of the member of his family to whom his letter is addressed:

"The company was too large for general conversation, but every now and then we at our end paused to listen to Brougham and Lyndhurst chaffing each other across the table. Lyndhurst said, 'Brougham, you disgraced the woolsack by appearing there with those plaid trousers, and with your peer's robe, on one occasion, put on over your chancellor's gown.' 'The devil,' said Brougham, 'you know that to be a calumny; I never wore the plaid trousers.'   'Well,' said Lyndhurst, 'he confesses the two gowns.   Now, the present Lord Chancellor never appears except in small clothes and silk stockings.'   Upon which Lady Stanley observed that the ladies in the gallery all admired Lord Chelmsford for his handsome leg.   'A virtue that was never seen in you, Brougham,' said Lyndhurst."

One of the most interesting things in the book is Bismarck's description of parliamentary warfare.   Bismarck and Motley were college companions at Gottingen and Berlin in 1832-3, and the friendship then formed continued throughout life.   In a note jotted down in the Chamber (about 1864), Bismarck says: "You have given me a great pleasure with your letter of the 9th, and I shall be very grateful to you if you will keep your promise to write oftener and longer.   I hate politics, but, as you say truly, like the grocer hating figs, I am none the less obliged to keep my thoughts increasingly occupied with those figs. Even at this moment while I am writing to you, my ears are full of it. I am obliged to listen to particularly tasteless speeches out of the mouths of uncommonly childish and excited politicians, and I have, therefore, a moment of unwilling leisure which I cannot use better than in giving you news of my welfare. I never thought that in my riper years I should be obliged to carry on such an unworthy trade as that of a parliamentary minister. As envoy, although an official, I still had the feeling of being a gentleman; as (parliamentary) minister one is a helot. I have come down in the world, and hardly know how.

"April 18.—I wrote as far as this yesterday, then the sitting came to an end; five hours' Chamber until three o'clock; one hour's report to his Majesty, three hours at an incredibly dull dinner, old important Whigs, then two hours' work; finally, a supper with a colleague, who would have been hurt if I had slighted his fish. This morning, I had hardly breakfasted, before Karolyi was sitting opposite to me; he was followed without interruption by Denmark, England, Portugal, Russia, France, whose ambassador I was obliged to remind at one o'clock that it was time for me to go to the House of phrases. I am sitting again in the latter; hear people talk nonsense, and end my letter.

"All these people have agreed to approve our treaties with Belgium, in spite of which, twenty speakers scold each other with the greatest vehemence, as if each wished to make an end of the other; they are not agreed about the motives which make them unanimous, hence, alas! a regular German squabble about the emperior's beard; *querelle d'Allemand.* You Anglo-Saxon Yankees have something of the same kind also. Do you all know exactly why you are waging such furious war with each other? All certainly do not know, but they kill each other *con amore*, that's the way the business comes to them. Your battles are bloody; ours wordy; these chatterers really cannot govern Prussia, I must bring some opposition to bear against them; they have too little wit and too much self-complacency—stupid and audacious. Stupid, in all its meanings, is not the right word; considered individually, these people are sometimes very clever, generally educated—the regulation German University culture; but of politics, beyond the interests of their own church tower, they know as little as we knew as students, and even less; as far as external politics go, they are also, taken separately, like children. In all other questions, they become childish as soon as they stand together *in corpore.* In the mass, stupid,—individually, intelligent." This inimitable description would apply to more than the Prussian Chamber.

We might continue our extracts, did we not fear to encroach too far on the domain of our "useless but entertaining" contemporary, *The Green Bag.* So we will conclude with a reference to the letter which ended Mr. Motley's functions as Minister to Austria. Somebody whose very name was unknown to him, wrote a letter to Mr. Seward in 1866, charging Motley with being "a thorough flunky," and the like. A copy of this contemptible communication was formally addressed to the Minister, with a request for an explanation, and Motley resigned in disgust. "No man can regret more than I do," writes the chagrined ambassador, "that such a correspondence is enrolled in the Capitol among American State papers." United States secretaries have not all yet acquired a correct notion of what is decent or dignified in State papers.—(*Montreal Legal News.*)

Editorial Department.

CHIEF-JUSTICE FULLER.

According to the *Albany Law Journal*, "the press is making itself too familiar with the Chief-Justice's family affairs. He is considering whether he shall shave off his moustache. This is his own affair (or off-hair, as the case may be), but we hope he will not cut it off, in spite of the wishes of his brethren. The *Chicago Herald* pertinently and impertinently says, 'It is another case of the fox which lost its tail.' Then his daughter has eloped and got married. We should think a man with seven of the same sort left, would not worry much over that. It seems not a bad way to reduce the surplus. And then he should reflect how Eldon stole his 'Bessie'—(God bless her!)—out of a second-story window, and how Judge Cooley discovered no constitutional limitation of his right to elope with his best girl." The *Scottish Law Magazine* says of the remainder of the paragraph in the Law Journal, that it forms a singular commentary upon the opening sentence, and reminds one of the sapient parent who counseled his offspring to avoid profane swearing, as it was "a d—— bad habit."

Judge. What are the requisites of a valid will?

Applicant. Can't tell 'em all, Judge, but I remember one is that it must be read at the burial over the grave of the testator.

Judge. What is a fee simple?

Applicant. I guess about two dollars and a half.

Judge. What is the largest estate in land?

Applicant. A very large estate would, in this country. be about one thousand acres.—(VIRGINIA LAW JOURNAL.)

NOTES OF TRAVEL.

BERLIN TO ZURICH—SOJOURN IN ZURICH—PROFESSOR GUSTAV VOLK-MAR.—The trip from Paris to Berlin has been already described, and something said about Berlin. [Law Times for July, 1888.]

After a stay of two months in that City, I took the train for Zurich on the 29th of January, 1885.

During the first hour out from the City, we passed a good many groves of pines, which were being grown with care. During the forenoon, many villages could be seen at a distance, but there were not many on the line of the road.

In the middle of the day, we were traversing an open country. The want of timber was manifest from the fact that in the towns the houses, however small, were nearly all built of brick.

Before noon, we had crossed the Elba, which has here become a large river. The fields are under cultivation, but there are no fences. We pass mines of coal, silver and lead. The mines are indicated by large heaps of excavated earth.

In the afternoon the country became rougher. with a bold outline of hills in the distance, some of them covered by a small growth of timber.

We now begin to see the old castles on the distant hills. Some of these are very beautiful. Toward night-fall we passed one close to the track, which was very interesting. It filled the bill of the old castles we read of. There were the craggy rocks all around—there was the tower on the top, and there was the heavy gate under the rocks, on a level with the ground.

In the evening came to Basel, on the Rhine, where we were transferred, after waiting an hour or more.

The next morning I found myself in Switzerland. The country is here hilly, almost mountainous, and the scenery picturesque and romantic. Zurich is a handsome city build in a rugged region of country. During the day I called at the house of Gustav Volkmar, Professor of New Testament Exegesis in the University of Zurich, and President of the Society of Critical Historical Theology. I had been in correspondence with him and with the Society.

The Professor was not at home, but I met his daughter, an accomplished young lady, who has translated some German works into the English language. Her father could read the English, but could not speak it.

He was then seventy-five years of age.

The next day I formed the acquaintance of the Professor, and found his companionship so congenial, that I determined to remain some weeks. During the time, I listened to the lectures of Professor Volkmar in the University, and attended a meeting of the Historical Society, of which I had the honor of being made a member. Previous to my admission, every member was a graduate of the University of Zurich. Professor Volkmar, the President, is well known as one of the most critical scholars of Europe, and is the author of many works connected with the early history of the Christian Religion. The Society held stated meetings, at which papers were read by the President, by Pfarrer Lavater, Pfarrer Kupferschmidt and others.

The lectures of the President to his class, were sufficient to mark him as a pronounced liberal. He took occasion in one of his lectures to explain to the class that there could not have been an eclipse of the sun at the time of the crucifixion, because it was at the time of the full moon. This I thought was good science but weak theology.

At another time, he asked the class what was the nature of the resurrection of Christ, and when one of the students answered, "Es war eine erscheinung," the old gentleman replied, "Das ist recht." On returning from the class, I asked him, if the resurrection was only an appearance, how he explained the rolling away of the stone from the tomb. He replied, "There was no tomb. Jesus was put to death as a malefactor, and such were denied burial." Some of our divines would be shocked at these doctrines, but Professor Volkmar is paid by the State as a religious teacher. I asked him if the more orthodox professors did not make war upon him. He replied that they had done so in former years, but had concluded to let him alone. They went their way, and he went his.

The last day I was in Zurich, we took a long walk together. I had contracted not only a friendship, but an affection for him, and felt sad at the thought of leaving him. Returning from the walk, we took a seat on a bench near that magnificent lake, admired by all travelers. I told him we should probably never meet again in this life, but I hoped nevertheless that we should meet again, and asked him if he did not believe in another state of existence.

The old man turned upon me his large full eye, with a suddenness that was almost startling. "Why do you ask this?" he said. I replied, I had no object except simply to know his opinion. "Well," said he, with deliberation, "that is something I know nothing about. All the teachings of Jesus related to this life. The Kingdom of God which he was seeking to establish, was to be upon this earth. To live again, is something to be hoped, but nothing is revealed to us upon the subject. The arguments in favor of a future existence must be drawn from outside the gospels."

After spending two months in Zurich and vicinity, two weeks of which were passed in the delightful scenery in the neighborhood of Lausanne, I took the cars for Paris. On the route from Zurich to Paris, I passed through German Alsace. It is very level, forming a striking contrast with the Swiss country. We passed many small villages on the way, some of them presenting quite a charming appearance. Many of the houses were very old, some of them looking as if they were about ready to fall to pieces. Some of the small churches were very handsome, the steeples presenting perfect models of Gothic architecture. The villages are compactly built, very few houses being seen in the broad tracts of country lying between them. The grape is here a prominent product. Nearly all the west sides of the hills are covered with vineyards. The country is noticeably destitute of timber. After traversing the districts of Belfour and Vessoul, we came into Chaumont, where wheat and other small grain is grown.

In the afternoon we passed through a broad expanse of country, mostly under cultivation—worked by the men and women, and boys and girls living in the villages. Many people were working in the large fields, with no house in sight. These people, when they have done their day's work, go one, two, three miles, to a small and poor cottage, or hovel. By the time they have put out and taken care of their teams, it is bed time. The next day the same thing over. They are not working their own land. They are tenants. The owners live mostly in the cities—many of them in Paris.

Is this a safe basis for a republic? These people must be ignorant. There is no indication of improvement, physical or intellectual. They are not safe sovereigns. Here, in the farming tenantry, as well as in the populace of the cities, lies the danger to the French Republic. It is not more dangerous than was the slavery element in this country, and scarcely more dangerous than some elements yet existing in our large cities. We must not indulge in forebodings; but hoping for the best, let us join in the prayer of the French patriots, "Vive la Republique!"

In the evening of the 30th of March, 1885, I again entered Paris.

C. B. W.

The "Green Bag" gives us the following:

There was a very irascible old gentleman who formerly held the position of justice of the peace in one of our cities. Going down the main street one day, one of the boys spoke to him without coming up to his Honor's idea of deference.

"Young man, I fine you five dollars for contempt of court."

"Why. Judge," said the offender, "you are not in session."

"This court," responded the judge, thoroughly irritated, "is always in session, and consequently always an object of contempt."

This could be easily matched by a story current among the Illinois bar, concerning Mr. Fridley, an old and well known lawyer of this State, and Judge Caton.

It is said that Fridley, a little surprised, and a good deal irritated by a decision of Judge Caton, while holding court in Kane County, said in an undertone:

"That's a d——d pretty decision!"

"Mr. Fridley," said Judge Caton, who had been accustomed to the New York practice, "if you are not satisfied with the decisions of this court, you can take them to a court of errors."

"A court of errors!" cried Fridley. "My G—d! if this isn't a court of errors, I'd like to know where you'd find one."

————————

The following poem, by Eugene F. Ware, Esq., of Fort Scott, Kansas. is descriptive of the case of State v. Lewis, 19 Kan., 200, to the official report of which it is appended as a reporter's foot-note.

LAW—PAW—GUILT—WILT.—

When upon thy frame the law
Places its majestic paw,
Though in innocence or guilt,
Thou art then required to wilt.

STATEMENT OF CASE BY REPORTER.

The defendant while at large,
Was arrested on a charge
Of burglarious intent,
And direct to jail he went.
But he somehow felt misused.
And through prison walls he oozed.
And affected his escape.

Mark you, now: Again the law
On defendant placed its paw,
Like a hand of iron mail,
And re-socked him into jail—
Which said jail, while so corraled,
He by sockage-tenure held.

Then the court met, and they tried
Lewis up and down each side,
On the good old-fashioned plan:
But the jury cleared the man.

Now, you think that this strange case
Ends at just about this place.
Nay, not so. Again the law
On defendant placed its paw—
This time takes him 'round the cape
For affecting an escape;
He, unable to give bail,
Goes reluctantly to jail.

Lewis, tried for this last act,
Makes a special plea of fact.
"Wrongly did they me arrest,
"As my trial did attest,
"And while rightfully at large.
"Taken on a wrongful charge,
"I took back from them what they
"From me wrongly took away."

When this plea was heard,
Thereupon the state demurred.

The defendant then was pained
When the court was heard to say
In a cold impassive way,
"The demurrer is sustained."

Back to jail did Lewis go,
But as liberty was dear,
He appeals, and now is here.
To reverse the judge below.
The opinion will contain
All the statements that remain.

ARGUMENT AND BRIEF OF APPELLANT.

As a matter, sir. of fact,

Who was injured by our act,
Any property or man?
Point it out, sir, if you can.

Can you seize us when at large
On a baseless trumped-up charge,
And if we scape, then say
It is crime to get away—
When we rightfully regained
What was wrongfully obtained?

Please-the-court sir, what is crime?
What is right and what is wrong?
Is our freedom but a song—
Or the subject of a rhyme?

ARGUMENT AND BRIEF OF ATTORNEY FOR THE STATE.

When the State, that is to say
We, take liberty away—
When the padlock and the hasp
Leaves one helpless in our grasp.
It's unlawful then that he
Even dreams of liberty.

Wicked dreams, that may in time
Grow and ripen into crime.

Crime of dark and damning shape:
Then, if he perchance escape,
Evermore remorse will roll
O'er his shattered, sin-sick soul.

REPLY BY APPELLANT.

Please-the-court sir, if it's sin.
Where does turpitude begin?

OPINION OF THE COURT, PER CURIAM.

We don't make law. We are bound
To interpret it as found.
The defendant broke away;
When arrested, he should stay.

This appeal can't be maintained
For the record does not show
Error in the court below,
And we nothing can infer;

Let the judgment be sustained.
All the justices concur.

REPORTER'S NOTE.

Of the sheriff, rise and sing
Glory to our earthly king.

LAWYERS REPORTS, ANNOTATED. ALL CURRENT CASES OF GENERAL
VALUE AND IMPORTANCE DECIDED IN THE UNITED STATES, STATE AND
TERRITORIAL COURTS; WITH FULL ANNOTATION BY ROBERT DESTY. EDI-
TOR. EDMUND H. SMITH, REPORTER. ROCHESTER, N. Y., THE LAWYERS
CO-OPERATIVE PUBLISHING COMPANY. 1889.—We have received Book 2
of this work, which, in mechanical execution is equal if not superior to its
predecessors, while in other respects it is presumably not inferior.

This book comprises the first quarter of 1889, and has a complete index,
besides a resumé of the decisions, arranged according to subjects, under
the following heads:

1. Governmental and Political Relations.
2. Commercial Relations.
3. Contractual Relations.
4. Fiduciary Relations.
5. Domestic Relations.
6. Social Relations.
7. Property and Property Rights and Remedies.
8. Damages for Torts.
9. Criminal Law.

BEFORE AND AT TRIAL.—WHAT SHOULD BE DONE BY COUNSEL, SOLICI-
TOR AND CLIENT. BY RICHARD HARRIS, Author of "Hints on Advocacy,"
"Illustrations in Advocacy," "Farmer Bumbkin's Law Suit," etc., etc., etc
First American (from the second English) Edition. BY JAMES M. KERR.
Editor American and English Railroad Cases; American and English Cor-
poration Cases; Benjamin on Sales, etc. For sale by Williamson Law
Book Co. (Successors to Williamson and Higbee), Rochester, N. Y.

This is a handsomely printed volume of 400 octavo pages. We have received it too late for more than a mere mention in this number. We may
have occasion to say more about it. hereafter.

HON. JAMES KENT, L. L. D.

THE CHICAGO LAW TIMES.

VOL. III.]   OCTOBER, 1889.   [No. 4.

JAMES KENT.

James Kent * was born July 31, 1763, in that part of Dutchess County then called the precinct of Fredericksburgh, now in the County of Putnam, in the State of New York. His grandfather, the Rev. Elisha Kent, a native of Suffield, in the State of Connecticut, married the daughter of Rev. Joseph Moss, of Derby, and was for some time a minister of the Presbyterian Church at Newtown, in that State. He removed, as early as 1740, to the southeast part of Dutchess County, then wild and uncultivated, but which gradually increased in population, and became known as Kent's Parish. He continued to reside there until his death, in July, 1776, at the age of seventy-two.

His eldest son, Moss Kent, who, as well as his father, was a graduate of Yale College, commenced the study of the law under Lieutenant-Governor Fitch, at Norwalk, Connecticut, and was admitted to the bar, in Dutchess County, in 1756. In 1760 he married the eldest daughter of Dr. Uriah Rogers, a physician at Norwalk, by whom he had three children: James, the subject of this memoir, Moss, who was a member of the Senate of New York for four years, afterward a member of Congress, and first judge of the Court of Common Pleas of Jefferson County, and Hannah, who married William Pitt Platt, of Plattsburgh. They lost their mother in 1770, and

*In preparing this article, we have drawn largely from a sketch of Chancellor Kent, in the second volume of the National Portrait Gallery, by Longacre and Herring, N. Y. and Phil., 1835.

their father died in 1794, at the age of sixty-one.

When five years old, James, the eldest son, was placed at an English school, at Norwalk, and lived in the family of his maternal grandfather, until 1772, when he went to reside with an uncle, at Pawlings, in Dutchess County. Here he acquired the first rudiments of Latin.

In May, 1773, he was sent to a Latin school, at Danbury, Connecticut, under the charge of the Rev. Ebenezer Baldwin.

After the death of Mr. Baldwin, in October, 1776, he was under different instructors, at Danbury, Stratford and Newtown, until he entered Yale College, in September, 1777. At these different schools he was remarked as possessing a lively disposition, great quickness of parts, a spirit of emulation and love of learning. The pious puritans among whom he lived, were sober, frugal and industrious, and the strict and orderly habits of those around him had their influence in forming his own. From their example and the impressions received at that early age, he acquired that simplicity of character and purity of morals which he ever afterward preserved, without losing his natural vivacity and playfulness of temper. He has often mentioned the delight he experienced on his periodical returns from school to his home, in rambling with his brother among the wild scenery of his native hills and valleys. The associations then formed rendered him an enthusiastic admirer of the beauties of nature, and in after life, during the intervals of business, he made excursions into every part of his native State, through New England, and along the borders of Canada, visiting each mountain, lake and cascade; and while gratifying his taste for simple pleasures, preserving and invigorating his health.

In July, 1779, in consequence of the invasion of New Haven by the British troops, the college was broken up, and the students for a time dispersed. During his exile, having met with a copy of Blackstone's Commentaries, he read the work of that elegant writer, with great eagerness and pleasure, and it so excited his admiration, that at the age of sixteen, he determined to become a lawyer.

He left college, after taking the degree of bachelor, in Sep-

tember, 1781, with high reputation. After passing a few
weeks at Fairfield, to which place his father had removed on
his second marriage, he went to Poughkeepsie, and commenced
the study of the law, under the direction of Egbert Benson,
then attorney-general of the State of New York, and afterward
one of the judges of the Supreme Court.

His strong and decided attachment to jurisprudence could
not fail to insure his success. Besides the books of English
common law, he read the large works of Grotius and Puffen-
dorf, making copious extracts from them, and as a relaxation,
perusing the best writers in English literature, of which his
favorite portions were history, poetry, geography, voyages
and travels. He was temperate in all his habits, was a water-
drinker, and engaged in no dissipation, not even joining in
the ordinary fashionable amusements of others of the same age.
He was very far, however, from being grave, reserved or austere; but was uniformly cheerful, lively, and communicative.
The love of reading had become his ruling passion, and when
he felt the want of amusement, "he better knew great Nature's
charms to prize," and sought it in rural walks, amidst objects
that purify and elevate the imagination.

In September, 1784, he took the degree of Master of Arts at
Yale College, and in January, 1785, was admitted an attorney
of the Supreme Court. He went to Fredericksburgh, with the
intention of commencing the practice of his profession there;
but the solitude of that retired place soon became insupportable, and in less than two months he returned to Poughkeepsie.
There, in April, 1785, he married a Miss Bailey, a lady a few
years younger than himself, with whom he lived in the uninterrupted enjoyment of domestic felicity.

He possessed, at this time, little or no property, but living
with great simplicity in a country village, his wants were few,
and were supplied with little expense. Young, ardent and active, he felt no anxiety for the future, but engaged with increased alacrity in professional business and literary pursuits, so
as to leave no portion of his time unemployed.

In 1787, he resolved to renew and extend his acquaintance
with the Greek and Roman classics, which he had entirely neg-

lected after leaving college. When it is considered that the only Greek book at that time read by the classes in that seat of learning, was the Greek Testament, and the only Latin works, Virgil, the select orations of Cicero, and some parts of Horace, we may easily imagine how imperfect must have been that part of his education, the defects of which he was determined to supply.

He began a course of self-instruction, with an energy and perseverance that mark a strong and generous mind. That he might lose no time, and pursue his various studies with method and success, he divided the hours not given to rest, into five portions: rising early and reading Latin until eight, Greek until ten, devoting the rest of the forenoon to law; in the afternoon two hours were applied to French, and the rest of the day to English authors. This division and employment of his time were continued with little variation until he became a judge. By this practice he was under no necessity of encroaching on those hours best appropriated to sleep, and preserved his health unimpaired.

If his mind became weary in one department of study, he found relief by passing to another; "from grave to gay, from lively to severe." He read Homer, Xenophon and Demosthenes, with great delight. Though he afterward relinquished the pursuit of Grecian Literature, he continued to read the best Latin and French authors, and many of the former more than once. As large public libraries, if any then existed, were not within his reach, he began a collection of books, which he gradually increased to several thousand volumes; a very large library for those times. He has often said, that next to his family, his library had been to him the greatest source of enjoyment.

In April, 1787, he was admitted a counselor in the Supreme Court. He soon entered with ardor into the discussion of the great political questions which then absorbed the attention and agitated the minds of all. He could not long remain neutral between the two contending parties, and after a careful examination of the arguments of each, he joined the federal side. He soon became the friend of Jay, Hamilton, and other eminent men of that party, with whom he uniformly acted, and to whose principles he afterward adhered.

In April, 1790, he was elected a member of the State Legislature for Dutchess County, and again in 1792. In the session held in the City of New York, he took an active part in the contested election case of Chief-Justice Jay against Clinton, who had been returned as elected Governor of New York. His writings on that occasion attracted much attention, and he became favorably known in the City. He was at that time nominated for Congress from Dutchess County but his competitor, who adhered to the opposite party, succeeded by a small majority. During his attendance in the legislature, his principles and conduct were so highly respected, that he was urged by his friends to remove to the City, where he might find greater scope for the exercise of his talents, and more lucrative business in his profession. He accordingly removed to New York, in April, 1793. The first month of his residence in the City was embittered by the loss of an only child, and for a time his prospects were clouded with sorrow.

In December, he was appointed professor of law in Columbia College, and commenced the delivery of lectures in November, 1794. The course was attended by many respectable members of the bar, and a large class of students. In the following winter he read a second course; but the number of his hearers having diminished, he was discouraged from delivering another. The three preliminary lectures were afterward published, but the sale of them did not reimburse the expense of publication. The trustees of the college conferred upon him the degree of doctor of laws, and he afterward received similar honors from Harvard University and Dartmouth College.

In February, 1796, he was appointed a master in chancery, and there being, at that time, but one other, the office was lucrative. In the same year he was elected a member of the legislature from the City of New York. He delivered an address before the society for the promotion of agriculture, arts and manufactures, at their anniversary meeting in New York, on the 8th of November, 1796, which is inserted in the first volume of the transactions of the society. In this address was foreshadowed the progress the country has made since that time.

In March, 1797, he was, without solicitation, and quite unexpectedly to himself, appointed recorder of the City. This, being a judicial office, was the more acceptable as well as the more honorable; and being allowed to retain that of master, the duties of both were so great, and the emoluments so considerable, that he gradually relinquished the more active business of his profession, to which he was not strongly attached. From constitutional diffidence, or habits of study, he appeared not to feel confident in the possession of the powers requisite to ensure pre-eminence as an advocate at the bar.

In 1798, Governor Jay, who knew his worth and highly respected his character, offered him the office of junior judge of the Supreme Court, then vacant, which he accepted. This appointment gratified his highest ambition. It placed him in a position where he could more fully display his attainments, and have a wider field for the investigation of legal science. In accepting the office, he relinquished, for a limited income, all the flattering prospects of increasing wealth that had opened to him during five years' residence in the City. Though most of his friends doubted the wisdom of his choice, he never regretted it. And all who feel interested in the pure and enlightened administration of justice, have found reason to rejoice that he followed the dictates of his own judgment, in a matter so important to the honor and happiness of his after life, and upon which depended so much of his subsequent usefulness.

On becoming a judge, he returned to Poughkeepsie, but in the following year, he removed to Albany, where he continued to reside until 1823.

When he took his seat on the bench of the Supreme Court, there were no reports of its decisions, nor any known or established precedents of its own, to guide or direct his judgment. The English law books were freely cited, and the adjudications of English courts regarded with the highest respect, and in most cases, they had the force of authority. The opinions of the judges were generally delivered orally, with little regularity, and often after much delay. The law was in a state of great and painful uncertainty. He began by preparing a written and argumentative opinion in every case of sufficient importance to become a precedent. These opinions he was ready to deliver on the day when the judges met to consult on the decisions to be pronounced by the court. The other judges, pursuing a similar course, also gave their reasons in writing, supported by legal authorities.

As he read with a pen in his hand, extracting, digesting, abridging, and making copious notes, the practice of writing opinions was easy and agreeable. Besides making himself master of all the English adjudications applicable to the points under examination, he frequently brought to his aid the body of the civil law, and the writings of eminent jurists of the countries in which that law prevails; especially in the discussion of questions arising on personal contracts, or of commercial and maritime law, the principles of which have been so admirably unfolded and illustrated by Domat, Pothier, Valin, Emerigon and others. Like Seldon, Hale and Mansfield, he thought law could not well be understood as a science without seeking its grounds and reasons in the Roman law. From that great repository of "written wisdom," he drew largely, engrafting its sound and liberal principles on the hardy stock of the English common law. Thus commenced that series of judicial decisions which have enriched the jurisprudence of New York, and shed their influence on that of other States.

In 1800, he and Mr. Justice Radcliffe, were appointed by the Legislature, to revise the Statutes of the State; and in January, 1802, their edition of them, comprised in two volumes octavo, was published.

In July, 1804, he was appointed Chief-Justice of the Supreme Court, in which he continued to preside until 1814. His opinions are contained in sixteen volumes of Reports, from January, 1799, to February, 1814; and the judgment of the public has long since been formed on their merit and importance.

In February, 1814, he was appointed chancellor. The powers and jurisdiction of the court of chancery were not clearly defined. There were scarcely any precedents of its decisions, to which reference could be made in case of doubt. Without any other guide, he felt at liberty to exercise such powers of the English chancery as he deemed applicable under the Constitution and laws of the State, subject to the correction of the Court of Errors, on appeal.

The causes before the court were managed by a few lawyers. He opened wide its doors; and his kindness and affability, his known habits of business and promptitude of decision, attracted many to the court. The number of causes rapidly increased, and it soon required the strenuous and unceasing efforts of his active mind to hear and decide the cases brought before him. Besides his attendance during the regular terms of the court, he was at all times easy of access at his chambers; so that no one ever complained of delay in the hearing or decision of his cause. He considered the cases in the order in which they were presented or argued, and did not leave one until he was fully prepared to deliver his judgment upon it. He read the pleadings and depositions with the greatest attention, carefully abstracting from them every material fact; and having become familiar with the merits of the cause, he was able, unless some technical or artificial rule was interposed, by his own clear moral perception to discover where lay the equity of the case. Not content, however, with satisfying his conscience as to the justice of his decision, he was studious to demonstrate that his judgment was supported by the well established principles of equity to be found in the decisions of the courts of the country from which our laws have been derived. His researches on every point were so full as to leave little or nothing to be supplied by those who might afterward wish to have his decisions re-examined or to test the correctness of his conclusions.

Accustomed to take a large view of jurisprudence, and considering law not as a connection of arbitrary and disconnected rules, but rather as a science founded on general principles of justice and equity, to be applied to the actions of men in the diversified relations of civil society, he was not deterred, but animated, by the novelty and intricacy of a case; and while his mind was warmly engaged in the general subject, he sought rather than avoided difficult points, even when the discussion of them was not essential to the decision of the main question between the parties; so that nothing was suffered to pass without examination. His judicial opinions are, therefore, uncommonly interesting and instructive to all, but especially to those who have commenced the study of the law, and aspire to eminence in that profession. The decisions in chancery are contained in seven volumes of Reports.

On the 31st of July, 1823, having attained the age of sixty years, the period limited by the Constitution for the tenure of his office, he retired from the court, after hearing and deciding every case that had been brought before him. On this occasion, the members of the bar residing in the City of New York, presented him an address. After speaking of the inestimable benefits conferred on the community by his judicial labors for five and twenty years, they say:

"During this long course of services, so useful and honorable, and which will form the most brilliant period in our judicial history, you have, by a series of decisions, in law and equity, distinguished alike for practical wisdom, profound learning, deep research and accurate discrimination, contributed to establish the fabric of our jurisprudence on those sound principles that have been sanctioned by the experience of mankind, and expounded by the enlightened and venerable sages of the law. Though others may hereafter enlarge and adorn the edifice whose deep and solid foundations were laid by the wise and patriotic framers of our government, in that common law which they claimed for the people as their noblest inheritance, your labors on this magnificent structure will forever remain eminently conspicuous, commanding the applause of the present generation, and exciting the admiration and gratitude of future ages."

A similar address was presented to him by the members of the bar in Albany, and also by those from the different counties of the State, attending the Supreme Court in Utica, in August following. In the latter, reference was made to the entire revolution which had been accomplished in the administration of equity; and it was compared to a similar revolution in the English chancery, affected by Sir Heneage Finch, afterward Earl of Nottingham, who became chancellor in 1673.

In the same address, they refer to their intercourse with him as a judge—to his personal kindness, his pureness and gentleness of heart, and the uniform and uninterrupted course of generous, candid and polite treatment which had marked his intercourse with the bar.

In these addresses, the bar were led to express a doubt as to the wisdom of that clause in the political constitution of the State, which "compelled him, in the full enjoyment of his intellectual faculties, to relinquish a station he had filled with such consummate ability."

In August, he visited the Eastern States, and soon afterward determined to remove to the City of New York, open a law school and act as chamber counsel. The trustees of the college again offered him the professorship of law in that institution, which he accepted; and in 1824, he prepared and delivered a series of law lectures on a more comprehensive plan than that pursued in his former course. He also gave private instruction to students who resorted to him from various parts of the United States. His parental kindness toward the young, and the frankness and affability of his manners, won their affection without diminishing their respect; and his conversation and example could not fail to inspire that ardor and emulation so conducive to their progress and success.

His high reputation as a judge, induced many, not only in the city, but in distant places, to consult him on difficult and important questions, and, instead of the brief answers usually returned by counsel, he gave full and argumentative opinions. Many causes actually pending in court were, by the agreement of parties, submitted to his final decision. He had continued, for some years, thus usefully and agreeably occupied, when, having discontinued his law lectures, he began to revise and enlarge them for publication; and in November, 1826, appeared the first volume of the "Commentaries on American Law." This volume includes three parts: the law of nations, the government and constitutional jurisprudence of the United States, and the various sources of municipal law. The second volume was published in November, 1827, the third in 1828, and the fourth in 1830. The last three comprise the law concerning the rights of persons, and personal and real property.

He treated the several subjects comprised under these extensive and most important titles—the rights of person and the rights of property—in a manner more full and satisfactory than Blackstone; and introduced many others not found in the work of that author, with numerous references, quotations and illustrations, the result of his various and extensive reading, highly pleasing and instructive to the student. The subjects of private and public wrongs, which occupy the third and fourth volumes of the English commentator, Chancellor Kent left untouched.

The work of Sir William Blackstone, by the elegance of its style, its lucid arrangement and finished execution, is so well adapted to render the study of the law attractive, that it has been for many years very properly placed in the hands of every student. But an American work, exhibiting our own Constitution, laws, institutions, usages, and civil relatior had long been wanted. In the full maturity of his understanding, with a mind long habituated to legal investigations and researches, and with sound and enlightened views of jurisprudence, he was fitted, better, perhaps, than any other man of his age, to execute such a work.

The first edition of the Commentaries having been exhausted, he published a second in April, 1832, carefully revised and much enlarged.

Having been elected President of the New York Historical Society, he delivered, by request, a public discourse, at their anniversary meeting, on the 6th of December, 1828. In this elegant and instructive address, he noticed the principal events in the history of the colony and State of New York, to the end of the Revolution.

At the request of the Phi Beta Kappa Society of Yale College, a literary association formed in 1780, of which he was an original member, and comprising the most distinguished graduates of that institution, he delivered a public address, at the anniversary meeting, September 13, 1831. This discourse, in which he takes a historical review of the college from its origin in the beginning of the last century, and sketches the characters of its pious and learned founders, supporters and instructors, is replete with generous feelings and just sentiments on literature and education. Alluding, toward the close, to his own class, of whom twelve (out of twenty-five) were then living, and most of those present, he said:

"Star after star has fallen from its sphere. A few bright lights are still visible; but the constellation itself has become dim, and almost ceases to shed its radiance around me. What a severe lesson of mortality does such a retrospect teach! What a startling rebuke to human pride! How brief the drama! How insignificant the honors and 'fiery chase of ambition,' except as mental discipline for beings destined for immortality."

Chancellor Kent had four children, one of whom, a son, was also a lawyer. One died in early life. He was happy in his family, amiable, modest, and candid in his social intercourse. With a sound constitution, strengthened and preserved by temperance and moderate exercise, he enjoyed almost entirely uninterrupted health to the close of his career.

He died December 12, 1847, at the advanced age of eighty-four. Few men have left a more valuable legacy to the world.

THE OREGONIAN CASE AND THE
AMERICAN COURTS.

The *Albany Law Journal* is very indignant at our strictures upon the action of the Supreme Court of the United States in this case. Our contemporary does not profess to be in possession of any account of the case other than our own, which it quite justifiably rejects as *ex parte*; and accordingly its indignation rests not upon knowledge of the merits of the controversy, but upon inherent conviction that the Supreme Court could not possibly do anything to deserve our censure. Now we frankly admit that our language was warm—warmer than is usual or generally desirable in legal criticism, but the moral aspects of the question, of which our contemporary is not in possession, were, we think, such as to justify no inconsiderable heat.

The *Albany Law Journal* speaks of Scottish capitalists being over-reached. We still prefer our own description that it was a case of Scottish investors being swindled. The story is short and simple. A company is formed in Dundee for the construction and letting of a railway in Oregon. To this company a capital of some £500,000 is subscribed, not for the most part by wealthy capitalists, but by hard working people, who have made their money by patient industry, and are anxious to better themselves and increase the hard-earned provision for their families. The company go to Oregon under a law which purports to give to foreign corporations the same rights and powers as domestic corporations of the same kind enjoy. By and by negotiations are entered into with a native company for a lease of the line. The native company is incorporated under a statute which allows of incorporation for any lawful purpose, and one of the purposes expressly set forth in its articles of incorporation, is the taking a lease of a railroad. The bargain is completed. The American company enter into possession. A year or two pass, and then this company, having devastated the property, calmly announce that they répudiate the bargain. An action is begun, and the Circuit Court of the United States rejects the contentions of the repudiators as "frivolous," and sustains the lease.

An appeal is taken to the Supreme Court of the United States, and, after years of delay, that august tribunal sustains the repudiation, sets aside the lease, and in effect gives legal sanction to a barefaced breach of an honorable bargain. The result brings ruin and misery to hundreds who honestly invested their savings in a lawful enterprise, conducted by upright and honorable men, and who went to the United States, and entered into transactions there, confident that the privileges which statute expressly promised them would be upheld, and that bargains honestly made were safe to receive enforcement at the hands of the Federal Courts. We venture to affirm that such a result is unworthy of a rational or civilized system of jurisprudence.

Now it may be objected that this may all infer a stricture upon American law, but that it warrants no reflection upon the Supreme Court, which we are bound to assume correctly interpreted the law. This would be a just observation, if the American Court had been obliged unwillingly to give effect to a clear statutory provision. But the very contrary was the case. The difficulty of the Court was not to have to give effect to the statutory provisions, but to get over them. The natural reading of these provisions was admittedly all in favor of the Scottish company, and a strained construction had to be put upon them in order to permit of the result finally reached. The inference is obvious that this result was in accordance with the Court's conception of natural law or abstract justice. We do not accuse the Court, as our contemporary suggests, of being venal or partial; but we do accuse it of being warped by prejudices and possessed by prepossessions quite unworthy of an enlightened jurisprudence.

The way in which the judgment was reached may be recapitulated in a single word. It was not disputed that the American company was incorporated under a law which expressly provides that any lawful enterprise mentioned in the articles of incorporation shall be within the powers of the corporation. It was admitted that amongst the purposes expressly mentioned in the articles of incorporation were both the construction and the hiring on lease of a railroad. In this state of the law and of the facts, the United States Court held that, notwithstanding the apparently clear provisions of the general statute, it was unconscionable to suppose that a company should have power by such a statute both to construct and to hire railroads; and accordingly they held that the company in question had no power to hire a railroad. Again, the Scottish company came to Oregon under a statute the plain intent of which was to give to foreign corporations the same rights and powers as domestic corporations enjoy. It was not disputed that this was the natural interpretation of the language used. But, again, in face of the language of the statute, the United States Court held that it was unconscionable to suppose that such powers were really conferred upon a foreign corporation.

The whole story suggests a reflection which must often be present to the minds of those on this side of the Atlantic who have business relations with America. Why is it that such a sense of insecurity prevails in regard to all American investments? Why is it, for example, that it is easier to get 6 per cent. over real property in America, than 4 per cent. in this country? It is not that America is distant, for the electric wires and the ocean racers have brought America very near to our doors. It is not that America is a back-going country, for her expansiveness is tenfold greater than our own. It is not that American government is unstable, for her Constitution has stood the test of a century. But it is because of the insurmountable dread that the negotiations will be vitiated by a swindle, and that the swindle will be one for which the law will give no remedy. This dread is born of experience.

The history of British investments in America is strewn with memories of swindles, for which the American Courts have been powerless to find redress. There are plenty of swindlers, in all truth, on this side the Atlantic, and an investor in a new company needs to be careful to whom he entrusts his money. But the investor on this side need be troubled with no apprehensions, that though the swindle be found out, the law will refuse to give him a remedy against it. The swindle may escape detection, the swindler may be unable to make good the loss; but it will not be the fault of the law if the wrong is not remedied. Now, why should it be otherwise in America? The Americans are of the same race, and their jurisprudence has the same traditions as our own. One can well understand an old system, such as the Roman law was before Prætorean intervention, or such as our land system was forty years ago, being warped by restrictions and technicalities which often render it impossible for the Court to give a remedy against undoubted wrong. But it is astonishing that it should be so with a young jurisprudence like that of America, and that these cases of wrong, against which there is no legal remedy, should abound.—(*Scottish Law Magazine.*)

AMENDMENTS TO THE FEDERAL CONSTITUTION.

In former numbers of this magazine, [See LAW TIMES for April and July], I have considered two of the amendments which were proposed in the 50th Congress; the Blair Amendment relating to public schools and to the teaching of the principles of the Christian religion, and the Springer Amendment relative to marriage and divorce. But these are not a tithe of the amendments which have been proposed. The adoption of them all would make a curious patch-quilt of the document framed by our fathers.

I will proceed to mention the other proposed amendments, briefly examining some of the more important. Their number will astonish those who have not kept themselves informed upon the subject.

PROHIBITION AMENDMENT
PROPOSED BY SENATOR BLAIR OF NEW HAMPSHIRE.

This is another of the schemes to change our form of government; and it requires not a very close scrutiny to see that it involves the most radical change of all.

In order to realize the radical character of the transformation in the frame-work of our government which would be effected by this amendment, it is only necessary to examine the decisions of the Supreme Court of the United States, and observe upon what ground the laws of the States prohibiting the manufacture and sale of intoxicating liquors, have been sustained by that high tribunal.

In Brown v. Maryland, 12 Wheaton 446, decided in 1827, Chief-Justice Marshall held that the importer of liquors upon which duties had been paid in accordance with an act of Congress, could not by a State law be subjected to a license for the privilege of selling them, so long as the liquors remained in the original casks or packages in which they had been imported; but after the package had been broken or after the first sale had been made, they became subject to tax or the owner subject to license under the State law.

Twenty years later, in 1847, the celebrated "License Cases" came before the Court. These were, Thurlow v. Massachusetts, Fletcher v. Rhode Island and Pierce v. New Hampshire; consisting of appeals taken by the first named parties respectively, who had been convicted of selling without license, in their respective States. The cases were argued and decided together. They were considered of great importance, and were argued exhaustively and with great ability. Chief-Justice Taney delivered the opinion, and the judgment was concurred in by all the judges, though they did not agree on all the points under discussion; separate opinions being filed by Justices McLean, Catron, Daniel, Woodbury and Greer.

The State law was sustained in each case, on the broad ground that it was a legitimate exercise of the police power of the State.

"The license acts of Massachusetts," said Justice McLean, "do not purport to be a regulation of commerce. They are essentially police laws. Enactments similar in principle are common to all the States."—(5 Howard, U. S. Sup. Ct. Rep. p. 588.)

Again: "If the foreign article be injurious to the health and morals of the community, a State may, in the exercise of that great and conservative police power which lies at the foundation of its prosperity, prohibit the sale of it."—(Ibid. p. 592.)

"I admit as inevitable," said Justice Catron, in his separate opinion, "that if the State has the power of restraint by licenses to any extent, she has the discretionary power to judge of its limit, and may go to the length of prohibiting sales altogether, if such be her policy."—(License Cases, 5 Howard, 610.)

See also opinion of Justice Woodbury in the same cases.

Speaking of the police powers of the States, he said: "The powers seem clearly to exist in the States, and ought to remain there."—(Ibid. p. 630.)

The License cases had been so ably discussed, and so thoroughly considered by the Court, all the judges participating in the decision, that they were considered as settling the law upon the subject. It was not until 1873, that the question, in a somewhat different shape, came up again, in Bartemeyer v. Iowa, 18 Wallace, 132.

Justice Miller, giving the opinion of the Court in that case, said, that up to the time of the adoption of the 14th Amendment, the regulation, or even the total prohibition of the liquor traffic, had been considered as falling within the police regulations of the States, left to their judgment, and subject to no other limitations than such as were imposed by the State Constitution or by the general principles supposed to limit all legislative power.

"All rights are held subject to the police power of the State;" said Justice Bradley, in Beer Co. v. Massachusetts, 97 U. S. Sup. Ct. Rep. p. 32; (1887).

In the same case it was held, that "as a measure of police regulation, looking to the preservation of public morals, a State law prohibiting the manufacture and sale of intoxicating liquors, is not repugnant to any clause of the Constitution of the United States."—(97 U. S. 25, 33.)

We come now to the cases which have attracted so much attention of late years.

The first was Foster v. Kansas, decided in 1884. Chief-Justice Waite, giving the opinion of the Court, said:

"In Bartemeyer v. Iowa, 18 Wall. 129, it was decided that a State law prohibiting the manufacture and sale of intoxicating liquors, was not repugnant to the Constitution of the United States. This was re-affirmed in Beer Co. v. Massachusetts, 97 U. S. 25, and that question is now no longer open in this Court."—(112 U. S. Sup. Ct. Rep. 206.)

In this case, the Court affirmed the judgment of the State court, removing from office one Foster, who had neglected and refused to prosecute persons who were guilty of selling intoxicating liquors in the county, in violation of a statute of the State known as the prohibitory liquor law.

In Mugler v. Kansas, 123 U. S. 666, decided in 1887, Justice Harlan, giving the decision of the Court, said: "The question now before us arises under what are, strictly, the police powers of the State, exerted for the protection of the health, morals and safety of the people. * * The exercise of the police power by the destruction of property which is itself a public nuisance, or the prohibition of its use in a particular way, whereby its value becomes depreciated, is very different from taking property for public use, or from depriving a person of his property without due process of law. In the one case, a nuisance only is abated, in the other, unoffending property is taken away from an innocent man."—(123 U. S. 668, 669.)

In Kidd v. Pearson, decided last year, the decision in Mugler v. Kansas was affirmed.—(128 U. S. 1.)

What is the police power of a State, which is so often referred to in these decisions?

"By public police and economy," says Blackstone, "I mean the due regulation and domestic order of the kingdom, whereby the individuals of the State, like members of a well governed family, are bound to conform their general behavior to the rules of propriety, good neighborhood and good manners, and to be decent, industrious and inoffensive in their respective stations."—(Black. Com. IV, p. 162.)

"The acknowledged police power of a State," said Justice McLean, in his opinion in the License Cases, "extends often to the destruction of property."—(5 How. 589.)

Justice Greer, in the same cases, speaking of the police power, said:

"Without attempting to define what are the peculiar subjects or limits of the power, it may safely be affirmed, that every law for the restraint or punishment of crime, for the preservation of the public peace, health and morals, must come within this category."—(Ibid. p. 631.)

Such is the police power of a State. Now it is proposed that his power be surrendered and transferred to the general government, in one of the most important branches of its exercise.

In the first place, a State has no right to surrender such a power. To do so, would be equivalent to abnegating its jurisdiction over its own citizens.

"A State cannot part with its police power."—(Wm. Wharton Smith, in a Treatise on Private Corporations, Phil. 1889, p. 25.)

This doctrine has been applied so as to sustain a State in passing laws in the nature of police regulations, which are apparently in violation of a contract, evidenced by a charter of a private corporation.

"It has been often decided by the American courts, Federal and State, that the State cannot barter away, or in any way curtail its exercise of any of those powers which are essential attributes of sovereignty, and particularly the police power, by which the actions of individuals are so regulated as not to injure others; and any contract by which the State undertakes to do this, is void, and does not come within the constitutional protection."—(Tiedeman's book on the Limitations to Police Power, p. 580.) See also Bank of Columbia v. Oakly, 4 Wheat. 235; Ex parte N. E. and S. W. R. R. Co. 37 Ala. N. S. 679; Ward v. Farwell, 97 Ill. 593.

In Stone v. Mississippi, 101 U. S. 816, the Supreme Court of the U. S. said, in substance, that a State could not divest itself of its police power. See also Butcher's Union Co. v. Crescent City Co. 111 U. S. 751, and New Orleans Gas Co. v. Louisiana Light Co. 115 U. S. 650, 672.

"The Legislature cannot part with any of the police powers of the State which are matters that affect the public peace, public health, public morals and public convenience."—(Farmers Loan and Trust Co. v. Stone, 20 Fed. Rep. 270; Allerton v. City of Chicago, 6 Fed. Rep. 555; in Re Wong Yung Quy, 2 Fed. Rep. 624; Beer Co. v. Massachusetts, 97 U. S. 25.)

A State has no more right to transfer its police power to another government than to a private corporation. In either case, it abnegates its authority, and ceases to be a State.

But, it will be asked, has the United States no police power? Certainly, it has full power over the territories, over the District of Columbia, and over American vessels on the high seas. It has also throughout the Union, even in the States, so much police power as is necessary to perpetuate the existence and to carry on the operations of the national government. It has thus much power and no more, and more cannot be given it without breaking up entirely our federative form of government.

The use of alcoholic liquors as a beverage is a great—a crying evil. I would it were entirely prohibited in every place under the exclusive jurisdiction of Congress, and by State authority in every State in the Union. The proposed amendment provides that "the manufacture, importation, exportation, transportation, and sale of alcoholic liquors as a beverage shall be, and hereby is, forever prohibited in the United States, and in every place subject to their jurisdiction."

Now such an amendment could not be carried into execution, for vagueness and uncertainty. Who is to decide what alcoholic liquors are imported into this country "as a beverage?" The casks are not marked, one, "This is to be used as a beverage;" another, "This is for medicinal purposes," etc. All the federal government does is to authorize the importation of the liquors; and the Supreme Court says, that under a proper construction of the Act of Congress, a State cannot tax the liquors in the hands of the importer or require that he take out a license for the privilege of selling them, so long as they remain in the same form—the same casks or packages in which they were imported. But the moment they come within the jurisdiction of a State, they become subject to State laws, with the single exception named. After the packages are broken, or after the first sale, the authority is complete. And even if the first sale should be made for the purpose, on the part of the purchaser, of retailing the liquor as a beverage, he would be powerless to carry out that purpose in a prohibition State, and should he undertake to do so, the liquor would be destroyed. How, then, can the Committee say, as they do in their Report, that "at the present time the police power in the States is fettered and thwarted in its efforts to suppress this evil within the limits of the States, respectively, by the national guaranties of protection to transportation and the rights of manufacture and sale existing in all the States and localities which decline to impose the necessary restrictions?" —(50th Congress, 1st Session, Senate Report, No. 1727, p. 3.)

The police power of the States is not thus fettered and thwarted. The State of Kansas, for instance, has full power, and can carry out the power, to destroy any intoxicating liquor which any one may attempt to sell as a beverage, whether it was brought into Kansas from Europe, or from the State of Missouri; subject only to the limitation mentioned.

At most that limitation constitutes but a partial obstruction, and that obstruction can be made still less, without any amendment of the Constitution, by an Act of Congress, regulating the size of the packages containing imported liquor.

Upon the hearing before the Senate Committee, Mrs. Bittenbender argued with much apparent force, in favor of national prohibition, as a necessary consequence of the decision of the Supreme Court of the United States in the late case of Bowman v. The Chicago Railway Company, 125 U. S. 472. The decision in that case was that the statute of Iowa forbidding railways, under a penalty, from bringing intoxicating liquors into the State, was unconstitutional; as infringing upon the power of Congress to regulate commerce between the States; and it was urged by Mrs. Bittenbender that this decision demonstrated the inability of a State to protect itself from the evil effects of an indiscriminate sale of intoxicating drinks without the aid of the general government. But in the first place, it is by no means certain that the decision will remain the permanent law of the land, since it was reached by a bare majority only of the Court. Justice Lamar did not sit on the hearing of the case, and of the other eight judges, three, including Chief-Justice Waite, dissented. If one other judge had gone with them, the court would have been evenly divided, and the judgment instead of being reversed, would have been sustained.

Even if the opinion of the majority should hereafter be adhered to, the consequence at most is but an obstruction, to a certain extent, requiring more vigilance on the part of the

State, in order to carry out her prohibitory laws. For, according to this decision even, after the first sale has been made so that the liquors may be considered as a part of the general property of the community, the State has full jurisdiction ov them. A partial and temporary obstruction of that sort, not sufficient to justify the State in abnegating its police pow in favor of the federal government. As a general rule, peopl engaged in wholesaling liquors will not take them into a prob bition State, because there the demand for them is so much less

The Report states that "there are members of the commi who concur in the report recommending the submission of th proposed amendment to the States, who do not, by such action indicate their approval of the adoption of the amendmen as a part of the Constitution, nor that they would themselv advocate its ratification by the legislatures of the States; bu in deference to the immense mass of petitions for this amend-ment of the organic law, coming from the people in all parts of the country, and believing that an opportunity should be given to them to be heard upon the merits of their cause in the forum of the States, where alone it can be heard and de-cided, the majority of the Committee would deem a refusal to submit the proposed amendment to the States for considera-tion, analogous to a denial of the right of a party to be heard in court upon a question of private right."—(Ibid. p. 1.) Af-terward it is stated in substance, that to refuse to give the petitioners the right to go before the people of the States on the question, would be a denial of the right of petition.

It is difficult to see how such a position can be maintained, in the face of the wording of the fifth Amendment to the Con-stitution, which provides for Congress proposing amendments to the Constitution "whenever two-thirds of both houses shall deem it necessary." If a member of Congress does not deem an amendment necessary, and would, for that reason, oppose it in his State, how can he, in the conscientious discharge of his duty, vote to submit the proposition to the action of the States? If he is afraid of the "immense mass" of petitioners, the best way to placate them is to advocate prohibition in his own State.

The right of petition is not denied. A certain portion of the citizens of a State have not a right to advocate before their State Legislature, a Constitutional Amendment which less than two-thirds of the members of Congress deem necessary. Such citizens have the full right of petition in their own State. Having exercised that right, but without avail, they go before Congress, and ask for an amendment compelling their State to do that which it is unwilling to do voluntarily. That is not such a right of petition as is recognized and protected in the State and Federal Constitutions.

A Prohibition Amendment, word for word the same as Senator Blair's, was introduced in the House by Mr. Dingley, of Maine.

BIGAMY AND POLYGAMY.

Senator Cullom has introduced the following amendment:

"ARTICLE XVI. Section 1. The only institution or contract of marriage within the United States, or any place subject to their jurisdiction, shall be that of the union in marriage of one man with one woman; and bigamy or polygamy is forever prohibited; any law, custom, form or ceremony, civil or religious, to the contrary notwithstanding.

"Sec. 2. No State shall pass any law, nor allow any custom, form or ceremony of marriage, except in obedience to and conformably to the institution of marriage as herein defined and established; but otherwise the regulation within each State, of marriage and divorce, and civil and criminal jurisdiction over those subjects, shall belong to the several States as heretofore.

"Sec. 3. Congress shall have power to enforce this article by appropriate legislation."

The manifest object of this amendment is to prevent the establishment of polygamy in Utah as a State institution, after the Territory shall have been admitted into the Union; since no such amendment is required in reference to the States now in the Union, monogamy being recognized both by the common law and by State legislation, as the only valid marriage relation.

The objection to adopting such an amendment with express reference to Utah, is two-fold.

In the first place, it is an applied admission, that when such a safeguard has been established, Utah may be admitted; whereas it ought not to be admitted as a State, so long as it maintains its present attitude, and continues to evade the anti-polygamy law already passed by Congress. Nay further; it ought not to be admitted so long as the controlling influences in the Territory are in favor of polygamy. So long as that is the case, such an amendment would not be a sufficient guaranty.

In the second place, the disease is too deep-seated to be reached by this amendment. Polygamy is not, as many suppose, the only objection to receiving Utah as a State. Polygamy is only an eruption on the surface of the religio-political body. The vital trouble is, that in the valley of Salt Lake has been established a religious hierarchy, with political pretensions entirely antagonistic to the Republic. There has never been a day since Brigham Young led the Mormons into that valley, when the conformity of his "people" to the laws and institutions of the United States, has been more than a mere matter of form. The theory is that these are God's chosen people, who have come up to Mount Zion, where they are to establish an independent government, which is eventually to absorb all the nations of the earth. The "gentiles," by which term they mean all outsiders, and especially the people of the United States, they look upon as their mortal enemies and their legitimate prey.

The Territory of Utah ought never to be admitted into the Union, until that element in the population is in a minority; and in a minority so decided that it is likely to remain permanently in that position. That is the only reliable guaranty for its good behavior.

Senator Dolph, of Oregon, has also introduced a joint resolution as follows:

"Congress shall have power to legislate upon the subjects of marriage and divorce by general laws applicable alike to all the States and Territories, and neither bigamy nor polygamy shall exist or be permitted within the United States or any place subject to their jurisdiction."

This is the Cullom Amendment and the Springer Amendment combined; and since both those have been examined, this needs no further consideration. In the House, Anti-Polygamy Amendments were introduced by Congressmen Ezra B. Taylor, of Ohio, Springer, of Illinois, Stewart, of Vermont, Culberson, of Texas, and Breckenridge, of Kentucky.

WOMAN SUFFRAGE.
AMENDMENT INTRODUCED BY SENATOR BLAIR.

The general government has already taken jurisdiction over the suffrage question in reference to the colored race, and has thereby established a precedent. But the Fifteenth Amendment is practically inoperative in the very States for which it was principally intended.

A Woman Suffrage Amendment was introduced in the House, also, by Mr. Reed, of Maine.

THE VETO POWER.
AMENDMENT PROPOSED BY SENATOR STEWART.

This amendment provides for passing a law by a majority vote over the Presidential veto. If the President disapprove the act, he is to return it with his objections, as at the present time, but it then may become a law by being passed by a majority of each house.

We do not think the people are prepared to dispense with the guaranty against hasty legislation, which is afforded by the presidential veto. The veto power may, it is true, be abused, and so may any of the powers confided to any public officer. All the reasons which operated on the minds of the framers of the Constitution, in providing for the veto power, remain in full force.

ELECTION OF PRESIDENT AND VICE-PRESIDENT
BY THE PEOPLE, AND RESTRICTION TO ONE TERM.

Senator Cockrell, of Missouri, introduced an amendment to be substituted for the first section of the second article of the Constitution, providing that the President and Vice-President be chosen every four years by the people, and that the President be ineligible to a second term. In case of failure to elect, the choice is to be made by the two Houses in joint session.

The object of having electors voted for by the people was, partly to guard against any irregularity in making direct returns of votes for President and Vice-President, and partly to preserve the representation of States, two of the electors standing in the place of the two Senators, and representing the whole State. The officer thus chosen would be President, not only of the People of the United States, but of the States themselves. Such an election is a solemn acquiescence in the result of the several States, and is equivalent to a pledge on the part of each State, to abide by the decision of the whole people, thus expressed.

It appears to be an eminently proper mode of choosing the chief executive, and it is difficult to see any improvement in the mode proposed by Senator Cockrell.

Upon the one term question, people are divided. There is much to be said upon both sides.

In · the House, Mr. Townshend, of Illinois, proposed an amendment, providing for the election of the President and Vice-President every four years by the people, and the canvassing of the votes by the Supreme Court of the State. If no person have a majority of all the votes cast, then a second election is provided for.

An amendment having a similar object was introduced by Mr. Browne, of Indiana, but the electoral representation is, by an ingenious process, preserved, without requiring electors. An amendment somewhat similar, was proposed, also, by Mr. Marsh, of Pennsylvania.

Mr. Stone, of Kentucky, proposed, as an amendment, that the President and Vice-President be chosen by the people, every fourth year, and that the votes be counted by the board authorized by the laws of the State to count the votes for State officers. An amendment offered by Mr. Springer, provides for the election of President and Vice-President by the people; the term to be six years, and the President to be ineligible to a re-election. The scheme of Mr. Springer also preserves the electoral representation in the choice of President and Vice-President.

ELECTION OF SENATORS BY THE PEOPLE.

This Amendment was introduced by Senator Mitchell, of Oregon, who proposes to strike out the word "legislature" in the first clause of section three of Article one, and substitute in ·

lieu thereof the word "people;" so that said clause shall read as follows:

"The Senate of the United States shall be composed of two Senators from each State, chosen by the people thereof for six years; and each Senator shall have one vote."

This amendment, like many of those introduced into the last Congress, is aimed against State sovereignty or State authority. Its object is, to have it understood that the United States Senators are to be directly responsible to the people, without any responsibility to the State as such. As at present elected, they are responsible both to their State and to the people of their State; to the State, inasmuch as they are elected by the body holding the legislative power of the State, and to the people, inasmuch as the legislature is elected by the people. Amendments for the election of Senators by the people, were introduced in the House by Mr. Townshend, of Illinois, Mr. Weaver, of Iowa, Mr. Hermann, of Oregon, and Mr. Oates, of Alabama.

SIX YEARS TERM FOR THE PRESIDENCY.

Senator Butler, of South Carolina, proposes an amendment, making the Presidential term six years instead of four.

Such an amendment, if adopted, should have incorporated in it the words, "and shall be ineligible to a second term."

In the House an amendment for six years with this very proviso was introduced by Mr. Neal, of Tennessee. Also by Mr. McComas, of Maryland. The amendment of Mr. Springer, already noticed, is the same, with the added provision of election by the people.

EIGHT YEARS TERM FOR THE PRESIDENCY AND INELIGIBILITY TO RE-ELECTION.
BY MR. HUDD, OF WISCONSIN.

REPRESENTATION IN THE DISTRICT OF COLUMBIA.

Senator Blair introduced the following:

"ARTICLE XVI. Sec. 1. The District of Columbia shall be entitled to representation in the Congress of the United States by one Senator, and by one or more Representatives, according to the rule of apportionment established by Article XIV of the Constitution. Said District shall also be entitled to as many electors for President and Vice-President of the

United States as it has members of Congress: Provided, that such representation in Congress shall not participate in joint convention of the two Houses, nor in any proceeding touching the choice of President or Vice-President, nor in the organization of either House of Congress, nor speak or vote upon any question concerning the same.

"Sec. 2. Congress shall provide by law, the time and manner of choosing the Senator, the Representative or Representatives, and the electors authorized by this article."

THE FOURTH OF MARCH
TO BE CHANGED TO THE LAST TUESDAY IN APRIL.
PROPOSED BY SENATOR HOAR, OF MASSACHUSETTS.

Term of members of Congress to end at the same time.

This Amendment was proposed in the House, by Mr. Lodge, of Massachusetts. Mr. Crain of Texas, proposed an amendment, fixing Dec. 31, as the end of the Congressional term, and another to the same effect, with April 30 as the end of the Presidential term.

The other amendments introduced in the House, are as follows:

By Mr. Springer, of Illinois:

Congress, as far as practicable, to pass general laws.

By Mr. McComas, of Maryland:

The States to have full power of taxation over corporations, notwithstanding any provisions in their charters.

By Mr. Davis, of Massachusetts:

Congress to have power to limit the time of daily employment of persons in manufactories and other industries.

By Mr. Dibble, of South Carolina:

Providing for a Second Vice-President.

By Mr. Phelan, of Tennessee:

Congress to have power to aid the public school systems of the several States, to the extent of ten millions annually.

By Mr. Peters, of Kansas:

Congress not to have power to repeal any of the Rebellion War pension laws.

By Mr. Johnston, of North Carolina:

The House to consist of 250 members.

By Mr. Mason, of Illinois:

Widows and spinisters who are property-holders, to have

the right to vote and hold office.

By Mr. Wheeler, of Alabama:

One third of each House to constitute a quorum.

By Mr. McAdoo, of New Jersey:

Presidential electors to be chosen on the 3d Tuesday of October, and no other officers to be voted for on the same day, except Congressmen.

These are the amendments proposed to the 50th Congress. The immense number of them, no less than 44 in all, involving some thirty changes more or less in the Constitution, show how many defects there were in the instrument framed by the Convention over which George Washington presided, and of which so many eminent statesmen were members—defects, most of which have only been discovered after the lapse of a hundred years.

Most of these amendments have no merit whatever; and others, seemingly meritorious on their face, when closely examined, are found not to be of such utility and importance as to justify a change in the fundamental law. Probably the best thing Congress could do would be to reject the whole batch until the rage for amendments is over, and then if there is any one that is particularly desirable, take it up, discuss it with much deliberation, and if, in the language of the Constitution, it be "deemed necessary," submit it to the States for consideration.

No doubt it is the illusive idea that a member, by voting for an amendment, does not necessarily commit himself to its necessity, that has caused such a flood of them to be poured upon Congress.

Charles B. Waite.

THE TRIAL OF WILLIAM PENN FOR PREACHING THE GOSPEL.

William Penn, the son of Admiral Penn, was born on Great Tower Hill, in London, on the 14th of October, 1644. His mother was a Dutch lady whom the Admiral had met in one of his voyages to the Low Countries, and owing to his constant employment on the sea, the mother and son were left alone very much of the time during the early years of young William.

England was just at that time all torn up by the civil war in which the Parliament was arrayed against the King, and royalist and country parties were marching up and down the land to the terror of all quiet citizens. No one could tell how the strife would end. The battle of Marston Moor had been fought in the previous summer, and King Charles I. had been virtually dethroned. London was nothing but one huge encampment, and it was thought best for the "Dutch wife," as the old Admiral always called her, and young William, to retire into the country. Accordingly they went to Wanstead, in Essex. near Chigwell, two very remarkable places for their historical associations as well as for the beauty of their surroundings.

Old Wanstead House was in its glory. It had been rebuilt by Lord Chancellor Rich and had received Queen Mary just before her coronation; had been visited by Queen Elizabeth for four or five days, and had witnessed the marriage of the Earl of Leicester with the Countess of Essex—the bridegroom being at the time lord and master of the domain. Chigwell too was renowned for its stately palaces, its magnificent churches and schools, and it was in this region that Penn passed the first eleven years of his life. Here he received his first knowledge of the rudiments of learning and received his initiation into the classics. He early became acquainted with the great questions that divided the people, and having learned of the cruelties and the oppressions of the "established church" factions, he imbibed notions of independence which he took with him to Oxford. There they got him into difficulty, which ended with his leaving the University and eventually becoming a Quaker.

His father, when he became acquainted with his vagaries, was greatly exasperated and turned him out of doors. But when he himself became involved in difficulties, he became reconciled to his son, and forgave him when he found that it was impossible to convince him of his errors or turn him from his chosen way.

He did not believe in Laud or Laudism; thought that the fate of Charles I. was not undeserved, and that Cromwell did much to make royalty respect the will of the people. He believed that the final triumph of the people would be supplemented by "The rise, race and royalty of God in the soul of man." He became a disciple of George Fox, was persecuted, thrown into prison and abused, but he never faltered or feared the results.

He studied law in Lincoln's Inn, and between the influences of the Holy Spirit and Magna Charta, he became strong in the faith and in the righteousness which that great charter of liberty would aid mankind in attaining.

He was accused of heresy, and at the instigation of the Bishop of London was thrown into the Tower, where he remained for several months. Here it was that he first tasted the real sweets of martyrdom, and here it was that he wrote his celebrated treatise, "No Cross no Crown." While he was in the Tower, a servant came to tell him that the Bishop of London had declared he should either recant or die a prisoner. "Thou mayst tell my father," he replied, "that my prison shall be my grave before I will budge a jot; for I owe obedience of my conscience to no mortal man."

It seemed at that time as if the devil himself had taken possession of the rulers of men, and that such a thing as toleration and liberty of conscience were utterly unknown. The whipping post, the parish stocks, pelting by infuriated mobs, and impositions of enormous fines; these were cruelties inflicted on Quakers year by year. Different statutes were brought to bear upon them, and where no specific law could be produced, it was easy to require the oath of allegiance, which exposed them to six months imprisonment.

Their meetings were disturbed by lawless hoodlums, and unconscionable brutes, who marched in a body to the places of worship at the sound of drums and fiddles. Women had their hoods torn off and little boys were beaten with a cat-o-'nine tails. More than fifteen hundred were thrown into prison, and many died there, because they could not furnish bonds to procure their liberation. Three hundred and fifty died in jail within a little over ten years after 1660. Altogether, according to Penn's calculations, more than five thousand perished for the sake of religion. The reigns of Charles II. and James II. furnished hideous examples of their wrongs, the accounts of which are preserved in their "Canons and Institutions" and in "those grim and ponderous folios, among the records of their society, where they stand as if ready for the judgment day." It is curious how this most harmless sect was persecuted both in England and in the New World—how they were driven out of Virginia and denied even the commonest offices of hospitality.

Penn spent some time in Ireland, in managing and looking after his father's estate, and on the continent; visited the Low Countries, traversed Germany, passed a year at Paris and saw persecution there in all of its forms. He early formed the project of obtaining an interest in the Western Hemisphere, where he and his people might live in peace and worship God as they saw fit.

This vision, which first dawned on his mind in his youth, he was enabled through the Providence of God partially to realize. Although he never lived to behold the dawning of the Great Republic, he did live to tread the soil of the new world and to lay the foundations of a commonwealth which links his name forever with all that is good and great in this world—as lasting as time and eternity itself.

Few men living—indeed few Americans know or realize what an impetus he gave to religious freedom in his struggles through that long night of oppression, which characterized the reigns of Charles II. and James II., and few realize what he did for the protection of human rights by his open defiance of unjust judges and cruel persecutors who strove to destroy him and his friends under the forms of law. His position was in some respects like that of Cromwell, for he led all mankind by his boldness and his daring, and defied all of his oppressors. He succeeded in breaking down the prejudices of caste and exposing to open day the iniquities which characterized all trials by courts which were organized solely to convict.

To trace out the life of this most extraordinary man would require a volume. His life was replete with incidents of the most thrilling interest.

We have selected one only at this time which we deem of the greatest importance, and that is his trial "for preaching to an unlawful, seditious and riotous assembly" in front of the "Friends' Meeting-House" in Grace Church Street, London, in 1670.

It was in this year that the infamous "Conventicles Act" was renewed, which prevented all dissenters from worshiping as they saw fit.

Penn and his followers had suffered much up to this time, but he was not aware that armed force was to be used to prevent his people from peaceably assembling, until he repaired to the "meeting-house" in Grace Church Street, when he found it closed and guarded. He made up his mind to preach to the crowd in the street. Another friend was with him, William Mead, a London linen-draper. Soon after the discourse had begun, both the preacher and his companion were arrested under warrant from the Lord Mayor, and immediately dragged off to Newgate.

What followed forms a curious chapter in the history of English jurisprudence. The prisoners were arraigned at the

Old Bailey, not as is sometimes supposed, for a breach of the Conventicle Act, but as we have said, for "preaching to an unlawful, seditious and riotous assembly." After two days adjournment of the court, a preliminary examination took place, at which time Penn and Mead appeared in the dock with their hats on. These were knocked off their heads, but the officers were told to put them on again, when the court proceeded to assert his dignity in the following manner:

RECORDER.—"Do you know where you are?"

PENN.—"Yes."

REC.—"Do you know it is the King's Court?"

PENN.—"I know it to be a court, and I suppose it to be the King's Court."

REC.—"Do you know there is respect due to the court?"

PENN.—"Yes."

REC.—"Why do you not pay it then?"

PENN.—"I do so."

REC.—"Why do you not put off your hat then?"

RENN.—"Because I do not believe that to be any respect."

REC.—"Well, the Court sets forty marks apiece upon your heads, as a fine for your contempt of the court."

PENN.—"I desire it may be observed that we came into the court with our hats off (that is taken off) and if they have been put on since, it was by order from the bench, and therefore not I, but the bench should be fined."

After this episode, a formal indictment was found against Penn and Mead, and on the 1st of September, 1670, they were placed upon trial at the Old Bailey, before the Recorder and Lord Mayor of London. It is one of the most remarkable trials on record. Penn planted himself squarely on the Constitution—declared that the Conventicle Act was contrary to all the provisions of Magna Charter, and was void.

He claimed for every Englishman four fundamental rights as descending to him from the Saxon period: 1. Security of property; 2. Security of person; 3. A voice in the making of all laws relating to property or person; 4. A share, by means of the jury, in the actual administration of the civil law. These rights had been attacked in Penn's person, and were vindicated by Penn's courageous action. He defended himself with great spirit and ability, though the court seized every opportunity to browbeat and confuse him.

The Recorder, in reply to Penn's calm request, that he would inform him by what law he was prosecuted, and on what law the indictment was grounded, replied violently, as follows:

"You must not think that I am able to sum up so many years, and ever so many adjudged cases, which we call common law, to satisfy your curiosity."

PENN.—"This answer, I am sure, is very short of my question, for if it be common, it should not be so very hard to produce."

RECORDER, (angrily)—"Sir, will you plead to your indictment?"

PENN.—"Shall I plead to an indictment that has no foundation in law? If it contain that law you say I have broken, why should you decline to produce it, since it will be impossible for the jury to determine, or agree to bring in their verdict, who have not the law produced by which they should measure the truth of the indictment?"

REC. (passionately)—"You are a saucy fellow; speak to the indictment."

PENN.—"I say it is my place to speak to matters of law. I am arraigned a prisoner. My liberty, which is next to life itself, is now concerned. You are many against me, and it is hard if I must not make the best of my case. I say again, unless you show me and the people the law you ground your indictment upon, I shall take it for granted your proceedings are merely arbitrary. * * *"

REC. (waiving this critical point)—"The question is, whether you are guilty of this indictment?"

PENN.—"The question is, not whether I am guilty of this indictment, but whether this indictment be legal. It is too general and imperfect an answer to say it is common law, unless we know both where and what it is; for where there is no law there is no transgression; and that law which is not in being, so far from being common law, is no law at all."

REC.—"You are an impertinent fellow. Will you teach the

Court what law is? It is *lex non scripta.* That which many have studied thirty or forty years to know, would you have me tell you in a moment?"

PENN.—"Certainly, if the common law be so hard to be understood, it is far from being very common; but if the Lord Coke in his Institutes be of any weight, he tells us that 'common law is common right,' and common right is the great charter privileges confirmed by various enactments."

REC.—"Sir, you are a very troublesome fellow, and it is not for the honor of the Court to allow you to go on. * * * My Lord, if you do not take some course with this persistent fellow to stop his mouth, we shall not be able to do anything to-night."

LORD MAYOR.—"Take him away! Take him away! Put him into the bale-dock!" And in the midst of a vigorous appeal to the jury, he was forcibly removed to the extreme end of the court, where he could neither see nor be seen.

The Recorder then proceeded: "You, gentlemen of the jury, have heard what the indictment is; it is for preaching to the people and drawing a tumultuous company after them; and Mr. Penn was speaking. If they shall not be disturbed, you see they will go on. There are three or four witnesses have proved this—that Mr. Penn did preach there, that Mr. Mead did allow of it. After this, you have heard by substantial witnesses what is said against them. Now we are on matter of fact, which you are to keep and to observe, as what hath been fully sworn, at your peril."

Here Penn from the bale-dock interrupted, in his loudest tones: "I appeal to the jury who are my judges, and to this great assembly, whether the proceedings of the Court are not most arbitrary, and void of all law, in offering to give the jury their charge in the absence of the prisoners? I say it is directly opposed and destructive to the right of every English prisoner, as declared by Coke in the 2nd Institute, 29, in the chapter on Magna Charter."

REC. (with an affectation of humor)—"Why you *are* present. You *do* hear, do you not?"

PENN.—"No, thanks to the Court that commanded me into

the bale-dock. And you of the jury, take notice that I have not been heard; neither can you legally depart the Court before I have been fully heard, having at least ten or twelve material points to offer in order to invalidate the indictment."

REC.(furiously)—"Pull. that fellow down! Pull him down! Take him to the hole. To hear him talk doth not become the honor of the Court."

After the prisoners had been "haled away" to the squalidest of all the squalid dens in England, the "hole" in Newgate, the Recorder commanded the jury to agree in their verdict according to the facts sworn. They retired for consideration; but instead of returning immediately, as the judges anticipated, tarried thirty minutes—sixty minutes—an hour and a half! Then entered eight of the jurors, saying that they could not agree. The Recorder demanded the other four, and immediately poured out upon them a flood of vituperation.

The jury withdrew a second time; and after two hours absence, returned with a verdict of "Guilty of speaking in Grace Church Street."

An attempt was made to coerce or cajole them into altering it to "unlawful speaking;" but they manfully refused. "We have given in our verdict; we can give no other." They were sent back a third time; whereupon they sent in a verdict, "Guilty of speaking to an assembly met together in Grace Church Street."

In a storm of passion, the Lord Mayor pronounced their foreman, "an impudent, canting knave." The Recorder exclaimed:

"You shall not be dismissed till you bring in a verdict which the Court will accept. You shall be locked up, without meat, drink, fire or tobacco. You shall not think thus to abuse the Court. We will have a verdict, by the help of God, or you shall starve for it!"

PENN.—"The jury, who are my judges, ought not to be thus menaced. Their verdict should be free—not forced."

REC.—"Stop that fellow's mouth, or put him out of the Court."

LORD MAYOR (addressing the jury)—"You have heard that

he preached; that he gathered a company of tumultuous people; and that they not only disobey the martial power, but the civil also."

PENN.—"That is a mistake. We did not make the tumult; but they that interrupted us. The jury cannot be so ignorant as to think we met there to disturb the peace, because it is well known that we are a peaceable people, never offering violence to any man, and were kept by force of arms out of our own house. You are Englishmen," he said to the jurors, "mind your privileges; give not away your rights."

The jury were then locked up, and the prisoners carried back to Newgate. The next morning (Sunday), the Court was again crowded, and with anxiety chequered by hope, the public awaited the re-appearance of the jurors. At seven o'clock their names were called over, and the Clerk once more inquired if they had agreed upon a verdict. They replied in the affirmative. "Guilty or not guilty?" "Guilty of speaking in Grace Church Street."

LORD MAYOR.—"To an unlawful assembly?"

BUSHEL.—"No, my Lord; we give no other verdict than we gave last night."

LORD MAYOR.—"You are a factious fellow; I'll take a course with you."

BUSHEL.—"I have done according to my conscience."

LORD MAYOR.—"That conscience of yours would cut my throat."

BUSHEL.—"No, my Lord, it never shall."

LORD MAYOR.—"But I will cut yours as soon as I can."

REC. (jestingly)—"He has inspired the jury; he has the spirit of divination; methinks he begins to affect me! I will have a positive verdict, or else you shall starve."

PENN.—"I desire to ask the Recorder a question. Do you allow the verdict given, of William Mead?"

REC.—"It cannot be a verdict, because you are indicted for conspiracy; and one being found 'Not Guilty,' and not the other, it is no verdict."

PENN.—"If 'Not Guilty' be no verdict, then you make of the jury and of the Great Charta a mere nose of wax."

MEAD.—"How? Is 'Not Guilty' not a verdict?"

REC.—"It is no verdict."

PENN.—"I affirm that the consent of a jury is a verdict in law; and if William Mead be not guilty, it follows that I am clear, since you have indicted us for conspiracy, and I could not possibly conspire alone."

Once more the unfortunate jurors were compelled to retire—only to persist in the verdict already given. The Recorder, carried by his wrath beyond the bounds of decency, exclaimed, "Your verdict is nothing. You play upon the Court. I say you shall go and bring in another verdict, or you shall starve; and I will have you carted about the city as in Edward the Third's time."

FOREMAN.—"We have given in our verdict, in which we are all agreed; if we give in another, it will be by force, to save our lives."

LORD MAYOR.—"Take them up to their room."

OFFICER.—"My Lord, they will not go."

The jurors were constrained to withdraw—actual violence being used—and locked up without food and water. Exposed to this harsh treatment, some weaker minds wavered, and would have given way but for the courageous resolution of Bushel, and others like Bushel, who understood the importance of the question at issue. So when, on Monday morning, the Court once more summoned the jurors, there was not, though they had fasted two days and nights, a traitor or coward among them. Wan and worn were they, with hunger, fatigue, and a not unnatural anxiety; but determined to do justice to their fellow-men, arraigned, as they knew, on a false charge.

CLERK.—"Gentlemen, are you agreed upon your verdict?"

JURY.—"Yes."

CLERK.—"Who shall speak for you?"

JURY.—"Our foreman."

CLERK.—"Look upon the prisoners, what say you; is William Penn guilty of the matter whereof he stands indicted in manner and form or not guilty?"

FOREMAN.—"You have your verdict in writing."

CLERK.—"I will read it."

REC.—"No, it is no verdict. The Court will not accept it."

FOREMAN.—"If you will not accept of it, I desire to have it back again."

THE COURT.—"The paper was no verdict, and no advantage shall be taken of you for it."

CLERK.—"How say you; is William Penn guilty or not guilty?"

FOREMAN (resolutely).—"Not guilty."

REC.—"I am sorry, gentlemen, you have followed your own judgments and opinions rather than the good advice which was given you. God keep my life out of your hands. But for this the Court fines you forty marks a man, and imprisonment in Newgate till the fines are paid."

PENN.—"Being freed by the jury, I demand to be set at liberty."

LORD MAYOR.—"No, you are in for your fines."

PENN.—"Fines! What fines?"

LORD MAYOR.—"For contempt of court."

PENN.—"I ask if it be according to the fundamental laws of England that any Englishman should be fined except by the judgment of his peers? since it expressly contradicts the 14th and 29th chapters of the Great Charter of England, which says, 'No free man ought to be amerced except by the oath of good and lawful men of the vicinage."

REC.—"Take him away; put him out of the court."

PENN.—"I can never urge the fundamental laws of England, but you cry out, 'Take him away! Take him away!' But this is no wonder; since the Spanish Inquisition sits so near the Recorder's heart. God, who is just, will judge you all for these things."

The prisoners and the jurors refusing to pay the fines so arbitrarily inflicted upon them, were removed to Newgate. The latter, at Penn's instigation, immediately brought an action against the Lord Mayor and the Recorder for having imprisoned them in defiance of law and justice. It was argued on the 9th of November, before the twelve judges, who unanimously decided in favor of the appellants.

They were immediately released, and Penn went forth triumphant, having struck an effectual blow in vindication of the liberties of the subject.

Penn's position in regard to the rights of man was, as we have said, an advanced one, and to promote liberty was in his estimation, to obey the gospel; not to do it, was to reject the gospel. Persecution he held to be not merely impolitic, useless and unreasonable, but also thoroughly anti-christian. Judging people by their conduct, not by their creed, esteeming meekness and charity as first fruits of the Spirit—he looked upon persecutors, whether orthodox or heterodox, whether churchmen or dissenters, as alienated from their Maker and as enemies to their race.

He retired for a time into the country, but had not been long at home, when once more he was arrested, through the petty spite of Sir John Robinson, lieutenant of the Tower, the nephew of Archbishop Laud, and again committed to the Tower. This miscreant had sat as one of his judges at the Old Bailey, and felt keenly the mortification that he was subjected to, by reason of the acquittal of Penn, and he resolved to get even with him.

He found out that there was a Quaker meeting-house in Wheeler Street, where Penn sometimes preached, and he accordingly laid a trap to have him arrested upon some trumped up charge. Having had him brought before him, he dismissed the original charge, and then demanded that he should take the oath of allegiance, which he knew Penn would not do, as he was opposed to all oaths.

He loaded Penn with insults, but Penn looked down upon him with contempt, and calmly replied: "Thy words shall be thy burthen and I trample thy slander as dirt under my feet." Discomfited and enraged, Robinson ordered Penn to be committed to Newgate for six months; and what Newgate was, can be best told by Ellwood, the Quaker, who had been a prisoner there.

"When we came" says he, "to Newgate, we found that side of the prison very full of *Friends*, who were prisoners there before us, as indeed were all other prisoners about the town; and our addition caused a still greater throng on that side of

Newgate. We had the liberty of the hall, which is on the first story, over the gate, and which in the day-time is common to all the prisoners on that side, felons as well as others. But in the night we all lodged in one room, which was large and round, having in the middle of it a great pillar of oaken timber, which bore up the chapel which is over it. To this pillar we fastened our hammocks at one end, and to the opposite wall on the other end, quite round the room, in three stories, one over the other; so that they who lay in the upper and middle row of hammocks were obliged to go to bed first, because they were to climb up to the higher by getting into the lower ones. And under the lower range of hammocks, by the wall sides, were laid beds upon the floor, in which the sick and weak prisoners lay. There were many sick and some very weak, and though we were not long there, one of our fellow prisoners died." This was the "Hell Hole," as it was then called, to which the gifted Penn was committed by a miserable wretch, who had been empowered to exercise judicial functions. There he remained for some time.

When his term of imprisonment expired, he went for rest to the continent, with George Fox, Robert Barclay and George Keith; saying that it was a great consolation to him in his troubles, that "If we suffer with Him we shall also reign with Him."

On his return to England, he became the fast friend of Algernon Sidney, and aided him in his candidacy for the House of Commons. He mourned the awful and untimely death of Sidney with sorrow, and with feelings almost of despair. It was at this period, when liberty seemed almost to have fled from the world, that Penn turned his thoughts to the Western Hemisphere. His father, at his death, had large claims in the Crown for moneys advanced, and Penn claimed a settlement; but as the King had no money to pay, he was willing to make over to him lands among the benighted heathen in America. Months however, elapsed before anything definite could be determined. At length, as Penn says in a letter to his friend Turner, dated March 14, 1681, "After many waitings, watchings, solicitings and disputes in council, this day my country was confirmed to me under the great seal of England, with large powers and privileges, by the name of Pennsylvania, a name the King would give it in honor of my father."

Penn was made "proprietary of the domain." The manner in which he received this grant and the spirit that influenced him is best expressed in his own words. He says: "Let the Lord guide me by His wisdom and preserve me to honor His name and serve His truth and people, that an example and standard may be set up to the nations; there may be room there though none here."

After due preparation, he set sail for America, and on the 24th of October, 1682, Penn reached "the Capes," and on the 28th, landed at Newcastle. The ceremony of taking possession of the country allotted him, is recorded as follows: "Penn produced two deeds of enfeoffment, and John Moll, Esq. and Ephraim Hannan, gentleman, performed livery of seisin, by handing over to him turf and twig, water and soil, and with due formality the act was recorded in a document signed with nine names." Penn afterward held "a court," and the inhabitants gave a pledge of obedience.

He entered into a treaty of "amity and friendship," immortalized by the hand of the painter, West, a native of the very city that he founded. At the very first meeting of a representative assembly of the province, Penn caused it to be declared that "If any person shall abuse or deride any other for his or her different persuasion and practice in matter of religion, such shall be looked upon as a disturber of the peace and be punished accordingly." He also provided for "a proper observance of the Christian sabbath, trial by jury, purity of elections, and legal taxation."

There is something of a romance connected with the place where the first assembly of Penn's province was held, and it is this: Penn had, in exploring the country, been to New York, and returning to his possessions, he arrived at a place called Upland, when, turning to a Quaker friend, named Pearson, who had come with him in the "Welcome," he said: "Providence has brought us here safe; thou hast been the companion of my perils; what wilt thou that I should call this place?

Pearson said, "Chester;" in remembrance of the city whence he came; and there it was that the first legislative assembly was called.

Penn was well pleased with the country at the very start, and in giving a description of it to his friends at home, he says: "The land is like the best vales of England watered by brooks; the air sweet; the heavens serene like the south of France; the seasons mild and temperate; vegetable productions abundant; chestnut, walnut, plums, muscadel grapes, wheat and other grain; a variety of animals, elk, deer, squirrel and turkeys weighing forty or fifty pounds, water-birds and fish of divers kinds, no want of horses; and flowers lovely for color, greatness, figure and variety."

Penn sailed from America on the 12th of August, 1684, and reached his native shores on the 3d or 4th of October.

A few months afterward, Charles II. died, in February, 1685, and was succeeded by James II., the last male of the line of Stuart. James II. was compelled to abdicate, when the Prince of Orange landed at Torbay. This prince lived on very friendly terms with James II. whom he knew while a boy, as the Duke of York.

When William III. and Mary ascended the throne, Penn was arrested and tried for treason, but he was acquitted. He was again charged with conspiracy to recall James II. but acquitted. He retired into obscurity in 1691, to avoid constant trouble and persecution. In 1699, he revisited America, but returned to England in the middle of December, 1701. Two months after, William the III. died and Anne ascended the throne. She was the daughter of James II., the friend of Penn's father, and even more a friend of his son. But difficulties seemed to multiply around him with advancing years.

Through the villainy of his agents in America, notably one Ford, who acted as his steward, and the waywardness of his son, he was arrested on some fraudulent claims, and thrown into the Fleet prison, where he spent some nine months, or "in the limits thereof," under surveillance.

James Logan, a friend of Penn, in a letter dated Aug. 13, 1706, written to one Thomas Callowhill, says: "Never was there any person more barbarously treated, or baited with un-deserved enemies. „He has been able to foil all attacks from public adversaries, but 'tis his fortune to meet greatest reverses from those that were most to him."

It has been beautifully said: "God darkens this world to us that our eyes may behold the greater brightness of His kingdom."

Penn died at Ruscomb, a suburban village, not far from London, on the 30th of May, 1718. He was buried in the burial ground of Jourdan's Meeting-House, midway between Beaconsfield and Chalfont, St. Giles. "It stands upon rather high ground, but its site is in a dell surrounded by meadows and brushwood." There the founder of Pennsylvania sleeps in the same grave with his wife, Hannah, who survived him till the year 1726, and next to that of his first love, Gulielma Maria. Letitia and Springett, her children, rest just behind their father and mother, and close by are the remains of Isaac and Mary Pennington.

The founder of one of the greatest commonwealths in the New World, a commonwealth that now constitutes the very keystone of the arch of this republic, he was called upon in the prime of his youth and manhood, to vindicate in his person the fundamental principles of all free governments, by a most terrible contest against human hate and arbitrary power.

For expounding the gospel of Christ, he was pounced upon in open day, in the city of his birth, by minions more brutal and heartless than the savages he was afterward to encounter in the wilds of America. He was subjected to taunts and in-sults which had not been exhibited to a prisoner at the bar since Coke was attorney general and Raleigh stood at bay and fought for his life, against overwhelming odds. By his wis-dom, his acuteness, his dauntless courage, and the righteous-ness of his cause, he won the hearts of the jurors who had been impaneled for the purpose of convicting him, and he conducted himself with such circumspection and adroitness that he over-awed the infamous judges that sat to try him, put them to open shame, and covered them with eternal infamy and dis-grace.

The result was one of the greatest triumphs of the age, and although he did not wholly free himself and his friends from persecution, he left such an impress upon the times, that it has ever since been cited as a warning to all persecutors, whether kingly or judicial in their character.

It is no wonder that since kingly prerogative has ceased to be the rule, that all Englishmen should delight in insisting, that as between man and man, there shall be "fair play."

It is the glory of England in her patronage of the arts, to adorn her public buildings by frescos and paintings illustrative of scenes and incidents in her history that are worthy of remembrance and commemoration.

In the corridors of "The New Palace of Westminster," where sits her immortal House of Commons, are paintings which represent the lineage of her Kings and Queens, great battles by land and sea, and the struggles of the people for free government.

There the God of Light smiles on the fruitful earth, and angels hold shields emblazoned with the armorial bearings of the barons who wrested Magna Charta from King John.

There are scepters and orbs, emblems of royal power, with crowns; the scales indicative of justice, mitres and croziers, symbols of religion, and blunted swords of mercy, and there one may read the story of the Saxon, the Norman, the Plantagenet, the Tudor, the Stuart, and the Hanoverian Houses.

There "The Spirit of Justice," "The Spirit of Religion" and "The Spirit of Chivalry" are all commemorated. There the attention of the observer is arrested by that noble fresco of "Prince Henry acknowledging the authority of Judge Gascoigne," and of "Speaker Lenthal asserting the privileges of the House of Commons against Charles I. when the attempt was made to seize the five members." There the mind of the American is carried back to "The Embarkation of the Puritan Fathers to New England," and the landing of the Mayflower.

There, too, in the great Hall of St. Stephen, which now forms the long entrance to the House of Commons, on either side, raised aloft on pedestals, which stand out in bold relief, are marble busts of the wisest and the best statesmen of former days, to whom England owes her gratitude for their patriotism and virtue. There are Selden, Hampden, Lord Falkland, Lord Clarendon, Lord Somers, Sir Robert Walpole, Lord Chatham, Lord Mansfield, Burke, Fox, Pitt and Grattan—but Cromwell, Eliot, Vane, Algernon Sidney, John Milton and William Penn have been omitted.

As you wander through the mausoleums of the dead, and through those long galleries filled with the treasures of art and with the busts and portraits of those who labored, fought and perished in the one great cause of freedom and truth, there come before us the great trials of those forgotten heroes, who were immured in prison, and died upon the block, and their memories will be hallowed by men of every kindred and every tongue in the Old and the New World.

But not in Westminster Abbey, nor in the ancient hall of St. Stephen, not in the corridors of the House of Lords or Commons, is there one incident or one scene which has been there commemorated by the hand of the sculptor, or with the brush of the painter, either on canvas or by fresco, which surpasses in thrilling interest or in its results, the defense of William Penn when arraigned by the partisan judges of Charles II., for attempting to preach in front of the old Quaker Meeting-House in Grace Church Street.

Elliott Anthony.

THE WOMAN LAWYER.

By Dr. Louis Frank.

Translated from the French, for the Chicago Law Times, by Mary A. Greene, LL.B., of the Suffolk, [Mass.] Bar.

IV.

CRITICAL EXAMINATION OF THE QUESTION.—As it seems to us impracticable to make a general and systematic exposition of the subject of the woman lawyer, we shall confine ourselves to examining in succession the various objections which may be raised to the admission of women to the bar. In an impartial analysis we shall show how slight is the foundation of each of these possible objections. We are persuaded that those who are not alarmed at innovations, those whose common sense is not obscured by foolish prejudice, those who are enlightened, guided and persuaded by reason alone, will conclude with us, that no serious ground exists for opposing the practice by a woman of the profession of advocate.

In the first place, it is necessary to discover whether, as the Belgian Pandects claim, the profession of advocate is a public function.—(Pandectes belges, Avocat. no. 10, 10 bis, col. 852 et 853.)

In our opinion, there can be no doubt on this point; an advocate is not a functionary; he merely practices a profession.

From the fact that the advocate takes the oath required of him by Article 14 of the decree of 1810, modified by Article 2 of the decree of July 20, 1831, one cannot conclude that he is a functionary, for, if that deduction were admissible, it would also be necessary to infer from the fact that Article 312 of the code of criminal practice compels a juror to take a special oath, that a juror is a public functionary, in the ordinary sense of the word. Yet this second conclusion would be truer and more rational than the first, since our penal code gives to a juror, by reason of his duties, a special protection by Article 282—a protection which the advocate does not enjoy.

If the advocate were a functionary in the administration of justice, he would hold an executive power, vested in him by reason of his functions. This was the established system in Austria, prior to 1868, where, as we have already stated, the advocate was nominated by Government. At present, advocates are functionaries in but one country, namely, Japan, where they are nominated and appointed by a decree of the Minister of Justice.

If the advocate were a functionary, any injury which might be inflicted upon him in or during the performance of his duties, could be punished by the imposition of a penalty for the insult. Such is not the case.

Moreover, a foreigner, who is incompetent in Belgium, to discharge any public function, could not be an advocate.

To complete the demonstration, that the opinion of the Belgian Pandects is erroneous, one last argument will suffice.

The law of May 26, 1848, declared a parliamentary mandate to be incompatible with the functions and employments paid for by the State, ministerial functions excepted. The Chamber of Representatives decided that an advocate of a ministerial department, an advocate receiving a salary from the State, could be a delegate. Whence we are warranted in concluding, *a fortiori*, that any advocate whatever, not an attaché of a ministerial department, and not receiving a fixed and definite salary from the State, cannot in any wise be considered a public functionary.

Having said this, we do not believe it necessary to recall, on the authority of Dalloz, the distinction made by Dupin, Procurer-General, and admitted in law, between the oath of the advocate and that of the functionary.—(Dalloz, Répert. vo. Avocat, nos. 48, 277, 68, 73. Cass. fr. 23 Sept. 1831. Id. vo. Serment, no. 39.)

. Besides, even in case the profession of advocate should be
held to be a public function, women would have still a right to
practice it, seeing that no provision, either constitutional or
legal, excludes women from public functions. By force of
Article 6 of the Constitution, all Belgians, male and female,
are equal before the law. All are "eligible to civil employments, with such exceptions as may be established by law to
meet special cases."

Therefore, supposing that the profession of advocate does
constitute a public office, a special law would be needful to
pronounce against woman her incapacity to discharge that
function.

Is it true, as some may possibly say, that an express and formal provision of law can alone qualify woman for the practice
of an advocate's profession?

In Belgium, four thousand women are now in the service of
the State, as teachers, regents, school directors or inspectors of
instruction. And there are not only female public functionaries
among the corps of educators, but also in the civil service of
the departments of Government.

In 1869, M. Jamar, Minister of Public Works, proposed, at
a session of the Council of Ministers, that women be admitted
to the corps in his department. After a lively debate, the
question was decided in favor of women. At the beginning of
1888, according to a census taken by us, the Minister of Railroad, Postal and Telegraph Service had two hundred and forty
women in his department. Now, the Belgian legislature has
never interposed for the purpose of granting to women the
right to become public functionaries. Why should a law be
necessary to enable a woman to practice the simple profession
of advocate, when a law has never been considered indispensable
in order to admit women to the civil service?

In order to exclude women from the bar, it is not sufficient
to prove that the profession of advocate is a *public function*; it
is further essential to prove that in conformity with the Roman
law, the act of assuming the defense of another, constitutes a
virile office, which the feminine sex cannot fill; Alienam suscipere defensionem virile est officium, et ultra sexum muliebrum

esse constat.—(Lex 18, Cod. II. 13 [12].)

Now, all the prohibitions by which the Roman law restrained women have disappeared from our modern legislation. Woman can carry on a banking business, although the Roman law had declared her incapable of so doing; she can be a witness, a surety for another, and can also intervene in justice.

There are no longer any traces of the Velleian Decree remaining in our laws: there is no longer any edict *de postulando*, which forbids women to appear in the courts as mandatories; moreover, the *virilia officia* exist no longer in the sphere of civil relations.

By what right, therefore, and in the name of what principle, is any one to forbid, at the present day, a woman to practice the profession of advocate?

The decree of December 14, 1810, concerning the profession of advocate and the discipline of the bar, does not indicate, as a cause of disability, the fact of belonging to the feminine sex. In order to disprove the right of woman to be an advocate and to practice as such, our opponents will doubtless claim, that the spirit of the decree must be invoked, and will search for this spirit in the opinions expressed by Napoleon on the subject of women.

"It is enough," wrote the Emperor, "to teach girls to cipher, and to write the principles of their language so that they may know how to spell: They should be taught a little geography and history, but good care must be taken not to show them any Latin, or any other foreign tongue."

If, in our day, this opinion of Napoleon must be adopted, we must begin by excluding women from the universities. We must close, in Belgium, the preparatory schools for girls, and must suppress, in France, the lyceums for girls, in operation since 1881.

It is an un undeniable fact that Napoleon I. had a small opinion of educated women. He seems indeed, on this point, almost to have shared the opinion of a certain duke of Brittany, mentioned by Montaigne. Some one spoke one day to this prince of his approaching marriage with Isabel, "who had been plainly brought up, with no instruction in polite literature." He replied that "he liked her the better for that, and that a woman knew enough, if she knew how to distinguish her husband's shirt from his doublet."—(Montaigne, Du Pédantism, Liv. I, ch. XXIV. Moliere, in his well known verses, was inspired by this historic remark. Les Femmes Savantes, Acte II., Scene VII.)

Napoleon estimated a woman's worth by her fruitfulness. We recall his very offensive repartee, when Madame de Stael asked him what woman, either in the past or the present he most esteemed. "She, Madame, who has produced the most children!" An excusable speech from the lips of a conqueror, hungry for flesh to feed his cannons.

The *Memorial of Saint Helena* contains a series of curious opinions of Napoleon, wherein the emperor, as Taine depicts him, appears as a brutal man, bestial and sensual. This one passage from the Memorial is more instructive than any number of opinions we might cite.

The emperor applauded the Oriental maxims. He strongly approved of polygamy, claiming that nature required it, and was very skillful and fluent in proving it. "Woman," he said, "is given to man in order to bear children. Now one woman alone cannot be sufficient to a man, for this purpose. She cannot be his wife when she is pregnant; she cannot be his wife while nursing; she cannot be his wife when she is ill; she ceases to be his wife when she can no longer present him with children : therefore, man, whom nature restrains neither because of age nor any one of these inconveniences, ought to have several wives. * * * And, after all, what have you to complain of, ladies? Do we not recognize the fact that you have a soul? You know there are philosophers who have decided that.

"Would you aspire to equality? * * * But that is foolish; woman is our property; we are not hers, for she gives us children; man does not give them to her. She is his property, as the fruit-tree is the property of the gardener.

"It is a want of judgment, vulgar ideas, and lack of education alone that can induce a woman to believe herself the equal of man. Moreover, there is nothing dishonorable in this difference; each has properties and obligations; your proties, ladies, are beauty, graces, seductiveness; your obligations, dependence and submission."—(Mémorial de Sainte Hélene, tome IV., p. 102.)

If the personal views of Napoleon should prevail, we should be compelled to overturn the fundamental principles of our law, while the decisions of jurisprudence would have to be modified. For example, we should have to restore polygamy, since the emperor admits plurality of wives; nay more, judges it indispensable.

If, in a matter of strategy, the opinion of the great general should be cited, we should not be able to contradict it; but in a juridical matter, the competence of the emperor appears very questionable.

Besides, is it not strange that *advocates* should desire to comment upon and complete the decree of December, 1810, by basing their arguments on the opinion of Napoleon, who never concealed in the least his sovereign contempt for them as a class?

His letter addressed to Cambacéres is a proof of the profound disdain with which Napoleon viewed the bar.

"I have received a draft of a decree concerning advocates. * * * I should like much better to take strong measures against this heap of boasters, and makers of revolutions, who are nearly all of them inspired only by crime and corruption. While I have a sword by my side, I shall never sign such an absurd decree. I wish the tongue of every advocate might be cut out who should employ it against the government."—(Pandects belges, Avocat. col. 830.)

Napoleon himself brands as absurd the decree he signed. We share his opinion, and do not desire to weaken it by any comments.

To sum it all up, Napoleon did not like childless women; on the other hand he detested advocates, and in his eyes a woman advocate would have appeared the sum of all abominations, and the most frightful of monstrosities.

In whatever concerns the interpretation of the decree, the emperor's opinion cannot be decisive; therefore we need not give any further attention to it.

The silence of the decree, we shall be told, must be supplemented by inspiring ourselves with the spirit of our legislation.

So be it. Let us first consider the character of our public law.

Title II. of the Constitution establishes the rights of the Belgians, and makes no distinction between the sexes. Article 6, already cited, proclaims the equality of the Belgians who are eligible to civil and military employments, saving those exceptions established by law for special cases. (Evidently, women are excluded from military service. To enter the army certain physical conditions must be met. Moreover, the law of the military, in its Articles 2, 35 and 40, particularly, speaks only of *men*, eligible and fit for service.)

Our public law establishes but one sole privilege of masculinity, that of Article 60 of the Constitution, which has for its object the prevention of the extinction of the house of Saxe-Coburg by the accession of a woman to the throne. Males, to the perpetual exclusion of females and their descendants, are alone capable of sitting upon the throne of Belgium.

However, though a woman cannot be Queen and head of the State, the Chambers would have the right to call her to the regency, during the minority of a prince.

A woman, in Belgium might discharge all kinds of public functions. For instance, there is no law which would prevent the King from appointing a woman to be a *Commissaire d'Arrondisement.*

Our provinces, which in the past were ruled by Margaret of Austria, Mary of Hungary and Margaret of Parma, might still, in our own day, be governed by women. Moreover, a woman, in Belgium, could be a minister, seeing that, in order to be a minister, it suffices to be a Belgian, and more than three millions of women possess this qualification.

In case our Chambers should pass a law excluding women from public functions, it would yet be necessary to amend the Constitution, in order to shut them out from the office of minister.

Let us now analyze the spirit of our private law.

Run over the Code. Thus our opponents will say, read particularly Articles 37, 148, 214, 215, 217, 373, 980, 1421, 1449, 1538. Does not the disability of woman clearly appear there? And would you desire that this inferior being, this subordinate, this subaltern, should have power, as advocate, to undertake the defense of the interests of a third party?

Certainly, we cannot possibly deny the fact, our Civil Code is strongly impregnated with the prejudices of the canon law against women. We do not consider this to be the time or place to bring an indictment against the Code and display all its strange contradictions. Why, to cite one example only, does the law allow a woman to be a declarant as to acts before the civil authorities, when that same law forbids her to testify to the identity of a declarant and to the truth of the declarations of another? Why cannot a woman be a subscribing witness to documents in the civil courts, when she can be to acts of notoriety which often serve to re-establish the civil power, as on the day following the outrages of the Commune?

In 1802, the testimony of women was accepted and was customary. Madame Dessirier, wife of Colonel Delelée was qualified to sign as witness, the certificate of the birth of Victor Hugo. To-day, she would be disqualified. Why? Not a single jurist has the power to say. The Code has thus sanctioned the principle of the inferiority of woman.

We will leave to the greatest of our jurists the work of criticising the labors of the legislature of 1803.

"The authors of the Code," writes M. Laurent, "declared themselves in favor of the subordination of women. When recourse is had to the prefatory works, one is astonished to find them silent on a question of such importance. The reporter and the orator of the Tribunat say not a word about it; indeed, the Tribunat was silenced by a *coup d'etat*. Portalis alone deals with the question, and he treats it with a species of contempt. 'There have been lengthy discussions,' he says, 'as to the preference or equality between the two sexes. Nothing is more vain than these discussions.' No, these discussions are *not* vain, for a principle is in question which should govern the relations between husband and wife, and from principles is the entire law constructed." * * *

What he says next is foreign to the question. "Force and boldness are on the side of the man; timidity and modesty are on the side of the woman." Well, what of it? Is it not so without marriage as well as during marriage? If that justifies the subordination and incapacity of a married woman, she should always be held in subordination; put her then, whether young girl or widow, under tutelage; and if you recoil from the consequences of your principles, drop at once your *timidity* and *modesty*, your *force* and *boldness*, for these antitheses are but words, and it is not by words that the difficulties of the law can be adjusted.

The interpreters of the Code Napoleon have in this matter a dryness which is only exceeded by the insufficiency of the arguments they advance, when it occurs to them to give arguments. "This is so because it is so," says Montaigne. And I greatly fear that this argument has the mastery; it is so convenient to invoke the power of fact when dispensing entirely with reason.—(Laurent. Avant-projet de revision du Code Civil, 1882, Tome I. p. 425 et seq.)

Therefore, following the expressions of M. Laurent, words, nothing but words, antitheses of words, which are not judicial reasons—these are the sole argument of those whose purpose it is to legalize woman's inferiority.

Will any one rely on the want of definite enactments of the Code, in order to contest a woman's right to practice at the bar, when, in the several countries of Europe, the legislatures, ashamed of the work of their predecessors, are hastening with all speed to efface the inequalities of law, and to restore to women the rights of which the egotism of men has deprived them?

Italy has just recognized the right of women to testify in public and private (Italian law of Dec. 9, 1877); the Hungarian legislature has qualified them to become members of family councils (Art. 157 of the Hungarian law of July 4, 1877, concerning tutelage and trusteeship), and England, more generous to women, has gone further yet. She has, in the domain of the domestic relations, brought about a veritable revolution of incalculable extent. The law of August 18, 1882, in effect January 1, 1883, abolished all marital authority in that country. Married women have the right to hold property and to dispose of it, and to contract, as if unmarried.—(The Married Women's Property Act, 1882.)

And now, when in every country, the cause of women's enfranchisement is triumphing, when reason has at last regained its ascendancy over vain prejudices too long respected, will any one come forward in Belgium, to invoke against women the text of a few superannuated and unjustifiable enactments?

It is true that it is not our business to formulate in this place our criticisms upon certain principles of our Civil Code, nor to demand its revision. We have but to interpret the spirit of existing laws, and that is what we are now about to do.

The spirit of the Civil Code does not appear to us to be impregnable or an invincible argument against the admission of women to the bar.

To facilitate our demonstration, we shall make a distinction between the situation of an unmarried woman of adult age, and that of a married woman.

A simple comparative table of the legal condition of the unmarried woman, and of the minor, will show better than the most brilliant dissertations, the value of the argument drawn from the spirit of the private law.

SITUATION OF THE MINOR.	SITUATION OF THE WOMAN.
Witnesses brought to attest documents in the civil courts must be of age.—(Art. 37, C. C.)	Witnesses brought to attest documents in the civil courts must be of the masculine sex. —(Art. 37, C. C.)
Witnesses to wills must be of age.—(Art. 980, C. C. Art. 9, loi du 25 vent. an XI.)	Witnesses to wills must be males.—(Art. 980, C. C. Art. 9, loi du 25 vent. an XI.)
Minors cannot be guardians, nor members of family councils, unless they are fathers or mothers.—(Art. 442.)	Women cannot be guardians, nor members of family councils, unless they are mothers or ascendants.—(Art. 442.)
A minor cannot adopt a	A woman may adopt a

child.—(Art. 343.)

A minor cannot be an official guardian.—(Art. 361.)

A minor above the age of sixteen, may dispose by will of only so much of his property as equals half the amount of that of which an adult may by law dispose.—(Art. 904.)

A minor has no power to contract.—(Art. 1124.)

A minor, not emancipated and not duly authorized cannot enter into commerce.—(Art. 4 C. Comm.)

A minor cannot be a manager or agent of commercial organizations.

An admitted principle in Belgium down to the present day;

A minor may be an advocate.

child.—(Art. 343.)

A woman may be an official guardian.—(Art. 361.)

A woman may dispose of her entire property by will or by gift *inter vivos.*—(Art. 902.)

A woman has power to contract.—(Art. 1123.)

A woman may enter into commerce.

A woman may be a manager or an agent of commercial organizations.

The principle sought to be imposed;

A woman cannot be an advocate.

For instance, the *Societe anonyme* of the founderies of Andenne, is managed by a woman, of remarkable intelligence, Mme. F. Moncheur de Mélotte, a member of the general society and deputy-manager of the above named organization.—(Supplement to the Moniteur Belge of July 21, 1886, no. 1250, p. 812.)

As to the married woman, the Code strikes her with a certain kind of incapacity, resulting from marital authority. In the sphere of the domestic relations, the Code has established the principle of the supremacy of the husband and the subordination and vassalage of the wife. The husband appears to be the head of the family, the lord and master of the wife, by force of the ancient precept of the canon law; *vir caput est mulieris.*

This principle of the precedence of the husband during mar-

riage is no hindrance to the practice of the profession of advocate by a married woman. At the very most she could only be
required to receive from her husband authority to practice.
In such a case, should the authority be general or special? In
our opinion, the authority could not be special, for the wife,
before undertaking a defense, could not be placed under obligation to keep her husband informed of the smaller details of
every case she manages, since that would be a violation of professional secrets. Moreover, the spouse of the woman lawyer
might himself be an advocate, and the representative of the
interests of the adverse party, so that one of the pleaders, the
husband, would have, through his knowledge of the entire case
of his adversary, a considerable advantage over the other pleader.

Authority to practice as advocate, then, should be general,
as it is, to enter into commerce.—(Art. 220, C. Civ.)

We do not intend to discuss in this place, the principles
of the Civil Code as to this matter of marital authorization.
We consider that, to practice the advocate's profession, a married woman needs not to be authorized. Marital authorization
is required for a certain class of acts, not for all—it is necessary
to acts which might endanger the patrimony of the wife.
(There is one exception. A wife cannot acquire any honorary
title without the authorization of her husband. Reasons of
etiquette and of great propriety have inspired this provision.
It is just that a husband should know the causes for the bestowal of bounty upon his wife.)

The wife may, by herself alone, provided her appearance in
court be not in question, perform any acts not involving *acqui-
sition, alienation* or *obligation.*—(Mourlon, Cours de droit civil,
tome I., p. 420.)

To appear in court, that is to say, to figure as a party in an
action at law, she needs to be authorized, because in a hazard-
ous suit, she might involve and endanger her patrimony.

But a woman advocate cannot possibly imperil her property
or that of her family, or prejudice any of them, since an advocate shoulders no responsibility by reason of the advice or
counsel he gives, and is only answerable for his fraudulent or

criminal conduct. By force of the general principles of the law, an advocate who is a married woman would be bound by all the obligations entered into by her, even by the consequences of a crime or tort committed in the exercise of her profession.

A married woman will have no more need of marital authorization in order to practice at the bar, than she now has in order to be admitted to the government staff of educators or to the civil service.

A married woman to appear as a party in a suit, must be authorized. A woman advocate, as well as a woman physician or pharmacist, would require her husband's consent to bring an action to recover her fees.

The advocate who presents a case is a mandatary, some of our adversaries will say. Now, a married woman cannot accept a mandate without her husband's authority. The husband, moreover, could always revoke his authority. Practically, the woman advocate could relieve herself from her obligation to plead gratuitously, by causing her husband to revoke the necessary authority.

An advocate, we reply, is not a mandatary—his functions amount to a mere assistance. Our opinion is based upon conceptions and recollections of the very history of the law. In Rome, the *cognitor*, afterward called the *procurator*, alone had the duty of representing the parties in the various stages of procedure. The part of the *advocatus* was limited to an assistance of his client by his influence, his counsel and his eloquence.—(Maynz, Cours de droit romain, tome II., p. 255, note 21.)

The system of the Belgian law is the same. The attorney alone is a mandatary. It is he who represents the parties, who prepares the pleadings and states the issues. He is the *dominus litis*, the master of the suit; upon him alone falls the responsibility for the course of the proceedings.

The advocate has so little of the character of a mandatary, that from the instant the attorney at the trial, makes oath to the issues, he cannot escape from them and is bound by them, and the judges decide, not upon the statements and arguments of the advocates, but solely upon the issues between the parties.

The advocate then is merely an assistant. Evidently there is one exception, in the case of an advocate of the Court of Cassation, who performs the duties of an attorney in the Supreme Court.

The advocate, if he were a mandatary, would be liable for any error (Art. 1992 C. C.), but in fact, he is only answerable for fraud or crime; hence he is not a mandatary.

Even if he were a mandatary, a married woman would not need the authorization of her husband to accept and discharge the mandate, for a mandate may even be given to a person incapable of binding himself to an obligation.

If the woman advocate, with the connivance of her husband, should succeed in freeing herself from the obligation of gratuitous defense incumbent upon established advocates, the Council of the Order would inflict upon her the penalty of a prolongation of the preliminary *stage* and could even refuse to enroll her upon the tablet of the Order.

One final objection might still be raised concerning the married woman.

A wife, by Art. 214 of the Civil Code, is obliged to live with her husband and to follow him wherever he thinks fit to reside. A woman lawyer might then be constrained to remove her office to any place where it should please her husband to establish his domicil.

As a matter of fact, the question is of slight importance, for if any woman advocate, for any reason which the Council of the Order would not accept as valid, should go to establish herself in another jurisdiction, the present rules of the bar would be applied; by *omission* the name of that woman would disappear from the tablet, and that would be the end of the matter.

If the objection were in the slightest degree a serious one, it would be necessary to forbid a married woman to become a public merchant, under the pretext that she might be obliged to follow her husband. Married women ought also to be excluded from the staff of educators and from the civil service, if they might find themselves compelled to abandon their duties in order to accompany their husbands.. Lastly, a minor ought no longer to be eligible to the bar, since he is bound to live with his parents.—(Art. 374, C. C.)

Without doubt our opponents will try to keep women away from the bar by arguing from a provision of Article 203 of the Belgian law of June 18, 1869, concerning the organization of the judiciary.

In the lower tribunals, every advocate, they will say, may be called upon to occupy the bench. Now, that law intended to exclude women from judicial functions. Therefore a woman cannot be an advocate.

This syllogism, which at first sight seems unexceptionable, has, unfortunately, for the theorem of our adversaries, the serious inconvenience of containing an inexact major, and an incorrect minor premise. The conclusion, it is almost useless to state, is scarcely worth more than the premises.

Is it true that women are excluded from judicial functions? Can any one show us the Belgian law which pronounces their exclusion?

Is it true, on the other hand, that every advocate may be called upon to occupy the bench?

Perchance our adversaries have invoked the aid of Article 203 without understanding it!

This article says, "In default of a substitute, there may be called, in the lower tribunals, a Belgian advocate, of the age of twenty-five years, an attaché of the bar, and in default of such a person, an attorney, a Doctor of Law."—(Art. 203, alin 2.)

An advocate to be called, must fulfill four conditions: (1) He must be a Belgian, (2) of the age of at least twenty-five years, (3) an attaché of the bar, that is to say, in active practice, (4) tainted with no physical or intellectual infirmity, which would unfit him for the performance of judicial duties.

Whence we conclude that four classes of advocates are disqualified: (1) advocates of foreign nationality enrolled upon the tablet of advocates practicing at a Belgian Court or tribunal, (As to foreign advocates in Belgium, see Pandects Belges, Avocat, nos. 27, 34, 35, 112, 649. M. M. Arntz Baze, formerly Batonnier of the bar of Agen, and many others, although of foreign nationality, have practiced the profession in Belgium); (2) advocates less than twenty-five years of age; (3) those possessing the title of advocate, but not in practice; (4) advocates who, by reason of physical or other infirmity are disqualified to perform the duties of a judge, as, for instance, the deaf, or the blind, who, nevertheless are capable of practicing an advocate's profession.

Up to the present time, would any one ever have dreamed of refusing the oath, and the enrollment, whether upon the Stage or the Tablet, to an advocate of any one of the four classes above indicated, under the pretext that he did not fulfill the conditions required for a possible future exercise of the duties of substitution on the bench?

Woman, we think could be called upon, as no provision of law forbids her to exercise judicial powers. If, however, there were such an exclusion, or if one were about to be pronounced, women would then form a fifth class of advocates disqualified for the office of substitute.

To our opponents who invoke against the admission of women to the bar, the spirit of the French decree of 1810, we oppose, in favor of women, the spirit of the Belgian law of May 20, 1876, concerning the bestowal of academic degrees.

During the debate upon this law, a proposal was laid before the Chamber favoring the free exercise of the profession of advocate with no condition or safeguard by diploma or otherwise. In its session of April 6, 1876, by 63 voices against 43, and 2 not voting, this proposal was rejected by the Chamber.—(Ann. Parlem. Session 1875–76, chamb. des représ, p. 768.)

The law of 1876 was enacted for a limited period, and the legislature has been obliged to prolong it by several renewals. This temporary and transitory law was designed, in the minds of its authors, to facilitate the establishment in this country of absolute freedom in the liberal professions. The speeches made in the Chamber by M. M. Jacobs, Woeste, Malon and Frere-Orban leave no doubt on this point.

This law of 1876 has not for its object the regulation of

higher instruction alone, it also determines the legal effect of academic degrees.

Let us inquire into the intent of the legislature of 1876, and particularly into that of the supporter and defenders of the law.

It was M. Frere-Orban who presented to the Chamber the project which became the law of 1876. The honorable Minister of State defended his plan with all the breadth of view and wonderful talent which he is wont to bring to the parliamentary debates, and since he was, to use an English parliamentary expression, the mover, the chief supporter of the law, it is in his speeches that the desires of the legislator are most clearly and plainly to be discerned; and it is there that we must seek for the spirit of the law.

M. Frere-Orban said in the Chamber: "This is not to be a rule for the freedom of the professions. Very true, it is not to be an absolute rule for the freedom of the professions. But what can approach more nearly to the freedom of the professions than the system I propose? Do not forget, gentlemen, that this is a question of the practice of the professions and not of eligibility to a public office.—(Id. p. 727.) * * *

"What will be conferred by the diploma?

"The power to practice the profession of advocate or of physician. As to offices, the value of titles must be weighed by the executive power. The legislature is to impose such conditions as it sees fit for admission to offices.

"For the practice of the profession, the title is indisputable and definitive. For access to office, it may be disputed, it may be pronounced insufficient; the law may require further qualifications.

"And now, I repeat, this will not be a system of absolute freedom of the professions, but nothing will come nearer to it. * * *

"The profession of advocate or of physician will be practiced only under certain conditions determined by the law.

"An authorization will be necessary, to be given by a Council (commission for confirmation), established to examine whether the diploma given—stating that the person has pur-

sued studies for the required period of time in an establishment
for higher education—is the actual proof that these studies
were pursued.

"When the diploma has been registered (confirmed), (by an
amendment offered by M. Delcour, Minister of the Interior,
the word registry (enrigistrement) was changed in the law to
confirmation (entermement); one may practice the profession.
This is the system. The obstacles are reduced then, as to the
practice of the profession, to the smallest limits."—(Ann. Parlem. p. 728.)

In the session of April 7, just before the Chamber took a
vote upon the law, M. Frere-Orban spoke again, for the purpose of emphasizing once more the purport of the new law.

"The distinction we-have made," said he, "between the practice of the profession and eligibility to offices remains in full
force, and thereby offers the means of remedying evils, should
any arise.

"As to the profession, the diploma duly confirmed gives an
indisputable, unassailable, irrevocable title; as to eligibility to
office it is disputable, it can be attacked, considered insufficient
by the executive power, and submitted by law to conditions in
order to frame a title to admission to office. • • •

"The State, now as always, remains master of the right to
impose any conditions of access to public employments, and
especially of entrance to the magistracy, which it may consider
necessary for the common welfare."—(Ann. Parlem. p. 779,
col. 2.)

The academic degree obtained, the diploma duly confirmed,
the profession may be practiced. The law neither imposes nor
requires any other condition.

Every Belgian academic authority has given to this law
of 1876, the interpretation we have here indicated, and they
have recognized the right of women to obtain academic degrees.

The Royal Academy of Medicine of Belgium, has on its part,
also, pronounced itself in favor of the rights of women.

The Academy, by maintaining a neutral position, has decided the question of women physicians submitted to them.
That is to say, they have not discussed the question whether it

is desirable for women to practice medicine, nor whether they possess the necessary qualities for it. They confine themselves to a literal interpretation of the Belgian law.

Here is an extract from the report of the discussion:

"Every one agrees in the opinion that no legal obstacle exists in Belgium to the practice of medicine by women. They have an incontestable right, and no one dreams of denying it to them, to pursue such studies as they please, and to take the degree of Doctor of Medicine, Surgery and Midwifery, the degree of Pharmacist and every other legally established degree.

"They have only, as our colleague, M. Crocq well says, to prove their capacity before the juries established by law, which does not forbid their admission.

"It is, therefore, not necessary that the law now in preparation concerning the bestowal of academic degrees, should expressly grant to women the right to practice not only medicine and pharmacy, but also *any liberal profession whatever.*"—(Extract from the journal L' Art Medical, September, 1884.)

Let us take note of this important fact, that the Academy of Medicine, at the time of this discussion, had several members who belonged to the Legislature.

In 1880, the commission of confirmation, a part of which was composed of several eminent magistrates of our Supreme Court, acknowledged that no individual could be excluded from academic degrees by reason of sex. With no debate or difficulty, the commission confirmed diplomas held by women, among others that of Mademoiselle Popelin (sister of Mlle. Marie), and thereby yielded to women access to the liberal professions.

To sum up, we cannot sufficiently insist upon this point, that the system of the law of 1876, is not a rule of absolute freedom in the professions, but is a modified system in the nature of an adjustment, merely imposing, for the practice of the professions, one condition only, that of a diploma duly confirmed.

Now, women may take academic degrees.

The commission of confirmation acknowledges the validity of their diplomas.

The degree taken, the diploma confirmed, women have the

right to practice any of the liberal professions, including that of advocate.

Let us now examine the objections of secondary importance which may be raised against our position.

In his famous diatribe, designed to justify the legal inferiority of woman, Andreas Tiraquellus cast upon women the odd reproach of inability to keep a secret; *nesciunt arcana retinere mulieres.*

How could any one admit to the bar, so our adversaries will say, a sex which in its very nature is garrulous and wanting in discretion?

We protest at the outset against this unflattering estimate of the feminine character. To bring an accusation to that effect against women in behalf of men, is an easy matter, but the men would have much difficulty in proving that loyalty and discretion are their especial attributes.

We do not desire to discuss this objection from the psychological point of view; just one legal consideration will suffice to reduce the argument to its proper valuation.

Article 458 of the Belgian Penal Code reads as follows:

"Physicians, surgeons, health officers, pharmacists, midwives, and all other persons to whom by reason of their situation or profession, secrets are confided, who, except in cases where they are called upon to testify in court, or in other cases where the law obliges them to reveal these secrets, shall reveal them, shall be punished by an imprisonment of not less than eight days nor more than six months, and a fine of not less than one hundred nor more than five hundred francs."

This article will apply to women lawyers, as it now does to three classes of women: midwives, women physicians and women pharmacists.

Would any one ever have thought of denying to either one of these three classes of women the right to practice, for the specious reason that they were not likely to keep the secrets which might be confided to them because of their professional character?

If a women lawyer, forgetful of her duty, should be foolish and imprudent enough to commit an indiscretion in connection.

with a suit conducted by her, the Council of the Order, as custodian of the honor of the bar, would inflict upon her, as upon any other advocate, the disciplinary penalties applicable to such a state of affairs, and in addition, the culprit would come under the provisions of Article 458 of the Penal Code.

But we shall be told, also, if an equality of rights really existed between the two sexes, an equality of obligations ought to result therefrom. The equality of obligations of the sexes is untenable; the inequality of obligations justifies a limitation of equality in the exercise of rights.

Under the ancient law, this argument could have been invoked. Women were smitten with a certain amount of incapacity, but, in compensation, they enjoyed divers advantages. The penalty which could be imposed upon them was always inferior to that inflicted upon men for a like infraction of law.

"Women are frail by nature," said the ancient law, which from the repressive point of view, was favorable to them. From the inequality of rights resulted, to their advantage, an inequality of duties.

In our day, it is no longer thus. The privileges of the feminine sex have disappeared from our laws; women by the same title as men, are compelled to pay impost duties; for the treasury, in the collection of taxes, knows no distinction of sex. In repressive matters there are no longer provisions specially applicable to women; our criminal law no longer considers the fact of belonging to the weaker sex an excuse or an extenuating circumstance. The social duties of the sexes are identical.

But, the reply will be, woman escapes military duties. It is evident that our military laws do exclude women from the army; these provisions apply only to *men* eligible and fit for service.

Nevertheless, in time of war, women can be called upon to perform a special mission, it may be in the administrative department, or in sanitary commissions; the law can even compel them to pay a war-tax. This was formerly done in Rome, when in time of war, the law obliged women to sell their jewels to re-imburse the public treasury.

If women are not compelled to do military service they do contribute to the fund for military expenses without getting any profit from it, for the military positions are all held by men, and the women get nothing in return from the fund.

Besides, if men, by their own foolishness have taken upon themselves the entire burden of army duty, for the purpose of rending each other asunder in inhuman and fratricidal strife, nature has imposed upon women a much more onerous and noble duty: that of maternity.

Every year, thirteen thousand men in Belgium are rallied around the flag, while more than seventy-five thousand women risk their lives to perpetuate the race, and this too, in the interest of the nation and of humanity.

Even the numerical proportion is not to the credit of the men.

The obligation of military service cannot possibly be invoked as an argument against women, since personal military service is not required in our country, and among the seven hundred advocates at the bar of Brussels, not more than three or four could be cited, who, otherwise than by a little money, performed military duty for the country.

Finally, if personal military service were required in Belgium, this would not be a sufficient reason for excluding women from the bar, for in many countries where personal military service is customary, women none the less have the right to become public functionaries, and a foreigner who is no longer bound to military obligations (except in the cases cited in Art. 7 of the military law of July 30, 1881), can practice the profession of advocate in Belgium.

The Turin Court of Appeal invoked against Signora Poet "the very grave danger to which the magistracy would be exposed, of being the object of suspicion and calumny every time that the scales of justice should turn in favor of the party for whom a woman advocate had pleaded."

In other words, a woman at the bar would be a menace to the morality and reputation of the judges.

But in a criminal trial, does not the accused appear in court? In a divorce trial, are not the spouses obliged to present themselves before the judge and to appear publicly in the court-room?

And cannot a woman plead her own case? Cannot the beautiful prisoner, the beautiful client, the beautiful pleader exercise over the advocate of her opponent and over the judges that fascinating influence which some persons affect to fear on the part of the beautiful advocate?

Besides, is the physical beauty of woman the only corrupting power in the world?

In Belgium, where unfortunate party considerations are an important factor in judicial nominations, where the magistrates often owe their advancement to the caprices of political majorities in our provincial councils, could not calumniators accuse certain judges of listening more favorably to the plea of a party leader, of whose influence they might stand in need, than to that of a modest pleader without influence?

In a country like ours, where, to the shame of our Parliament be it said, our magistrates do not receive from the State a salary proportionate to the importance of their functions and their conspicuous public position, might it not come to pass that unsuccessful pleaders would suspect their judges of allowing themselves to be bought over by richer pleaders?

Money, honors, decorations, promises of advancement, are not these the most powerful instruments of corruption in the hands of pleaders destitute of a sense of honor and without shame?

We should not have allowed ourselves to raise this objection if the Court of Appeal at Turin had not committed the blunder of invoking the corruptibility of the magistracy, as an argument against the admission of women to the bar.

As for ourselves, we have a much higher opinion of the magistracy of our country, which has never failed to prove itself inaccessible to every immoral and dishonest influence.

"It would be unbecoming and villainous," says the decree of the Turin Court of Appeal, "to see women descending into the arena of the forum, taking part in the midst of the bustle of public procedure, exciting themselves in discussions which easily carry one beyond bounds, and in which one could not show towards them all the respect which it is proper to observe toward the more delicate sex. Moreover, a woman might at times be compelled to deal *ex professo*, with questions which the excellent rules of polite society do not allow to be discussed in the presence of respectable women."

This argument is, under a new form, a reproduction of that text of the Roman law which forbade women to plead, because it would be opposed to the modesty and reserve befitting their sex.

The Turin Court seems to overlook the laws of human nature. The world moves, ideas change, and customs, far from being immutable, become modified. The progress of civilization ought to prevent our considering it a thing contrary to modesty and the destiny of the feminine sex that women should mingle in the assemblies of men.

If, as the Turin Court feigns to fear, an advocate, in the flow and excitement of debate, should so far forget the most elementary rules of etiquette and gallantry as to allow himself to omit the deference which every gentlemanly man owes to a woman, there is not a single tribunal that would hesitate a moment, to recall such a misguided advocate to a respect for proprieties.

Because an advocate might some day be wanting in politeness to a feminine colleague, we cannot see why, in view of the slight likelihood of such an occurrence, this should be a reason for pronouncing the exclusion of women from the bar.

As to the third point raised by the Turin Court, if it were well founded, it would be necessary to prevent women from undertaking medical studies, but at the present time most countries, even the most conservative, recognize their right to practice medicine. Is it not much more opposed "to the modesty and reserve" imposed on women, to see our fair competitors, side by side with young men pursuing courses of medical study, and in attendance in the dissecting room? In all such places, women, young girls, are allowed, almost every day, to listen to lectures from professors who do not restrain themselves on account of their feminine auditors, from "analyzing physiological phenomena, dissecting the generative organs, separating the principal constituents of urine, or from discussing the mysteries of syphilis."—(Ad. Wasseige, De l'exercise de la medicine parles femmes. Inaugural address at the University of Liege, 1886, p. 25.)

Besides, just as women physicians do not select as a specialty, the treatment of the various maladies pertaining solely to the masculine sex, so women lawyers will not seek to make for themselves a reputation, by appearing in scandalous causes, which moreover, are only of occasional occurrence. (In the United States, in the States where there were formerly mixed juries, women were excused from sitting during the trial of scandalous cases.)

The Turin Court has also mentioned "the risk which the gravity of legal proceedings might run, if one should sometimes see the toga covering the strange and *bizarre* garments which fashion often imposes upon women, or the cap placed upon not less extravagant coiffures."

This fear of the Italian magistracy seems entirely chimerical. A woman who shows enough stability of character to pursue to completion her legal studies, will not become fickle and frivolous at the bar. Her seriousness is a pledge that she will not try to render herself ridiculous by senseless adornments. Be assured, we may trust women for their skill in remaining women, even at the bar.

This reason of the Turin Court, appears to us even more *bizarre* than the garments of which they speak. Pray, when did fashion become a legal argument?

The robe worn by a deformed and misshapen advocate, is it not more ridiculous than the toga which covers the shoulders of a woman? The plea made by a stammerer, or an advocate whose tones resemble the voice of a chorister in the Sistine Chapel, does not this much more than the presence of a woman at the bar, excite a hilarity prejudicial to the dignity of judicial debates?

If the argument of the Turin Court had anything of a serious character, we ought to adopt in Belgium that provision of the German law as to advocates which excludes from the bar all persons tainted with physical infirmities.

Akin to this argument of costume, is the matter of wearing a moustache and whiskers.

A decree of the legislature of Paris in 1540, forbadë advocates and judges to wear beards and moustaches. Ah! some of our despairing opponents will triumphantly exclaim, behold the proof that the profession of advocate is a virile office! It might have been so in 1540, but no one will pretend that this decree of that epoch has not fallen into desuetude. Besides, the wearing of the moustache is *prohibited*, so that such an argument could only have been invoked against women in case the contrary prescription had been imposed.

On the other hand, lawyers, says Article 6 of the decree of Nivose, An. XI., still in force, shall wear either long or clipped hair. If we are to adopt as true the famous definition of which Schopenhauer, the most rabid of mysogynists, has given us, of woman ("Woman has long hair and short sense"), they much better than men, could fulfill the condition of Article 6 of the Decree of Nivose.

It will be objected that a woman would be an advocate incapable of performing all the duties demanded of the profession; the party which she might defend could not call her to the duties of arbitrator; she would be an advocate disqualified for nomination as magistrate, or for becoming a member of a jury, or of a Council of the Order, since the Council is occasionally called upon to act as judge, and a woman could not be a judge.

We shall not attempt in this place to solve the problem as to whether a woman can be called to the duties of arbitrator.— (Dalloz, Arbitre, no. 332.) We confine ourselves to the recollection of the hesitancy of jurisprudence in this respect. But even if woman were considered incapable of rendering a judicial award, this incapacity would in no wise take away her right to practice at the bar.

Is a woman incapable of being an advocate because she does not fulfill the conditions requisite to become a member of a jury? Are foreign advocates and Doctors of Law less than thirty years of age, better qualified than women to be members of a jury? Jurors, moreover, are not chosen from among advocates exclusively. · Engineers, doctors of medicine, of science, of letters, make up a class of citizens proper to be chosen as jurors. Should a woman be forbidden to become a physician, because she might be placed on the list of jurors?

Must woman be excluded from the bar, because she could not be nominated as magistrate? There is no law forbidding the King to appoint a woman to judicial offices. A court of appeal would have no right to refuse the oath of office to a woman merchant, for instance, nominated as consular judge and appointed by the King.

At the time of the discussion of the law of 1876, M. Frere-Orban, with the most exact precision, drew the distinction between the practice of the profession of advocate and eligibility to judicial functions.

All those whose moral character is unquestionable, and who hold a diploma of a Doctor of Law, duly confirmed, possess all the requisite qualifications to become members of the bar, while the qualifications required for admission to the magistracy are quite different. The advocates constitute a class of persons from whom the King may make a selection to fill vacancies in the judicial corps, but the Crown has power to choose also from other classes of persons.

The admission of a woman to the bar will not compel the government to nominate her for a magistrate; the executive power remains free to nominate its judges as it sees fit, and if it fears social revolt, it will not impose women judges upon its citizens.

The practice of the advocate's profession is entirely independent of the question of eligibility to the magistracy. This is so well settled that it is a fact that a foreigner can be an advocate in Belgium, although he is excluded from judicial offices, Belgians only being eligible to these latter.

By admitting that the woman lawyer might be looked upon as an incomplete advocate, we do not concede in any wise that she should be excluded from the bar. Is a woman forbidden to become a public trader? And yet a woman is but an incomplete merchant, for she cannot be enrolled upon the list of consular electors, nor according to the theory of our opponents, is she capable of being called to membership in a commercial tribunal.

We have two special cases to consider. First, that of a married woman lawyer, whose spouse is likewise a member of the bar. Husband and wife might be intrusted with conflicting interests in the same cause. Let us even suppose that the parties, have confided to their counsel, privileged documents not to be communicated to the adverse party.

In such an event professional secrecy might be violated. By reason of their situation, the spouses might by a fortuitous chance or otherwise, gain a knowledge of the contents of these secret documents.

A more unlikely circumstance cannot be imagined, for the adversaries would be too much interested to be guilty of the imprudence of revealing to their spouse their respective points of defense. Brothers, or a father and son very frequently practice at the bar at the same time, and one never sees such near relatives appear in court in behalf of opposite interests.

In the western States of America, according to information furnished us by Miss Robinson, there are at present, twenty law offices presided over by husband and wife. In most of the eastern States, this is impossible, as the laws do not allow a partnership between husband and wife.

In Belgium, the usage of the bar prescribes permanent partnerships between advocates. As a father and son, dwelling under the same roof, would not be looked upon as partners, so an office occupied in common by husband and wife ought to be allowed, for there would not be anything of a speculative character in it, or of the nature of a commercial enterprise, which is the real reason for the interdiction of such partnerships.

The other case is that of the woman lawyer whose husband is a judge. The Italian Code of Civil Procedure, Article 116, sec. 10, states that objections may be made to the judge in the following case: "When one of his relatives or connections in the direct or collateral line to the third degree, undertakes the exclusive defense of a cause as advocate or attorney." If the legislature had thought of admitting women to the bar,

they would have indicated, among the reasons for challenging
the judge, the marriage relation existing between the judge
and his wife, acting as advocate for one of the parties. This
consideration, which escaped the attention of the Turin Court,
might have been invoked in Italy, against the admission of
women to the bar.

Our Code of Civil Procedure has nothing of the kind; it fails
to mention as a reason for challenging a judge, the relation-
ship or alliance between judge and advocate, hence the preceding argument which has its *raison d'etre* in Italy, cannot·be
used by our opponents.

A son may plead before his father, the magistrate; a wife
could also do so before her husband, who most assuredly would
have the tact to decline to sit as judge during the trial.

But our opponents will further urge, the work at the bar,
the intellectual toil, so intense, continuous and absorbing,
would it not injure the health of a woman? Those peculiar
and periodic conditions to which the laws of nature subject her,
would these not interfere with her endurance of the fatigue of
the profession? Would she not be prevented from the prompt
performance of her legal duties?

Advocates, as a general thing, are complaining that the
number of new associates seems to increase proportionately to
the decrease in the number of suits brought, and most of them
lament this state of business stagnation. The work at the
bar then, is not so absorbing as our·adversaries would have
us think, doubtless to help out their case.

The fitness of woman for a medical career or that of a pharmacist is recognized, yet physicians and pharmacists must hold
themselves at the disposal of their patients at every minute
of the day and night. Do not these professions occasion much
severer fatigue than that of the advocate?

The health of women is thought of too late. If this pity
which some persons pretend to feel for the sufferings of working women were sincere, it ought to be exercised toward those
who, five hundred feet beneath the surface of the earth, are
risking their lives in the mines, and avaricious employers should
be forbidden to abuse the strength of women by putting upon

them tasks which are beyond their strength. Before denying women access to the bar on the ground of their health, we ought to prevent them from poisoning themselves in factories, in unhealthy workshops and weave-shops, where anæmia, chlorosis and consumption are permitted to make their frightful ravages upon emaciated frames, whose health is decaying, while hardly any one cares for the sickly offspring to which they give birth.

As to the peculiar physiological conditions which have been invoked, are not the millions of women who earn their living by their labor, subjected to them? (The Rector, M. Wasseige invokes these physiological conditions as an argument against the practice of medicine by women. Discours rectoral, 1886–7, p. 17 et seq.)

Are female students assigned to particular times for their examinations? Do classes have a holiday when their teachers are ill? Are the patients in hospitals left to treat themselves, during the periodical illness of the internes?

Do the thousands of women who practice medicine, leave their patients to die when they are suffering from catamenial disturbances? (In New-York and Brooklyn, there are more than 900 women practicing medicine at the present time.)

In those courts in the United States where women practice as lawyers, is the regularity and expedition of procedure interfered with? And however numerous may be the peculiarities which differentiate the Yankee race from ours, I do not know that American women are subject to other physiological laws than those affecting our Belgian women.

FEDERAL SUFFRAGE.

THE LAW OF FEDERAL SUFFRAGE; an argument in support of. By Francis Minor, of the St. Louis Bar.

After noticing the decision of the U. S. Sup. Ct., in *Ex parte* Yarbrough (110 U. S., March, 1884), when *Minor v. Happersett* (21 Wallace, U. S.) was distinguished, the author goes on to say, as a result of that decision, that "Men do not vote for members of Congress by reason of their sex, or because they are men, but because they are citizens of the U. S. and members of the national body politic. The right of women to vote is based on the same ground and for the same reason. They constitute a part of the 'people' or 'citizens.' There is not a word as to the sex of the electors."

There has been a surprising change, during the past few years, on the subject of woman suffrage.

When it does come fairly into politics, the opposition will be able to furnish no better arguments, than fear for existing institutions, for the position of women in society (not in the community), and for the future of practical politics as a lazy way of getting a living. There will be a parade of the same impure statements as greeted the co-education of the sexes; there will be the same old chivalrous talk as an apology for the ownership of the wife or daughters; texts will be wrenched out of the Book of books; all the devices of conservatism will be worked over again; until the daring and novelty of a change will make a break somewhere, and then a few years will make woman suffrage an accomplished fact. Then women will be found to be the most conservative of all the voters.—*Current Comment.*

INJURY TO PASSENGER FROM UNKNOWN CAUSE.
PRESUMPTION OF NEGLIGENCE.

A question of considerable novelty in the law applicable to common carriers of passengers arose in the case of Pennsylvania Co. v. McKinny, decided recently by the Supreme Court of Pennsylvania, and reported in 17 Atlantic Reports, 14. It appears that the plaintiff, while a passenger on a train in rapid motion, was struck over the eye by a hard substance, thought by surgeons to be coal, and was severely injured. Another train was at the time passing, and the engine was opposite plaintiff. There was no evidence to show where the missile came from. The operators of plaintiff's train testified that they knew nothing to cause it, and those of passing trains testified that nothing was thrown or escaped from their trains. There was evidence that the appliances and machinery of the trains were in good order.

In his charge to the jury the Court, among other things, said: "The rule of law, as applicable to this case, is that the mere happening of an injurious accident to a passenger while in the hands of the carrier will raise *prima facie* a presumption of negligence, and throws the *onus* that it did not exist on the carrier."

"Under this principle and the facts in this case, the jury will begin their consideration with the fact established that the injuries were the result of negligence of the defendant. This fact must be rebutted or answered by evidence. In other words, the defendant must show by evidence that it was not negligent. If it has not done this the verdict must be for the plaintiff." In immediate connection therewith, he said to the jury: "It is your duty, of course, to consider all the evidence in the case and to come to a conclusion on this question of negligence. If you find that the defendant was negligent, then the question of damages must be considered by you."

Mr. Justice Sterrett, delivering the opinion of the Supreme Court, admitted that the rule stated by the trial court was well settled and of general application in cases of injury to passengers while in the course of transportation, and that the only question was whether it is one of such universal application that it can be invoked without proof of something more than the mere fact of an injurious accident to a passenger while in the hands of the carrier in the absence of any admission or evidence tending to connect the carrier or its servants or any of the appliances of transportation with the happening of the injury.

"The rule in question has been frequently recognized, and the presumption of negligence applied in a variety of cases, among which are stage coach accidents, resulting from breaking an axle, etc., railroad accidents, including derailment of cars, collisions, breaking of machinery, falling of berths of sleeping-cars, violent out-break among other passengers on train, explosion on passenger vessels, etc.: Christie v. Griggs, 2 Camp., 79; Stokes v. Saltonstall, 13 Peters, 181; Ware v. Gay, 11 Pick., 109; Hipeley v. Railroad Co., 27 Am. & E. R. Cases, 287; Feital v. Middlesex R. R. Co., 109 Mass., 398; Edgerton v. Railroad Co., 39 N. Y., 229; Sullivan v. Railroad Co., 30 Pa. St. 237; Railroad Co. v. Wolrath, 8 Am. & E. R. R. Cases, 371; Railroad Co. v. Pollard, 76 Pa. St., 510, 513; Spear v. Railroad Co., 119 Id., 61; Packet Co. v. McCool, 8 Am. & E. R. R. Cases, 390; Laing v. Colder, 8 Pa. St. 481; Holbrook v. Railroad Co., 12 N. Y., 236; Railroad Co. v. Anderson, 94 Id. 351; Story on Bailments, 592, 601; Sherman & Redfield on Negligence, §§ 280a, and notes.

"In nearly every case in which the rule under consideration has been applied, it will be found that the injury complained of was shown to have resulted from breaking of machinery, collision, derailment of cars, or something improper and unsafe in

the appliances of transportation or in the conduct of the business, and not from any cause wholly disconnected therewith.
* * * If a passenger seated in a railroad car is injured in a collision by the upsetting of the car, breaking of a wheel, axle, or other part of the machinery, he is not required to do more, in the first instance, than prove the fact and show the nature and extent of the injury. A *prima facie* case for plaintiff is thus made out, and the *onus* is cast on the carrier to disprove negligence. It is reasonable that it should be so, because the company has within its possession and under its control almost exclusively the means of knowing what occasions the injury, and of explaining how it occurred, while, as a general rule, the passenger is destitute of all knowledge that would enable him to present the facts and fasten the negligence on the company. * * *

"When a passenger is injured by any accident connected with the means or appliances of transportation, there naturally arises a presumption that it must have resulted from some negligent act of omission or commission of the company or some of its employes; because, without some such negligence, it is very improbable that the accident would have occurred. That is the basis on which the presumption rests, and it stands as proof of the negligence until it is successfully rebutted. It arises not from the naked fact that an injury has been inflicted, but from the cause of the injury, or from other circumstances attending it.

"It follows from what has been said that the learned judge of the Common Pleas erred in directing the jury to begin their consideration of the case 'with the fact established that the injuries were the result of the negligence of the defendant.'"

The decision in the above case is very able and convincing, but it is, in my judgment, fallacious and erroneous. The common law obligation of a common carrier, is that he shall deliver at its destination the property received by him, without damage while in his hands, unless prevented by the act of God or the public enemy. Mr. Justice Wright, of the New York Court of Appeals, in Michaels v. N. Y. Cent. R. R. Co., 30 N. Y., 564, speaking of the "Act of God" as used in the case of carriers, says: "All the cases agree in requiring the entire exclusion of human agency from the cause of the injury or loss. If the loss or injury happen in any way through the agency of man, it cannot be considered the act of God; nor even if the act or negligence of man contributes to bring or leave the goods of the carrier under the operation of natural causes that work to their injury, is he excused. In short, to excuse the carrier, the act of God, or *res divina* must be the sole and immediate cause of the injury. If there be any co-operation of man, or any admixture of human means, the injury is not, in a legal sense, the act of God." See, also, Proprietors, etc., v. Wood, 4 Doug., 287; Chicago, etc., R. R. Co. v. Sawyer, 69, Ill., 285; Caldwell v. N. J. Steamboat Co., 47 N. Y., 282; Bulkley v. Naumkeag, etc., Co., 24 How., 386; Hayes v. Kennedy, 41 Pa. St., 378.

The liability in respect to passengers is somewhat different. His undertaking amounts to no more than that so far as human foresight and care can reasonably go, he will transport them safely. He is not liable if injuries happen from sheer accident or misfortune which could not have been prevented by the greatest degree of care, foresight or judgment.

It was not claimed that the accident to McKenney was caused by the act of God, and although there was no evidence to show where the missile came from, it was more rational to suppose that it was carelessly thrown by the fireman on the engine which was opposite the plaintiff at the time he was hit, than that it fell from the clouds or was the result of some natural cause. McKenney was seated in the passenger coach in the seat provided him by the defendant. He had no say as to the mode or manner of running the train. He was as absolutely under control of defendant's servants as if he were a statue, and yet when injured under such circumstances, must he do more than to prove the fact and show the nature and extent of the injury? We think not. We think the learned judge of the Common Pleas was right in saying: "The jury will begin their consideration with the fact established that the injuries were the result of negligence of the defendant."

The traveling public believe that if injured while in the

course of transportation without any fault of their own, the common carrier is liable in damages unless he can show that the accident arose from natural causes or that it could not have been prevented by the exercise of the greatest vigilance, foresight and judgment. We think this is good law and that courts should long hesitate before relaxing the rule in the slightest particular.

The basis of the rule which exempts a common carrier for liability for injury to a human being, under circumstances which would render it liable for injury to a domestic animal or for the destruction of a keg of beer or a barrel of whisky, can hardly be traced to a divine origin. There should be no difference in the rule respecting the obligation of the common carrier, whether the thing carried be freight or passengers, unless it be shown that the passenger injured did something which probably brought about or contributed to the injury.— *Chicago Law Journal.*

A KAFIR LAWSUIT.

A Kafir in the witness-box is often a surprise to those who know little or nothing of the traditions of the Kafir race. The ease with which the ordinary native parries the most dexterous cross-examination, the skill with which he extricates himself from the consequences of an unfortunate answer, and above all, the ready and staggering plausibility of his explanations, have often struck those who come in contact with him in the law courts. He is far superior, as a rule, to the ordinary European, in the witness-box. Keen-witted and ready, he is yet too cautious ever to answer a question the drift of which he does not clearly foresee, and which when he understands, he at once proceeds, if necessary, to forestall by his reply. As a result, the truth of his evidence can only be sifted by very careful proceeding on the part of the cross-examiner, and by keeping him in the dark as much as possible to the bearing of his answers upon the subject-matter of the suit. Whether this dialectic skill is innate in the Kafir, or whether it is the result of long cultivation, it is difficult to say, but as some proof of the former, we subjoin a very interesting extract from a book now unhappily becoming rare, viz. Colonel Maclean's "Handbook of Kafir Laws and Customs, compiled from Notes by Mr. Brownlee, Rev. Dugmore and Mr. Ayliff," which will, we venture to think, throw a great deal of light upon the present abilities of the descendants of those whose judicial customs fifty years ago, are so graphically described in the following words:

(418)

"When a Kafir has ascertained that he has sufficient grounds to enter on an action against another, his first step is to proceed, with a party of his friends or adherents armed, to the residence of the person against whom his action lies. On their arrival they sit down together in some conspicuous position, and await quietly the result of their presence. As a law party is readily known by the aspect and deportment of its constituents, its appearance at any kraal is the signal for the mustering of all the adult male residents that are forthcoming. These accordingly assemble and also sit down together within conversing distance of their generally unwelcome visitors.

"The two parties perhaps survey each other in silence for some time. 'Tell us the news,' at length exclaims one of the adherents of the defendant. should their patience fail first. Another pause sometimes ensues, during which the party of the plaintiff discuss in an undertone which of their party shall be 'opening counsel.' This decided, the learned gentleman commences a minute statement of the case, the rest of the party confining themselves to occasional suggestions, which he adopts or rejects at pleasure. Sometimes he is allowed to proceed almost uninterrupted to the close of the statement, the friends of the defendant listening with silent attention, and treasuring up in their memories all the points of importance for a future stage of the proceedings. Generally, however, it receives a thorough sifting from the beginning; every assertion of consequence being made the occasion of a most searching series of cross questions. The case thus fairly opened, which occupies several hours, it probably proceeds no further the first day. The plaintiff and his party are told that the 'men' of the place are from home, that there are none but 'children' present, who are not competent to discuss such important matters. They accordingly retire with the tacit understanding that the case is to be resumed next day.

"During the interval the defendant formally makes known to the men of the neighboring kraals, that an action has been entered against him, and they are expected to be present on his behalf at the resumption of the case. In the meantime, the first day's proceedings having indicated the line of argu-

ment of the plaintiff, the plan of defense is arranged accordingly. Information is collected, arguments are suggested, precedents sought for, able debaters called in, and every possible
preparation made for the battle of intellects that is to be fought
on the following day.

"The plaintiff's party, usually reinforced both in mental and
material strength, arm the next morning, and take up their
ground again. The opponents, now mustered in force, con-
front them, seated on the ground, each man with his arms at
his side. The case is resumed by some advocate for the defendant requiring a restatement of the plaintiff's grounds of
action. This is commenced perhaps by one who was not even
present at the previous day's proceedings, but who has been
selected for this more difficult stage on account of his debating
abilities.

"Then comes the tug of war; the ground is disputed inch by
inch; every assertion is contested, every proof attempted to be
invalidated, objection meets objection, and question is opposed
by counter-question, each disputant endeavoring with surprising adroitness to throw the burden of answering on his opponent.
The Socratic method of debate appears in all its perfection,
both parties being equally versed in it. The rival advocates
warm as they proceed, sharpening each other's ardor, till from
the passions that seem enlisted in the contest, a stranger might
suppose the interests of the nation at stake and dependent upon the decision. When these combatants have spent their
strength, or one or other of them is overcome in argument,
others step to the rescue. The battle is fought over again on
different ground, some point either of law or evidence that had
been purposely kept in abeyance, being now brought forward,
and perhaps the entire aspect of the case changed.

"The whole of the second day is frequently taken up with this
intellectual gladiatorship, and it closes without any other result than an exhibition of the relative strength of the opposing
parties. The plaintiff's company retire again, and the defendant and his friends review their own position. Should
they feel that they have been worsted, and that the case is one
that cannot be successfully defended, they prepare to attempt

to bring the matter to a conclusion by an offer of the smallest satisfaction the law allows. This is usually refused, in expectation of an advance in the offer, which takes place generally in proportion to the defendant's anxiety to prevent an appeal (to the Chief). Should the plaintiff at length accede to the proposed terms, they are fulfilled, and the case is ended by a formal declaration of acquiescence."—*The Cape Law Journal.*

FINDING THE VERDICT.

In one of the earliest trials before a colored jury in Texas, the twelve gentlemen were told by the judge to retire and "find the verdict." They went into the jury-room, whence the opening and shutting of doors, and other sounds of unusual commotion were heard. At last the jury came back into the court, when the foreman announced: "We hab looked eberywhar, Jedge, for dat verdict—in de drawers and behind de doors; but it ain't nowhar in dat blessed room."

Department of Medical Jurisprudence.

EDWARD B. WESTON, M. D., EDITOR.

THE SO-CALLED ELIXIR OF YOUTH AND ITS ABSURD PRETENSIONS.

It is now more than two months since the news of Brown-Séquard's alleged method of rejuvenating the aged reached this country. The subject is one that naturally appeals to public interest, since a long life and a vigorous old age have always been among the chief objects of human desire, and consequently it has received a much greater share of newspaper attention than is usually bestowed on medical topics. This is most unfortunate, for the public discussion of such an absurdity, tends only to bring scientific medicine into ridicule.

The method is on its face preposterous; its vaunted effects are impossible and ridiculous. It is opposed to all known physiological and biological laws, and had it not been bolstered up by the reputation of a Brown-Séquard, it would scarcely have been heard of outside of the Paris society where it was proposed, and no one would ever have looked upon it in any other light than as the foolish conceit of an old man, in whose mind the dreams of returning youth had assumed the counterfeit of reality. Supported as it was, however, by the weight of an authority hitherto respected in the world of medicine, it was necessary that it should be tested cautiously and in a proper way, and that the method should not be actually condemned until it had been proved as worthless, as were its pretensions extravagant. For unreflecting and obstinate scepticism in matters medical is as illogical as unreasoning credulity.

The experiments reported by Dr. Loomis in another column are sufficient, we think, to satisfy the demands of legitimate prudence. In fact, the subject has already received more attention than it has deserved. The results of these experiments seem to show that the injected material may, in certain cases, act as a mechanical stimulant, but that is all; they fail utterly to support the extravagant claims of physical and mental rejuvenescence which have been put forward in behalf of this method. What these experiments do not so clearly show, since they were conducted with a proper regard for surgical cleanliness, is the imminent risk of septic poisoning or of tuberculous infection to which the subjects of such injections are exposed in the hands of incautious operators.

It is high time, therefore, to call a halt in this matter, unless scientific medicine is to be made ridiculous in the eyes of the public. If there are any not yet convinced of the worthlessness of this method, let them continue their experiments as long as they wish, but let them do so removed from the public gaze and out of sight of the newspaper reporters. It is repugnant to true science to parade such crude and untried theories before the public, as though they had received the stamp of authoritative approval, and in the name of this science we protest against it. The daily press is awakening to the true issues involved, and will in its own effectual way bury the theory out of sight, as soon as its falsity and absurdity have been made manifest.— *N. Y. Medical Record.*

THE MAYBRICK CASE.

Some singular dicta have crept into the discussion of the Maybrick case by the British medical journals. The details of the case are as follows: Mr. Maybrick, a hypochondriac patent medicine taker, arsenic eater and secret drinker, was, after a visit to the races, where he ate and drank heartily, and was wet through, taken ill with vomiting and stiffness in the legs. He was treated for gastro-intestinal catarrh by several physicians and given small doses of ipecac and Fowler's solution, bismuth, carbolic acid, cerium oxalate and similar remedies to relieve gastric distress. As constipation was present, cascara sagrada was administered. Sulphonal was given to secure slumber. The patient was doing well up to three days before death, when diarrhœa attended by tenesmus set in. Four days before death, suspicion of arsenic poisoning was raised by an interested party, but on examination of the excreta no trace of arsenic was found. From this time on the patient was kept under surveillance, but on the first day thereafter, he grew rapidly worse and died two days later.

The British medical journals with their usual bias for the prosecution, have summed up in favor of arsenic poisoning, albeit leading forensic experts like Tidy, whose work on "Legal Medicine" is an Anglo-Saxon standard, Fritzgerald and Kinkhead, claim that death was caused by ordinary gastro-enteritis. Small quantities of arsenic were found by Stevenson in the intestines, liver and kidneys, by the use of tests long since abandoned by toxicologists as defective. Had no arsenic been medicinally given the patient, and had he not been an arsenic-eater, this finding, despite its defective origin, might have been of value, but in the light of these facts, it becomes valueless, especially when the defective nature of the tests is remembered.

The British Medical Journal lays down as a starting point, that vomiting, attended simultaneously with diarrhœa, in an adult, is indicative of poisoning. Every American physician of any experience will take issue with this dictum. Vomiting, attended simultaneously with diarrhœa, may result from a chill, from nephritis, from malarial hepatic disease, from hepatic cirrhosis, from bad water, from impure food, and in certain persons, from cold. This dictum has therefore no value, moreover it has no bearing on the case. The vomiting of Mr. Maybrick did not occur simultaneously with his diarrhœa. Dr. Tidy claims that since pain was absent, gastro-intestinal disease was not of arsenical origin, and this claim is certainly a justifiable one, especially in view of the facts of the case.

In view of the facts given, the only ones bearing on the medical aspects of the case, the conservative scientist could find but one verdict as regards the arsenical theory—not proven. Mrs. Maybrick's immorality has no bearing on the scientific aspects of the case, nor has the amount of arsenic found strewn lavishly over the house after suspicion had been aroused by a person inimical to the accused. On the clinical symptoms, post-mortem findings and toxicological results, "not proven" would be the only justifiable verdict.—*Medical Standard; Chicago.*

THE MURDERER'S GUILT AND THE SURGEON'S RESPONSIBILITY.

A legal decision of considerable interest to surgeons was rendered not long since in a murder trial in Liverpool. A man named Vaughan was tried for the murder of a Mr. Godfrey, whom he had struck on the back of the head with an adze, inflicting a scalp-wound behind the ear. The injured man was taken to a hospital, and there developed symptoms of compression of the brain. It was thought that the skull was fractured, and on consultation the surgeons determined to trephine. This was done, and the man died in consequence, apparently, of hemorrhage from a large vessel opened during the operation. At the post-mortem examination it was found that there had been no fracture of the skull. At the trial the defense claimed that death resulted directly from the operation, and was not to be attributed to the original injury. The judge ruled, however, that this claim was inadmissible, as no culpable want of skill or negligence on the part of the surgeons could be proven.

Such questions have arisen before, and are liable to be raised in any case in which the murdered man does not die within a very short time after the injury has been inflicted. If the wounded man is saved by timely treatment, the defense is very willing to profit by the surgeon's skill, though seldom ready to acknowledge its agency. But if treatment is unavailing in saving life, it is the surgeon, they say, and not the assailant who has killed the man.

There is a precedent in the English courts for this ruling, which is cited by the *The Lancet* in its comment upon the Liverpool case. Edward Lawless Pym was tried at Southampton, in the year 1846, for the murder of a Mr. Hawkey, and had the advantage of being defended by Mr. Cockburn (afterward Chief-Justice of England). Mr. Pym had shot Mr. Hawkey in a duel and wounded him. An operation was subsequently performed, and the wounded man died. Mr. Cockburn proposed to show that the operation performed was unnecessary, and that without it the patient might have lived. But the presiding judge, Mr. Justice Erle, after consulting with Baron Rolfe, laid it down as law that "where a wound is given which, in the opinion of competent medical advisers, is dangerous, and the treatment which they adopt is the immediate cause of death, the party who inflicted the wound is criminally responsible."

This ruling would seem to be a very just one, and moreover, one that will ultimately be of benefit to the accused in similar cases. For the surgeon, assured that the death will not be laid to his door, can accept the responsibility of treatment with greater confidence, and the success of his efforts will not be jeopardized by nervous apprehension of failure.—*N. Y. Medical Record.*

EXECUTION BY ELECTRICITY.

The warfare that has been waged between the supporters and the opponents of the electrical execution law of New York State, has given rise to the most conflicting kind of testimony regarding the lethal force of the agent required to be used hereafter. Those who oppose the law are, at the same time, in most instances, persons whose interests lie in the more pro-

ˈfitable and popular uses of electricity for motor or illuminating purposes. By some strange logic of their own they seem to argue that if the electrical execution law can be, and is carried into effect, there will be a stigma placed upon the commercial applications of electricity.

In spite of a variety of statements to the contrary, it is probable that a trial of the means provided by the new law must be had in due time; and we have no fear that it will not prove adequate. Professor William H. Howell, of the Johns Hopkins University, says: "Anybody who has been unfortunate enough to have a very strong electric current pass through his system must suffer paralysis of some or all of the nerve centers. This may be temporary or may be permanent. If the paralysis does not affect the vital parts of the human mechanism, the patient may live.... The descriptions of the apparatus in the infliction of the penalty which the New York criminal is to suffer, show that there is little possibility of his escaping almost instantaneous death. His head is to be invested in a metallic cap, and the full strength of a very strong current sent directly through the centers controlling the mechanism of life. These must be immediately paralyzed, and the beat of the heart, as well as the breathing, cease. The brain must also be entirely paralyzed at once, and all consciousness be lost."

Such a statement will, to the medical mind at least, carry conviction. Until the test has been made, and the facts are found to contradict these scientific propositions, we shall expect to see the new law obeyed. The contracts have been entered into, we are informed, with our State officials for the delivery of a suitable electrical plant to each of the three prisons where the extreme penalty of the law will hereafter be administered—at Sing Sing, Auburn and Clinton. These prisons already possesss the steam-power sufficient to drive the form of dynamo that is ordered. The dynamo is said to be of the Westinghouse pattern of alternating current, electric-light machine; the pressure of the current will be equal to that used in the system of electrical illumination.—*N. Y Medical Journal.*

MEDICAL EDUCATION.

Every year, at some ot our medical associations, articles are read, addresses presented and discussions ensue condemning, in general terms, the lax methods adopted in medical education and practice. A general cry follows about the necessity of higher medical education; curriculums are discussed and certain evils condemned, but no medical Moses appears to lead the profession out of the swamps of ignorance and incapacity to the fair fields of knowledge and professional perfection. Numerous plans are suggested, and various doctors claim to have the necessary panacea; but ignorance still exists and incompetents continue to tread the avenues of the profession.

Dr. Wile, in a recent address before the American Medical Editor's Association, of which he was the retiring President, outlined his views, and suggested some methods by which the standard of medical education can be elevated. His subject was "Our Duties as Journalists, and the Reforms we should advocate." He claims that every year numerous incompetent men are sent forth from the various medical colleges in our country, ignorant of medicine and unable to use the English language correctly.

He contends that numerous institutions should not be permitted to grant diplomas to incompetent graduates; that State Boards of Health should be appointed by the Governors of each State, who should pass upon the merit, or want of it, in each applicant for graduation. He contends that as American physicians are prevented from practicing in foreign countries, so the ignorant foreigner should not be permitted to practice in this country.

There is much here that is worthy of consideration. These recommendations, if adopted, would be of advantage to the profession. The higher standard we reach, the more shall our knowledge enlighten the world. But "art is long and time is fleeting." Many years must pass ere perfection can be obtained. Let us build, but build slowly, that we shall not be compelled to tear down.

2. The more we consider this question, we are compelled to ask ourselves: Is our professional standard lower than that of other professions in this country? Are our members more ignorant than those of law or theology, when taken as a body? We do not believe the medical profession suffers in comparison with any other under the sun. How many lawyers are practicing who scarcely know the difference between *petit larceny* and *mayhem*? How many ministers occupy pulpits who think John the Baptist founded one or two evangelical churches and was the author of the Gospel of St. John?

This does not excuse ignorance in our own ranks, but it is a satisfaction to know that physicians have no exclusive corner on ignorance in this country.

Has the American physician any reason to be ashamed of his part in the world's advancement in medicine in the last one hundred years? Look at Rush, McDowell, Simmes, Battey and hundreds of others who are identified with medical progress, who have hewed their way to deathless fame and benefited the world by their researches and inventions. And yet it is scarcely a decade since all our medical schools were graduating a majority of their students who had attended two consecutive sessions of lectures. It will probably be said: These men mentioned were remarkable characters, and made themselves despite extraneous surroundings. This is the very application we desire to make from what has gone before. There must be an individual determination to overcome difficulties in order to insure success and ability in any profession. If this is not inherent in a student, neither three, five or seven years can make him a competent practitioner.

3. If each member of the profession were determined to elevate the practice of medicine, it would be impossible for unworthy and incompetent men to secure entrance. Every candidate for medical degrees should be compelled to furnish his chosen college an endorsement from a preceptor, whose standing in the profession should be investigated. Before permitting the student to enter upon the study of medicine, the precep-

tor should know positively that his preliminary education was sufficient to qualify him for professional life. He should be examined by the faculty of the college where he selects to receive instruction, and proven qualified in those primary branches which are essential for success in all the avenues of life.

Colleges, too, should be compelled to maintain a high standard of medical education, and the examination of candidates for graduation, should be conducted by a medical board not identified with the faculty or the alumni. Prejudice or favoritism should be unknown in the graduation of students from schools of all kinds.

Another reform in medical colleges should be established. Fees for diplomas should be at once abolished, and the lecture fees made sufficient to meet the deficiency produced by such abolishment. A student who labors faithfully, and successfully passes the examination, deserves his diploma as a gift from the hands of his alma mater, and if he cannot acquire a grade necessary to qualify him for graduation, the faculty will not strain a point in order to secure the graduation fee, and turn loose upon the community an incompetent physician.—*Medical Advance, St. Louis.*

THOMAS JEFFERSON AND THE UNIVERSITY OF VIRGINIA.
By H. B. Adams, Ph. D.

This is one of a series of volumes issued by the United States Bureau of Education, giving the history of educational institutions. No. 1 was largely devoted to the history of the College of William and Mary, of Virginia, and the current No., 2, is principally devoted to the scheme of Jefferson for the founding of the University of Virginia; and it certainly presents a pleasant picture of the Virginia statesman in his efforts for higher education in his own State. He was hardly behind the New England sentiment, which favored State aid for higher education, and local taxation for support of primary schools. For fifty years he struggled against the selfishness of the wealthy class in behalf of the "holy cause of the university," and to this day Jefferson is the foremost figure of the promoters of educational interests in Virginia. During his diplomatic residence in France, he made a study of European universities, and he caught the French spirit in the educational sphere quite as much as in the political.

It is remarkable that when France lost her territorial influence and control in the West, some of the leading spirits made earnest efforts to impress upon the United States, French thought and French educational methods through a Southern university. The story in the volume reviewed, of Chevalier Quesnay's project of a university under the patronage of Jefferson and other Virginian leaders, reads like a romance. He was the grandson of the famous court physician of Louis XV., and served for some time in our army of the revolution.

It was to be a French academy he would found, to be equipped with French professors. Richmond was to be its seat. Its corner-stone was laid June 24, 1786. Quesnay then returned to France to complete his plans for an intellectual and educational union between France and the United States. This was at a period when Rousseau and the Encyclopedists dominated French thought, and there was great danger that they would become potential in the Southern States. But that influence was checkmated in time by a current of "Scottish Presbyterianism proceding from Princeton College."

Jefferson's bill of 1779 provided for the foundation of common schools for both male and female children, ten years in advance of the time when even Boston gave a place to female children in her public schools. In connection with his system was a system of township government and taxation, after the type of that of New England, whose power he felt in the hostility of New England to his own policy when at the head of our government. Referring to this concentrated power in townships, and to its energy at the time of the Embargo, Jefferson said he "felt the foundation of the government shaken under his (my) feet by the New England townships." Quesnay's plan did not mature, and it is very remarkable that, in 1794, the French faculty of the College of Geneva, Switzerland, proposed to Jefferson to transfer that college to Virginia. Jefferson favored it, and endeavored, unsuccessfully, to influence Washington to second the scheme; but the Virginians did not sustain Jefferson in this project. And it is well, for it was far better for American institutions to represent the American spirit, than to start under the auspices of French philosophers.

Jefferson was, as is well known, an advanced liberal in religion, yet it is matter of interest to find that he favored placing the ethical education of children upon a theistic basis. He says: "The proofs of the being of a God, the creator, preserver, and supreme ruler of the universe, the author of all the relations of morality, and of the laws and obligations, these, I infer, will be within the province of the professor of ethics." He even favored the establishment, in the immediate vicinage of the university, of theological classes by different sects, which he thought would create a spirit of toleration, "and make the general religion a religion of peace, reason and morality." Here he anticipated, in large degree, the policy of several of our leading universities. It certainly is pleasing to see the intense democratic leader of American politics, who represented all the bitterness in controversy characteristic of the early period of the Republic, devoting his old age, as well as his early years, to the promoting of that higher education which is the glory of a commonwealth, and to see his early philosophic hardness—for such it was—softening as he advanced in years, until toleration and charity and social "sweetness and light" chastened and subdued all the harsher elements of his nature.

Much of the volume we have noticed treats of the influence and power of the University of Virginia, which the author of that paper regards as the transcendent intellectual influence in the South.

A continuation of this series, which shall embrace the higher educational history of the whole country, presented with equal intelligence and breadth, as appears in the volume before us, will be a valuable contribution to the literature of the country. —*Buffalo Medical and Surgical Journal.*

Editorial Department.

Alexandria to Palestine—Greece—Spain.

Before leaving Alexandria, I ascertained that by taking the Austrian steamer to Jaffa, I could stop a week in Palestine and then proceed to Athens. But if the steamer should be taken a week later, the stay in Palestine would have to be two weeks instead of one, making me two weeks later in Greece, and disarranging my subsequent plans of travel. So I resolved to take the Austrian steamer.

On the 17th of December, 1886, we embarked on the steamer Danae, for Jaffa. After passing the custom-house there was a swarm of Egyptians struggling to get possession of the baggage, so as to get the fee for taking it on board.

The natives look upon travelers as legitimate prey, and it is very difficult to avoid payment of the most extortionate charges. Even the custom-house officers or employees who volunteer the passenger's protection, sometimes make themselves parties to the abuses which are practiced. It is a crying evil which calls for correction from the law making powers on the Mediterranean.

On the morning of the 19th, we arrived at Jaffa, having stopped several hours at Port Said.

At Port Said, the houses, fronting on the sea, with their bright contrast of colors (the windows and some other portions being painted green or red, and the body of the house white), presented a motley and picturesque appearance.

A dignitary of some kind was being conveyed ashore from one of the vessels, and on the small boat in which he was seated was what might be called a band. The music resembled a Scotch bag-pipe, accompanied by a base drum. A large crowd had assembled on shore to do honor to the public functionary.

There was also music on our vessel, consisting of the performance of a Turk on a rattle and a tambourine. It was a chant, ending frequently in the chorus, "Alla-hoo-ah, Alla-hoo-ah."

The poor Egyptians who were loading coal on one of the steamers, had to go on the run, not only with the empty baskets, but many of them with the baskets loaded.

Under a splendid sky we sailed over this inland sea, arriving at Jaffa, as stated, on the 19th of December.

This City contained from twenty to twenty-five thousand inhabitants, composed largely of Jews, with many Syrian Christians.

Stopping at a hotel I asked of the landlord the expense of going to Jerusalem. He would take me there, stay two days and return, for 125 francs. But that would not, of course, include my meals and hotel bills. To go to Jerusalem merely, would cost 50 francs in one carriage, and 40 in another not so good. I told the landlord I would take a walk about the City. Would I have some one with me? No. I had better. "No!" (Somewhat emphatically.)

Fearing the result of the walk, he took me into the back yard, and showing me the second class carriage, offered to take me in it for 15 francs. I insisted upon my walk, however, and walking to Cook's Office, purchased a good cushioned seat for 12 francs. In a few hours, I was on the road to Jerusalem.

The Arabs are a fine people—honest, industrious, and moreover, very religious. For a mile or two out of Jaffa, the road was lined with trees and plants of tropical growth—the palm tree, the date, the olive, and the orange trees, loaded with fruit ripening in the December sun. The earth rejoiced in its luxuriousness of vegetation.

But this did not last long. Soon we began to cross vast, open plains, with no fences and no habitations, though mostly under cultivation. This was the character of the country until we reached the mountains—two thirds of the way to Jerusalem.

At 5 or 6 in the evening, we reached Ramla, a place of 4 or 5,000 inhabitants, and after supper proceeded to the foot of the mountains, where we halted for about 3 hours.

It was an Arabic public house: a stone building resembling a brick or or lime-kiln; the entrance corresponding with the arched opening in which the fuel is put.

Inside was wood, etc., and animals. Men were sitting around on the ground near a small fire. I went up the stone steps, to the second story and entered a room comparatively aristocratic. Stretching myself on a bench, covered with plain upholstering, I tried to sleep. But the night was chilly, and the scenes were so strange and exciting, that sleep did not come.

About 3 A. M., after drinking a small cup of very sweet coffee, and paying the moderate fee demanded, we resumed our journey.

The road in the mountains was in some places not only steep, but exceedingly rough. The passengers frequently walked, though they were not required to do so.

About 9 o'clock in the forenoon, we arrived at Jerusalem, the stony hills having continued up to the very city. There was no vegetation, except the olive tree. This is here about the size of a large apple tree, and grows sometimes from the very rocks themselves. And this is Jerusalem, the holy city, inhabited by Jews as in days of old. How it came to be built upon these rocky hills is a constant source of wonderment, especially to one who finds it difficult to adopt the theory of Mr. Spafford, who was presiding over a religious colony, most of whom, like himself, came from Chicago. His explanation is that in ancient times all these hills were covered with dense forests. I asked him for the evidence.

"Why," said he, "this country was given by the Almighty to his chosen people for an inheritance. Would you give your son something not worth having? These hills, in their present condition, would be very undesirable. Therefore, they must have been covered with a luxuriant growth of timber." How such a growth could have been supported upon the sterile rocks, he did not explain.

Almost the only fuel used here, consists of the limbs and roots of the dead or decaying olive trees. The trees are of a stunted growth. The fuel obtained from them is very dear, and gives out but little heat. The expense of bringing coal from Jaffa, is about equal to the price of it in that city. Some charcoal is brought on mules, from the valley of the Hebron.

I visited the Mount of Olives, and saw the stone from which Christ is said to have ascended into heaven. I then descended into the City, and visiting the Mosque, saw the stone from which Mohammed is said to have ascended. On the stone are shown the foot-prints of the angel, who sustained and assisted the prophet before his ascent. I saw the Valley of Jehoshaphat, the Dead Sea and the River Jordan. I passed through the

Garden of Gethsemane, and into the Church of the Virgin Mary, where devotees were paying homage at her tomb. Afterward, visited the Church of the Holy Sepulcher, and was shown what purported to be the tomb of Christ.

I took supper with Mr. Spafford and his "family" or society. Every thing was pleasant. There were about twenty of them. They had been living under the same roof for about 5 years.

During my stay, I visited Bethlehem, which was a repetition of the olive crowned hills; though here they were less sterile—more beautiful and picturesque. There were also some fertile valleys between.

AN ARAB DINNER.

While in Jerusalem, in company with Mr. Spafford, I took dinner with an Arab sheik, or chief. He lived in a two story stone house, on the side of the Mount of Olives. We ascended two or three flights of stone steps, built outside the house, and were ushered into a room somewhat luxuriously furnished, there being plenty of sofa seats and lounges. In one corner of the room was a bed. We were seated about a low table, upon which soon appeared a round, flat cake of bread for each guest, and one for the host. There were five in all. The bread had been baked on hot stones, and was very good. Then came a large platter, with four dishes of food. In the center of the platter was a plate containing small pieces of meat, well cooked. There was a dish containing rolls, about an inch thick and four to six inches long, having on the outside cabbage leaves wound round, like the outside of a cigar. The inside consisted of meat and rice, properly cooked and seasoned. The whole was very palatable. There was another dish containing what appeared to be carrots; but in some mysterious way the outside of the carrots was gone, and the place was supplied also by meat and rice. Then there was a bowl of olives. The rolls we ate with our fingers. Then came the dessert. It was served on a platter about two feet in diameter, and consisted of a delicious pudding, covered over the top with almond meats. The drink was water. After dinner, rose water was passed round for the hands and head.

Jerusalem had at that time 45 or 50,000 inhabitants, and was growing rapidly, the accessions being principally Jews, from all parts of the world.

After an interesting sojourn of a week in Palestine, I took steamer for Athens, by the way of Smyrna.

On the second of January, we passed Cape Colonna, where we could see the twelve remaining pillars of the Temple of Minerva, built by

Pericles, about 450 years before Christ.

As we approached Piraeus we could see Athens in the distance, and the Acropolis very distinctly. Here, before us, was the home of the philosophers, among whom were some of the most profound thinkers the world has ever produced. It was with mingled feelings of pleasure and sadness, and with some confusion of thought that I placed my foot upon this classic soil.

In Athens I passed the month of January. It has been too often and too well described, to justify me in attempting a description. Athens is a beautiful, modern city. There are many ancient ruins of interest. There are no paintings worth speaking of, and not a single complete piece of ancient statuary did I see while in Athens. These I was told had all been removed to London by Lord Elgin. If so, the English government should do that justice to Greece, which France has done to the various European governments whose cities and villages had been despoiled by Napoleon, of their choicest works of art.

One of my visits to the Acropolis was made by moonlight. The moon was shining gloriously through one of the clearest of Grecian skies, and the solemn splendor of the scene, as we ascended the marble steps of the Propylæon, no words can describe. Here were the majestic and still beautiful witnesses of the greatness and splendor of ancient Greece. No ruins in Rome can compare with them in beauty and completeness of preservation; nor in the many remains of the most splendid architecture.

All the way from the Propylæon to the Parthenon, and in every direction around this noble structure, were broken columns and massive blocks of marble, as well as smaller pieces, ornamented in the handsomest manner known to architectural art. There were thousands of pieces, any one of which would be a valued treasure in an American museum

On the fourth of February I embarked in a French vessel for Marseilles. Thence in a Spanish vessel for Malaga, encountering on the way a terrific gale—the worst storm which had been known on the Spanish coast for twenty years. We touched at Barcelona, where I attended the theater; also at Valencia, Alicante, Carthagena and Almaria, and arrived at Malaga, Feb. 20, 1887.

From Malaga I proceeded to Grenada, and visited the Alhambra. Thence to Madrid, where I witnessed a bull fight, during which five bulls were slain by the matadores.

After a stay of two weeks in Spain, I turned my course, for the third time, toward Paris.   C. B. W.

BOOK REVIEWS.

COMMENTARIES ON AMERICAN LAW. BY JAMES KENT. IN FOUR VOLUMES. VOLUME I. NEW AND THOROUGHLY REVISED EDITION BY WILLIAM M. LACY, OF THE PHILADELPHIA BAR. PHILADELPHIA: THE BLACKSTONE PUBLISHING CO. 1889.

This is a handsome edition of the work of the great American Commentator, whose portrait and a sketch of whose life appear in this number of the LAW TIMES. It appears as part of the "Text Book Series," which is published monthly by the Blackstone Publishing Company, at $15 per year. Appended to this volume are the Articles of Confederation, the Declaration of Independence, and the Constitution of the United States.

Speaking of this work, the author says:

"Subsequent to the last edition issued under supervision of the author, important changes have occurred. Of the international questions by him so thoroughly discussed, some, arising anew from the peaceful intercourse and hostile conflicts of sovereign powers, have received further consideration and more authoritative decision. Within the nation still greater changes have taken place. In addition to the gradual progress of national progression, the country has recently been subjected to a great political revolution, whose causes may have passed into history, but whose effects are appearing in constitutional and legislative provision. Aside from this, the fabric of national and State legislation, which, at the author's death, had been reared upon the underlying principles of our legal system, has been extensively altered and increased; while the decisions by whose light he was guided, have been multiplied a thousand fold. Read without frequent reference to these changes, his work, originally remarkable for its fullness of treatment, would be inadequate to the exposition of American law."

The deficiency here adverted to the author supplies by notes, which add much to the value of the work.

TENURE AND TOIL; OR RIGHTS AND WRONGS OF PROPERTY AND LABOR. BY JOHN GIBBONS, LL.D., OF THE CHICAGO BAR. PHILADELPHIA: J. B. LIPPENCOTT COMPANY. 1888.—This is a well-written book upon an important subject. The subject itself has been well considered and treated in an exhaustive manner.

Some idea of the scope of the work may be formed from the headings of its principal divisions:

Book I. The Right of Property and the History of Tenures.

Book II. The Origin, Growth, and Decadence of Feudal Tenures.

Book III. The Right of Property and the Stability of Tenures.

Book IV. Labor; its Wrongs and their Remedies.

Book V. Limitation of Ownership and Prohibition of Trusts.

Book VI. Distribution of Population and Division of Property.

The author devotes some of the chapters of the first book to Dr. Glynn, and two chapters of the third book to the fallacies of George's Land Tax theory, and to George's self refutation.

Discussing, as it does, in a calm and thoughtful manner, the great problem of the day, this work deserves to be extensively read and studied.

A TREATISE ON THE LAW AND PRACTICE OF FORECLOSING MORTGAGES ON REAL PROPERTY, AND OF REMEDIES COLLATERAL THERETO. WITH FORMS. BY CHARLES HASTINGS WILTSIE, OF THE ROCHESTER BAR. ROCHESTER, N. Y., WILLIAMSON LAW BOOK COMPANY, SUCCESSORS TO WILLIAMSON AND HIGBIE; 1889.—This work is published in a single volume of over a thousand pages. It is stated in the preface that it is not a second edition of the author's first treatise on "Parties to Mortgage Foreclosures and their Rights and Liabilities," but that it is distinctively a new treatise; covering every part of the law and practice of foreclosing mortgages, from the complaint, through the distribution of surplus moneys, and including such collateral remedies as the appointment of a receiver.

"It is adapted to the practice of every State in the Union, and especially of those States where foreclosures are conducted by equitable actions and sales. Over eight thousand cases have been cited; about one-third of these have been taken from the reports of the State of New York. Every case cited has been tested and examined three different times, with a view to making the work accurate in details, as well as exhaustive, and as far as possible original."

Acknowledgment is made to James M. Kerr, Esq., (who will be recognized as a contributor to the LAW TIMES), for assistance in preparing a large part of the work; without whose assistance the author says, it would hardly have been possible to prepare the book with that exhaustiveness, completeness and accuracy by which it is characterized.

LAWYER'S REPORTS, ANNOTATED. BOOK III. ALL CURRENT CASES OF GENERAL VALUE AND IMPORTANCE DECIDED IN THE UNITED STATES, STATE AND TERRITORIAL COURTS; WITH FULL ANNOTATION, BY ROBERT DESTY, Editor. EDMUND H. SMITH, Reporter. Burdet A. Rich, Editor in Chief of the United States and General Digests, and the several Reporters and Judges of each Court, Assistants in Selection. Rochester, N. Y. The Lawyer's Co-Operative Publishing Company. 1889.

We have heretofore had occasion to call attention to the value of these reports. This volume is improved in mechanical execution, while in other respects it is presumed to be not inferior to its predecessors.

In the "Current Comment and Legal Miscellany," published in Philadelphia, is a very good sketch and portrait of our lamented and distinguished fellow citizen, Leonard Swett; but one may look the article through in vain for any evidence that he ever lived in Chicago, a place not once mentioned.